PRESENTED TO

_____

BY

_____

DATE

_____

BLESSINGS ALL MINE
WITH 10,000 BESIDES!

Frederick L. Kosin

ECS
MINISTRIES
The Word to the World

Blessings All Mine With 10,000 Besides!
Frederick L. Kosin

Copyright © 2006 ECS Ministries

ISBN 1-59387-062-0

First Edition 2006

Published by:
  ECS Ministries
  P.O. Box 1028
  Dubuque, IA   52004-1028
  web: www.ecsministries.org

Frederick and Jenny Kosin
P.O. Box 7505
Florence, SC 29502
web: www.FrednJenny.com

Cover Design:
  Glenn Andrews, AndrewsCreative
  email: glenn@notjust.co.za

Printed in the United States of America

Dedicated
to the many folks who
have sat, survived or slept through
sermons, preaching, sharing, teaching,
arguments, discussions, panels, devotions,
lectures and personal conversations and responded
with "Uhu, Ummmm, Unah, Ug, Ump, Oh," a few "Amens,"
an occasional "I never heard that before," an isolated applause,
many a thank you and a lot of silence, to my expositions, illustrations,
exhortations, alliterations, invitations, remonstrations, and occasional
accusations relating to the subject of this series of meditations
in churches, chapels,
halls, homes, prisons,
missions, sanctuaries,
cathedrals, boats and
the open air to family,
friends, fellowships and
a few foes during meetings,
seminars, conferences, retreats,
and advances, in most every state
of the union and more than seventy
foreign countries during fifty years of ministry.

"THANK YOU!"
I couldn't have done it without you!

Introduction

A Few Thoughts

This book is a summary of blessings given to us in the Lord Jesus Christ. These blessings are ours because we possess Christ. They are promises that are being fulfilled by Christ who lives in us. Each meditation is designed to be a spiritual meal which, if absorbed into your heart, appropriated into your thinking, and applied to your behavior, will bring development. This spiritual growth will point people to Christ because our life is the vehicle by which God makes an invisible Christ visible. Consider these mediations as a sheaf of blessings. Like a field waiting to be harvested, each blessing is available for our claiming. Cut the sheaf, remove the chaff, and feast on the wheat.

Some people may wonder why God gives us these blessings. Is it so that we can become spiritually fat? Far from it! Paul told Timothy, "Meditate on these things; give yourself entirely to them, that your progress may be evident to all." If a person gives themselves entirely to "fatty" food, it will be evident to all when they gain weight. If believers give themselves to biblical truths, it will be apparent as their faith grows, their understanding develops, and their behavior is transformed.

You will notice that the prayer at the end of each meditation does not conclude with the word "Amen." It is omitted so you, the reader, can respond to God based on what He has taught you, thus embarking on a life of thanksgiving.

One powerful and practical question that will soon arise in the mind of the active reader is, "How do I make these blessings mine?" In answer, consider the digestive system. Intake of food is normal and repeated regularly. Once the food has passed the lips the mouth masticates, the throat swallows, the stomach digests, and the blood stream dispatches nutrition to the organs while the unnecessary is passed off in waste. We grow by this process. Eating is essential. The same process is necessary in the spiritual life. Jeremiah wrote, "Your words were found and I ate them" (Jeremiah 15:16). Truth must be taken in. That is the goal and purpose of *Blessings All Mine With 10,000 Besides!*

Repetitious reading of the Bible is absolutely essential and imperative. If you are not engaged in some program of memorizing Scripture, it will be more difficult to grow. Meditation is a conscious review, from memory, of Bible truths and principles. Without memorization, meditation is almost impossible.

The result of absorption in our minds is the spontaneous response of the mouth from the heart's storehouse. Jeremiah went on to say, "Your Word was to me the joy and rejoicing of my heart." From your heart will flow rivers of "joy and rejoicing" because the truth is received, believed, memorized, meditated on, and manifested. Your life, lived from the truths stored in your mind, cannot be hidden from the eyes of others.

Worldly programs have stolen these principles of mental and spiritual exercise and used them to promote self. They encourage a prospective laggard to begin positive thinking and repetition. "I can do it" has been copied from Philippians. "You have it all" has been taken from Ephesians. "I am a winner" is plagiarized from 2 Timothy. "I am free" is taken from the lips of Jesus.

What is ironic is that worldly programs take these aphorisms and urge the slow starter to begin repeating and believing them in his life and business dealings. They use concepts from Scripture, taking Christ and God out, and promote them as self-help, motivational strategies or for the worship of self. They turn the truth of God into the lie and cause people to believe in themselves rather than in God. If they can do this with success in the business world, we, who believe the One who is Truth, should be able to more effectively repeat the truth, live the truth, and be changed by the truth.

Yet, although the principle is simple and direct, it demands much mental determination to learn and grow. The ultimate goal is maturity and likeness to Christ—the One who lives in us and empowers us to live like Him.

Read the daily verse and meditation. Write out a portion of the verse that speaks to you about that day's blessing, listing the specific gift. During the day review the verse and truth you learned. Respond to God in prayer, worship, confession, and thanks. Share the truth with someone who will accept accountability for you as you share what the Lord is teaching you. Refrain from arguing with the way the truth is presented or approached. The Lord will speak to you through the Scripture even though you may not always find the way it is presented comfortable. Expect to be challenged by the Scripture. At the end of the day, thank the Lord again for the blessing you employed that day.

Foreword

"Christ is in the believer. He indwells the heart by faith, as the sun indwells the lowliest flowers that unfurl their petals and bear their hearts to his beams. Not because we are good. Not because we are trying to be whole-hearted in our consecration. Not because we keep Him by the tenacity of our love. But because we believe, and, in believing, have thrown open the doors and windows of our nature. And He has come in.

"He probably came in so quietly that we failed to detect His entrance. There was no footfall along the passage; the chime of the golden bells at the foot of His priestly robe did not betray Him.

"He desires to be in us as His Father was in Him, so that the outgoing of our life may be channels through which He, hidden within, may pour Himself forth upon men. But there is a reason why many whose natures are certainly the temple of Christ, remain ignorant of the presence of the wonderful Tenant that sojourns within. He dwells so deep.

"Through the Holy Spirit, Christ dwells, as of old the Shechinah dwelt in the Most Holy Place, closely shrouded from the view of man.

"We repeat here our constant mistake about the things of God. We try to feel them. If we feel them, we believe them; otherwise we take no account of them. We reverse the Divine order. We say *feeling*, FAITH, FACT. God says, FACT, FAITH, *feeling*. With Him feeling is of small account—He only asks us to be willing to accept His own Word, and to cling to it because He has spoken it, in entire disregard of what we may feel.

"I am distinctly told that Christ, though He is on the Throne in His ascended glory, is also within me by the Holy Ghost. I confess I do not feel Him there. But I dare to believe He is there: not without me, but within; not as a transient sojourner for a night, but as a perpetual inmate: not altered by my changes from earnestness to lethargy, from the summer of love to winter of despondency, but always and unchangeably the same. And I say again and again 'Jesus, thou art here.'

"When God's secrets break open they do so in glory. The wealth of the root hidden in the ground is revealed in the hues of orchid and scent of rose. The hidden beauty of a beam of light is unraveled in the sevenfold color of the rainbow.

"So when we accept the fact of His existence within us deeper than our own, and make it one of the aims of our life to draw on it and develop it, we shall be conscious of a glory transfiguring our life and irradiating ordinary things such as will make earth, with its commonest engagements, like a vestibule of heaven.

"Such glory, the certain pledge of the glory to be revealed—is within reach of every reader of these lines who will dare day by day to reckon that Christ lives within, and will be content to die to the energies and promptings of the self-life so that there may be room for the Christ-life to reveal itself.

"When this mystery, or secret, of the divine life in man is apprehended and made use of, it gives great wealth to life. If all the treasurers of wisdom, knowledge, power, and grace reside in Jesus, and He is become the cherished and honored resident of our nature, it is clear that we must be greatly enriched. It is like having a millionaire friend come to live with him.

"And we cannot live such a life till we have learnt to avail ourselves of the riches of the indwelling Christ. The grace of purity and self-control, of fervent prayer and understanding the Scriptures, of love for men and zeal for God, of lowliness and meekness, of gentleness and goodness—all is in Christ; and if Christ is in us, all is ours also. Oh that we would dare to believe it, and draw on it, letting down the pitcher of faith into the deep well of Christ's indwelling opened within us by the Holy Ghost.

"But if only we would meet every call, difficultly and trial, not saying as we so often do, 'I shall never be able to go through it,' but saying, 'I cannot; but Christ is in me, and He can,' we should find that all trials were intended to reveal and unfold the wealth hidden within us, until Christ was literally formed within us and His life manifested in our mortal body II Cor 4:10."

F. B. Meyer

❧ ───────────────── ☙

Usually a Foreword is done by someone who is alive and knows the author. On this occasion I could not ask Mr. F. B. Meyer (1861-1929) to write a Foreword. Instead I have taken the liberty of extracting some very pertinent thoughts from an extremely helpful book that has blessed me over the past 40 years. I found myself consuming these thoughts, digesting them, appropriating them for myself, repeating them, and dispensing them. I have appreciated the encouragement I have received as others enjoyed them as well.

The above selection is from the book by Frederick. B. Meyer entitled: *Steps into the Blessed Life*, published by Henry Altemus, copyright 1896.

F.L.K.

January

THE "ALL THINGS OF GOD" TO GET YOU GOING

". . . as newborn babes, desire the pure milk of the word . . ."
1 Peter 2:2

Pardon for sin and a peace that endureth,
Thy own dear presence to cheer and to guide:
Strength for today and bright hope for tomorrow,
Blessings all mine, with ten thousand beside!

Thomas O. Chisholm

January

A New Born Baby

Oh, how sweet to hold a new born baby. What a marvelous miracle God gives when a child is born and handed to us for care. And no other biblical metaphor gives us a clearer picture of the fullness of blessing that we have in Christ when we are born again.

The completeness of the body and soul is an astounding credit to the creative genius of our God. The baby of 7 or 8 pounds is born with all that he or she needs for life. These permanent ingredients include dozens of organs, 206 bones, hundreds of muscles, thousands of nerves, and millions of cells.

What is so remarkable is that, as the child grows to adulthood, there is no need to exchange the child-sized organs for adult-sized ones. Everything grows as the necessary ingredients are applied to the body. Good food, regular exercise, fresh air, adequate sleep, and the application of challenges, interaction, social exchange, spiritual adjustment, and discipline make the child a man or woman who is well-rounded and capable of meeting the demands of society. There is no need for upgrading the bones or organs. All that was there at birth is there at death.

Spiritual life is just as complete at the spiritual birth. The needed ingredients for believers are employed by the application of truth and the challenges for expanding our capacities to trust God more and more.

The girl who wants to perform gymnastics cannot exchange her muscles for stronger or better ones. The boy who wants to play basketball does not go back to the hospital to get longer legs and bones. Each learns to use what they were given at birth. We do not ask for more strength, either. What the child and the believer need to do is to exercise and challenge what they already have. For the believer, strength is found in Christ, who is our strength. Although we have strength, we need to develop and direct it in a way that is pleasing to God, who gave us strength in Christ.

The New Testament uses the body and its soul as an illustration of our life in Christ. A new-born baby is hungry for milk. Young men are strong. Fathers and mothers are mature. Old immature believers are a disgrace to the provision that God has given for growth. But a balanced diet of reading His Word and of prayer will feed our spiritual tissues. The exercises of obedience, evangelism, and self-discipline strengthen our spiritual sinews. Regular fellowship with our local church of believers builds us into men and women who are useful to the body of Christ.

This collection of meditations is a look at some of the resources for spiritual life that were given to us at spiritual birth. The comparison will take the form of many different metaphors, but it examines how those gifts, capacities, and abilities need to be accepted, appreciated, developed, employed, and exhibited.

Few of us are really happy with our physical bodies. We blame our parents, our culture, our country, and God. We covet others' abilities, build, skin color, mental acumen, and physical prowess. But most aspects of our physical make-up cannot be changed. They must be accepted as God's gifts to us, to the church, and to the world. Similarly, the Lord gave us, in Christ, the resources we need to serve in the sphere where He has placed us. Like children, however, we often ask for more than He has given. Each day's meditation will examine a special gift that God has given for which we should be thankful as we learn how best to appropriate and to expand the usefulness that the Lord expects of us. Every believer needs to acknowledge that God has adequately blessed us all at spiritual birth. We will grow when we develop and use the blessings to the highest possible good for the glory of Christ.

Some believers, after reading the introduction, will set this book down and not accept the biblical challenge of learning what they have in Christ, preferring to continue to ask and plead with God to give them something they already have in Christ. Others will accept the challenge of growing up "to the measure of the stature of the fullness of Christ," just as a mature adult learns to accept the gifts and abilities, strengths and weaknesses, given by God through his parents. A choice in life, both physical and spiritual, faces us all.

Take these blessings of life and enjoy the growing experience. But remember: growing pains and growth are the flower and fruit on the same tree.

The Promise of God's Presence

Behold, I am with you and will keep you wherever you go,
and will bring you back to this land; for I will not leave
you until I have done what I have spoken to you.

Genesis 28:15

One of the most common prayers from our lips, repeated almost without thinking, is "Lord, be with . . ." We then mention ourselves or someone else who needs a "special portion" of God's nearness. Why do we pray this prayer when the promise of God's presence is prolific in every part of His Word?

Genesis 28:15 is the first of many promises that can be found in the Scriptures declaring the fact of God's presence with His people. The greatest resource for life is the presence of God with, or in, those who are His. God cannot be closer to His own than to dwell in them.

In the Old Testament, the promise of God's residence is repeated dozens of times—long before the promise of the Holy Spirit was given to Christ's disciples as a permanent, personal possession—reminding believers of every age that God has chosen to dwell with them in every circumstance of life. In Hebrews 13:5 the author summarizes this by quoting God as saying, "I will never leave you nor forsake you." He uses the strongest possible negative in the original language to convey this truth.

Is it that we want to have some *physical* evidence of God's presence? Do we want some miraculous *demonstration* that He will keep His promise? Or are we simply in a habit we find very hard to break? To pray "Lord, be with . . ." is "an exercise in unbelief" in the most foundational truth of our salvation. We who have been born again by the Holy Spirit should never question whether God lives in us when we read His promise so many times.

> God cannot be closer to His own than to dwell in them.

Although we create long lists of Scripture that proclaim this fact, as believers we should not need God to tell us more than once. He is faithful who promised Joshua, "as I was with Moses, so I will be with you." And yet, through the Holy Spirit, even the newest Christian has a far fuller expression of the presence of God than either Moses or Joshua had. As believers, we cannot have more of God than He has given to every one of His children.

— ❧ ⎯⎯⎯⎯⎯⎯⎯⎯⎯⎯⎯ ☙ —

Father, thank you for giving me all that You are by dwelling in me through Christ, Your Son. I confess I do not always believe this and thoughtlessly ask You to be with me. I desire to live every day in the joy of Your presence which You will never take away from me.

Our "Box" of Spiritual Blessings

Blessed be the God and Father of our Lord Jesus Christ, who has blessed us with every spiritual blessing in the heavenly places in Christ.

Ephesians 1:3

We often quote this verse to remind ourselves of the adequacy of our blessings for life. It can be a challenge to accept this verse by faith, although the message is crystal clear: we have every spiritual blessing in Christ! This means that all the spiritual blessings that are resident in Christ are ours as well. Since God has given us Christ as the sum and substance of our salvation, all that is found in Him is ours. The first chapter of Ephesians goes on to list numerous blessings that are included "in Christ."

Have you ever played this old trick when giving someone a small but valuable gift? You begin with a small, attractively-wrapped box, which you then put inside a bigger box (also nicely wrapped), then in another, until the final box is quite large, decorated with excessive wrapping. Opening the gift is half the fun; each box is unwrapped only to find another, and another, until the gift itself is finally discovered.

God has given us Christ, who is like the initial big box. Inside each of the succeeding boxes is a further discovery of some other aspect of His wonderful blessing. Today's Scripture reading does not specify what each individual blessing is, but instead gathers them up in one glorious "package," which is Christ Himself. Our spiritual blessings are infinite in scope, just as the person of Christ is infinite.

All the spiritual blessings that are resident in Christ are ours as well.

Obviously, this gift from God does not include material or physical blessings. Christ is not health, wealth, a luxury car, a bulging bank account, an influential career, insulation from disease, or many of the other *things* we want. Requesting such things in prayer often confuses need with greed; it confuses wants with what has already been given by God in the person of His Son. Blessings that are in Christ are strength, love, grace, peace, meekness, gentleness, sonship, a spiritual inheritance, and many more.

A couplet helps us remember the all-encompassing gift of Christ: "He *is* what He *gives,* and what He *gives* He *is*!" The blessings of Christ are not given independent of Him or in addition to Him. It is unbelief that wants God to give us resources for life in addition to all our spiritual blessings in Christ.

⁎ ──────────────── ⁐

Father, You have given me all that is in Your Son. I accept these blessings by faith and begin today to appropriate them for Your glory and the blessing of Your people.

Nourishment for Life

*All Scripture is given by inspiration of God, and is
profitable for doctrine, for reproof, for correction, for
instruction in righteousness, that the man of God may be
complete, thoroughly equipped for every good work.*

2 Timothy 3:16-17

The Word of God is the greatest source of food for development and growth in the life of the believer. What a privilege to have this great book in our hands and hearts! It is a fountain of truth for all who dip their cup in its fullness to satisfy their every thirst. How blessed to be able to pick up this handbook of life and know the Holy Spirit is ready and willing to be of comfort and help to those who trust Him.

The Word of God is the source for knowing the things that have been freely given to us. Its Author is our Teacher so that we might know the things that have been given to us by God. We cannot grow in the Christian life if we reject this book as the sole authority in areas of faith and practice.

> *What a privilege to have this great book in our hands and hearts!*

One of the reasons we are unaware of what the Father has given us is that we are not reading the "operator's manual" for employing the abundant life He has given. We are ignorant of the inventory our Father has bestowed so generously in each of His children. Even when the Word itself points out to us that we have been blessed with this gift, we tend to disregard it. The Lord Jesus said to the Father in John 17:14, "I have given them [His disciples] Your word . . ." The Bible is the premiere documentation that all these blessings are actually ours as well.

Our walk of faith begins by accepting the promises and principles of the Word of God. The truth of the Word helps us take our first steps when we learn its doctrines. It will reprove our faltering steps, correct our false steps, and strengthen our forward steps by its instruction in righteousness. It is profitable!

The Scriptures are entirely complete. They also fully reveal their truth to anyone who applies his or her heart to their wisdom. Most of us do not need a greater revelation, but a willingness to obey what we already know. God is waiting for us to offer submissive hearts to the guidance He has so fully presented in the living pages of His Word. He longs to see us complete and thoroughly equipped for every good work He has given us.

❧ ──────────── ☙

Father, thank you for this great book You have given me. I confess I am not as addicted to it as I should be. Thank you for giving me Your Teacher, the Holy Spirit. I submit to His instruction today.

The Blessing of Citizenship

Now, therefore, you are no longer strangers and foreigners, but
fellow citizens with the saints and members of the household of God.
Ephesians 1:19

Traveling today is not as easy as it used to be. There are many surprises! We faced some in spite of the words we received as we left a travel office for one recent trip: "No problem!" said the agent. But when we tried to enter our destination country, new forms and requirements, additional pictures, and other procedures were demanded. This resulted in delays and a practical test of our patience.

The believer has received a "heavenly passport," fully authorized and stamped in the precious blood of God's dear Son, the Lord Jesus Christ. The gift of God, eternal life, is a living "visa," secured by Christ's resurrection and delivered to us at the point of conversion. There are no special forms to complete, no added requirements, no changing regulations, and no delays or waiting for approval.

Maybe we'll go on a "group tour," when "the Lord Himself shall descend from heaven" as our "Tour Guide" to usher us all together into the presence of His Father, "and thus we shall always be with the Lord." Or maybe we'll leave by individual invitation, laying our head down for the last time and finding ourselves absent from the body and present with the Lord. Whatever our "travel arrangements," they are all made. We need no paperwork. No payment. No pleading. All we have to do is enter!

What a blessing to have citizenship arranged by the Lord, appointed by the Scriptures, and available whenever He calls us home. Home! Not a foreign country, but the home He has been preparing for us. No uncertainties—no need to wonder if someone is going to be there to pick us up. No need to exchange money—we sent that on ahead long ago! No need to ask directions to our new dwelling. No need to be concerned about the culture, currency, or cuisine. No need to ask what kind of clothes to wear, for His righteousness is adequate and fits all His children.

Some of the sweetest words a weary returning traveler hears from the immigration officer are, "Welcome home!" Our Father will welcome us home as citizens of heaven. How much He wants us there. Even so, come, Lord Jesus!

        ಬಿ ———————————— ಚಿ

Father, I confess I do not long to go home as I should because I love this world too much. Help me set my affections on things above and turn away from the things of this earth. Thank you for my passport and visa that guarantee my entrance into the eternal home You have prepared for me.

Discovering God's Treasure

. . . in whom are hidden all the treasures of wisdom and knowledge.

Colossians 2:3

When we were children, one of the fun things we would do was have a treasure hunt. Someone would hide a treasure at the end of a long list of clues. After being divided up into teams, we would be given the first clue. Each team would then decide where the clue led. When we found another clue, we followed that until we found the "treasure" which—more often than not—wasn't of much real value.

In Christ are hidden all the treasures of wisdom and knowledge. To seek such true treasure is no game; this is a serious "treasure hunt." Like gold that is hidden in the earth and must be found and mined, so these two blessings of the Christian life are hidden in Christ. And just as mining gold is worth it, so mining the "wisdom and knowledge" hidden in Christ is worth it.

> *Mining the "wisdom and knowledge" hidden in Christ is worth it.*

A huge expense is often invested to find the minerals that are hidden deep in the heart of the earth, but there is no need to look elsewhere in search of wisdom and knowledge—it is all in Christ. There's no problem finding it; the problem is believing that the treasures of wisdom and knowledge are found *only* in Christ. When we believe this, we are able to appreciate and appropriate the riches that are resident in Him.

When seeking real wisdom, we are easily confused. Is it to be found searching the libraries and literature of the world? Paul adds to his profound, inclusive directions for the miner by saying in 1 Corinthians 1:30 that Christ "became for us wisdom from God—and righteousness and sanctification and redemption." *All* the treasures are resident in Him. Although we may be tempted to mix the "treasures" of this world and those of Christ, we must remember that the resulting alloy reduces the value of such treasure to ashes.

The tools of discovery include reading about the One who *is* true wisdom and *displays* true wisdom, memorizing the details of gems found in Him, meditating on the nuggets of wisdom explained by Him, practicing the art of thanksgiving for the principles of wisdom He has exposed to us, and surrendering our minds to the development and display of the glories of His wisdom and knowledge.

Father, I acknowledge I have not sought Your wisdom as I should. I have been satisfied leaning on my own understanding. I open my mind to Your truth and the understanding of Your mind so the mind of Christ will be revealed through me.

Filled to Overflowing

*For in Him dwells all the fullness of the Godhead
bodily; and you are complete in Him.*

Colossians 2:9-10

As children, filling a glass as full as possible with some special juice was a challenge. A further challenge was to get that very full glass to our lips without spilling a drop. The goal was to fill the glass so full that just one more drop would make it spill. Selfishness prompted us to not only want as much as possible, but to always want more than the others!

Because each believer has the indwelling of the Holy Spirit, each believer can enjoy all the fullness of Christ. One of the most powerful reminders of God's provision for our Christian experience is that, since we have Christ, "we are complete" or "filled full" with all the resources that are found in Him. It is hard for us to believe that this reservoir of blessing is always full. Because we doubt this truth, we pray for more, wonder why we do not have enough, and compare ourselves to others who seem to be "fuller." But God has given us all the fullness of Himself in His Son, and His reservoir never drains dry.

> *God has given us all the fullness of Himself in His Son.*

The swimming pool at a mission school in Zambia is filled with water from the Zambezi River. A gate is opened and the flow of the mighty Zambezi fills the pool. When it is full, it overflows back into the river. The fullness of the river is always adequate for the pool.

When we receive Christ, the door is opened and the flood of His fullness overwhelms our emptiness. It is not repeated prayer that opens the door. Receiving Christ as Savior opens the door! It is not more of Christ that we need, but stronger faith to believe He has already given us all He is and has. Believing that all the fullness of God is imparted to us at salvation is to accept His flood and then to wash, drink, walk, and swim in Christ's adequacy. It is our choice whether or not we allow that flowing river to fill us so we "swim" in all His fullness.

A river cannot give its fullness without giving itself. There may be some areas of our lives where we find huge displays of self. To remove these is to allow the fullness of God to fill what was previously filled with self. His fullness is ours to appropriate. He has opened the floodgates to all that Christ is and to all He has to give.

౪ ──────────── ౸

Father, I confess I do not realize or partake of Your fullness as I should. I now empty my life of self and choose Christ to overwhelm that emptiness created by my confession. Thank you for filling me with all the fullness of Christ.

Reflections

But we all, with unveiled face, beholding as in a mirror the
glory of the Lord, are being transformed into the same image
from glory to glory, just as by the Spirit of the Lord.

2 Corinthians 3:18

There is nothing we have to do to make a mirror work! No switch. No button to push. No warm up necessary—simply step in front of it and it reflects. Sometimes we forget this as we stand in front of the mirror of God's Word praying, "Teach me! Speak to me!" When we trusted Christ as our Savior, the great Physician removed our spiritual blindness and brought us into the glorious light of His presence. God's mirror is ready to serve us if we will simply stand in front of it with open eyes.

Physically speaking, we do not always like what we see in the bathroom mirror. Pimples and other imperfections. Another gray hair. A few deeper lines and wrinkles. Because we loathe the direction in which the body is going and do not enjoy this process, we try to cover up with paint and powder. The mirror of the Word gives a picture of reality, too. As a mirror, it serves two purposes: it shows me what I am, and it shows me what Christ, who is the glory of God, is like. All the beauties and glories of the perfect Man are fully displayed in God's Word for our open eyes.

Day by day I see more that the Holy Spirit wants to change!

Pinned to the wall by the door of our Army commander's office was a life-sized picture of a perfectly dressed soldier. Next to it hung a full length mirror. The mirror showed me what I looked like; the picture showed me what I *should* look like. I was expected to change whatever I saw in the mirror to conform to the picture: straighten my tie, level my awards, align my creases, polish my shoes, line up my belt buckle, tilt my cap. Only then should I go in to see my commander.

As believers, we look into the mirror of the Word and see the Savior. The Holy Spirit who lives in us points out the differences between my Lord and me, then urges and gives the strength to change so that I become more like the Master. Day by day I look, and day by day I see more that the Holy Spirit wants to change. Day by day I grow into the likeness of Christ, transformed from the inside by the Spirit applying the Word of God to me.

Father, thank you for revealing the beauty of the Lord to me in Your Word. I confess I do not look like Him as I should. I surrender to Your Holy Spirit to change in me what He wants to change today.

Step into the Sonshine

If we live in the Spirit, let us also walk in the Spirit.

Galatians 5:25

The word "if" in our text is what grammarians call a "first class condition." Translating the word as "since" gives us a better handle on the absolute certainty of the life we live in and by the Holy Spirit. "Since" we have the Spirit, we should live, or walk, in that same life. The availability of the Life of the Spirit is uninterrupted. He never leaves us nor departs from us. But because we do not physically see Him, we are often more dependent on those we do see than the Spirit who lives in us. So many of us, therefore, live in our own strength and by our own wisdom, pleasing our own selfish natures.

The blessing of the indwelling Spirit is like the blessing of the sun. I occasionally ask a group of students to look outside and tell me if the sun is shining. If the day is very cloudy, most will say, "No, the sun's not shining." But it is! We can't stop the sun from shining. We can't stop the Spirit from living within us, either, but we can fail to live in the Spirit's sphere. The "clouds" of unbelief, disobedience, carelessness, disregard, or just forgetfulness of His presence cause us to live in and by ourselves.

On a cold and cloudy day, wind might blow away the clouds to allow the sun to have its warming effect on us. In the spiritual realm, we *do* have a choice. We can remove the clouds of doubt, we can determine to obey, we can think on divine things and decide we will habitually walk in the sphere of the Spirit. We make a choice whether to walk where the sun shines on us or where a building casts a shadow. We *choose* to fill our minds with the blessings of the Son and to enjoy the warmth of His presence and the fullness of His blessing. As we do this, we will enjoy, radiate, and reflect the glory of the Lord.

> *We can decide that we will habitually walk in the sphere of the Spirit.*

We cannot change the sun shining or the Spirit living within us, but we can decide where we walk—in our own power or by the life of the Spirit who is always available to us. We begin that walk of faith by saying "thank you" to the Father for providing His amazing Life! The Holy Spirit of God is permanent, personal, and available!

ಬ ──────────────── ಜಿ

Father, thank you for the gift of life which is communicated to me by Your indwelling Spirit. I realize I walk in the shadows by choice. I choose by faith to walk in Your power and vitality.

Egg-stravagant Giving

And my God shall supply all your need according
to His riches in glory by Christ Jesus.

Philippians 4:19

This verse is often quoted by believers when they become aware of their "needs." They empty their purse or wallet on some unnecessary, extravagant item and then run to this verse for cover. The context, however, precludes these and other misuses of it.

This precious promise of God was for the Philippian believers who, in a state of deep poverty, gave so liberally that they did not have much of anything left for themselves. Their giving made them poorer. In accepting the riches of their liberality, Paul reminded them of God's complete responsibility to meet their needs.

After we have given sacrificially (as the Philippians gave) we can present this verse with confidence to our great God as one of His blessed promises. Our biggest hindrance to claiming this promise is the difficulty of knowing the difference between need and greed. Let us not come to God asking Him to meet our needs when we have not even determined what our needs are. Let us not come to God pleading this verse if we are living in the lap of luxury and pleasure. Let us not come to God expecting His glorious commitment until we have given to the point of pain or sacrifice.

It is true that God has promised to meet our needs, and His riches in glory are infinite in scope and variety to meet every circumstance of His children. But to hastily claim this verse because we do not think we have what we should have for our life or ministry is inconsistent with the message in both this verse and its context. We should learn from and follow the example of the Philippians who gave beyond their ability and pleaded with Paul to accept the gift when he knew it was much more than they could afford to give.

In our travels we have learned this lesson from Paul's standpoint in accepting the Philippians' precious gift. On one occasion we received a gift of an egg or two from a very poor widow who lived out in the bush. Although this widow needed it more than we did, because it was given as unto the Lord, we accepted it and thanked God for His promise to her. Is it safe, or right, for the poor to give like this? It is the only safe and right thing to do. When we give sacrificially, this promise of God is for us.

ဆ ———————————— 03

Father, thank you for meeting all my needs in Christ. I confess I confuse my needs and wants. I surrender my needs to You and deny my wants as I learn to give as the Philippians gave.

The Source of Every Good Thing

*That the sharing of your faith may become
effective by the acknowledgment of every good
thing which is in you in Christ Jesus.*

Philemon 6

What is a "good thing"? We hear discussions of how a movie was good, an actor was good, or food was good. At the same time, the apostle Paul confessed in Romans 7:18, "I know that in me (that is, in my flesh) nothing good dwells." Human good is the lowest element on the triacular scale of excellence (good, better, and best).

Philemon learned from Paul's personal letter to him that the good things which were evident in him were actually a display of the "good things" that are in Christ Jesus. Paul commended Philemon for many gracious characteristics that could only be the result of the life of Christ being manifested in his mortal body. Among the things Paul saw in Philemon's life were his love, the sharing of his faith, and the way he refreshed his fellow believers. No doubt he had other attractive qualities that are desirable in all saints.

Paul is enunciating here a lovely principle—God wants to work out His good in the life of each believer. It begins by acknowledging that the resources of "every good thing" are in fact found in Christ. "Acknowledging" is what Paul does when he confesses that no good thing dwelled in his flesh. It is when we think we are "pretty good" that the "good things" of Christ become overshadowed by our proud selves. Acknowledging that we are a display case for the beauties of Christ removes any vestige of our wanting to outshine the lovely characteristics that only He can produce. When the Judean churches observed the dramatic change in Paul after his conversion, he reported in Galatians 1:24 that "they glorified God in me."

These lovely "good things" will be working in us and out of us as we confess that we are dependent on the indwelling Christ for this display. Philemon's faith in the availability and employment of these good things was the key to their being observed by others.

James wrote, "Every good gift and perfect gift is from above, and comes down from the Father." Christ came down from the Father as the good and perfect gift for everyone who receives Him and all He is. Accept the truth that "good things" are available for display because Christ is the source of "every good thing."

☜ ———————————————— ☞

Father, I have tried to show good things in my own strength. I surrender my life today as a stage on which Your "good things" can be openly and fully revealed. Thank you for using my feeble being as a means of showing Christ to the world.

Dying to Live

I have been crucified with Christ; it is no longer I who live, but Christ lives in me; and the life which I now live in the flesh I live by faith in the Son of God, who loved me and gave Himself for me.

Galatians 2:20

When Christ went back to heaven to sit at the right hand of God, He continued to limit Himself to human flesh as His personal revelation on earth. Although He is resident in glory now, He has chosen to live His life through the bodies and personalities of God's children. In the same way that, during His lifetime, Christ made the invisible Father visible, so now the absent Christ is made present and visible through the lives of believers. The key words for our meditation today are "Christ lives in me." It is easy to forget that Christ is a person who is real, living, feeling, thinking, acting, and working.

Many Scriptures remind us that when we believe in Jesus Christ for salvation, He comes to dwell in our lives. John 1:12 reads, "But as many as received Him [Christ], to them He gave the right to become children of God." Since Christ is in us, He is in us to "do His good will." He is resident in our lives to be a real, living, feeling, thinking, acting, working person. It is not possible to have only a part of Christ or to have only a portion of His mind, emotions, or will. I have all of Christ! Yet the question remains: Does Christ have all of me?

Crucifixion is a dramatic way of saying I must die to all my own efforts to save myself as well as to display a living Christ. He is waiting for me to admit that I cannot live His life in my own strength. He cannot and will not project His life through our lives without our surrendering all we are to Him for His use. This is why Paul says, "It is no longer I who live . . ."

> *I have all of Christ! Yet the question remains: Does Christ have all of me?*

The choice is ours. We can try to live the life of Christ in our own effort or we can die to our own energies and allow Christ to use our minds, emotions, and desires as means of making His resurrected life known through our human flesh.

Father, thank you for the presence of the Lord Jesus in my life. I give Him my life, my mind, and my whole being so that He can use my body and soul to display Your love, Your joy, and Your peace. Thank you for using me as a means of showing that He lives in me.

Appreciating Our Sonship

*And he said to him, "Son, you are always with
me, and all that I have is yours."*

Luke 15:31

Our text is a remarkable statement from the lips of the faithful father in the parable of the prodigal son. It is all the more gloriously enhanced because the son to whom these words were addressed was not the returned and repentant prodigal, as part of his reinstatement, but rather the unrepentant son, the "elder brother" as he is often called, who was angry at his father for openly welcoming back his "prodigal brother" and fully restoring him to favor.

What astonishes us is that the father gives his angry son, in the midst of his anger, a comprehensive and unqualified statement of truth. The elder brother hears that beautiful word "son" which reminds him of his own permanent relationship to his father.

> *Sonship does not depend on behavior, but on birthright.*

One of the first responses of the prodigal as he came to his senses was, "I am no longer worthy to be called your son." It is not unusual for a believer who has fallen to worry about how his behavior may have injured his relationship with his Father. The prodigal went through a difficult curriculum of life lessons before truly appreciating the sonship that his own behavior had caused him to fear was in jeopardy. It is not his relationship that was as risk, however, but the enjoyment of it.

Of course, from the father's perspective, the prodigal's sonship was never in question. It was his lifestyle that gave the prodigal reason to question if he deserved to be called by the father's name. We, too, can lose our assurance of the Father's love through careless living. The elder brother was not so much concerned about that relationship as about a celebration with his friends. Even when we do not value our sonship, it is still there for our enjoyment. The elder brother may have appreciated his sonship more if he had gone through the degradation his younger brother experienced. Some believers who know a lot of truth can nonetheless be unappreciative of these blessings because, while they know them in their minds, they are not enjoying them in their hearts.

In the parable, it is clear that not only is the prodigal still a son, but the elder brother is as well. Sonship does not depend on behavior, but on birthright. It is *appreciation* of sonship that often depends on behavior, as the prodigal learned. Sonship is a permanent, personal position.

൭ ———————————— 03

Father, thank you for making me Your child. I confess my behavior does not always reflect my appreciation. Your faithfulness to me is the basis of my enjoying this relationship.

Reconciliation for One and All

Now all things are of God, who has reconciled us to Himself through Jesus Christ, and has given us the ministry of reconciliation.
2 Corinthians 5:18

One of the least-practiced provisions of God is reconciliation. People leave churches, husbands and wives divorce, and brothers and sisters in Christ prefer to live in alienation from one another rather than be reconciled as the Bible provides.

God has reconciled us to Himself. The word *reconcile* means "to thoroughly change." God has changed us. Without the death of Christ there would exist a state of antagonism between us and God with no solution to the problem. Christ's death made a way of access. Man's condition was changed from being without any avenue to God to being able to receive the offer of full salvation through Jesus Christ.

2 Corinthians 5:18 does not say that *God* changed or was reconciled; it was man who moved away from God when he sinned in the Garden of Eden, bringing death and alienation. Because of his sinfulness, man had to be changed from a position where he could not be saved to one where—by means of the cross—he can now be saved through faith in Christ.

Reconciliation was one of God's foundational works in His plan to provide salvation through Christ. It was always part of His plan. This means that the death of Christ was effective for all who lived before the cross as much as for those who live after. The work of God reached back as well as forward. The door that was shut by the sin of Adam was opened by the death of Christ. It was, in fact, opened as soon as it was shut (when Adam sinned) because of what God was going to do at the cross.

The glorious truth is that *all* people stand reconciled to God by what Christ did in His death for us. Anyone can come to Christ under the banner of "Whosoever will!" Nothing more needs to be done in regard to this aspect of God's provision of salvation. The application of reconciliation, however, is *provisional* for all, but *actual* for everyone who responds with the obedience of faith, just as verse 20 challenges: "Be reconciled to God." This is the action of my heart and will when I change my mind about Christ. But this decision is only possible and effective because God made a thorough change so that *anyone* can come to Christ.

Thank you Father, for reconciling me to Yourself through Christ when He died for me. You have opened the way at a great price so I could come through the narrow road that leads to Life.

Glorious Promise and Blessing

. . . that the blessing of Abraham might come upon
the Gentiles in Christ Jesus, that we might receive
the promise of the Spirit through faith.

Galatians 3:14

The source of this glorious promise goes all the way back to Abraham, the father of the faithful. Consider the blessing God gave to Abraham in the dawn of divine revelation. It is significant that what Abraham grappled with by faith 4,000 years ago is ours by the same exercise of faith today.

To Abraham's seed, the scope of God's blessing to Abraham was largely material, including the land in which he dwelt, multiplied descendants, and general personal blessings. The blessing to the whole world through his heir, however, is the premiere aspect of God's blessing that was repeated to Isaac and Jacob. This was fulfilled in the person and work of Christ, and it will provide a final demonstration to Israel in the millennium, when Christ will reign as the Son of David and King of Israel. For us who live 2,000 years on this side of the cross, the blessing of Abraham is the spiritual resources for all who exercise faith in Abraham's greatest Son, Jesus Christ (Galatians 3:16).

We are blessed in Christ because He is the fulfillment of God's blessing to Abraham and his seed. We who are Gentiles enter into those blessings spiritually. Israel as a nation still awaits the enjoyment of these blessings. We who live by faith in Christ now partake continually of what Abraham was looking for and died without enjoying. But Abraham did not ask or plead; instead, he quietly expected the fruition of God's promise.

We do not ask, plead, or pray for these blessings but partake, enjoy, and appropriate them because they are resident in Christ. The blessings that await Abraham's seed in the future are dependent on the sovereign plan of God for the nation of Israel. Our blessings are fully ours in Christ, and they will be ours to enjoy into eternity, when full blessing is realized.

We have the added gift of the Holy Spirit, whose primary ministry is to help us understand, appreciate, and appropriate the blessings poured out on us in Christ. The book of Galatians is clear in reminding us that all the blessings of Christ are the personal and permanent possession of everyone who exercises faith in the God of Abraham. *He* waited, looking forward to Christ. *We* worship, looking back to Christ. As Galatians 3:29 says, "If you are Christ's, then you are Abraham's seed, and heirs according to the promise."

ဆ ———————————————— ଏ

Father of Abraham, thank you for blessing me as You did Abraham. Because these blessings are resident in Your Son, I am drawn to rest in His provision for my every need. I therefore claim these blessings by faith!

Grace: An Abundant Ration

And of His fullness we have all received, and grace for grace.

John 1:16

*G*race is one of the most familiar words in the believer's vocabulary, and rightly so, because it is one of the most repeated words in the Holy Spirit's language. The fact that the Greek word translated as "grace" and "gift" is the same gives insight into the special blessing of the grace of God. Christ is "full of grace and truth." Repeatedly we are reminded of the adequacy of God's grace. Few believers would consciously pray for more grace in the face of these verses, but many would think nothing of asking for more gifts.

The fullness of God's grace is resident in Christ and communicated to us when we receive Christ. It is impossible to receive Christ without receiving the fullness of His grace. Can we receive a seed without receiving the life of the seed and its capacity for growing and multiplying? We do not receive a seed and then have to ask for its life.

When God gave us Christ He gave us all the gifts found in Christ. John says we have received "grace for grace." Translators have struggled with how to adequately render the word "for" to convey the abundance of supply: *instead of, in place of, on top of, used up for.* Each has its own nuance of meaning, but each concludes there is profusion and surplus.

We do not need to ask for grace/gifts. Rather, we should appreciate and appropriate what is our daily ration. This storehouse of grace is made available to all equally. No believer has more than another. The newest believer has as much as the oldest. A baby's lungs can be filled from the first scream just as a mature adult's can be filled while jogging. Their capacity may be different, but the supply is equal. Appropriation is the key. If we are still appropriating the same amount of grace we needed as a "baby" when we are mature, we have not grown.

This storehouse of grace is made available to all equally.

Many times Paul greeted his readers with "Grace *be* with you." The *"be"* is in italics in many versions of the Bible, indicating it was added by translators. My suggestion is that we substitute *"is"* for *"be"* to indicate the fullness of God's gift of grace to us in Christ. *Grace* is with you because *Christ* is with you. I have all grace because I have Christ. My appropriation is enlarged by faith in the resources of His gifts and His grace given to me.

&⁜ ⁜⁜ ⁜⁜⁜ ⁜⁜⁜⁜ ⁜⁜⁜

Father, I confess I have often asked for the grace You have already given. I am sorry for failing to enjoy the adequacy of Your gift. Today I begin to live in the fullness of Your abundant grace.

Come to the Comforter

*Blessed be the God and Father of our Lord Jesus Christ,
the Father of mercies and God of all comfort, who
comforts us in all our tribulation, that we may be able to
comfort those who are in any trouble, with the comfort
with which we ourselves are comforted by God.*

2 Corinthians 1:3-4

Our world is perforated by difficulties and hardships. Few people would say that they have no trials. Money does not insulate us from them. Medicine does not totally protect us. Education cannot. Possessions do not. Troubles happen to us no matter what we do to ensure they are kept at bay. Yet we usually think that it's our Father who sends blessing and the enemy who sends troubles. However, the one who allows tribulations (and may, in fact, send them) is our Father. Regardless of their source, if we did not experience troubles and trials in life, we would not need the Father of mercies and the God of all comfort.

*God knows
what we
need before
we come.*

When our children fall or hurt themselves, they come running back to us. They do not ask for comfort; they just fling themselves into our arms, knowing we are ready to give what is our nature to give: a soothing word, a warm embrace, a pat of knowing care, a kiss of love. Soon, the tears are gone and the hurt is healed.

When we face the trials and tribulations of life allowed by the Father, we run to Him and fling ourselves into His arms and He gives what is His by nature. We need not ask Him to comfort us; He is the God of all comfort. Comfort comes from Him and is ministered to us by the Comforter, the Holy Spirit.

Too often we run to a human source of comfort without realizing that all true comfort is found in the God of all comfort. Go to Him first! He is waiting for you! He knows the trial because He allowed it or sent it. He is like the mother who sees her child fall and waits for him or her to come. God is waiting for us to come because He knows what we need before we come. As we open our hearts, He reminds us of His love, His care, and His protection. We do not need to ask for mercy or comfort. Since the Father is there, mercy is there and comfort is there. Draw deeply today for your every sorrow from the adequacy of His comfort available in Christ.

₮ ———————————— ℣

Father, I am learning to thank You even for my tribulations so I can know more fully Your comfort. You are my perfect Father.

Peace that is Resident and Evident

"Peace I leave with you, My peace I give to you;
not as the world gives do I give to you. Let not your
heart be troubled, neither let it be afraid."

John 14:27

Peace was one of the greatest gifts Christ gave His disciples before He left them. If we knew all that was going to happen, we might arrange to bypass trials or change direction so that we would not have to go through these uncomfortable experiences. But God does not reveal to us the next day's trials ahead of time. In place of that knowledge, we are offered His peace.

Peace is a settled conviction that the Lord knows my life and is shaping events to teach me more about Himself. Peace is depending on the presence of the Prince of Peace in the problems of life. Peace is knowing that the Father will not bring more into my life than He gives grace to handle. Peace is knowing God, because He is the God of peace!

But peace is a gift that we must accept by faith. We do not ask for peace; we believe it is ours because the God of peace resides in us. The gift of peace is ours because of the ministry of each Person of the Trinity. The Father is the source of peace because it is His nature and He longs for His people to enjoy it. The Son died on the cross to make peace possible to everyone who believes. The Holy Spirit lives in us and is the distributor of the peace promised by Christ. Trusting Christ as Savior results in justification that in turn results in the addition of peace with God to every believing heart. We *have* peace! Do we enjoy it? Count on it? Appreciate it? Appropriate it?

Peace is not only *for* us, but also to be shown *through* us. Perhaps more than anything else, the world is looking for peace. World peace is the goal of many nations. Personal peace is the cry of every heart. The world is looking at believers to see if we truly believe that peace is possible in the midst of trial, trouble, and sorrows. The Father wants to be able to point to

> *Peace is not only for us, but also to be shown through us.*

His children and show the world how true believers can be at peace while enduring the problems of life. Do our lives manifest the peace God has given us in the trials that He allows into our lives?

    ₧ ———————————— ℯ

Father, thank you for Your peace which is permanently resident in my life. I unnecessarily carry a load of cares because I fail to believe Your peace is always mine. I now claim Your peace and thank You for filling me with Your peace today.

Joy . . . Abundant Joy

Rejoice in the Lord always. Again I will say, rejoice!
Philippians 4:4

Rejoicing is a glorious provision of God for His people. Some of the Lord's last words to His disciples were, "These things I have spoken to you, that My joy may remain in you, and that your joy may be full." The words the Lord was speaking were to be the basis of their joy. Not experience or prosperity, but what He said. If we limited our meditation just to what He said we would still have sufficient reason to be filled with His joy. As it is, we have the entire Word of God to rejoice in, know, and study.

In today's text, Paul reminds us of the direction of our meditation: "in the Lord." Paul, like his Lord, was in dire straits when he spoke of joy to the Philippians. He was in prison, chained to guards all day and night. The Lord Jesus was facing the rejection of his disciples, the hatred of the Jews, and the suffering inflicted from His Father on the cross.

It is easy to blame our circumstances and surroundings for living in the doldrums. But because the Lord has given us a full revelation of Himself in the Scriptures, we have no excuse for living without joy. We may not find it in ourselves to rejoice in our circumstances— that comes with maturity—but we can choose to be filled with the knowledge of the Lord and, in so doing, our hearts will overflow with rejoicing. Paul adds in Colossians 1:9 and 11 that being filled with the knowledge of God's will results in the spontaneous fruit of joy.

> *The display of joy is an accurate barometer of spiritual health.*

The dietician says, "You are what you eat!" Spiritually, too, as you feed on the blessings of God, your life will radiate the joy of the Lord. This joy will fill your mind, and your face will respond with a radiance that can only be explained in terms of what your mind is meditating on.

You choose what goes into your mouth, and you choose what goes on in your mind. What goes in your mouth influences your physical health; what goes into your mind determines your spiritual health. The display of joy is an accurate barometer of spiritual health. Feed much on spiritual truth and it will not only set you free from the fears and anxieties of life, but will also fill your heart with rejoicing in the Lord.

❧ ⸻ ☙

Father, thank you for giving a full revelation of Your Son for my meditation. I choose to fill my mind with the glories of His person and to rejoice in Him.

Armed for Victory

*Put on the whole armor of God, that you may be able
to stand against the wiles of the devil. . . . take up the
whole armor of God, that you may be able to withstand
in the evil day, and having done all, to stand.*

Ephesians 6:11, 13

It is a rather daunting day when a person joins the military. All civilian attachments are set aside as a new uniform and provisions are issued, and a new lifestyle is embraced. The adjustments of the first few days can easily shake one's comfort level.

When we trust the Lord Jesus Christ as our Savior, we too leave behind a familiar life and lifestyle for a new environment. The old deeds may be hostile to our attempts to change our conduct and performance. In view of that hostility, God "issues" military paraphernalia suitable for spiritual conflict and victory. Every piece of armor we need for our protection and for defeating the enemy is given to us by the One who won the battle on our behalf, the Lord Jesus Christ. The command in today's text is to use each piece. The inventory of the armor is carefully delineated by the apostle Paul so we can know what has been given us in Christ.

*The words "put on"
and "take up" indicate
our responsibility to
prepare for battle.*

Many believers do not learn until far along in their Christian experience that they possess this complete armor, let alone how each piece fits for battle. Some do not receive training in how to use it for a victorious life. Others are given a distorted view of what victory is, believing that it comprises casting out demons and claiming wealth and health. Defeat is most often traced to failure to take up our armor. We must carefully appropriate and fit each piece. We must be aware that without the armor we are vulnerable to the world, and to the devil in particular.

Each piece, especially the shield of faith, is directly related to the use of our faith. Ours is neither a prayer for armor nor a prayer for victory, but a prayer of confession of our *need* for the armor. Employing the armor is an act of faith expressed by the mind and executed by the will in the attitudes and actions of life. The words "put on" and "take up" indicate our responsibility to prepare for battle. Just as taking clothes suitable for the climate is an act of the will based on the knowledge the mind has gained through investigation, so we must deliberately arm ourselves with Christ.

☙ ——————————— ❧

*Father, thank you for equipping me for spiritual battle. By faith I take each
piece of armor You have provided and choose to act in the awareness of my
opposition and Your protection. Thank you for victory in Christ.*

Our Wondrous Oneness

For we, though many, are one bread and one
body; for we all partake of that one bread.

1 Corinthians 10:17

In biology text books, we learn that the composition of the human body is a wonder of creation, confounding even the most advanced scientists. There are 206 bones in the body, but this number dwarfs in comparison to the number of cells and molecules it is composed of. Even when we reduce the picture from a body to a single organ, the molecular construction remains mind-boggling. God, knowing all, reminds us that there are an untold number of members in His family, one body, of which His children are members in particular.

The important thing to remember is the *oneness* of the body of which all believers are a part. For those who are associated with a small church, for a missionary seeking to reach the "one's and two's" in a difficult land, for a secret believer in a North African country, low numbers are often a cause for disappointment. What should be remembered is that any great number is comprised of smaller parts. Although some people use the word "body" carelessly by referring to "the body" as a local church in Boston or Bombay, the Word of God is clear: there is one universal body of all time, and believers in local fellowships are collectively members of that one body, the body of Christ. The blessing of oneness is a foundation of strength to all who believe.

> *The blessing*
> *of oneness is a*
> *foundation of strength*
> *to all who believe.*

The Lord Jesus said, "Whoever eats My flesh . . . has eternal life." No matter where the "flesh" of Christ goes, all who partake of Him share that same life. Each local church teaches this universal truth every time they break the bread and partake of the cup. And when we learn and grasp the fact that we are united to every other believer who has partaken of the Lord Jesus by faith, it becomes a source of great personal comfort.

No gathering on earth has been organized to accommodate the whole body of Christ at one time, but the thought brings a sense of the greatness and grandeur of His body. We are partakers of it by faith in a risen Christ. "Because I live, you shall live also" places the resurrection at the center of God's means of sharing the life of His Son in His body.

ꙮ ——————————— ꙮ

Father, thank you for giving me the life of Your Son and so making me one with You, with Him, and with all other believers. I rejoice that You have joined me to every believer from the beginning of the church.

Realizing Our Riches

. . . the eyes of your understanding being enlightened; that
you may know what is the hope of His calling, what are
the riches of the glory of His inheritance in the saints.

Ephesians 1:18

The crown jewels are on display in the Tower of London for visitors to marvel at and behold. Placed behind glass under lock and key, their security is vigilantly guarded. At the end of the day, all guests are ushered out and the building closed down only to open the next day to allow another long line of people to come and "ooh and aah." Even the Royals who own them only get to see and wear their regalia on special or official occasions.

What would you do if you were offered as many of the royal jewels as you would like from the vault where they are stored? And what would you do with them if you got them? The spiritual eyes that the Lord opened when we trusted Him for salvation are capable, by faith, of perceiving the riches of His inheritance. Imagine yourself literally receiving from the Lord's hands the riches He has amassed for you as a result of His work on Calvary. Surely you would receive all you could use from His hand. If you then stored them under lock and key at home, they would be useless. But if you wore them and enjoyed them, they would lose none of their splendor or beauty, but gain more glory for being displayed.

Our riches in Christ are freely given us by the Lord Himself. From His throne in heaven He offers the glorious riches of His inheritance to those in His family. The infinite riches of Christ's glory are waiting for us, not just to know, but to partake of and enjoy every day. We can return again and again to receive a further consignment of blessing for our enjoyment and use. A daily supply. A moment-by-moment installment. Never a fear of rejection. No insufficient supply. No one offered more than another. No line in which to wait. No payment we need to make. No need to share, as all have the same opportunity. Free to take and free to use. We cannot live His life without these riches that are provided in, and dispensed from, Christ Himself!

Why do we live in spiritual poverty?

Knowing this, how different our approach to the Lord and His throne will be. Our text today assures us that we can go beyond knowing about Christ's riches to being aware that they are for us to freely take and employ for His glory. So why do we live in spiritual poverty?

       ଅଠ —————————————— ଔ

Father, thank you for opening the heavens, Your home, and Your hands to me
so that all the riches made possible by Calvary are available to me.

Defending the Faith by Faith

. . . above all, taking the shield of faith with which you will
be able to quench all the fiery darts of the wicked one.

Ephesians 6:16

When I was in military training, every soldier had to have a rifle for the day's exercise. The whole company lined up near the armory to get a weapon. As each soldier filed past the armory, he grabbed a rifle which was his for the day. He carried it, marched with it, kept it clean, protected it, and learned to use it. If war broke out, he needed to know all about his weapon and be responsible for its care and effective use. In war a soldier fights with his weapon, as well as eats and even sleeps with it by his side. His rifle is a constant companion.

The shield of faith is ours—one of several pieces of armor available to the believer, given to us at conversion. The training necessary to use it effectively begins the moment we believe. This vital piece of armor needs to be taken up in our spiritual hand, held in front of us, and moved from side to side as we see the "fiery darts of the wicked one" heading our way. Training in the use of the shield can be tedious, but is a necessary exercise in the use of our faith. That training involves knowing what we believe and being prepared to contend earnestly and defend courageously the faith we possess.

Training is an exhausting exercise; it tires our whole being. If we do not commit to this training, we will easily set the shield and sword down, just as Christian did in *Pilgrim's Progress*. When our armor is on the ground, we are unprepared and become vulnerable to the darts of the enemy. The Lord exhorted His disciples who were sleeping, "Rise and pray, lest you enter into temptation." The danger is *not* "taking" the shield of faith because we are asleep, distracted, or exhausted by training or conflict.

When our armor is on the ground, we become vulnerable to the darts of the enemy.

This shield is capable of quenching *all* the fiery darts of the wicked one. The illustration is of the enemies' darts being extinguished when they meet the water-soaked leather shields of the Roman soldier. Satan's darts are aimed at our faith, as Peter learned from the Lord Jesus in Luke 22:32: "I have prayed for you, that *your faith* should not fail" (emphasis added). The shield of faith (what we believe) is like water to fire: the dart is extinguished and stopped and falls harmlessly to the ground. The shield of faith can cover every vital part of our being—especially our heart. Victory is by faith!

☙ ———————————————— ❧

Father, thank you for providing my shield of faith. I take it now and determine to hold it fearlessly in today's conflict.

The Price of Giving the Priceless One

He who did not spare His own Son, but delivered Him up for us
all, how shall He not with Him also freely give us all things?

Romans 8:32

E valuate the two gifts mentioned in this verse and compare the cost associated with them. The first gift is God's own Son. The second is condensed into the words "all things."

The cross of Christ is the central evidence of the price God was willing to pay in order for believing humanity to be counted as His children. In considering the cost of fulfilling such an objective, God willingly gave the ultimate price—His only Son. There was no other way for Him to bring many sons to glory.

When writing these words, the apostle Paul may have had in mind the amazing story of God commanding Abraham to sacrifice his only son on a mountain three days' journey from home. When Abraham's obedience was evident, God intervened and stopped Abraham's hand, saving the life of his son Isaac. God spared Abraham what He would not spare Himself. On Calvary, heaven was silent when Christ bore our sin in His own body.

God delivered His only Son to wicked men, to unjust Romans, to angry Jews, to willful scribes, to depraved priests, to an immoral crowd, in order that He might claim us as His own children. This was the supreme sacrifice. God Himself then poured out His anger against our sin on His beloved Son. God made Him "to be sin for us."

Although the resurrection is not mentioned in this verse, it is the reason God can then, through a living Christ, give us all things. He gave up His Son and with Him gave us all that was provided by Christ's death and resurrection.

What are the "all things" He has freely given to us? We can conclude that the term "every blessing" (of which we read in Ephesians 1:3) is a summary of all that we have in Christ. God gave us His Son and all that is in Him. The cost to give His Son was His Son's life. The cost of the "all things" is included in the sacrifice of Christ. But we must not separate what Christ is from what Christ gives. God does not give us Christ without giving "all things" that are in Christ.

These are not things we pray for, earn, or deserve. They are gifts. Our task is to learn of the gifts, say "thank you," and employ them.

℔ ———————————— ℳ

Father, thank you for giving Christ to me. I accepted Him as my Savior; I
commit myself to know the blessings found in Him.

Channels of Love

A new commandment I give to you, that you love one another;
as I have loved you, that you also love one another.

John 13:34

One of the gifts the Lord Jesus gave His disciples on the night He was betrayed was a "new commandment." We do not usually view a command as a gift, yet such a gift worked out in obedience will transform the life of every disciple. To fail to love one another is to live in disobedience. Loving one another is, therefore, not optional for any believer!

Our casual reaction is, "I can't love everyone! Besides, some people are really hard to love." In ourselves, we cannot love some folks that have particularly difficult idiosyncrasies. But Christ loved all of His disciples, even though some had personalities we might find "hard to love"—people like Peter, James, and John who thought so highly of themselves. And since loving one another is a command, the Lord expects us to obey—not to argue, compromise, or even complain that some are hard to love.

Take your eyes off what you cannot do and focus on Christ who has done it. Rather than looking at your inability to love, look in the other direction at His adequacy and power to love others through you. Obedience flows from faith in the person of Christ, who not only gave the command but is the source of this kind of love. We are not asked to generate this love, but simply to pass it on!

> *We are not asked to generate this love, but simply to pass it on!*

By faith, bask in Christ's unconditional and constant love for you. Soak your soul, marinate your mind, and wash your will in it. In ourselves we are helpless, but through His strength we can be the means Christ uses to love others. We accept His love and pass it on, untainted by our own ill feelings or unappreciative heart. Then love—*His love*—will spontaneously flow in abundance to "one another," and we will have kept His commandment.

Christ's love was sacrificial. His love through me will be sacrificial! His love was selfless, universal, and painful. It caused Him loss and cost His blood. His love through me will be selfless, universal, and painful and may cause me loss and perhaps cost blood. "Give as 'twas given to you in your need . . ."

ಬ ———————————— ೞ

Father, You loved me more than anyone by giving Your Son Jesus Christ for me. He has loved me without end. I now surrender to Him to be Your vehicle to show that same love to some unloving and unlovely person. Bring someone into my life that needs Your love. I give myself, my time, and my resources to You so that others will know Your love.

Desiring What God Desires

*Who desires all men to be saved and to come
to the knowledge of the truth.*

1 Timothy 2:4

If God "desires all men to be saved," why doesn't He do it? What is He waiting for? God could not want all to be saved without making adequate provision for all to be saved. The knowledge of the truth has been revealed in the Word of God, but His program of saving men is dependent on believers *communicating* that truth. We have possession of it and are responsible to get the message out. As we obey the commission to "Go," we know that the Lord is working with us.

We do not need to persuade God to save, or even to be willing to save, because we are reminded that He is "not willing that any should perish but that all should come to repentance" (2 Peter 3:9). We need to persuade *ourselves* that He is ready to save all who come to Him by Christ Jesus. God is waiting on us!

If we desire all men to be saved, as God does, then the harmony of purpose will work all things according to His own will. Perhaps we must ask ourselves: Do we desire all men to be saved? Do our lives and behavior reflect that longing of God's heart? Does how we spend our time, energy, and resources indicate that we believe this message?

We may find ourselves pleading with God to save someone who has not surrendered in faith to Christ. The Holy Spirit works in harmony with the living seed of the Word to convince and convert the hearts of men and women. As we teach Sunday school, God is waiting for all to come to know the Way. As we give out a tract, the Holy Spirit is desirous

God desires all to be saved. Do we?

that the recipient open his ears to the Truth. As we pray for heathen in a far-off country, God wants each one to believe in Christ as the Life. As we preach the gospel, the Lord is willing that none perish. As we give sacrificially to missions, it indicates our desire that all should be saved. God is revealing His grace to all who will hear. It is the hearer who must choose to listen, receive, believe, and accept the truth in Christ.

God desires all to be saved. Do we? Is God waiting for us to be more earnest and faithful as we call on His name in faith for the salvation of the lost?

— ೞ ⸻ ೮ —

Father, I choose to give evidence of Your desire to save all people by telling one person today of Your offer of the Truth in Christ.

Full and Final Forgiveness

*. . . who being the brightness of His glory and the express
image of His person . . . when He had by Himself purged our
sins, sat down at the right hand of the Majesty on high.*

Hebrews 1:3

Our world is not very conscious of sin. It is aware of failure, weakness, and so-called "white lies," but most of our society finds little time to mull over the existence or the effects of personal sin. In fact, so many live with sin that they have little conscience about it.

For the believer, being cleansed of sin is one of the greatest blessings we can know. In *Pilgrim's Progress,* Christian had an exhilarating experience when his sin rolled off his back, down the hill, and into the hole at the foot of the cross. If we harbor doubts about the full forgiveness of our sin, we cripple our Christian experience and carry the burden of fear that those sins will again be brought up before God. Christ's full sacrifice set God free to forgive all our sin.

The enemy hounds many believers into thinking that if sin is not confessed, it is not purged. Several Scriptures remind us that the work of Christ on the cross guaranteed sin would never again be brought against any believer. To serve God without fear requires a sound conviction that, in the words of an old song, "All my sins are gone, All because of Calvary." The peace that replaces fear makes it possible to go on my way rejoicing, believing that, because I have been completely cleansed, I can serve the Lord acceptably.

The Lord is seated in heaven because the Father has received Christ's sacrifice as adequate in atoning for the sin of the world. The Father seats His Son because Jesus has satisfied all the demands of God's character that had been offended by our sin. The seated Son at the Father's right hand is also adequate for me who had angered His holiness. Since God is satisfied, I can be satisfied as well. That satisfaction is the basis on which I can serve the Lord with joyfulness.

Because we are cleansed, we serve out of devotion to the Son who purged our sin. What joy! What rest! What peace! What forgiveness! What cleansing! What satisfaction!

         ❧ ———————————— ☙

Father, thank you for accepting the work of Your Son on the cross as adequate payment for my sin. I rejoice in that cleansing and reject any suggestion of the enemy that my sin still remain and need further purging. I stand in awe of Your Son seated on my behalf and celebrate the full and final forgiveness of all my sin.

Through a Glass Clearly

*. . . according to my earnest expectation and hope that in nothing
I shall be ashamed, but with all boldness, as always, so now also
Christ will be magnified in my body, whether by life or by death.*

Philippians 1:20

For those with failing eyesight, a magnifying glass is a constant companion. What a blessing to put one in front of the list of Joneses in the telephone book and actually be able to pick out the right one!

A magnifying glass makes what is invisible (or unreadable) to the naked eye visible. Christ, who is invisible to the world's eye, is waiting for us to "put ourselves in front of" Him so others can "read" Him. Christ is in us, and our body and life is the glass that God uses to make Him known to the world around us. My behavior stands between Christ and the world's eyes.

> *Christ is in us
> and visible to
> the world.*

Just as we pick up a magnifying glass to look at something closely, so the world "picks us up," places us in front of Christ, and reads Him in terms of our lives. As a believer with Christ resident in my body, I am always giving the world a view of Christ. It may not be what He wants or is pleased with, but it takes place nevertheless.

Sometimes a magnifying glass needs to be cleaned so it can be more effective. Since Christ is in us and visible to the world, all we are and all we do should reveal or magnify Him. If we keep our behavior clean and put our lives in front of Him, the world will see Christ clearly. If our lives are dirty through unconfessed sin, our glass is dirty and the view the world has of Christ will be clouded. Many of us give a distorted view of Christ because of the condition of the glass (our lives). For this reason, many are turned away from Christ as a result of what they see through us. We are, therefore, to be tools suitable and ready for the Master's use.

The blessing is that Christ lives in us and has chosen us to be the "magnifying glasses" the world uses to get to know Him. "Christ will be magnified" says Paul. We do not need to pray for Him to use us! He is waiting for us to be used. What a responsibility! What an opportunity! This is the kind of responsibility and opportunity no angel ever had.

                            ✠ ──────────── ✠

Father, thank you for revealing Christ to me through those who helped me come to Him as my Savior. I surrender my life to be cleansed so others will see Him clearly. I place myself at Your disposal in this world so the lost will see Christ.

Our Perfect Example

For I have given you an example, that you
should do as I have done to you.

John 13:15

No other leader can say this to his disciples in good faith (although Paul did tell the Corinthians to imitate him, even as he imitated the Lord). One of the unique features of the life of Christ is its perfection. In the context of today's verse, the perfect example He set was humble service to a group that included the lowest of men, Judas Iscariot. This is the first gift of seven the Lord mentions in the Upper Room Discourse of John 13-17.

Our Lord's example never changes. As we study His life, we are continually reminded of the unwavering character of His walk here on earth. If a friend were to say "follow me," we might well follow for a brief time or in one area of life. But there is always the possibility they will fall or leave the path.

The example of the Lord was for all time and every area of life. It's as if He says, "Live as I lived, love as I loved, serve as I served, care as I cared, speak as I spoke, walk as I walked, do good as I did good, die as I died." The list is endless, since His life is infinite. He never asks us to do what He had not done and done perfectly.

His living in us makes it possible to follow His example.

The more we explore His life, the more we are compelled to say with Pilate, "I find no fault in this man." The goal is to do as He did because we are the only ones who can make the absent Christ present to our world. As Christ made the invisible Father visible in terms of His life, we are commanded to do the same for the risen Christ through our lives. His living in us makes it possible to follow His example.

As we surrender our lives to the indwelling Christ, He will live through us and the world will know Christ is indeed alive in us. The Lord Himself says in Matthew 5:16, "Let your light so shine before men, that they may see your good works and glorify your Father in heaven." He who gave the example gives the power to follow it. Our faith in Christ's presence sets His power free in our beings to demonstrate that we can follow Him.

ဆ ——————————— ☜

Father, thank you for the perfect example of Christ's life so clearly described in Your Word. I surrender my being today to His power and light so the world will see that Christ is alive within me.

Giving and Getting

You were bought at a price.

1 Corinthians 7:23

Ownership is a great feeling. It is not always satisfying, but it is often a consummation of a long held desire. We see something in a store we would like to possess. We save. We crave. We may covet. We imagine it in our hands and home. Eventually we purchase it and take it home and place it prominently for all to see.

Christ bought us. He longed for us. He contemplated our position. He paid. He owns. He possesses us. Like a slave bought at the market and taken home for service, there is no dispute as to ownership. It's not a matter of *whether* we belong to Him—we just do.

Of course, we can fight that relationship and struggle every time He gives a command, or we can surrender all we are and have to Him and then find He will release all He is to us. We cannot have one without the other. Consecration to Christ will set us free from the slavery to sin and release all the blessings of being His possession.

The difference between enjoyable service to Christ and painful slavery to sin is a choice we make. The first response to the fact of God's ownership is to enunciate that truth over and over again. I am His! He owns me. I belong to Christ. This repetition brings a willingness to accept the condition God has established. When my mind and heart accept this relationship, I start to understand my purpose in life. When I begin to enjoy the blessedness of this union, I then learn to be released from slavery and the sin that so easily beset me.

I am Christ's servant by ownership; I choose to be His from my heart. Rejecting the idea of His ownership does not change the fact; accepting the fact does change my mind! Submitting to my position produces joy in service and releases all the blessings of my intimate relationship with Christ.

> *I am Christ's servant by ownership; I choose to be His from my heart.*

We may want Christ to release all His blessings without surrendering all our willingness, but that cannot be. As we hand over all we are to Him, He is willing to hand over all He is to us. Our consecration affects the enjoyment of our completeness in Him. "Give it all to Jesus!"

❮❯

Father, thank you for purchasing me by the blood of Your Son. I am Yours. I choose to be Your servant and offer You all that I am and have.

Resurrection's Guarantee

And if Christ is in you, the body is dead because of sin,
but the Spirit is life because of righteousness.

Romans 8:10

The fact of Christ's indwelling is not in question in this text (or in any other New Testament passage). The "if" in Romans 8:10 should be read as a positive truth, not one which questions the validity of God's promise to give His Son to dwell in each believer. "*Since* Christ is in you . . ." would be a suitable translation of this important facet of our great salvation.

Christ takes up His residence in everyone who believes the gospel, which includes the fact of Christ's death for our sin and His resurrection for our justification. The resurrection is God's seal on the finished work of Christ. Without the resurrection, Christ cannot dwell in anyone. "If anyone does not have the Spirit of Christ, he is not His" is the fact that precedes our text in verse 9.

Paul is making it very clear here, as he does elsewhere, that the indwelling of Christ in the body of the believer does not silence the activity of sin in that body. The body still contains the sin nature, and the sin nature will continue to do its work of causing the body to pass through death. Death is the end result for all who have a sin nature, just as Hebrews 9:27 says, "It is appointed to men to die once, but after this the judgment." Romans 5:12 also reminds us of the universality of sin and death.

Just because we become believers does not remove the sin nature or its effects on our bodies. True, some believers will escape death in the body if they are "alive and remain until the coming of the Lord," but death is sure for all others. Believers and unbelievers alike suffer the same diseases and death. For every birth with a sin nature there will be a death. Let us not be occupied, though, with the fact of the death of the body so much as with the fact of the indwelling of Christ.

Death cannot hold us any more than it could hold Christ.

The living Christ gives us resources to deal with advancing age and its accompanying diseases and death. Christ gives us life that is eternal, life that carries us out of the clutches of death. We will pass through death, but death cannot hold us any more than it could hold Christ, because we are in Christ.

℘ ———————————— ℭ

Father, thank you for the completeness of my salvation. I rejoice in the fact that Christ is living in my body. Even when I face death, I claim His resurrection as a guarantee that I will not be held by death.

Walking in the Light

But if we walk in the light as He is in the light, we
have fellowship with one another, and the blood of
Jesus Christ His Son cleanses us from all sin.

1 John 1:7

The forgiveness of sin is an integral part of the work of salvation for every believer. The conversion experience cannot take place unless we are first aware of our sin, and aware that we need forgiveness. The foundational work of Christ on the cross was to bear our sin in His own body on the tree. The resurrection of Christ makes it possible for God to forgive all the sin of any who come to Him by Christ.

The forgiveness of sin establishes a relationship of sonship that is eternal and cannot be broken. God becomes our Father and we His children because He bestows His life in us by His living Son and through the Holy Spirit.

Many who have trusted Christ for salvation are conscious of the continuing pattern of sin in their lives. Without solid biblical teaching, they may think that such sin will break the relationship established at conversion. This thought suggests the need for a second work of grace or a repeated salvation experience.

But the Scriptures are clear that a second salvation cannot be accomplished. It further declares that the relationship cannot be broken. Rather, our fellowship with the Father and His Son can be injured and needs repair, and this repair is only possible as we confess our sin, as verse 9 teaches.

The instruction in 1 John 1:7 reminds us that the continual fellowship with the triune God is the catalyst for a consciousness of sin and the subsequent confession and restoration of fellowship. The blood of Jesus Christ is adequate for full, final, and perfect cleansing of all sin. John does not instruct us to "ask for forgiveness." But taken together our guidance is clear: fellowship with a holy God is injured if we go our own way and live in disobedience. The loss of fellowship should be so poignant that we do everything possible to restore that fellowship. Our part is confession and turning away from our careless living which is painful to our Father and His Son. The Father's part is cleansing and restoration of fellowship.

Walking in the light is a guarantee that the light of His presence will expose any inconsistency in our lives and cause us to turn from that behavior to the cleansing power of His Light. His blood indicates that God justly forgave my sin. His light shines on our lives as we walk in harmony with the Father.

‸ ———————————— ℣

Father, thank you for the continual fellowship that You offer me. I confess
that I fail in maintaining fellowship. I choose to enjoy Your presence today.

February

ADDITIONAL BLESSINGS TO CHANGE YOUR "THANKING"!

". . . the first principles of the oracles of God . . ."
Hebrews 5:12

God now brings thee to His dwelling,
Spreads for thee His feast divine;
Bids thee welcome, ever telling
What a portion there is thine.
John Nelson Darby

February

The Birds of the Air

It is amazing what intricate care the Father provides for the birds of the air. The best-known biblical reference to this care is that the Father knows the fall of every sparrow. Stop and consider the enormity of this statement. It causes us to stand in awe of the Father's care for us because He also says we "are of more value than many sparrows."

Sparrows are found throughout the world in many different environments. God chose that common bird to remind us of the distinction between the lowliest of His feathered creations and the highest of His earthly creatures, those made in His own image.

Birds do not need our help to live. God built into the culture of our winged friends some simple lessons, useful for all who choose to follow Christ. Over and over, God uses the birds to teach us of His care, His provision, His knowledge, their purpose, their interaction with society, and their birth and death.

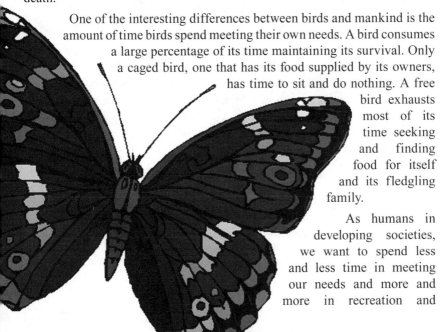

One of the interesting differences between birds and mankind is the amount of time birds spend meeting their own needs. A bird consumes a large percentage of its time maintaining its survival. Only a caged bird, one that has its food supplied by its owners, has time to sit and do nothing. A free bird exhausts most of its time seeking and finding food for itself and its fledgling family.

As humans in developing societies, we want to spend less and less time in meeting our needs and more and more in recreation and idleness. Is that progress? Birds fulfill their purpose by building their nests, feeding, raising, and training their young, and singing a gladsome song for our enjoyment.

The example for us is the carefree existence of birds that live out their life under the watchful eye of their Creator, unlike the anxiety and frustration of human conflict and pressure. Birds seem to play their games of tag, follow the leader, and "watch out for the cat!" But God clearly provides for their needs, at the same time allowing them to face the fears of getting caught in the claws of some preying feline.

Relationships are one of the contrasts that the Lord wanted to point out to us. He is the birds' Creator—but He is your Father! If, as Creator, He shows meticulous care for the lowly sparrow, will He not, as our Father, bestow on us a greater level of care and make available a greater level of provision, fostered by a greater investment, coupled to a greater goal? Surely, since we know this to be true, our acknowledgement of these facts should cause us to trust His provision and care as the birds do.

The birds of the air preach a practical sermon to any observant believer. These birds, like the lilies that they rest beside, do not toil or spin, yet their needs are all provided. The significant part of their day spent in seeking, feeding, and preening, shows us that, as children of the Father, we too are, moment by moment, to draw for our needs from the abundance that our Father has laid before us. Birds fulfill their duties daily as they search for their own food; so, too, we are to fulfill our own responsibilities by feeding ourselves from God's holy Word.

God chose the eagle to help us understand the need for development from a state of total dependence to one of self-reliance (Deuteronomy 32:11). But that self-reliance is not devoid of dependence on the Creator's provision and care. The little eaglet does not like to be disturbed from its cozy nest. He is no doubt filled with fear, flailing his wings as he descends toward the canyon floor at an alarming rate. What comfort when the strong wings of his mother are spread as a net for her fearful, falling offspring. He is borne upward, to be dumped back into the nest, which becomes increasingly uncomfortable as the mother removes some of the "down comforter" each time he leaves it. She does this so that the baby bird will not want to stay home when the Creator has ordained that he depart.

Our Father has done the same for us. He has made all the arrangements for our growth and, at the same time, made all the provision for our development. The resources are all available. The appropriation is dependent on our industrious application of truth to the situations of life which our Father allows. Reliance on Christ is a growing appreciation of all that is available in Him. Count on the faithfulness of the Father as the bird does on its faithful Creator.

Crucified to the World

*But God forbid that I should boast except in the
cross of our Lord Jesus Christ, by whom the world
has been crucified to me, and I to the world.*

Galatians 6:14

The cross of Jesus stands as the central masterpiece of the Word of God for our salvation. The resurrection of Jesus Christ is the greatest demonstration of divine power on behalf of man's needs. But the New Testament is clear—the one is ineffective without the other.

When Christ died, I died with Him. The absolute identity of the believer with Christ in His death is the basis of most blessings available to us. The work of Christ on the cross was to destroy the works of the devil and to separate the believer from the influence of the sin nature, the power of the flesh, the judgment of the law, and the influences of the world.

Together with the flesh and the devil, the world stands as the primary enemy that the believer faces daily. This enemy, all around us, tries to coerce us to make it our source of self-preservation.

Our victory over the world is based on the irrefutable fact that, when Christ died, we died. Had Christ not been raised, He would be dead and we still in our sin. However, because Christ has been raised, we have been given His new life to direct our life. The world's power fades as we rely on the life of the Savior. The world does not go away, but the new life of Christ makes the world lose its attraction.

As Romans 6 says, we are raised "to walk in newness of life" rather than to walk "according to the course of this world," as we did before we were "crucified." We now can walk worthy of the life that we have been given by our resurrection with Christ.

> *The new life of Christ makes the world lose its attraction.*

The world has also been crucified to me at the cross of Christ. Crucifixion is a visible and vicious method of death. Death in itself means separation. It is separation from, rather than annihilation of, the world that is in view. The world is still around, but it has been crucified (separated) from me as a ruling force. I can, in the power of Christ, defeat its attraction and self-preserving talk. In place of occupation with this present evil world, God holds out to me the Father's world, the future world, the final world. I died to this perishing world so that I might live for the next world.

℧ ———————————————— ℣

Father, thank you for bringing me into union with Christ. I accept the death of Christ as my source of victory over this present world.

All Things

Therefore let no one glory in men. For all things are yours:
whether Paul or Apollos or Cephas, or the world or life or
death, or things present or things to come—all are yours.

1 Corinthians 3:20-21

God has given all things around us as our servants and teachers. This glorious statement seems so inclusive and helps us to realize the adequacy of the Lord to minister to us from every corner of His creation. It cannot be declared any more emphatically than God saying, "All things are yours!" Since these things are ours, we should bow in appreciation and learn in appropriation.

Seldom does Scripture delineate the things that are given as this verse does. Paul invites us to stand in the expanse of all that is allowed to come into our lives, and to realize that each comes from the hands of the Father Himself. The Corinthians were blessed with many "things," but they were not always thankful. Instead, they were sometimes argumentative, occasionally jealous, and often abusive of the wonderful blessings.

These Corinthian believers received the arguments of the apostle Paul and were tempted to set them aside because they were entranced by the eloquence of Apollos, as he masterfully laid down the grand doctrines of the faith. Cephas, on the other hand, was the superb expounder and exhorter of the lessons learned when walking with Jesus. All these, and many other teachers, were brought into their lives for their edification. We, too, often pick and choose among our favorite teachers, but all are given to us to bring us to maturity. Surely, we can hear God speak through each one.

The world around was unfolded to the Corinthians to help their progress in Christ. The lilies of the field taught them not to worry. The seeds of the ground reminded them of the resurrection. The sheep in their flocks spoke about the care of the Shepherd. The grass of the field illustrated the brevity of life. The birth of a baby brought life to the eye of the student and taught lessons of hunger, development, relationship, love, and growth. Every death reminded them of the shortness of life, the reality of sorrow, and the blessing of passing from our world to the Father's world.

The cosmos speaks about the glory of God. The present is the sphere in which I contact my generation. Because it will not endure, I focus on things that are to come: the Father's house, the face of Christ, and eternal life. All these things are mine.

જી ——————————— ও

Father, thank you for giving all these things to me. I confess that I often walk by them, with my eyes and ears closed to their teaching.

An Eternal Inheritance

*To an inheritance incorruptible and undefiled and that
does not fade away, reserved in heaven for you.*

1 Peter 1:4

A true inheritance costs nothing. It is a gift from a relative or friend that is distributed after he or she dies. Such an inheritance is disbursed according to the will and wishes of the deceased. Usually the will is written, signed, witnessed, and stored in a safe place. After the person's death, the will is read and the inheritance is disseminated to those mentioned in the will. Strictly speaking, no one can buy this inheritance, and normally, there is no request for an inheritance. It is a choice made by the testator during his lifetime.

Peter's letter was written as an encouragement to believers who had been scattered to the land that we now know as Turkey. Their faith in Christ drew severe persecution and drove them far from home in Israel. Many lost everything they possessed, and some found themselves sold as slaves. The suffering continued, even as they sought various means of livelihood.

The apostle Peter reminds them of the fact that, though they had lost everything in this life, they had an inheritance that is secure and significant in heaven. Peter reminds them that the promise of their resurrection is secure, even if they lose their life for Christ's sake. He urges them to glory in the fact that God is keeping them by His power. All these wonderful truths were used to encourage these believers to rejoice, despite their current suffering and persecution.

Making sure that your last will is carried out after your death is a serious problem. In our world, many families are unhappy with the way the inheritance is distributed. How can you make sure that your will is honored? Someone said, "Do your giving while you're living, then you'll know where it's going."

But what did God do about our inheritance in His Son? The Lord Jesus wrote His will in what we call the New Testament, stating the many blessings that He wanted distributed after His death. He died on the cross to make His will valid. He then rose from the grave to be the administrator of His own will. What a profound accomplishment for God and for us. All the resources of God in Christ are being dispersed through the Holy Spirit to every believer, as we exercise faith in Christ for those blessings. Believe that you have them, and you will enjoy and employ them. The initial offering, or earnest, of this inheritance is being distributed now. The rest is waiting until we see His face.

⊗ ———————————————— ⟨⟩

*Father, thank you for the inheritance waiting for me in heaven. By faith, I
partake of these blessings today, as I live for You in this world.*

A Beautiful Balance

For no one ever hated his own flesh, but nourishes and cherishes it, just as the Lord does the church.

Ephesians 5:29

We are cherished as the bride of Christ. If life does not go as we think it should, we begin to wonder if we are among the cherished. There is the temptation to compare our lives with the lives of others and wonder if some are loved more than others. Does the Lord show how much He treasures us by the "good times" that we have from Him? No. Rather, we are cherished by the Lord because His love is not varied in relation to His bride. The bride is cherished totally and completely. No member of the bride is loved more or less.

Not only does Christ cherish, but He also nourishes us as His church. Nourishment is an evidence of His deepest love. We give to our children what is best for their health. How blessed we are to know that our Bridegroom provides the nourishment that will produce a bride without spot or wrinkle or anything undesirable. Like God's care for Esther and the three friends of Daniel, His care is greater for His promised bride. We will be fairer than the children of men.

> *No member of the bride is loved more or less.*

Another blessing of Christ is that He provides nourishment, enabling us to grow up into full maturity. It is available and adequate for our every need. The table is loaded with all the best spiritual food for the bride. He loves her and died for her so that she will be a glorious church to Him.

The cherishing of a bride is emotional, whereas nourishment is largely physical. What a beautiful balance is provided for us by our wonderful Bridegroom! All His emotional support reminds us of His deep love, shown by His cross, where He gave Himself for the church. All the balanced nutrition of spiritual blessings is to be appropriated, so that we will be absolutely glorious in that day when we see His face for the first time. When we have attained that glory, it will be a glory that will never fade away.

All we need is set on the heavily-loaded table. Come and eat; stay and dine. Feast on His love and His deep care for our every thought. Bask in the evenness of His unchanging devotion to us as His bride. He has done all and waits for us to enjoy His feast, so that we will be emotionally, mentally, and spiritually beautiful in that day.

そ — ∽

Father, thank you for giving me a Bridegroom that cares so deeply for my every blessing. He has provided for every need that I have.

Submit to Your Head

But I want you to know that the head of every man is Christ, the head of woman is man, and the head of Christ is God.

1 Corinthians 11:3

Authority figures seem to be continually challenged by other people. The statements from God in this verse have been under attack for generations. Many people approach the message as being archaic and out of touch with social progress. The Bible must be adjusted, they say, not the culture reigned in from its wild pursuit of self-satisfaction.

But God did not make provision to accommodate man's shifting opinions. What He said or meant does not change. Those who do not accept this try to make the Bible say what they want, and seek to overthrow its authority altogether.

Today's verse is found in an area of Scripture that is specifically addressed to the church in its corporate functions. From other places in the epistles, Christ is established as the head of the church. From there, we can work upwards from man to God, and downwards from man to woman. The word "downward" is distasteful to some women, who reject the simplicity of this verse. But the very word "head" describes the issuing of authority, as well as the exercise of it in God's divine order.

The head of the physical body is never questioned. Direction, appropriation, absorption, instruction, and many other functions are largely limited to the head. What is significant is that God did not repudiate the truth of Christ's equality with Himself by saying that "the head of Christ is God." Christ took a place of submission in order that He might accomplish our salvation. It did not negate His divine attributes or His equality with the Father.

The entire structure of God's order is a blessing clearly laid out for all to accept. The specific truth that is enunciated provides order in the functioning of God's administration. The Lord is talking about His divine order, not the distribution of gifts, abilities, or even the proportioning of our spiritual blessings in Christ. All in Christ share the same divine resources.

> *The entire structure of God's order is a blessing.*

A woman, by willingly submitting to the man, does not renounce her individuality in God's sight. Rather, she is incorporating her God-given role to create a functioning marriage, home, church, and society. Denying her role and responsibility does not change the fact. Accepting the wisdom of it by faith leads to order and blessing.

ଚ —————————— ଔ

Father, You have placed me in the position of your appointment. I accept it and rejoice in Your wisdom. I choose to submit to my head.

The Power of Weakness

For though He was crucified in weakness, yet He lives by
the power of God. For we also are weak in Him, but we
shall live with Him by the power of God toward you.

2 Corinthians 13:4

Admitting weakness is the key to appropriating the strength that is Christ's. Paul takes us back to the life of Christ on earth. His humanness was evident in the early part of His ministry, when He sat on the well wearied from His journey. In the end of His life, He said, "I thirst." As God, He could easily have ministered to His own needs, but He voluntarily chose not to so that He might be exemplary and sympathetic to us in our pilgrimage.

Christ portrayed weakness and lived in dependence on His Father. Over and over again, He reminded His hearers that He did nothing apart from His Father's instruction. We have no problem accepting the fact of His weakness in suffering and death. We clearly understand that He lives by the power of God who raised Him from the dead.

But the statement that we are weak in Him confuses our minds, when other Scripture verses say that our strength is in Him and our power is through Him. Paul is identifying with the life of Christ. His connection is so close that he, too, will not use his powers to deliver himself from his foes. Paul did perform miracles, but he chose not to use them for defending himself or defeating those opposing the gospel. Like Christ, he appears weak and is willing to submit to anything, as his Savior did.

The demonstration of the power of God toward the Corinthians may refer to a future visit that Paul was hoping would take place. In that day, God might have appointed Paul to use that power for His defense. In that day, the power of God would be shown in accordance with the will of God.

The order of the day for the apostle was the same as that of His Lord. Christ was crucified in weakness and in seeming defeat. That is the lot of all who follow the Lord. Peter got it right when he summarized his discovery after the Holy Spirit came: "The sufferings of Christ and the glory that would follow" (1 Peter 1:11). Suffering first—glory later. Weakness now—power then. The power of God is not primarily demonstrated in amazing miracles. Perhaps the greatest sign of divine power is to love those that despitefully use you. Paul was defending his apostleship and he submitted to the same kind of weakness, even though he possessed the power of God.

Father, thank you for the example of the apostle in his life and ministry to the church. I choose to be identified with my Lord as well.

The Ministry of the Gospel

*Therefore, since we have this ministry, as we have
received mercy, we do not lose heart.*

2 Corinthians 4:1

Paul was a deacon. Although he may not have been an officially recognized deacon in a local church, he was a planter and servant of many churches. The word that he uses to describe his ministry is the word that is elsewhere translated "deacon." Such a person is a servant of the church and a minister in the body of Christ. Paul saw himself as a deacon to the entire church, not just to one local church. Here, he is reminding the Corinthians that He has a ministry which is a stewardship of the gospel of the Lord Jesus Christ.

Surely, he is not speaking of himself alone or just the church of Corinth. He is summarizing the responsibility of all in the body. Each specific duty in the body of Christ may be different, while the overall service is the obligation of the whole. We cannot say that we have no ministry. That is to call God a liar! We all have received a ministry.

As we consider the various operations within the body of Christ, we know that each believer has a special and unique responsibility for the effective ministry of the entire body—although not everyone in the body knows their gift and service. We may not be doing what we are supposed to do, or what we are called to do, or what we have been equipped to do, but we have been given stewardship of the good news of salvation in Christ.

Everyone who believes the gospel for themselves also receives it to give to others. Not all are called to "preach" the gospel. Not all of us do "personal evangelism" well. Not all of us can travel across the seas with the good news. Not all of us are asked to perform or serve in the same way, but all of us have received some aspect of making the good news known. When you receive something, the polite response is to say "thank you." That expression of our heart reinforces our understanding of our responsibility to make known the good news.

For many believers, presenting the gospel is a discouraging ministry. Most people do not want to hear. Others reject it. Some persecute those who bring it. A few receive it, and their lives are changed. Those people lift our hearts. The Lord gives us adequate mercy in the face of all who say no. What a message we have received. What a miracle we have received. What a ministry we have received. What mercy we have in our Lord Jesus Christ.

ଐ ———————————— ଓ

*Father, thank you for the blessing of a special ministry in the gospel of Your
Son. I accept that service and render it in Your power.*

Twin Blessings

Grace and peace be multiplied to you in the
knowledge of God and our Lord Jesus Christ.

2 Peter 1:2

Like twin sisters, "grace and peace" are used by Peter at the beginning of a very vivid description of the end times. His short letter, like that of Jude, introduces many figures of speech to warn of the impending judgment of God on a godless world. The cataclysmic destruction of the world is a source of worry and fear to many in our world today. Peter informs us about the physical world being burned up and disposed of, and he further warns that the spiritual conflict is escalating at an alarming rate.

Some Bible students suggest that "grace and peace" are two different greetings, one for Gentiles and one for the Jews. Peace is the formal greeting of "Shalom" among the Israelites, but, for believers of all races, the twin blessings are repeated time and again for our consideration.

The order is also important, as Peter reminds us of the grace that came to us ahead of peace because of the preaching of the gospel and the ministry of the Holy Spirit. This message was not understood by the Old Testament prophets or by Peter himself before the gift of the Holy Spirit. But, with the advent of the Father's gift, the beautiful array of blessings included in the word "grace" became a spring welling up in his own soul. Peter, like the other writers, did not wish the saints to miss the impact or the multiplicity of the gifts that God has presented to us in Christ.

Peace is the second blessing, and it, too, has a manifold impact on the life of all who believe. After the initial endowment of grace at salvation, which included "peace with God," the unfolding of His peace grows greater, even as the river of Ezekiel gets deeper and broader with every step. Who can measure His grace and peace?

But how do we grow into the appreciation and appropriation of these twins in our daily lives? The answer is clearly stated in this verse—"the knowledge of God and our Lord Jesus Christ." It is striking that neither grace nor peace are to be realized by our feelings or circumstances. So often we expect peace to only be present when trials and troubles are absent. On the contrary, the peace within is permanent, while the difficulties of life are temporary. One is dependent on Christ, the other on circumstances. Only by growing in the knowledge of Christ can we understand and enjoy the adequate supply of His grace and peace.

❧ ———————————— ❧

Father, thank you for the multiplicity of Your blessings in grace and peace. I acknowledge my need and claim these in Christ.

The Knowledge of Power

*That you may know . . . what is the exceeding
greatness of His power toward us who believe,
according to the working of His mighty power.*

Ephesians 1:19

A s was his custom, Paul told the church at Ephesus what he was praying for them. Most of the prayers of the epistles are directed toward the churches' appropriation of the blessings that God gave them in Christ. The specific request in today's Scripture refers back to verse 18 which says, "that you may know . . . what is the exceeding greatness of His power." To put it simply, Paul is asking that they might know the extent of the power that is available to them by faith in Christ—the power that is theirs.

> *As believers, we
> possess the power
> of God in Christ.*

It is not a prayer for power but for the *knowledge* of that power. A sheaf of verses can be quoted reminding us that, as believers, we possess the power of God in Christ. In spite of all these statements of God, one of the most common prayers that we repeat is for strength to live the Christian life. It is inconsistent with the Scriptures to ask for those blessings that God has already given us in the person of Christ. But, by habit, ignorance, immaturity, or unbelief, we echo the words again and again, not stopping to hear God say that His power is in us and we should know and appropriate it by faith.

How do we know, by experience, the strength that is available to us in Christ? There are several responsibilities. One is to study the Word of God and learn the blessings that are ours in Christ. That study is a lifelong commitment to knowing these gifts, thereby growing in knowledge. A second is to begin a practice in prayer of thanking God for every gift that we discover in His Word. The exercise of faith is a key ingredient in developing a reliance on Christ in all our activities. We must believe that God has given these gifts and, by active faith, draw from these resources for life and service every day. Confession of weakness in oneself is a mental activity that releases Christ's power in one's life.

This growth will not be based on feelings, but solely on faith in what God says. Too often, the prayer for strength is generated by feelings and not by an admission of weakness. His "mighty power" is available in Christ to any believer who admits his weakness and claims it by faith. We do not need more power. We must accept by faith and employ what He has already given.

⁂ ─────────────── ⁂

*Father, thank you for all the power of Christ which rests on me. I choose to
live in His strength today instead of pleading for more.*

The Primary Foundation Stones

*For there is one God and one Mediator between God
and men, the Man Christ Jesus, who gave Himself a
ransom for all, to be testified in due time . . .*

1 Timothy 2:5-6

The tri-unity of God, consisting of three distinct persons, is a concept that is impossible for our simple minds to comprehend, yet it is not so profound that we cannot accept it. God exists as one, but expresses Himself and appoints His work to each member distinctly. The Father is the source of all that God does. The Son is the one who accomplishes that work, and the Holy Spirit applies the work. The Father presents Christ as the mediator: "The Father sent the Son to be the Savior of the world." The Son is the one who accomplishes the fact: "He was manifested to bear away our sins." The Holy Spirit was appointed as the one who "will convict the world of sin."

> *God could
> not give less
> when the full
> and final act
> of substitution
> took place.*

Substitution is the primary foundation stone of God's salvation. It is a concept instituted by God in the Garden of Eden, promoted in the Levitical sacrifices, and perfectly carried out by the Man, Christ Jesus. Since substitution was appointed by God for the atonement of sin throughout the Old Testament, God could not give less when the full and final act of substitution took place. There is no other event that can be pointed to as the satisfactory substitutional sacrifice than the surrender of Christ on the cross. The fact of His act being voluntary is simply stated: He "gave Himself." The Father sent Him, but He went voluntarily. He offered himself by the eternal Spirit, entirely without coercion.

Substitution must also be for *all* because God says *all*! Several other Scripture verses repeat the same glorious truth of the full and complete substitution for all mankind. If substitution is not for all, then God must condemn all mankind to a lost eternity for whom He did not provide a substitute.

Redemption is the key aspect of God's provision. The word "ransom" teaches us that a price must be paid so that the redeemed ones can then be set free. Christ Jesus died as my substitute, fully paying the price so that, on the basis of my faith in that redemptive work, I am set free. God was satisfied that the full price was paid for all by Christ, and I am satisfied as well. There is no other god, no other mediator, no other substitute, no other testimony.

ଅ ———————————— ଔ

Father, thank you for sending Christ to be my substitute, and thank you that He stands as my Mediator before Your face. I glory in Christ my Savior.

Peace, Perfect Peace

*Now may the Lord of peace Himself give you peace
always in every way. The Lord be with you all.*

2 Thessalonians 3:16

One of the first gifts of salvation is peace between God and the sinner. The most profound statement of this peace is found in Romans 5:1: "Therefore having been justified by faith, we have peace with God through our Lord Jesus Christ." This is the end of God's animosity toward our sin, because God counts our faith as an adequate evidence of our confidence in His Word, regarding our sinfulness and the sufficiency of Christ's sacrifice. The relationship with God completely changes. God's peace, found in Christ, comes to rest in us as an abiding presence. We have peace since Christ, the Prince of Peace, is in us.

Today's Scripture seems to introduce several variables that could bring doubt to the timid and unsure soul. Does the word "may" indicate some possibility that the peace, which flows from the heart of Christ, may run dry or cease to flood our soul? Do we need to pray that the Lord of peace will continue to give peace? Might the God of peace desist, waiting for a new prayer for a fresh supply? The question itself sounds capricious. How can the only One who calls Himself the Lord be present, without His special virtue also being present? Is it possible to have a surgeon in residence without his skills of surgery? That is ludicrous. The Lord of Peace cannot be living in us without that peace flowing from His very person.

A new problem then presents itself to our thinking. Since the Lord of Peace is resident, why do we not always enjoy His peace? Is it His failure to give, or my failure to receive? Since there is no change in Him, it must be my unbelief or disobedience. If I do not claim the profusion of peace which He offers, I cannot blame Him. I do not need to pray for it; I need to confess my unbelief and sin in order that the enjoyment of His peace is resumed in every way. The surgeon is waiting for us to lie down and allow him to do his work. Christ is always waiting for us.

> *We have peace since Christ, the Prince of Peace, is in us.*

Paul goes on to write, "The Lord *be* with you all." The *be* is in italics to indicate that the translators tried to help us understand the implications. If we change the word *be* to *is*, we can relish the fullness of the Lord's presence and revel in the peace flowing from His heart. The Lord *is* peace, and He cannot be resident without His peace.

ཐ ———————————— ཐ

*Father, thank you for the abundance of peace found in Christ. I confess that
I do not cherish and employ it always. I claim peace today.*

A Safe Harbor

That by two immutable things, in which it is impossible for
God to lie, we might have strong consolation, who have
fled for refuge to lay hold of the hope set before us.

Hebrews 6:18

Is your life being overwhelmed by the storms of life that are sent or allowed by God? They are in your life because God wants you to find no refuge in the lies of the enemy or the false hopes of your society. The enemy of our peace and hope is luring us to seek a safe harbor in his lies, but no safety and no security are available in him.

Thus, into this climate, so polluted by the enemy and our own willingness to follow his footsteps, comes the God of all hope, who offers our failing souls two unchangeable characteristics: His oath and His absolute truthfulness as a double anchor. A ship must be tied, both bow and stern, to have hope of security in the refuge of a harbor.

Why does God use His absolute truthfulness as a basis of consolation during these storms? The reason is that the enemy of all this is "the Liar" who has projected his unchanging practice on mankind from the Garden of Eden to the present. We do not advance far in life without lying in various situations. A lie is thought to be the means of escaping problems and pressures, or a means of hope that our untrue words will somehow change the circumstances for the better. That is the lie of the enemy, but we so easily accept it as true. Many people in a hopeless situation lie in hopes of changing the unfortunate developments. The ultimate result is, "Be sure your sin will find you out."

The God of all consolation is and will be the only one who offers His person and character to all who flee. It is our responsibility to flee and find the refuge; His is to offer all that He is to us in our fear and anxiety. He is unchanging. It is we who change! It is our temptation to shop around in search of a safe harbor, even when we know that the only safe harbor is God. Flee, weary one, to Him and tie your fatigued soul to His strong support.

> *It is our responsibility to flee and find the refuge; His is to offer all that He is to us in our fear and anxiety.*

A safe harbor is the goal of those who know that a storm is on the way. Even those who are caught in the storm make every adjustment to go for the harbor. The storms allowed by God drive us to the refuge of our blessed Savior, who is the anchor of our soul.

ಬ —————————————— ಚ

Father, thank you for the storm that is raging in my life today. It has driven me from the rocks of the enemy to Your safe harbor.

The Occupation of Our Mind

Let the word of Christ dwell in you richly in all wisdom, teaching and admonishing one another in psalms and hymns and spiritual songs, singing with grace in your hearts to the Lord.

Colossians 3:16

Most of us would immediately point to the Bible as the Word of Christ. A few, however, may limit this term to only the words printed in red. No confusion is brought to our overall understanding if we say that the Scriptures in general are referred to by the phrase "the Word of Christ" for, if "the Word of Christ" is limited to those specific words that Christ spoke during His pilgrimage on earth, the term would have been plural—"words." Because it is singular, it refers to all that is presented projecting Christ in the Scriptures.

It is instructive to note that we are not urged to pray for the Word of Christ to dwell in us, but to allow it to fill and flood our capacities for meditation and instruction. The Word is available to us through the mind of Christ. The operation of our abilities is a choice which takes place in the throne room of our souls. We decide what will occupy our mind and emotions. We have a host of things waiting at the doors of our soul for the opportunity of feeding and filling our mind. Too often a conflict develops when the Word of Christ wants to influence our thinking and action, but instead we open the door to something totally incompatible with His thoughts.

Our ears should be committed to the voice of Christ, to hearing what He is saying. The oft-repeated statement of Christ reminds us of our responsibility when He says, "He who has ears to hear let him hear." We have ears in our head and in our heart, and we decide what will enter and what will stay. Paul says "let," which reminds us that we bear the obligation for the entrance and abundance of Christ's word in our heart. Obviously, the word "richly" means "fully" and perhaps suggests overflowing in bounty. Our Lord said, "for out of the abundance of the heart the mouth speaks."

When so much is filling and flooding our souls, the overflow will show up in our conversation with others and with God. What a joy to hear a believer, in the quiet moments of life, singing some truth that Christ has repeatedly taught him. The music of the church is designed to be carried from the meeting in the sanctuary of our heart. Not all tunes are suitable, but souls can repeat and reiterate grand teaching as they fellowship together. The key to the occupation of our mind is reading, memorizing, and meditating on the Word of Christ.

❧ ──────────────── ❧

Father, thank you for giving me the mind of Christ to know the Word of Christ.

14

FEBRUARY

BLESSINGS ALL MINE WITH 10,000 BESIDES!

The Perfect Sin Offering

For He made Him who knew no sin to be sin for us, that
we might become the righteousness of God in Him.

2 Corinthians 5:21

This summary of God's decision and action is one of the most profound statements of Scripture. The explanation of what God was doing when Christ hung on the cross is expounded in earlier verses. Paul discusses reconciliation so that we can better understand the staggering price paid for us to be fully reconciled to God. Because of the spiritual nature of this summary, God must then explain how it is possible for Him to thoroughly change sinful man in order that a relationship can be established that cannot be broken.

The problem was sin, dating back to Adam and Eve. Sin severed an intimate relationship which only God could repair. The action of God demanded the most precious investment in the restoration process. The interrelation of the Father and the Son in this proposal is simply stated, but behind it is the most expensive validation of God's love.

All that God does demands the involvement of each member of the trinity. The Son, who was fully and completely devoid of sin because He is God, was made a sin offering. The Holy Spirit's activity is seen in Hebrews 9:14, where it says that the Son offered Himself by the eternal Spirit to God. In 2 Corinthians 5:21, the Father seems to be portrayed as the one who placed mankind's sin on His Son. Note carefully that God did not make His Son a sinner. That would be blasphemous. He imputed our sin to Him. In our attempt to understand this, we must not go beyond the words of Scripture. "God made Him . . . sin for us." The words "to be" are in italics to aid the completion of the thought.

The emphasis of the word *sin*, used twice in this verse, is different. Christ was innocent of any sin. He was sinless, holy, pure, and stainless. The second use is as a "sin offering" for our sin. The fulfillment of the types of the sin offering in the Old Testament is seen in this one statement. Christ was the only satisfactory sin offering. God demanded of Israel an animal without blemish as the annual sacrifice. Christ was the sin-offering, presented once for all as the final sacrifice. Such a sacrifice does not need to be repeated, because God is satisfied. To show the adequacy of Christ's offering, God responds by clothing us in the righteousness of the same Christ who rose from the dead. A final display of His righteousness on us is the promise to all who enter into the sufficiency of the sin offering.

ଏଠ ———————————————— ଓଃ

Father, thank you for presenting the perfect sin offering in Your holy Son. I rejoice in the garments of righteousness given me in Christ.

The Equality of Sin

But the Scripture has confined all under sin, that the promise
by faith in Jesus Christ might be given to those who believe.

Galatians 3:22

The repetition of the fact that all have sinned is needed in cultures that excuse so many aspects of thought and behavior. Long before the word of the cross began to be preached, God announced His universal sentence of sinfulness: "There is none righteous." In addition to condemning all, God passes the sentence of death on the same world. The fullness of the word "death" may not have enlightened previous generations, because the full dawn of revelation only began to spread across the landscape of humanity after the cross.

Those who can only read creation, not having the Scriptures, are still without excuse under God's condemnation. How much more so are those who have the Scriptures also without excuse. It is true that one can look at a tree, an animal, or a sunset and not respond by saying, "I am a sinner." But the nature of man within confirms an innate desire to appease a deity, even if it is created by the culture in which people live.

The equality under God's storm of condemnation is designed to also bring equality of blessing by the promises of God. Since all men are equally slaves of the sin that invades and rules mankind, God offers a salvation of equal scope. God is not measuring how much more sinful one person or culture is than another. If man can contend that all are not equally lost, then God could be challenged because He only offers one equal salvation. It is clear— Scripture says that all are confined under sin, and the specific level of our wickedness is unimportant.

Elsewhere, this argument is not even engaged, because man is not lost because he has committed theft or murder, but "because he will not believe in the name of the only begotten Son of God." That judgment completely levels the field for sinners. That evenness should not cause a man to look at his brother, but at himself. It is true that man needs Christ because he sins. But he is lost because of unbelief.

Likewise, God's provision of His promises to all who believe contradicts the argument of the Jews, who thought themselves in a privileged position because of their ethnicity and history. Even though they are God's chosen people, they are far from God through unbelief. They must come, just as anyone else, to inherit the divine promises. Although both Jew and Gentile are under sin, both receive the same promise by faith in Christ Jesus the Lord.

☍ ──────────────────── ☌

Father, thank you for extending the same promises to me as You do to all who believe. I do not deserve any, but rejoice in them all.

You Are Needed!

*For we are God's fellow workers; you are
God's field, you are God's building.*

1 Corinthians 3:9

Three great responsibilities are presented to the church at Corinth. These opportunities to be involved in the work of the Lord are not limited to the local Corinthian church, but are expanded to all who are related to God by faith in Jesus Christ. We gather them together like a three-strand cord that holds us close to the Master. Yet we must remember that we are working under and for God, rather than being His co-worker, as though He were one of us.

We are companions in a team of workers. No one serves alone but is in harness with others, who have different duties and skills. This is not a job that we apply for, but one that we are installed in the moment that we trust Christ as Savior. All other believers are similarly employed, and they depend on us for our contributions. This is a statement of fact that we rejoice in and bear responsibility for. There is no thought of being excused from other companions who serve. We are workers!

> *The condition of the soil is more important than the skill of the sower.*

We are soil with properties and capabilities. The field seems inert but, in fact, is burgeoning with possibilities, as the parable of the sower so eloquently explores. The soil and seed are as intimately intertwined as possible. The seed without the soil must remain alone and unfulfilled; as John 12:24 states, "It abides alone." The soil without good seed will be overcome with weeds, whose seeds are endemic to any field. The condition of the soil is more important than the skill of the sower. As soil, we are responsible for what happens in our lives. We can bring forth food and fruit or thorns and briars. The soil has all the necessary ingredients for success and productivity. Rain, sunshine, and cultivation are offered by God. We receive all that we need to be prolific for the blessing of others and glory of God.

We are the house being completed. Each piece of the structure is being added and installed, as one after another comes to believe in Christ. Each beam bears a relationship to all others. Each plank or stone bears the weight of those above, and adds to the integrity of the whole structure. We do not think of a house as individual pieces but one edifice. Each of us is a member of one residence for God Himself; therefore, no one can opt out of his responsibility of bearing the blessing of functioning for God.

૪ —————————————— ૭

Father, thank you for employing me in Your overall plan for building the church of Jesus Christ. I choose to serve faithfully.

Comfort in Suffering

For as the sufferings of Christ abound in us, so our
consolation also abounds through Christ.

2 Corinthians 1:5

The One who allows suffering is the same One who causes comfort to abound. Suffering is universal to all cultures. No one can completely alleviate suffering, because sin is its cause. The suffering that comes to believers was promised to the disciples before Christ went to the cross. If we would stop seeking to escape trials, we would begin to enjoy God's comfort in the tribulation, for the only hope of full escape is the coming of the Lord Jesus Christ in power and great glory.

Those who trust Christ and acknowledge the sovereignty and superintendence of the Lord in their lives will endure sorrow. The blessing for us is that sufferings and persecutions are administered or permitted by the One who saved us. It is both biblically and practically erroneous to teach that, if a believer has enough faith, he will never face trials and his prayers will insulate him from suffering.

What, then, is our response to those who have placed their faith in Christ and still encounter suffering? What should we say to those who are enduring pain and hurt? Where should I stand today in the mixture of messages that come to the believer who is suffering? Many can only say "I'm sorry" and go on their way. A few say that they understand, but have they gone through what the person is experiencing? Others will say that they will pray, but what do they pray?

Paul, who endured more than most of us, provides a divine perspective on the controversy. Our Lord Jesus Christ endured the suffering normal to human beings. He accepted the hatred of men, which was more than most mistreatment. Uniquely, our Savior experienced pain and punishment from God for our sin. If we choose to follow Christ in life, we can expect to endure some of His sufferings. Paul could say that the suffering of Christ found a home in his body and soul. He seldom asked the church to pray for escape from suffering, but instructed them to accept such difficulty as part of their intimate association with Christ.

An additional point should be emphasized: consolation in the midst of our sorrow abounds in Christ. Comfort is found in Christ. Since I have Christ, I have the consolation needed for the suffering that is allowed. Paul teaches that the glory of God is better served by enduring suffering and partaking of Christ's consolation than by seeking deliverance from it altogether.

໐ ———————————— ଔ

Father, I trust Your wisdom to bring into my life the suffering that You choose.
I flee to Christ for the comfort found in Him.

Our Most Personal Resource

Therefore he who rejects this does not reject man,
but God, who has also given us His Holy Spirit.

1 Thessalonians 4:8

A person, by our understanding, has the capacities of mind, emotions, and will. We accept that these three make up the parameters of our soul. The ability to think, the ability to feel, and the ability to decide are characteristic of mankind, who was made in the image of God. When the Father gives the Holy Spirit in answer to Christ's prayer in John 14:16, we receive all of the Spirit that there is to receive and all the ministries that He has the capacity to perform in us and for us. The Holy Spirit is the most personal of all the resources that God has given us.

John 3:34 says, "God does not give the Spirit by measure." God does not divide the Holy Spirit and give His mind to some, His emotions to others, and His will to the rest. We can confidently say, "I have all of the Holy Spirit." The need in my life is to surrender all of my mind, my every emotion, and my entire will to the Spirit's control.

The Holy Spirit is sent to teach, comfort, guide, counsel, enlighten, strengthen, and reveal to us the capacities of Christ. Because we have the Holy Spirit, we have His guidance, His comfort, His counsel, and much more. In the same way, if we are in the company of a person, we have all the skills and abilities that he possesses. A doctor cannot be with me without his skills being present, as well. I need to believe that I have all of the Holy Spirit and, by faith, appropriate all the ministries that He is ready and waiting to dispense. He waits to demonstrate Christ's power in my life and acts in my life, based on my faith in God's Word.

> *He waits to demonstrate Christ's power in my life.*

The intricate link between the ministry of Christ and the ministry of the Holy Spirit must not be confused. The ministries are much the same. The "Spirit of Christ" is the Holy Spirit, who is the person of the Trinity who applies the work of Christ practically to each believer. I must believe that the Holy Spirit is in me and that He is ready and willing to do His work. If I will trust Him, He will respond to my faith by doing His work in me. I do not need more of Christ or the Holy Spirit; rather, the Holy Spirit wants to control more of me!

❦ ──────────── ❧

Father, thank you for Your Holy Spirit. I believe that He is in me, waiting to do His work. I submit my mind to His teaching, my will to His commands, and my emotions to His comfort as I read Your Word.

Living Power

For the word of God is living and powerful, and sharper
than any two-edged sword, piercing even to the division
of soul and spirit, and of joints and marrow, and is a
discerner of the thoughts and intents of the heart.

Hebrews 4:12

The most powerful message in the world is that God has made a way for sinners to become His children by faith in Christ. This authoritative message is contained in the living Word of God. The responsibility for those who have come under the power of the Word of God is to carry that same book to the ends of the earth.

Many look at the Bible as a book like any other, printed with ink on paper and available to those who wish to read it. Yet we can pick it up in our hands, turn its leaves, read its message, and know that God is speaking to our hearts and minds. Our spirit is touched by the Spirit as our eyes read. Our heart responds with "Amen" when God speaks. Our wills are challenged to obey the voice of the Lord, who proclaims our responsibility.

Literally speaking, the Bible is paper and ink; spiritually speaking, it is the Word of God. The source of the book is the living God. The author of the message is the living Spirit. The center of its truth is the living Christ. The Word came from the Father, by the Holy Spirit, and is about God the Son.

As I open the Bible, it knows what I am thinking. It knows the failure that I am experiencing. It reveals the guidance that I am seeking. It comforts my sorrowing heart. It uncovers my sin. It lists the blessings of my salvation. It is alive, because God is alive. When we sin and stray from the path of obedience, we first leave off the Word and prayer. Like Adam before us, instead of running to the source of healing, we run and hide from the voice of His Word. Even opening the leaves of this Book carelessly, my eyes can be drawn to a line that is like a spear that cuts my heart in conviction. On another occasion, it is like the surgeon's knife that slices away the cancer to bring healing. Again, it becomes a penknife that will remove a painful splinter, a kitchen knife that cuts the meat to prepare a glorious feast, and a sword that will battle with the enemy.

Today's Scripture does not direct us to pray for its power or its life. It is powerful! It is living! Our need is to come under its authority, to open its pages, listen to His voice, learn its meaning, love its message, and live its precepts. It will bring peace to the soul, joy to the spirit, health to the joints, medicine to the marrow, acumen to the thoughts, and love to the heart. It defends, dissects, discovers, destroys, and discerns. It is living!

&❦ ———————————— ❧

Father, what a glorious gift You have given. I accept it as living truth.

Building the Building

. . . having been built on the foundation of the apostles and prophets, Jesus Christ Himself being the chief cornerstone . . .

Ephesians 2:20

In this monumental revelation of the mystery of the church, Paul draws all believers under the one roof of the building. This building is being built of living stones, as Peter calls the saints. The Lord Jesus, as the Living Stone, has touched all who believe and imparted His life to each one. The accumulation of these living stones by God into a living entity established the church in Acts 2. Stones continue to take their appointed place as, one by one, they are quarried from humanity by God through faith in Christ. The metaphor of a building is used to help us visualize the mission of the church as a temple or lighthouse for the Holy Spirit to dwell in and shine from.

As stones in the temple, each of us is responsible to be joined to other believers, just as stones in a building are placed above, beside, and under other stones. No one is isolated in the building. Dependence and support make the integrity of the building viable.

> *Dependence and support make the integrity of the building viable.*

The overall plan, determined by the architect, establishes the alignment of the building by appointing the chief cornerstone. In a typical building, you might have four corner stones, but among the four is a preeminent cornerstone which would be set in a prominent place in the front of the building. In the church, Christ is that chief cornerstone. In the ancient building tradition, this foremost stone was larger and more responsible for the dimensions and definitions of the building. The foundation would be built to the ground level, then the largest stone would be moved into place. Strings would be drawn from its corners to establish the angles and specify the lines for the building.

The leaders of the nation of Israel, Christ said, would set Him aside from His divinely appointed position of prominence in the building. Yet He was chosen by God to be the most important stone in the church, the temple of God. Every doctrine of the church must be aligned with Him. Every teaching, every activity, every program, plan, song, meeting, goal, ministry, and every message must be in line with the person and work of the living Christ. His position is unchangeable and unchallengeable and must be recognized and established by every stone. Not one stone should be out of place, so that the building will give glory to Christ, who is the Light to the world.

ɞ ———————————— ☙

Father, thank you for taking me from among humanity and appointing me a place in Your building. I offer myself to shine in this world.

Forever Unchanging

Jesus Christ is the same yesterday, today, and forever.
Hebrews 13:8

Although this well-known verse is true, let's take a moment to consider several deeper aspects of the statement. The Bible says that Jesus "grew in stature and in favor with God and man." He also grew in knowledge. These elements of change are not in the character or essence that He possesses as God. To begin comprehending these distinctions, we first need to realize the impossible heights of these truths to our simple minds (read Romans 11:33-36).

As believers, we should focus on those aspects of His nature that are unchangeable, because that is what the Holy Spirit is trying to teach us. As to the attributes that He possesses as God, there can be no change. Jesus Christ is immutable as to His essential nature, substance, and personality. He made an irrevocable condescension to take a human body for the sake of our salvation. He now exists in a glorified human body, yet His birth was a permanent incarnation in human form. It was different in display than His presentation prior to His birth in Bethlehem. Still there is a man—a glorified Man—in the heavens today.

In His relation to us as believers, there is no change. He remains the head of the body and the Bridegroom to us as His bride. He is faithful to the promises, and will not fail. He is resident in us and cannot leave that position. He has made us His personal responsibility and will not deny us. He is the Shepherd, as we are the sheep; He cannot resign. He is the Master, we the slave; He cannot mistreat us. He is interceding for us before the Father, and He will not cease. He is coming back again to take us to Himself. He loves us, and will never wane in His devotion.

> *In His relation to us as believers, there is no change.*

Yesterday is the eternity that He enjoyed in the presence of the Father, dwelling in His glory, delighting in His every thought. Then He entered *today* and lived His life on earth in human form, including His ascension and present session. In human form as man, He is presently seated, having finished the work that God gave Him to do. *Tomorrow* He will rise from that seat and, at the Father's hour, will begin the consummation of all things. This will include His gathering of the church from the earth, and His final return to Zion in power and flaming glory, to rule as King *forever* and *forever*. Yes, He "is the same yesterday, and today, and forever."

⁎ ———————————— ⁏

Father, in a world of so much change, I thank you for the unchangeable One who is my Savior, my Shepherd, my Bridegroom, and my Lord.

Peace Is Mine

And the peace of God, which surpasses all understanding,
will guard your hearts and minds through Christ Jesus.

Philippians 4:7

The world is searching for peace between nations, peoples, families, races, genders, and ages. The keystone in the arch of Christian relations is peace with God. Laced through the Scriptures is the reminder that peace is found in a person and is not possible without Him. The nations are seeking peace on a scrap of paper, signed by world leaders. However, these auspicious documents often crumble like the parchment they are written on because the basis of such peace agreements is often couched in deception and selfishness. As one diplomat said, "Peace is so elusive!"

The God of peace has His hand in the affairs of men to prove that peace is a trait which belongs solely to God. Peace between God and man was shattered by sin in the garden, and peace between man and man was ruptured in the next chapter of Genesis, when Cain killed Abel. One

Christ died on the cross to establish a spiritual foundation for peace.

of the fundamental parts of God's salvation is peace between God and men, and between man and man. Christ died on the cross to establish a spiritual foundation for peace. When that is appropriated by faith, peace can reign in the hearts of men and women.

The previous verse commands us not to be anxious, but to pray. It does not say to pray for internal peace, which many do. We are to "let our requests be made known to God" by prayer. The spontaneous result is that "the peace of God . . . will guard *our* hearts and minds through Christ Jesus."

When this guard is at the door of our mind and the windows of our heart, it will keep anxiety, fear, and worry out and God's serenity within. Like the melodious voices of a hundred musical instruments blended together, it is there to orchestrate the peace which floods our mind from the Word of God, confirming the will of God, and uniting harmoniously my spirit with His Spirit.

Christ is the Commander of the thoughts of my mind and the feelings of my heart. "He is our peace," says the Holy Spirit in another letter. He is the "Prince of Peace" writes the prophet. The mind of Christ is a mind full of peace. The heart of Christ is a heart where peace reigns supreme.

ರು ———————————————— ೞ

Father, thank you for receiving my prayer requests. Your hearing them causes Your peace to reign in my soul.

The Gift of Suffering

For to you it has been granted on behalf of Christ, not
only to believe in Him, but also to suffer for His sake.

Philippians 1:29

The character of God is such that He is always giving. The gifts granted to us by God are numerous, but one of His special gifts is that of suffering. Because we are Christ's, we are granted the privilege of sharing in the sufferings of Christ. Obviously, it is not the suffering of the Lord for our sin on the cross, for no one could participate in His substitutionary work as the sin bearer. We are, however, one with Him in His body, and we can experience the sorrow and rejection that He is now experiencing. To suffer for His sake is to be so much like Him that, when the world wants to bring suffering to Christ, it must be done to those of us who belong to Him.

Could Christ have saved us without suffering? Of course not! Nor can we accept the delights of being one with Christ without accepting His suffering, because we are one with Him. Most of us do not know real suffering as a result of being one with Christ but, if persecution does come, we must remember that it is a gift from God.

Someone said, "We should be so close to Christ that, when they throw mud at Him, we get spattered." Paul heard Jesus say "I am Jesus whom you are persecuting," because the pain that Paul was inflicting on believers was felt by the risen Head of the church. When we believe, we accept the gift of suffering for Christ's sake, because we have received His life and taken His name. If others try to destroy His life, they will do so to us. It they try to defame His name, they will do so to us.

Peter writes that Christ left us an example that we should follow in His steps. Those feet never sidestepped the path of suffering. Paul wrote from his prison cell and was reminded of the special joy that he shared in being able to bear the reproach of Christ. The poor saints at Philippi also shared in the sufferings of Christ as they gave sacrificially.

Those feet never sidestepped the path of suffering.

We joyfully accept the gift of salvation when we believe on Christ, but we find it more difficult to rejoice in being granted the privilege of bearing suffering on His behalf. We want the joy of our salvation, but not the responsibility of bearing His shame and sorrow. Both gifts come from the same Giver and in the same package. Can we say "thank you" to both equally?

∞ ———————————— ∞

Father, thank you for Your many gifts. I accept joyfully every gift You give,
including suffering, if You see fit to send it to me.

The Light of Love

He has delivered us from the power of darkness and
conveyed us into the kingdom of the Son of His love.

Colossians 1:13

A transfer of monumental proportions took place the instant we believed the gospel. How were we to know the enormity of the work of God in saving us? The answer is seen in our own birth. How much did we know when we were born into this world? Our parents cared for us, and it took years to begin to understand what happened when we were born. The spiritual birth is similar to the physical. *"What happened when we believed?"* is a question that will continue to unfold before us as we grow to more fully know our Savior.

The previous kingdom is described as darkness. This concept is explained in several other pictures drawn by the divine artist. The condition of blindness is a consignment to darkness. One of the Messiah's proclamations was to give physical sight to the blind. This miracle is reserved only for the Messiah, which should have been indication enough that Christ was the promised One.

But darkness is not only a condition; it is also a power. The god of this world is described as the one who blinds the minds of those who do not believe. The freedom for movement out of such a kingdom is denied by the very nature of the condition. The enduring nature of the spiritual condition is further explained by Jude, who calls such slavery "the blackness of darkness forever." The idea of a king of darkness and a demonstration of his power to kill translates into the slavery that we all partook of before the delivering power of Christ came to us.

Christ is the deliverer who went into the strong man's prison and set at liberty those who were subject to bondage, conveying them from one kingdom to the other. We, in simple faith, responded to the invitation for liberty from slavery to sin, to death, to darkness, and to a host of other masters who held us captive—from darkness to glorious light, from death to eternal life, from dominion to liberty, from lust to love, from self to saint, from servanthood to sonship, from hate to holiness, from hell to heaven.

The gates of the kingdom of darkness were summarily opened by the King of Light, and He rescued all who would believe and closed the gates behind Him. He brought us into His banquet hall and established an illuminating banner over us of His Love. The Love of God rules in this kingdom.

☙ ———————————— ❧

Father, thank you for the demonstration of Your power to take me out from the control of darkness and enclose me in Your love.

The Son's House

. . . but Christ as a Son over His own house, whose
house we are if we hold fast the confidence and
the rejoicing of the hope firm to the end.

Hebrews 3:6

We are the household of God. That was a creation which was accomplished by the work of Christ on the cross and consummated when the Holy Spirit came in power to unite all believers in one holy organism. As people come to Christ for salvation, they are added to the house by the same Holy Spirit. It is an event that is simultaneous with every other operation of God in salvation.

A house has two different but related ideas. The building in which we live protects us from the elements and allows us privacy and comfort. God is not saying in this text, however, that the church is a temple-like building, a habitation for God by the Spirit. A house is also considered the household with all the members and activities that take place in the building. We sometimes make a distinction between a house, which is the building, and a home, which has been decorated and furnished to make life as comfortable as possible. Surely, the word "house" is a suitable picture, if it includes all that goes on in the home.

Today's Scripture mentions that the house is the concert of activities that gives the home life, light, and love. Surely, the household gives a glorious picture of the whole family of God: Christ the Son over the house, and we as brothers, sisters, fathers, mothers, and little children. All ages are represented, all levels of maturity, all gifts and abilities, all serving and functioning for the blessing of each other and the glory of the Son.

But the little word "if" seems to give some problem. If we do not hold fast, will we be asked to leave? If, in our youth, we lose confidence and ask hard questions, will we be left to wander the hills in search of truth? Suppose if, in our old age, we don't hang on as strongly as previously, will we be unceremoniously evicted from the house, though we have been there so long?

The word "if" is used here in Hebrews of fully turning from the cross of Christ and returning to the sacrifices of the law. Those who fall, by rejecting the Son and His sacrifice, prove that they never were members of the household. Rejoice that this house does not have a revolving door but the door of a vault, which opens to come in and is shut so that none can be put out.

❧ ———————————— ❦

Father, thank you for bringing me into Your household. I count my position
and privileges reason for my highest confidence and joy.

Infinite Grace

But to each one of us grace was given according
to the measure of Christ's gift.

Ephesians 4:7

Grace is one of the most common words in the New Testament. It is characteristic of God's name, His works, His words, His witness, and His generosity. God will give His grace unsparingly (Romans 5:20). Thus, God chooses to fill our minds with what He has given us by repeatedly telling us of all His blessings.

> *God chooses to fill our minds with what He has given us.*

Here, Paul gives full and clear testimony that each believer receives the same amount of grace. To help prevent the church from fighting about the proportions that each receives, God reminds each one of us that we have an adequate and equal supply.

A temptation that shows up in our talking and praying is that we just do not believe that we have enough of God's gifts. We are inclined to think that we know better, based on our feelings. Because we do not feel "full" of the grace of God, we think that we must be lacking. Our response to such feeling is to go to God in prayer and plead for more strength, peace, joy, grace, and comfort.

What is the measure of Christ's gift? Surely, we cannot come up with any other answer than the most lavish outpouring of all that He is, for He gives infinitely. John writes, "Of His fullness have we all received." Like the fountain which never runs dry, we can come, and there is always an adequate supply. Draw deeply with your bucket of whatever size, and it will be filled. Draw again and again, and it will be full time after time.

How is it that Christ has such an inexhaustible supply? The resurrection of our Savior put Him in a position to pour out abundantly all the resources obtained by His victory, pouring them into our emptiness, caused by sin.

Paul teaches that this grace was given at a specific point of time in our lives. We must conclude that His grace was given when we believed the gospel, referred to in Ephesians 3:6. We were given the river that flows in us and is available to us whenever we draw from it, which Jesus summarized in John 7 by saying, "out of his heart will flow rivers of living water." Christ gave Himself for us and is waiting for us to come, again and again, to draw as much as we need.

಄ ———————————————— ಆ

Father, You continually remind me of the adequacy of Your resources. You also tell me that it is all available to me. I draw deeply from Your supply given to me in Christ.

Are You Watching?

He who testifies to these things says, "Surely I am
coming quickly." Amen. Even so, come, Lord Jesus!

Revelation 22:20

The One who, above all, can make it happen has promised that He will come and receive us to Himself. For the third time in this chapter, the coming Savior has spoken through the apostle John, encouraging the church not to abandon the practical habit of looking for Him. The "Amen" announces the infallible prediction that the clock of

> *"He that shall*
> *come will*
> *come and will*
> *not tarry."*

God, which runs with eternal accuracy, will strike the day and hour fully known by God. "He that shall come will come and will not tarry."

It is easy in an unbelieving world to adopt the attitude that pervades every aspect of our society. We, too, can live as though the Lord will never return to catch away His waiting children. We, too, can add possessions to our already full abodes, as though man's life consists in the abundance of things that he possesses. We, too, can be lovers of pleasure more than lovers of God. We, too, can sleep in the day, as if the thief will never come. We, too, can allow our lamps to be snuffed out so that when He comes our lamps will not be trimmed. We, too, can set our affections on things below, rather than on the face of our Beloved. We, too, can be so busy that we can fail to fulfill our duty. We, too, can prostitute our talents on the success of the world and allow the church to flounder because of our spiritual indolence.

But, you say that He is not coming "quickly." If so, we might as well apply our hearts to the wisdom of the world. We might as well adopt the behavior of the unbelieving. We might as well refuse to "go into all the world and preach the gospel." We might as well store our wealth "where moth and rust corrupt and thieves break through and steal."

Can the word "quickly" mean that the time frame between His promise to John in the upper room and His physical appearance in the sky was to be immediate? If so, it has only been "two days," as Peter reminds us in his warning about the last days (2 Peter 3:8).

It is not so much our concern about the day, which no man knows, as it is with the responsibility that we have to "watch and pray lest we enter into temptation." We respond joyfully, "Even so, come, Lord Jesus!"

֍ ———————————— ֎

Father, thank you for the oft-repeated reminder that Your Son will be sent
from Glory to remove us from this world. I await His appearance.

The Lord's Obedient Bondservants

Masters, give your bondservants what is just and fair,
knowing that you also have a Master in heaven.

Colossians 4:1

It has always been the intention of God to change individuals in order that they will have an impact on others, rather than to change a whole nation with a blanket of dictums. Therefore, God did not order believers to release or set free their slaves because they were now Christians. No matter how powerful we might think such a command might have been to the unbelieving world, God did not say so. He did, however, choose such cultures to teach important lessons to all who received Jesus Christ as Lord of their life.

Through the master/slave relationship, God chose to help us understand that we should treat those under our control as our Master or Lord treats His own servants—not only with honor and justice, but also with love, compassion, and patience.

It is of greater consequence to most of us that the Lord Jesus said, "If the Son shall make you free, you shall be free indeed," than to remember that we are "bought with a price" and so do not own anything and are responsible to glorify our Master in heaven. The slave is owned and has no rights but to please and

We are "bought with a price" and so do not own anything.

serve his master. For believers, it is a blessing to own nothing and ascribe allegiance to our Master. The Lord Jesus Himself became man and took an even lower position by becoming a servant to accomplish the will of His Father. Can we expect to exempt ourselves from the path that the Lord trod? Or do we need to be reminded that, even if we do not have slaves, we still have a Master in heaven and are commanded to serve Him in a world of inequity and injustice?

Paul's words have a huge impact when we are reminded that some of the first words out of his believing heart were, "Lord, what do You want me to do?" These are the words of a bondservant to His Master. Many of us walk a long time in our Christian life before we are willing to trust our Master and say, "I'll do what you want me to do, dear Lord. I'll go where you want me to go!" The Lord Jesus reminded His disciples, just before He went to the cross, that the primary evidence of discipleship was obedience. We are the bondservants of the Lord Jesus Christ, and obedience is the hallmark of a servant.

꙳ ──────────────── ꙳

Father, thank you for saving me to serve You and Your Son, my Lord.

Baptized Into His Resurrection

Therefore we were buried with Him through baptism into death,
that just as Christ was raised from the dead by the glory of
the Father, even so we also should walk in newness of life.

Romans 6:4

Baptism is one of the fundamentals of most religions. Some form of identification or association is practiced to give a clear indication of the intention of a person to follow a specific creed or religious rite.

The baptism of John was used to identify Jews who were willing to repent of sin, seeking to restore the nation back into God's blessing. Christ went through John's baptism, not because of any sin, but to identify Himself with the repentant remnant of Israel.

Christian baptism has some of the same features. A believer is baptized to indicate his association with the Lord Jesus and other believers. The rite of baptism is a physical symbol of the spiritual transaction that occurred when the believer was baptized by the Spirit into the body of Christ. The picture is graphic as a person goes down into the waters of death and comes out again, having escaped death.

The death of Christ by itself was insufficient to obtain our salvation. The resurrection of Christ was essential for any of the value of Christ's work to be applied to us.

The effectiveness of His work is best described by our intimate union with Christ in the very action of the cross. In this context we are told that, when Christ died, we died; when Christ rose, we rose; when Christ ascended, we ascended with Him. That is perfect identification or union. When we plant a seed, it dies. When it dies it germinates and begins the growth process that continues by reproducing itself many times over through the tree. If the seed did not spring to life, there would be no seeds from the seed we planted.

If Christ were not raised, there would be no communication of His life to anyone. We died with Christ. We were raised in the newness of Christ's life. Our responsibility is to walk in the power of this new life. His life has been given to us. It is a gift! We do not earn it, nor are we worthy of it. But the resurrected Christ lives in us, just as the life of the seed that is planted lives in the seeds produced by the tree that came from that seed. It is not our life but His. Our physical baptism is a symbol of our spiritual planting and resurrection with Christ.

    ଊ ———————————— ଔ

Father, thank you for giving me the life of Christ through my death with Him.
I commit myself to live in the power of Christ who was raised from the dead
to live in me.

March

RESOURCES THAT ARE OFTEN FORGOTTEN BUT SORELY NEEDED

"... be transformed by the renewing of your mind ..."
Romans 12:2

Blessed with every blessing given,
Through His cross and resurrection.
All that God in Christ has placed,
I now have because of grace.

F. L. K.

March

A Stream Under the Kitchen

We were invited to the U.K. several years ago for ministry and, at the same time, went searching for my roots. We borrowed a car and came to Laddock in Cornwall. The old house, now more than 150 years old, was still standing near the remains of an old blacksmith shop that had once been operated by my great-grandfather. We saw the dilapidated house and the family name, Puckey, carved in the keystone in the arch above the front door.

Next to the old Puckey house was a four-hundred-year-old cottage that fascinated us. The owners came out to see who was looking at their thatched-roof home and kindly invited us in for a tour of their residence that has been in the family for a long time.

In the kitchen we discovered a most remarkable arrangement for getting daily water. In front of the sink was a wooden trap door about 18-inches square. It looked like a quick route out of the house in case of emergency. In fact, it was a door which opened to reveal a pool of water just below the floor. When the family needs water, they open the trap door and a few inches below lies the brim of a flowing pool of pure spring water.

This does not seem so amazing in our day of hot and cold running water. But, 400 years ago, that house was built right over the spring, and we were told that it has never run dry. We turn on the faucet in our house and water pours out, but that is arranged by human ingenuity. The spring under this old house is the Lord's doing, and it was marvelous to us.

When the Lord saved us, He planted us "by the rivers of water" so that we would bring forth fruit in each season. I saw the spring as a clear reminder of the Lord's giving us all the resources that we need for life, both immediately and eternally. Just dip into the exhaustless spring of His blessing for all our needs.

I was reminded of the popular chorus that says, "Flow, river, flow." My mind is transported to the banks of the powerful Zambezi River, hurriedly making its way to the sea. A thoughtless child may stand near the shore, saying at the top of his voice, "Flow, river, flow!" If the river had ears, it surely would laugh at the little boy, thinking that he could make the mighty Zambezi flow faster or in a different direction. The river might well respond with a chuckle, "Drink to your heart's content, my boy. There is enough for all!"

The chorus no doubt refers to the ministry of the Holy Spirit, who does have ears. What does He say to us, as we sing, "Flow, river, flow"? It must make Him sad to have given us abundance of water, like the spring under that house, and still hear us sing to the spring, "Flow!"

The Lord's own commentary is given to the woman of Samaria. "The water that I shall give him will become in him a fountain of water springing up into everlasting life." Again, He tells those at the feast in John 7, "He who believes in Me, as the Scripture has said, out of his heart will flow rivers of living water." He was speaking of the Holy Spirit.

What supply for our every thirst! Without request for more, or command to flow, the river of God's provision flows for every believer to enjoy. We need not go to the river, "come to the waters," or even lift the trap door, because the river is within all believers. He provides us with "rivers of living water."

Isaiah 55:1 says, "Everyone who thirsts, Come to the waters!" But, by means of the Holy Spirit, the waters have come to us. By faith, we dip our parched life in the boundless and endless supply for all our needs. The Holy Spirit is given to us, according to 1 Corinthians 2:12, so that we might know all the riches that God has given us in Christ.

The book of Revelation comes to a close with the invitation to "take of the water of life freely." No matter how often we come, or how much we take, the blessings of our great God flow eternally from Christ by the Holy Spirit. The desired response from our overflowing heart should be "the sacrifice of praise to God, that is, the fruit of our lips, giving thanks to His name." "Oh, the peace forever flowing . . ."

Drink deeply, beloved of the Lord! And when you come back for more, an adequate supply will still be there. How glorious is His provision!

He Cares

Casting all your care upon Him, for He cares for you.

1 Peter 5:7

This page of Scripture is wrinkled in many Bibles because their owners have come to it with wet eyes. The tears water the page as comfort is absorbed by the soul. These words come like a cold cloth on a fevered brow, a warm embrace from a loved one, and comfort from God who extends His comfort to all who claim this simple but poignant promise.

Many a house has this text on the wall gently reminding the occupants of its truth. The giver of every good and perfect gift showers any who simply lift their burdens to Christ and claim the truth: "He cares for you."

The basis of this care is prominently declared by the wounded hands of the Lord Jesus, who extends them to all who come to Him. "I will give you rest" are His promising words to all who are heavy laden. That is, rest *in* the burdens of life more than rest *from* the burdens of living.

It can sometimes be hard to "cast" our burdens on the Lord. Most of us without thinking will ask the Lord to lift the burdens. We pray for the burdens to be taken away. We plead for God to change our circumstances so that the cares of life will not be a part of our daily experience.

The Lord, far from removing our cares, is waiting for us to throw the burdens onto Him. This verse is so simply stated that we miss the impact: God asks us to do the casting, yet we ask God to do the removing! This is a very important lesson that Peter faced many years earlier. The Lord prayed that Peter's faith would not fail, but we wonder why the Lord did not pray to remove the temptation. We often ask God to remove the trial, affliction, temptation, or care instead of casting all our cares on Him.

There is not one who has come to Him for salvation for whom He does not care personally and intimately.

The action that is in doubt is our casting, not His caring! God is caring for us! There is not one who has come to Him for salvation for whom He does not care personally and intimately. He is waiting for you to take the cares and anxieties of life and remove them from your shoulder and lay them on His. Perhaps we say, as Peter did, "Do you not care that we are perishing?" Yet that is a contradiction to what Peter is now commanding us. God is waiting for us! Why will we not do our part? He cares for us!

ဢ —————————— og

Father, thank you for the sacrifice of Christ for my sin. I know that He cares for my burden and so I lift it off of my heart and place it on Him.

God's First Gift

*Now we have received, not the spirit of the world, but
the Spirit who is from God, that we might know the
things that have been freely given to us by God.*

1 Corinthians 2:12

The first gift promised to the followers of Christ was the Holy Spirit. The Lord Jesus said to His disciples before He died that He would send "the promise of the Father" who was the Holy Spirit. The third person of the triune God is sent from the Father through the Son into every believer in Christ.

Many other blessings are given to each believer, but no other gift is a person. The gift of Christ from the Father to all believers is accomplished by the presence of the Holy Spirit. Many times over, the Scripture repeats the blessing of having His Spirit in us. He is there as a personal, permanent possession. He is given, never to be taken away. He is also given not in measure but in all His fullness. And because He is a person, the relationship with Him is more intimate than any other blessing God gives.

> *Many other blessings are given to each believer, but no other gift is a person.*

The Holy Spirit is given to each believer so that we might know what God has given us as members of His family. When we begin to investigate the adequacy of our salvation, the Holy Spirit is there to inform us and introduce us to all the riches of His grace. Like a mother who teaches her child, the daily work of the Holy Spirit is to help us discover in the Word all the resources necessary for life. With love, tenderness, encouragement, and discipline, the Holy Spirit causes us to discover, appreciate, and appropriate each of the blessings given us at our spiritual birth. Through all of our Christian life, the Holy Spirit continues to reveal and rejoice with us as we by faith accept, appreciate, and employ each blessing.

These meditations are intended to assist the Holy Spirit in teaching us the meaning of each gift, training us in the use of the gift, and increasing our trust in the necessity of these blessings. Listening to and learning from the Holy Spirit increases our capacity to employ each of the riches of divine grace. God freely gives to us every blessing.

₭ ——————————— ∞

Father, thank you for the Holy Spirit. I choose to listen to Him as I read His unfolding catalogue of the blessings You have given me in Christ. I rejoice at each new discovery that I accept by faith.

Adopted into God's Family

*Having predestined us to adoption as sons by Jesus Christ
to Himself, according to the good pleasure of His will.*

Ephesians 1:5

Finding homes for children who can no longer be cared for by their natural parents due to the death of the parents, poverty, divorce, drugs, disease, or perhaps just lack of love falls to adoption agencies these days. One link that is common in almost every case is that the adoptions occur without any agreement on the part of the children.

The Greek idea of adoption was "son purchasing." It was used to fill a vacancy in the family with a slave purchased and brought into the family to receive all the privileges and blessings when he came of age. The Roman idea of adoption was "son placing" of the male offspring in the position of full responsibility and privilege in society. Adoption is a transaction fully understood and involving the whole family in a glorious ceremony. Lloyd Douglas describes this in his classic book *The Robe.*

In each case the "son" has no choice, nor can he pride himself on the father's choice. He receives his position of sonship on the basis of family line or his father's selection. We, as believers, rest in the work of the Father who brought us into His family. If we believe the truth of this transaction, we rest in its impact on us and bless the Father for such a wonderful plan.

Many adopted children fear that they will be rejected by their adoptive parents just as their real parents may have rejected them. The danger of wondering if we are worthy of being sons, based on our faith or behavior, only fosters fears that we may be rejected by the very One who chose us. We have been "predestined." This word means "to plan the end." God as the loving Father has planned our end—eternal enjoyment in the Father's house. "Eye has not seen nor ear heard" the things that the Father has reserved for His own family. We cannot be disinherited or disenfranchised. Nothing can "separate us from the love of Christ."

What a wonderful solution to the sin that broke up God's original family! Adam, His son, brought death, destruction, and distance into God's family. Christ, His Son, by His death and resurrection created a new family by providing adoption for all who believe. We are sons of the Father through no work of our own. We are adopted and have life, security, and closeness in this family through Christ.

℔ ———————————————— ∛

Father, thank you for creating Your family by adopting me into Your circle of acceptance, privilege, and position. I do not deserve this, but You have fully given me these blessings. I rejoice in Your provision for my family.

Christ, Our Strength

But the Lord stood with me and strengthened me, so
that the message might be preached fully through
me, and that all the Gentiles might hear. And I
was delivered out of the mouth of the lion.

2 Timothy 4:17

These are some of the last words of Paul to his beloved Timothy and to the church which has continued to read them with special comfort. He is summarizing the ordeal that he endured in his service to the Lord Jesus Christ. He stood alone in defending the faith when his associates forsook him in time of need. In this way, Paul walked in the footsteps of his Savior who saw one betray him and His eleven forsake Him and flee.

But the risen Christ stood by him in his hour of confrontation and was his strength for spiritual conflict. Paul reminded the Philippians, "I can do all things through Christ who strengthens me." He may not have known the full meaning of his revelation until he again faced the possibility of Nero's fury against Christ. Now, having had the joy of such provision, He says, "The Lord stood with me and strengthened me."

It is instructive that the Lord did not send twelve legions of angels but was Himself in and with Paul. This was not the result of prayer soliciting the Lord to "be with" him or asking for more strength; instead, the apostle appropriated the resources of Christ Himself. Here is the resurrected Savior fulfilling His promise, "Lo, I am with you always." In the hour of Nero's terror the greater comfort was available in the One who "is able to aid those who are tempted" because "He Himself has suffered."

We do not know the details, but the lion was hungry, roaring, and ready for a meal of Paul's body. The Lord chose to deliver him and to show His strength by making Paul's declaration of the gospel powerful to the Gentiles. Strength to do the will of God in the most difficult circumstances is the Lord's promise and is fully supplied as we rest in His adequacy.

Paul had proven Christ to be all things to him, whether it was in a shipwreck, receiving thirty-nine stripes, being naked, cold, robbed, beaten, stoned, hungry, thirsty, or facing false brethren as well as rioting Jews and Gentiles. It is useful to remind ourselves that the Lord did not keep him *from* these experiences but preserved him *through* them. Christ strengthens us for enduring the will of God. What is God bringing into your life today? Remember that Christ is your strength!

જી ——————————— ୧୨

Father, thank you for giving Christ to me. I confess my fear and worry but
claim His strength for all You send into my life today.

Living as Lighthouses for God

In whom the whole building, being joined together, grows into a holy temple in the Lord, in whom you also are being built together for a habitation of God in the Spirit.

Ephesians 2:21-22

We are parts of the building that is being assembled as God's dwelling place. The building is unfinished and is daily having components added as each person comes to faith in the Lord Jesus Christ. No one is left out and none can delay their addition to the overall structure.

This is one of three important metaphors used in Ephesians that help us understand the complete plan of God for His church. In this text Paul helps us understand that every believer is a stone in the building of God. The church is not just one nationality, one denomination, or one class of people. It consists of every individual who has received Christ and is a part of the building of God.

The temple is growing as, one-by-one, each person accepts Christ. The completion of the building is in the mind of God, and we can help its growth by inviting all to believe in Jesus Christ.

Peter reminds us that we are living stones in God's building. Those without Life and Light cannot be a part. We were like dead stones in the quarry of humanity. God reached down and lifted us out of the filthy clay and set us on the solid rock of Christ Himself. He placed His life in us and commissioned us to bring glory to the builder and to provide a dwelling place for His Spirit. He began a great work of molding and shaping us for the special place that He designed for us in His building.

We are members of the temple in harmony with many others who also are being added. People from every tribe and nation and kingdom and tongue are being added day by day.

We are not told what kind of building God is constructing, but perhaps a picture can be drawn of a lighthouse, since God is Light. Such a building is a warning to those who are passing on the sea of life. It is a refuge for those who are dragged from the pounding waves crashing on rocks below. It signals a harbor from the howling winds of life. It is a shelter from the lightning that strikes all around the tall slender building. It is what God is making us—a sanctuary for the Light of the World.

      ⅒ ———————————————— ⅓

Father, what a calling You have given me together with all other believers. I accept my role as part of the building in which the Spirit lives. I submit to the Spirit dwelling in me, calling the world to Jesus Christ.

We Change but God Does Not!

Like a cloak You will fold them up, And they will be changed.
But You are the same, And Your years will not fail.

Hebrews 1:12

God is unchangeable! He is the same no matter how much our emotions vary, no matter how little our faith may be, no matter how many times we fall, no matter how brave or weak our witness is, no matter how many fears or how dry our anointing or how empty our cup, regardless of how seldom we pray or how short our patience or how deep our devotion may be. Despite our shifting, changing character, God remains the same!

We spend so much time looking at ourselves that we tend to portray God in the light of our changeableness. In contrast we should be spending our time looking at Him and portraying ourselves in the light of who He is. Self-centeredness is a natural characteristic of man as a fallen being. When we believe the gospel, we receive God Himself into our life and a conflict begins between the old changeable self and our new unchangeable Life.

> *We spend so much time looking at ourselves that we tend to portray God in the light of our changeableness.*

Because we do not know anyone who is unchangeable, it is hard for us to attach this characteristic to God. We have no reference from which to work. God came into this world in the person of Jesus Christ to show himself in human form. Christ is God. God is the unvarying standard and we the changeable ones.

The world is changing and one day God will fold it up like a coat. God's duration is immeasurable. He will not fail because He is permanent and unchanging. When you fall and repent, will God be angry and turn His face from you? When you are weak and have made a mess of things, will you not find Him when you cry to Him? Will the river of His love be dry when you need his comfort the most? Will the storm be so severe that He will close the cleft in the rock? Will His arms be full and have no room for you when you come? No, my brother and sister! He does not change.

God gave His light to Moses, His power to Elijah, His protection to Daniel, His water to Israel, His joy to Nehemiah, His beauty to Esther, His patience to Job, His wisdom to Solomon, His peace to the disciples, and His guidance to Paul. He gave Christ to us. And in Him are all these blessings.

⊰ ⊱

Father, thank you for being always and forever unchangeable!

Escaping the Wrath That Is to Come

For God did not appoint us to wrath, but to obtain salvation through our Lord Jesus Christ.

1 Thessalonians 5:9

Judgment is an important part of God's sovereign intervention in the lives of His creatures. Sin must be punished; this has been a hallmark of God's justice from the beginning. No one will escape righteous judgment—yet the punishment that we deserved for sin was placed on Christ so that God might be "just and the justifier of all who believe in Jesus."

Paul wrote to the Thessalonians to instruct and comfort them regarding the return of Christ, particularly about when He will return to take His church out of the world before God's wrath is poured out on the unbelieving world. The church was worried about some who had died and might miss the departure of living believers. Paul answers their fear by giving a detailed sequence of events relating to the coming of Christ. The believers who had died would rise first and then the living saints would be caught up to meet the Lord in the air and be carried back to glory with Christ. A grand reunion is described that brought much comfort to the church and relieved them of the fear of being left behind.

The judgment or punishment of those left behind is a terrible consideration. The events of these catastrophic days are described in Revelation 6-19, where the terror and wrath of God are chronicled in much detail.

These believers had come to faith in Christ and were assured of the eternal life that is found in Him. They were enjoying salvation with all the blessings and riches that are found in their Savior, Christ Jesus. Their level of spiritual growth was profound and became an example for many to emulate. They turned to God from idols and were serving the living God.

Yet despite all this, these believers were overcome by a fear that perhaps they might have to endure the awful judgment of God on an ungodly people. They thought that perhaps the Lord was not going to take them out of the world before He set His angels loose to punish those left on the earth.

Paul's answer to those fears is that the salvation found in Christ includes the escape from God's wrath. How could God pour out His wrath on Christ as our substitute and then pour it out again on those who have believed and are part of His church? We have no appointment to "the wrath" as Paul speaks of it here. There is no punishment for any who are in Christ.

Father, thank you for promising an escape from Your wrath on the wicked. Christ bore my wrath. You have given me the blessed hope of being at home with You in heaven. I eagerly await Christ's return.

8

Displaying His Glory

For a man indeed ought not to cover his head, since he is the
image and glory of God; but woman is the glory of man.
1 Corinthians 11:7

The crowning display of God's creation is man. In the Garden of Eden, Adam was charged with disobedience and rebellion against the law of God, and God's glory was thereby defaced by Adam's sin. Eve did not bring sin into the world, it was Adam, and Adam alone, who brought down the wrath of Almighty God on the human race. The parallel thought is that the woman is the glory of the man. She was created for the man and is in many ways the finer specimen of the creative artistry of God.

Many in our "enlightened" society do not like these statements inscribed by God through the pen of Paul. Nevertheless, they are as true as any other dictum in God's Word. Although man will rephrase and paraphrase these words to dull their sharp edge, what God has said does not change. With equal authority God says that a male should not cover his head because he has been designated as the one to display the image and glory of God. In the same way a woman is instructed in 1 Corinthians 11:6 to cover her hair. Her hair is her glory and she is the glory of man, and these twin glories are to be covered when the glory of God is to be displayed.

Many people will claim that this teaching is merely the custom of the first-century culture. The teaching that a woman should cover her glory has been relegated to personal convenience, or described as an archaic interpretation of the text. Does changing the *We all exhibit* text or its meaning set aside the fact that man is the *the image and* glory of God and that woman is the glory of the *display the* man? Some will attempt to do so in an egalitarian, *excellence of* gender-neutral reconfiguring of God's order.

our Creator and Each person in the family of God, whether male or *Redeemer.* female, has a responsibility to display his or her God-given glory. It is a blessing to be chosen by God to reveal His glory to each other and to the angelic hosts. We all exhibit the image and display the excellence of our Creator and Redeemer.

                     ഇ ———————————— രു

Father, I am astonished that You would choose me to display Your glory.
I accept the duty with humility and commit my life to display Your glory
unhindered.

Are You Qualified or Disqualified?

Examine yourselves as to whether you are in the faith.
Test yourselves. Do you not know yourselves, that Jesus
Christ is in you?—unless indeed you are disqualified.

2 Corinthians 13:5

God does not tire of telling us that His Son is resident in all His children. Perhaps He repeats it because He knows that we may soon forget and try to live life in our own strength and wisdom. Maybe it is repeated because He is the fountain from whom all "blessings flow." He is the foundation on which all blessings are built. He is the soil out of which all His graces grow.

"Jesus Christ is in you." This statement can be stated as a fact as well as a question. Paul here is concerned that the Corinthians had an experience, but did not have Christ. He suggests that those without Christ are disqualified or unapproved. The word carries the connotation of the results of a test. A $100 bill is tested by streaking a special marker across its face. The response of the paper to the pen declares whether it is counterfeit or authentic, phony or real, fake or trustworthy. It cannot be both. Only two categories exist: approved or disqualified.

The presence of Christ is validated, not by feelings, but by a changed life.

The test of our life is the presence of Christ in our being. Paul is not questioning the work of God which places Christ in the life of every one who believes. That act of God is unchallengeable. What he is objecting to are people who call themselves Christians and say that they have believed when no evidence of a changed life is present. They have had some experience or attempted an imitation of Christ but have never received Christ. The lack of evidence declares that Christ is NOT in them!

Paul writes elsewhere, "Christ dwells in your heart by faith." The presence of Christ is validated, not by feelings, but by a changed life. Many speak of feelings as if that were proof of salvation, but Paul asks these people to put their life to the simple yet profound test—Is Christ in you? Because the enemy can counterfeit many aspects of the activities of believers, we must be very careful. The only way that a life can be truly transformed is by the person of Christ living His life through ours. We can even deceive ourselves and those around us. Test yourself! A life lived in the power of the flesh can seem satisfying but it is disqualified by God.

ℬ ———————————————— ℭ

Father, You placed Christ in my life when I believed. I surrender my life to Him to live His life in and through mine. I desire that there be no doubt to anyone that Jesus Christ is in me.

Shining the Light from Our Faces

For it is the God who commanded light to shine out of darkness, who has shone in our hearts to give the light of the knowledge of the glory of God in the face of Jesus Christ.

2 Corinthians 4:6

The creative act of bringing light into darkness was a glorious revelation of who God is. Before the creation of man and his environment, all was dark and empty—not dusk, but absolutely dark.

2 Corinthians 4:6 takes us back to the first day of creation where God said, "Let there be light." The world has never been without light since then. The sun was placed as a stationary sentinel to rule the day. Similarly, the moon, on its periodic journey reflecting the light of the sun, rules the night. The difference was the command of the Creator to the mightiest member of our solar system. This impersonal power responded in obedience, appearing to take off the wraps which might have shielded its display. Light and total darkness cannot exist in the same sphere; the light won out and darkness fled.

Light and total darkness cannot exist in the same sphere.

The birth of Jesus was the response of the Son of God to the Father commanding the Light of the world to shine in a darkened sphere. That light was seen in His walk, His ways, His words, His attitude, His actions, and His anger. Light was seen in His listening ear, His looking eye, and His loving lips. It was light displayed in His glorious face. Christ took upon Himself the form of a man so that the glory of God would be seen in a human face. No more perfect display of glory was visible for man.

And that face was marred more than any man's. They pulled the hair from His cheek. They pounded Him on the head. They spit on this face. They crushed a crown of thorns on that brow. They attacked His ears with bitter blasphemy. They offered His lips sour wine. All of this He referred to as the hour when He was to be glorified.

The Son is now raised, ascended, and fully seated in the glory of His Father. That face will never be abused again. How then can this glory be seen today? God has commanded that same light to shine out of the darkness of our society through our faces to give light by the knowledge of Christ. All that remains is for the light to shine out of us! If light were shined into a prism but did not shine out, no rainbow of color would be seen. The Light is in us!

       ও ———————————— ঙ

Father, thank you for giving the light of Christ in me. I offer my face as Your face to show the light of Your presence to the world.

Like a Hand in a Glove

And I thank Christ Jesus our Lord who has enabled me,
because He counted me faithful, putting me into the ministry.
1 Timothy 1:12

We are never encouraged to ask for strength. Paul tells Timothy that the Lord Jesus Christ Himself was the enabling force for all that he was called to do.

Our temptation is to look ahead to what we think is in front of us and then ask for "needed strength." Yet we are reminded that the Lord Himself is the enabler for every ministry that He gives. This thought demands a radical change of thinking. Even though we have Christ living within, we often think that we are inadequate to accept the ministry that He has given without asking for more strength. He is the strength and energy for the responsibilities that He gives.

Paul had many abilities which were his by birth and by training. Every child has potential communicated at conception by his natural parents. Each believer has spiritual gifts given at spiritual birth by the Holy Spirit.

The hand in a glove enables the glove to pick up a walking stick. The person of Christ in me enables me to carry out the ministry that He gives me. It is not the glove that wants to pick up the walking stick but the hand in it. It is the Lord who puts us into His work or ministry and chooses to use us. The glove does not ask a hand for strength but submits to the enabling of the hand. If there is total surrender the glove will respond, doing what the hand wants done.

And who gets the glory? The One who enables us. So again we are turned back to realize, "apart from me you can do nothing" as the glove can do nothing without the hand. How I tremble in unbelief thinking that the glove needs more than a hand to do what the hand wants to do.

The hand can do so much more than just pick up a walking stick. The hand is busy all day with a multitude of tasks. The hand will choose a different glove in surgery than in the workshop or the garden. Each glove must submit, yet some of us are like a leather glove left in the rain that has become sun-hard, stiff, and cracked. What kind of glove are you?

Father, you gave Christ to live in me so that He can do what He pleases through me. I confess that I have often wanted more than Christ. I now give my life unreservedly to Him to be in me all that He wants so that the ministry is entirely of Him.

God's Fullness in Human Form

*And without controversy great is the mystery of
godliness: God was manifested in the flesh, Justified in
the Spirit, Seen by angels, Preached among the Gentiles,
Believed on in the world, Received up in glory.*

1 Timothy 3:16

Immanuel, "God with us," was the announcement to the Old Testament world. The birth of Jesus was the primary fulfillment of that prophesy. In this cameo of the incarnation we have a summary of the events relating to the appearance of God as Man in the created world.

The greatest mystery is that *all* of God could be enveloped in a physical body. Nothing was adjusted in the baby's body to accept the incarnation of the fullness of the Godhead. He would grow normally to adulthood and in all of the ensuing years He would be a perfect revelation of the Father. Do we understand that the One who fills heaven is resident fully and completely in a body of flesh? We must bow in adoration and astonishment that God would go to that extent to restore His glory in human flesh.

As men saw the Lord walk, He was God in human form. As they listened to Jesus, they heard the Word of God. As they viewed Christ's miracles, they saw the power and glory of God. As they watched the tears of Jesus, they understood the emotions of God. It was this way in all His activity. The Father removed the veil from Himself and revealed to men His holiness in Christ's anger, His grace in becoming poor, His mercy in healing a widow, His peace in calming the storm, His mercy in giving life back to a son, His joy in accepting the cross, and His love in dying. Every aspect of the character of God was revealed. When Jesus knew their hearts, God's omniscience was revealed. When Christ was tempted and did not sin, they glimpsed God's holiness.

But how do we in human form lay hold of this mystery? The answer is that we believe on Jesus Christ and accept His salvation, and God comes to dwell in us in all His fullness. This does not make us God but is an incarnation of God in human flesh. The fullness of God dwells in Him and we are filled in Him. We cannot reveal all that He revealed because we are not God, but we can in a limited way reveal Christ because He lives in us. It took God in Christ to make the invisible God visible. It takes Christ in us to make an invisible Christ visible.

„ ———————————— ‘

Father, we marvel at Your fullness indwelling the human body of Christ. What a responsibility to be the residence of Christ Himself.

Flowing to the Hems of Our Garments!

But the anointing which you have received from Him abides in you, and you do not need that anyone teach you; but as the same anointing teaches you concerning all things, and is true, and is not a lie, and just as it has taught you, you will abide in Him.

1 John 2:27

How thrilling to read these comforting words that the anointing is present and enduring in us because we have Christ. The word "anointing" refers back to the official installation of Aaron as the High Priest of Israel. The anointing oil was poured on Aaron's head, and David tells us that it ran down on his beard to the hem of his garment (Psalm 133). On another occasion, Aaron was anointed with the holy oil on his right ear, right thumb, and right big toe. Each of these was to symbolize the consecration of the ministering capacities of Aaron to the work of the Lord, showing the abundance of the Lord's blessing!

It is humbling to know that when we received Christ as our Savior, the Holy Spirit was given to us in all of His power. His anointing is included with all the other aspects of His ministry to us. This anointing is a reminder that the ministry of teaching by the Holy Spirit is ours as a continuing fact. We sometimes pray that the Holy Spirit will anoint a particular speaker as he teaches from the Word. Yet the Holy Spirit has the capacity to teach every one of us. This does not mean that we should ignore a teacher of the Scriptures when the church gathers. But many who are not able to sit under the teaching of great Bible professors have gleaned the great truths as they sit under the teaching of the Holy Spirit in the secret place of the Most High. How refreshing to be taught by God!

> *It is humbling to know that when we received Christ as our Savior, the Holy Spirit was given to us in all of His power.*

His teaching is not the result of special prayer but the spontaneous ministry of the Spirit in the heart of any person who is teachable. He desires for us to come with open ears, eyes, and mouth—allowing Him to take the things of Christ and minister them to us. He will aid our memory. This Teacher abides in us and is not relegated to a classroom or conference pulpit. He waits for a learning, open heart that we might know the things given us in Christ. How exciting to know that we have been anointed in Christ by the Holy Spirit who abides in us!

ↁ ———————————— ☙

Father, thank you for anointing me with the oil of the Holy Spirit. I accept His instruction as a fulfillment of Your promised blessing.

14 MARCH

Enjoying the Peace of God

The things which you learned and received and heard and
saw in me, these do, and the God of peace will be with you.
Philippians 4:9

There are many titles which belong to God because of His character. Although we often use names without much insight into their meaning and connotations, God places high priority on the names that He gives Himself and those that He has given His people. Other names that God uses for Himself (The God of glory, God of hope, God of all grace, God of heaven, God of Hosts, God of all comfort) are descriptive of His activity or the qualities of His being.

This Scripture from Philippians 4:9 reminds believers of the many aspects of teaching Paul had left with them and they were to follow. He was their teacher, and they his students. He was the giver of truth, and they the recipients. He the speaker, and they the listeners. He the modeler of Christ, and they the imitators. He had designed a well-rounded array of methods for communicating the manifold grace of God.

We are dependent on the written Word, carefully orchestrated by the Holy Spirit, to minister the unsearchable riches of Christ. God has added to us the wonderful blessing of having all of the New Testament as well as the Old. We have far more access to the Scriptures than these Philippian believers. The Spirit helps us draw the concepts of behavior which Christ developed in Paul so that we also can profit from this epistle.

Paul is not suggesting that, if we do not learn, then the God of peace will leave. The only condition of the presence of the God of peace is saving faith. When Christ comes to live in us the God of Peace is in us!

> *If we do not learn, receive, and hear the Word of God, we will not enjoy the peace of God.*

The challenge is that, if we do not learn, receive, and hear the Word of God, we will not enjoy the peace of God. To live in disobedience is to bring the clouds of unbelief between us and the God of peace. Fellowship is broken but relationship is unchanged. In order for us to appropriate the peace of God we must learn the truth of God. To appreciate the peace of God we must receive the instruction from God. To apply the peace of God we must hear the voice of the God of peace. Learn, receive, and hear His Word today.

80 ———————————— os

Father, thank you for giving me Your peace as a permanent blessing. I choose to learn, receive, and hear Your voice so that I might enjoy Your peace.

Our Anchor—Sure and Steadfast

*This hope we have as an anchor of the soul, both sure
and steadfast, and which enters the Presence behind
the veil, where the forerunner has entered for us,
even Jesus, having become High Priest forever.*

Hebrews 6:19-20

In the Bible "hope" is not a conditional expectation dependent on circumstances which may change. We say that we hope to do something and realize that the weather, our health, our resources, or time may prevent us from fulfilling our hope. Biblical hope is classically described here as both "sure and steadfast."

The author has just reminded his readers that God has made a promise of blessing on which they can set their hopes. The anchor of the soul has been firmly placed in the very presence of God, and the two ropes connecting it to us are huge. These ropes, using the metaphor he chooses, are God's promise and His immutability or changelessness.

God made a promise to Abraham and all his seed, both physical and spiritual. That promise was confirmed by His oath. That "rope" is firmly attached between Christ, who is in heaven, and us on earth. The other "rope" is the fact that God is unchangeable—He is the same yesterday, today, and forever! Our hope, like two huge ropes holding a ship to the shore, is so permanent it cannot be changed or challenged.

Christ is intimately linked to us even though He is in heaven as the God-Man and we are on earth in the midst of the troubled waters of life. The ropes are not strained nor threatened. They are sure and steadfast.

What is changeable is our faith in these promises and covenants. We are the changeable ones. We are challenged by circumstances and temptations. We vacillate because of our unbelief and fear. Too often we evaluate the faithfulness of God on the basis of our faithfulness to Him. If we "do well" then we think that God should reciprocate with His faithfulness. That expresses our idea of hope. We have done our part and we "hope" that God will do His. This is denigrating to the One who has said with an oath that He will bless. He who is unchangeable has said that "we are blessed." God's blessing is dependent on Christ who, like a large anchor, is firmly imbedded in the rock of God's presence in glory. That anchor is attached to us by those immense ropes of God's character which are unchangeable and unchallengeable.

&) ———————————— C3

*Father, our hope is in you and your Son who is firmly seated in glory. His
position is unassailable. Your words are unchallengeable. Our Hope is in
Christ.*

Endowed with All Wisdom

If any of you lacks wisdom, let him ask of God, who gives to all liberally and without reproach, and it will be given to him.

James 1:5

The need for wisdom seems to be a regular acknowledgement among believers. Wisdom is the proper use of knowledge. Having wisdom presupposes that you have researched the facts, but that the facts by themselves do not give you adequate information to decide. This offer of God seems to be employed most often in the area of divine guidance. What does the Lord want me to do? With that question firmly in mind, a person will seek the wisdom of God.

Several thoughts should be considered when discussing wisdom. Scripture reminds us that true wisdom is found in Christ. James reminds us that "the wisdom that is from above is first pure, then peaceable, gentle, willing to yield, full of mercy" (3:17). Christ is the fullness of wisdom. In Christ, we are all endowed with His wisdom!

In Christ, we are all endowed with His wisdom!

In James 1:5 God invites us to ask Him and He will give abundantly and does not reproach us for coming or lacking. The prerequisite to this prayer is a believing heart. Explore all the information available to you. Gather as much understanding as possible. If, in the course of this gathering, the Lord does not reveal His will to you, then you are instructed to boldly ask for wisdom.

The text does not inform us how God will endow or communicate this wisdom. It is clear that He will not give us a feeling of its presence. We should not expect an emotional expression to indicate that we now possess wisdom. Faith must come into the exercise as I claim His wisdom. Establish unimpeded fellowship with God. Make sure that my motives are clear and pure. Acknowledge my lack of wisdom, then claim His wisdom by faith. An attitude of thanksgiving helps my heart to claim His gift of wisdom.

A decision can then be made in faith, accepting the fact that God is guiding my thoughts and helping me to make a choice that is in harmony with His wisdom. I cannot and must not later wonder whether I made the right decision. That is fostering unbelief which this chapter condemns. This blessing, like all others, is based on faith in the Word of God and in the person of Christ. I need. I ask. I receive. I claim. I thank. I decide. I act.

༄ ——————————————— ༈

Father, thank you for opening the reservoir of your wisdom to me as Your child. I confess my tendency to lean on my own understanding.

Workers Together in Grace

*We then, as workers together with Him also plead
with you not to receive the grace of God in vain.*

2 Corinthians 6:1

P aul is challenging the Corinthians to be sure that the blessing of God's grace is not only received but also appropriated or put to work in their lives. He follows his challenge by reminding them, "Behold, now is the accepted time. Behold, now is the day of salvation." Salvation is described as "receiving the grace of God." Grace is the blessing of salvation in an enormous array of gifts. God offers all these blessings provided through the work of Christ on the cross and made available by His resurrection.

The special blessing Paul is counting on is the activity of himself and God working in tandem to encourage people to accept the grace of God. An amazing picture comes to mind of God, the infinite worker, choosing to toil with a servant like Paul to accomplish His desires. Perhaps the image is drawn from the Lord's own visualization of serving together under the same yoke, "take my yoke upon you and learn of me." The encouragement of serving under the yoke with the Lord Jesus should produce a spontaneous enthusiasm for vibrant service.

Mark records in the last verse of his Gospel (16:29) that the disciples went on their way, preaching everywhere, "the Lord working with them and confirming the Word." The presence and power of the Lord in our ministry is a blessing which we seldom consider or perhaps even count on.

How is the Lord working in you to accomplish His will? Surely the convicting work of the Holy Spirit, as the gospel is preached, is a mighty and powerful activity bringing people to receive the grace of God. It is God who makes the hard points of truth easy to accept by the ignorant. God brings to bear on the lives of the lost their need of a Savior. God reminds them of their emptiness, their sinfulness, and the darkness of their heart. He opens their eyes to their blindness. He shows them the hardness of their heart. He shows them His wonderful grace.

God is working in the lives of those who need Christ as well as in the mind and heart of the preachers who are proclaiming the grace of God. The message is empowered. The memory is renewed. The compassion is sensitized. The mind is vitalized. This is the work of God using a committed vessel. We cannot do it without God working with us. Both God and man say, "receive the grace of God!"

—— ∞ ——

Father, thank you for using me as a worker together with You in Your ministry of drawing men and women to receive Your grace.

Sons by Natural Birth

For you are all sons of God through faith in Christ Jesus.
Galatians 3:26

God calls us all to be His sons! We are not mere slaves, bought as a piece of property, but sons, born into the family and the home. The word "sons" is not limited to the male members of the family of God but is gender inclusive of all believers, even though God uses the word "sons" instead of child.

How does a person accept and defend the position of sons? Galatians defines the concept of adoption, but the only source of sonship is to be born a son. The only clear defense of our sonship is the fact that we have the life of our Father in us. God goes to great lengths to teach us the truth that believing on Jesus Christ is the identifying exercise that places God's life in each believer. Regeneration is simultaneous with sonship.

The relationship of a father and son is based on the child receiving the life of the parents. There is no other way of actually injecting life into a fetus.

On the spiritual plane, the communication of life from God to each of His children is made possible only by the death and resurrection of Christ. Had Christ died and not risen from the dead, there would be no way of infusing His life into believers. It would be like a dead man having the capacity to conceive a child in a physical way.

So, sonship is not to be prayed for, earned, or produced by any effort of our own. It is a gift and a blessing to be enjoyed and appreciated. It is incumbent on us to live in the light of this lofty pronouncement. A son who is proud of his father and family often stands a little straighter with his head held a little higher as he contemplates the blessing of sonship.

We are the sons of God only by our faith in a living Christ who has given us His Father's life. We may be tempted to be proud of the fact that we belong. But no pride is suitable since the position of sonship is a gift in response to faith in Christ. What we do with that sonship is our responsibility. The fact that we are God's children is reason enough to redouble our efforts to please our Father. Remembering our position should produce thanksgiving. Contemplating this blessing will strengthen resistance to temptation.

Father, thank you for making me Your child. I do not deserve it but I delight in it. I did not earn it but I enjoy it. I am blessed by you.

The Doorway of Death

. . . who delivered us from so great a death, and does
deliver us; in whom we trust that He will still deliver us.
2 Corinthians 1:10

What is a great death? Is it the agony of a long, drawn out ordeal of cancer? Is it languishing in old age without friends and family? Certainly not! A great death is one without a resurrection, to go into the grave without Christ. That is a great death from which there is no resolution, no recourse or return. It is a death without a door to the other side, a death where you exist for all eternity separated from God, a death in darkness from which there is no escape.

Christ delivered every believer from death by guaranteeing resurrection, by building a door into the next life, by promising life on the other side of the valley, by covenanting to bring us through the river of death. God does not declare that we will not experience death but that we will not be held captive by death. We will not continue in death because of His resurrection. Although death can claim us, Christ reclaims us. Death grabs us, but cannot hold us. Death catches us, but will not imprison us. The gates of that prison will fly open of their own accord, and we will be guided by angels into the presence of Christ Himself.

Every day God delivers believers who die in Christ. These believers pass through the waters into the glorious blessing of our Savior's presence. Scripture reminds us that to be absent from the body is to be present with the Lord. The transition is instantaneous, but the door is still death. Keeping this perspective we do not fear for the believer entering through death's door. We do not need to weep for the one who, in a step, passes through death into true life eternal.

But what about those of us who are still alive and remain? Will He deliver? The answer is a resounding yes. For it will be even more glorious to go to Christ without going through death's door! We will be changed into His image without being sown in the grave of weakness. We will be transformed into His likeness for we shall see Him as He is. What a delivery from so great a death. This is guaranteed by His own resurrection. "Because I live you shall live also." As believers, we should yearn to be caught up to meet Him in the air. And we must remember that this could happen any time, "in the twinkling of an eye."

ଜ ———————————— ଔ

Father, thank you for the resurrection of Christ my Savior. I long to be with Him without death, but if through death, I will not fear.

Drinking from the River of Peace

*And let the peace of God rule in your hearts, to which
also you were called in one body; and be thankful.*

Colossians 3:15

" "I've got peace like a river in my soul" is part of a popular chorus which also reminds me that "I've got joy like a fountain" and "love like an ocean in my soul." The picture is glorious in its comprehensiveness. Each of the lines takes us to the abundance of water—whether a fountain, a river, or an ocean.

Peace is one of the primary fruits of our salvation. The prophesy of Isaiah regarding our Savior involved His ministry as "The Prince of Peace." He also wrote, "of the increase of His government and peace there shall be no end." And when Christ came He said, "Peace I leave with you, My peace I give to you." Romans 5 reads, "we have peace." Ephesians adds, "He is our peace." You would have to lose Christ to lose His peace! The blood of Christ guarantees that peace will never be in short supply.

The challenge of our text is not the possession of peace but the supremacy of peace. The little word "let" indicates that we choose whether peace rules. If peace does not rule, what does? Perhaps fear, worry, confusion, feelings, anxiety, doubts, and other intruders.

Our calling is to peace because it has been supplied in such abundance. It is like a river which flows beside your house. As a child you played here and drank of its pure water. As a youth you found it a joy to swim in. In manhood you harvested its wealth. Now, as an old man, you sit and rest in its beauty and draw from its abundance. For your whole life it has never failed. In the early morning it flowed silently by. In the heat of the day it refreshed. In the storm it filled its banks. In drought it was lower but adequate. It has always been there in every season of life. Draw deeply by faith and set fear aside.

> *Our calling is to peace because it has been supplied in such abundance.*

Unfortunately some live by the river but never draw from its wealth. Because they choose to be ruled by fears that it will go dry, they do not drink. Others worry that it will overflow and so build bulwarks against it. A few fear that it will be impure, and thus will not drink. How sad to be ruled by fear when peace is near—so near that He dwells in us and is waiting to be given His place of adequacy and authority. Allow Him to increase in your life. His peace has no end!

⌘ ──────────────── ⌘

Father, thank you for living in me and giving me Your peace. I drive fear out and in faith enthrone the Prince of Peace in my heart.

God's Will Is Already Revealed

For this is the will of God, your sanctification: that
you should abstain from sexual immorality.

1 Thessalonians 4:3

Many Christians earnestly desire to know the will of God. Some suggest that the will of God is like an elusive guide who, leading us through the maze of life, is hard to keep up with. Others envision that the will of God is found in a book whose language is written in a secret code known only to the high and holy.

Perhaps the primary problem in discerning His will is that we are not willing to do it. We see a clear expression of the will of God, as in our verse, and know that it will mean giving up a lot of thoughts, activities, and desires that we harbor in our heart. We are prone to select the things that we want to do, and we choose not to do those that cost us or inconvenience us or disturb our pattern of life.

Do you suppose that we cannot find the will of God because we are not doing what He asks already?

Do you suppose that we cannot find the will of God because we are not doing what He asks already? If a mother asks her child to do something and he refuses, will she leave that request undone and ask for something else? That would not be good parenting.

This specific aspect of the will of God goes much deeper than the physical act of fornication or adultery. Our Lord Himself said that when a man "looks at a woman to lust for her [he] has already committed adultery with her in his heart." The Lord does not separate the thoughts from the act. To do so would be contrary to the will of God. This is not something to be prayed about or studied and explained but we are to follow in the footsteps of Joseph in Genesis 39:12.

Sanctification is being set apart for God. These sexual temptations demand that I daily set apart my eyes, my thoughts, my physical desires, my mental images, and my heart. This aspect of the will of God does not change. There are some facets of God's will that might be new each day. How should I use my time today? Does God want me to take this trip? Should I spend my money this way? These are the daily revelations of God's will. But if I find those things hard to know, maybe I am leaving the command in this verse undone. Sanctification is the will of God!

⁣⁣⁣⁣⁣ ∎ ——————————— ∁

Father, I confess that I struggle with obeying this aspect of Your will for me.
Thank you for revealing it so clearly. I give myself to You today.

Members of One Body

For we are members of His body, of His flesh and of His bones.
Ephesians 5:30

The connection of the parts of our physical body is one of the most profound illustrations of the closeness of our bond in Christ and with all other believers. What a glorious blessing! The most intimate connections in our human body tell us of our permanent relationship with Christ in His body. Any doubt we might have can be dispelled by looking at our hand or finger. Our faith may fail but it is augmented by seeing the visible union of the members of our body.

Three words are used to describe this intimate connection: body, flesh, and bones. The use of the body is to help us understand the singleness of the one body. None of us has two bodies. All believers are united to Christ in one body. Occasionally we hear someone speak of their local church as "the body." This connotation defeats the plain statement of this verse and others announcing that there is only one body. It is true that a local church should be a microcosm of the universal church, but Christ only has one body just as you have only one.

The inability to separate the flesh from other members reminds us of the intimate connection of one muscle to another. No one can take a muscle from the others and leave it at home because it is tired of traveling. All the flesh makes one body. All belong to each other.

> *What is clear and comforting is that we are all permanently joined to Christ and to every believer.*

In the same way, the bones of the body are connected permanently for utility and harmony of movement, whether the smallest bone in the ear or the large hip bone. Even Ezekiel speaks of the bones being joined together, illustrating the future restoration of the nation of Israel. What is clear and comforting is that we are all permanently joined to Christ and to every believer. Do you doubt that you are a member of Christ? Be comforted by considering your body—your flesh and your bones. Union in the body of Christ is illustrated by the body you carry with you every day of your life.

℺ ———————————— ∛

Father, thank you for placing me in Christ and making me a member of His body. I celebrate my union with every other believer.

The Powerlessness of Fear

For God has not given us a spirit of fear, but of
power and of love and of a sound mind.

2 Timothy 1:7

We have power! That power is the same power that raised Christ from the dead. But we are often far more conscious of our weakness than of His power.

Fear flows from the old man and power flows in and through the new man. How many times has this scenario been repeated: We are called by God to do something for Him and our immediate response is fear! "I can't do that! I have never done that before! Get someone else, God!" Moses used a number of such excuses to exempt himself from the Lord's call. God's answer to him is much the same as that given here. "I gave you the power to do what I ask," God says. "I gave you my love to feel the hurt of other people. I gave you the mind of Christ to reason things out in a spiritual way. Now go do what I asked you to do!"

Fear comes from the enemy as he tries to hinder us in ministry.

Fear comes from the enemy as he tries to hinder us in ministry. As soon as sin came into the world fear came also. Fear is the opposite of the response that God desires. God is waiting for faith to be expressed in what He has said and what He has given. In place of fear, faith is believing that the Lord has called, directed, and empowered, and that He will enable me to accomplish His will.

John writes "fear has torment." Most of us have known times of severe fear! Our mind thinks wrong thoughts, we are paralyzed to act, our emotions rise in unexpected ways, we say things that we would not normally express, and we run in our mind and may run with our feet.

"Perfect love casts out fear" is the answer given by John. That is the love that God has given to all of us. God gives power to *my* will so that I can choose to do *His* will. He also gives me a sound mind so that I can think the thoughts of Christ. "Now go act on my behalf!" says the Lord.

A common prayer is, "Lord, give me strength." That prayer is borne out of fear—fear that I do not have the power in Christ. We do not need to ask or pray for additional strength or power. We need to set fear aside and claim the power of God resident in a risen Christ.

— ❧ ─────────── ❧ —

Father, thank you for giving me the power of Christ. I confess my many fears which are not pleasing to You. I choose to obey Your call.

The Will to Live—Eternally

And you He made alive, who were dead in trespasses and sins.

Ephesians 2:1

L ife and the desire to live is a God-given aspiration. People will do almost anything to continue living. Innate to our being is a hunger to live a long life. Every doctor is called upon by patients to do whatever is necessary to sustain or extend life.

The confusion in the mind of man between spiritual life and physical life clouds the offer of God to give eternal life. We are so bound by the world's philosophy regarding the permanence of physical life that we miss the need for life eternal. Although God calls on men to realize that in their natural sinful condition they are spiritually dead, the enemy has deluded the minds of men to think that the "here and now" is more important than what is conceived of as the "then and there." Is this life more important than the life on the other side of death?

> *God cannot Give Himself without giving His life.*

Paul begins his instruction about living in the world by reminding his readers that the first ingredient necessary is the life of God exchanged for our deadness. The words life and death need to be understood in the spiritual context of God's revelation. Our understanding of physical death confuses numerous references to death in the Bible.

We need the life of God. That life is in Christ! When a person believes that he is a sinner and receives God's forgiveness, he is moved from a state of death to a state of life. All believers are changed from being separated from God to being alive in God. That is salvation!

This life is in God's Son. The only way to obtain the life of God is by receiving Christ as our Savior from the sin and trespasses that held us in death. One of the greatest gifts of God is life. God cannot give Himself without giving His life.

This is a most wonderful transaction in the saving work of God. I am alive because God has taken up His permanent residence in my life. This life should be exhilarating and ennobling. I have a reason to live. I have a life to live. I have a Person to live for. I am alive unto God through the Lord Jesus Christ. We are made alive by the life of Christ.

ᴽᴐ ———————————————— ᴄᴪ

Father, thank you for giving me Your life. Help me to live every day empowered by that life.

Drink Deeply from the Reservoir

Therefore if there is any consolation in Christ, if any comfort of love, if any fellowship of the Spirit, if any affection and mercy . . .

Philippians 2:1

Paul lists five resources available in Christ for every believer. The word *consolation* is the term often used of the Holy Spirit. *Comfort* is a unique word suggesting stimulating forces or impetus from within. *Fellowship* is the common term for jointly partaking and sharing. *Affection* is usually seen to be metaphorically springing from our heart, which is the seat of such emotions. The word *mercy* refers to the absence of judgment that is due because of sin and failure.

All of these blessings are resident in Christ who has been given to every believer when they "receive" Him as Savior. Not often do we have such a list of resources so plainly declared. But it is good to remind ourselves that these are present for all believers every day of their peregrinations on this earth.

> *All of these blessings are resident in Christ.*

In the midst of loneliness, we can receive and display consolation from the Holy Spirit. When we are fearful of moving forward in the face of apathy or antagonism, we can draw on the strength found in Christ Himself who faced the cross. When we have more than we need, we can give as Christ gave and be humble enough to receive as our Lord did at the well in Samaria. The deep feelings of Christ for others can well up in us when we are faced with coldness of heart. The desire to repay evil for evil can be overcome by the outrageous display of mercy Christ has shown to us.

We need never question the availability of these blessings because they are part and parcel of all that is in Christ. We cannot receive Christ and not be given the character, compassion, and comfort that is Christ. We can, however, not know or partake of these, either through ignorance or independence of Christ. More often than not we try to offer these graces from our own experience or ability. That display pales in comparison to the kaleidoscopic manifestation recorded for us of Christ in the Gospels. We are here to make the invisible Christ visible by means of His life in us. Draw deeply from His infinite reservoir to give to those in need.

⸎ —————————— ⸎

Father, how can I ever fully know all the resources You have given me in Christ? I commit myself to learn these blessing and then to display and communicate them to others around me.

26

Loving the Unlovely

No one has seen God at any time. If we love one another,
God abides in us, and His love has been perfected in us.

1 John 4:12

God dwells in me! It is hard to fully comprehend that the God who inhabits eternity and fills the heaven of heavens abides in every believer. Yet God's presence in us should have the most profound impact on our every thought and deed.

Is the presence of God in us dependent on our loving other believers? When we stop loving a believer, does God depart? No! God does not come and go as in a revolving door, leaving us when we sin and returning when we confess that sin.

Perhaps we should say that the *fullness* of His presence is known when we love one another with a pure heart. If we sin and turn from love to hate, as John writes, the presence of God recedes to the innermost parts of our being. Failing to love our brother erects a wall through which God will not pass. He awaits our return to purity by repentance, for He wishes to be, not merely present, but preeminent.

God is waiting for us to acknowledge our polluted thoughts toward our brother and apply the blood of Jesus Christ which cleanses us from every sin. He will then make His presence known by filling and flooding our being and continuing His perfecting work in our life.

> *Perhaps we should say that the fullness of His presence is known when we love one another with a pure heart.*

We may plead with God to overwhelm us with His love so that we can show it to others, but He is waiting for us to offer a pure home for Him as the center of His activity. If our house is clean and prepared God will overflow every thought, every feeling, and every decision. Then the love of God will flow from our being and be manifest to everyone in the family of God.

Those closest to us can be the hardest to love. We have no problem loving those across the seas—but those we meet every day, those with annoying eccentricities or those who offer us criticism, those people can easily ruffle our feathers. But they are the ones who present a test of whether God is filling and flooding our house and showing His love out through the windows of our being. In this way they can see God in our behavior, our words, our works, and our love.

❧ ──────────── ☙

Father, You are abiding in me. I confess that I do not always offer You a clean house. I confess my emptiness and claim Your fullness.

Redemption, a Cornerstone of Salvation

*In whom we have redemption through His
blood, the forgiveness of sins.*

Colossians 1:14

Our salvation is like a pyramid that points up toward God, and the three cornerstones of that pyramid are redemption, propitiation, and reconciliation. Propitiation is God's satisfaction with Christ's work, while reconciliation is the complete change of man, making it possible for him to receive the value of Christ's work. Redemption deals with sin. Propitiation is in relation to God. Reconciliation is toward man.

Redemption is the payment for the sin of man, thereby allowing God to forgive his sin and set him free from bondage and slavery. The price mentioned here, and in other places, is "His blood." These words help us to grasp the enormity of the cost. The shedding of blood is seen as the pouring out of life. When Jesus was on the cross, He allowed His blood to be shed. He did not die from the loss of blood, but because He dismissed His spirit, which brought physical death. Yet the shedding of His blood was necessary as the evidence that He was pouring out His life for the sin of all mankind.

Hebrews 9:22 states, "Without shedding of blood there is no remission." Remission is the sending away or forgiving of sin. The blood of Jesus Christ had to spill from His body to demonstrate that He is human, and it also demonstrates the willingness of God to sacrifice the life of His Son for the sin of the world. Blood poured out tells of cost, loss, pain, sorrow, sacrifice, and the expense involved in setting man free from the punishment of sin. The sacrifice of Christ is clearly the punishment that God demanded for the sin of man. Christ accepted the responsibility of our sin as our substitute and willingly poured out His life.

The result for us is that God forgives the sin of everyone who comes to God by faith in Christ. The adequacy of Christ's sacrifice makes it possible for God to forgive *all* our sins. Paul tells us in Colossians 2:13 that God has "forgiven you all trespasses." *All* my sins are gone—past, present, and future!

> *The adequacy of Christ's sacrifice makes it possible for God to forgive all our sins.*

Our redemption is not solely in His work but also in His person. Our redemption is in Christ. If you have Christ, you have redemption. The blessing of forgiveness must not be separated from the Lord Jesus Christ.

₧ ———————————— ₸

Father, I cling to the full and complete sacrifice of Christ for my sin. Thank you for helping me not to continue living in sin.

Our Abundant Inheritance

For we have become partakers of Christ if we hold the
beginning of our confidence steadfast to the end.

Hebrews 3:14

The New Testament is clear that we can never lose possession of Christ. The writer of Hebrews tells us that our *partaking* of Christ can be diminished—but not Christ Himself. Nothing can separate us from Christ, writes Paul in Romans 8:39. Yet many believers begin to question whether they still have Christ in their lives if they are not living according to the standard described in the Scriptures, or if their lives are not in harmony with what they have been taught about the Christian life. Losing Christ and not partaking of the blessings in Christ are two very different things. To lose Christ is to lose salvation and that cannot happen because we are kept by the power of God the Father, God the Son, and God the Holy Spirit.

The New Testament is clear that we can never lose possession of Christ.

The danger in this verse is to stop partaking of the abundant resources found in Christ. This is a far too common circumstance. Many believers start well, feasting on all that God has given them in Christ. Yet then their hearts grow cold or are drawn away, and they seek satisfaction in someone or something else. As they lose their confidence in Christ, His Word, and His provision, they then begin to wonder whether Christ does in fact hold all the riches of God.

A person may be given a lavish inheritance from a rich relative and find enjoyment and fulfillment from those resources. But friends draw him away from those possessions to other attractions. The young person does not become disinherited, nor is the inheritance dissipated. He has lost interest and is finding fulfillment in something else. He no longer is partaking of the resources that his relative gave him.

So it can be among believers who start so well with great confidence and expectation. They come daily to the throne of grace and receive adequate supply for each moment of each day. But after a while they are drawn away from Christ to the world; they seek, but do not find, satisfaction from the world's offerings. There is no change in the supply, only a change in confidence and enjoyment from that supply. What great faithfulness and fullness there is in Christ. What tremendous abundance there is for our daily needs!

ℝ ———————————— ℞

Father, thank you for preserving for me the resources in Christ. Forgive me for seeking satisfaction elsewhere. I come and feast on the abundance You have offered me in Christ.

Three Branches of the River

Jude, a servant of Jesus Christ, and brother of
James, To those who are called, sanctified by God
the Father, and preserved in Jesus Christ.

Jude 1

Jude opens his book by reminding his readers of the blessings of their salvation. We who have believed can rest under the banner which Christ spreads for all "who are called." God has called, sanctified, and preserved us in Christ!

What comfort these first few words are to those who are tossed by the enemy into severe trials. What strength is drawn from these pillars of the faith by those challenged by false teachers. What courage is appropriated from these three beacons of light: called, sanctified, and preserved. What joy is tied to this three-fold cord for the faint at heart. How refreshing to come to the three branches of this glorious river!

God has called, sanctified, and preserved us in Christ. Here again the blessings of this aspect of our salvation are found in Christ. Our calling, our sanctification, and our preservation are secure because we have been placed in Jesus Christ.

The calling is that first work of God in the long chain of events that stretches from eternity to eternity. The calling of God took place long before we had any interest in the things of God. His work on our behalf became effective the day that God called and we responded to the drawing power of God. The day that we believed, we were born again and placed in Jesus Christ.

Being sanctified is the second ministry of God the Father. Jesus said, "sanctify them by your truth," and God has been working in our lives to bring us to Christ-likeness. Jude is not saying that we are entirely sanctified but that in God's sight we, in Christ, are as set apart as He. We seek to be as set apart on earth as we are in glory.

The third branch of blessing is the position of security and safety that we enjoy because God placed us in Christ. "If anyone is in Christ" he is as secure as Christ Himself. What a sanctuary, a haven, a harbor from the judgment of my foes, from the darts of the evil one, and from the thoughts of my own mind. I am preserved by God in Christ!

Drink and refresh yourself at each of these branches of the great river that flows from the throne of God. We were called by God in the past, sanctified in Christ in the present, and preserved in Christ for the future.

  ———————————

Father, these three marvelous truths buoy me up in the storms of life that come my way. Thank you for such a glorious plan of redemption.

Radiating Heavenly Wisdom

But the wisdom that is from above is first pure, then peaceable, gentle, willing to yield, full of mercy and good fruits, without partiality and without hypocrisy.

James 3:17

The beauties of true wisdom stand out in stark contrast to the wisdom which is all around us. The world's wisdom is earthly, sensual, and devilish, writes James. This description is an apt summary of the froth that comes from our society: the world is earthly, the flesh is sensual, and the devil is—well, devilish. That kind of wisdom is from below and is fabricated in the pit of the lowest parts of the earth.

The true wisdom which comes from above is the opposite. Heavenly wisdom is a characterization of the Lord Jesus Christ. He is pure, peaceable, gentle, willing to yield, merciful, full of good fruits, without partiality, and without hypocrisy. This eight-fold portrait is a partial presentation of God in the person of the Lord Jesus Christ.

How does this affect us in our pilgrimage in this wicked world? Christ is not here in the flesh to display all these fruits for the eyes and ears of the world. God has called us to be His family of lights in the world. He wants our behavior to exhibit that which cannot be found in the world.

Because God has given Christ to live in us, these same qualities should be found in us as well. The world generates their wisdom from below because of their orientation, which is worldly; similarly we should generate true wisdom from above, since our orientation is heavenly.

How does God give us these lovely commodities to distribute in our behavior? The simple answer is that He gave us Christ in whom are hid all these wondrous treasures. The practical answer is that we are to draw on these resources which were fully paraded by Christ during His earthly life. Are we then called to *imitate* these graces in our life which we have seen in Christ? Should we be capable of doing that, we would receive the glory for such an accurate counterfeit of Christ. That would not please God and should not please us either.

Rather, God has given Christ to us, and in doing so has given us the elegant qualities which He will display through our personality. People will be drawn to Christ in us as we radiate this wisdom. "They glorified God in me" was Paul's summary of his capability to point people to Christ. These beauties should be present in our everyday life since they are the graces of Christ.

ଅ ———————————— ଔ

Father, thank you for placing Christ and all His divine qualities in my being. I surrender my life to Him to display Your wisdom.

Held in the Grip of God

*Now to Him who is able to keep you from stumbling, and to present
you faultless before the presence of His glory with exceeding joy.*
Jude 24

God is able. We know that He is able, but sometimes we are tempted to ask, "Is He willing?"

A short look at the special object of this saving and keeping power—God's own children—should leave no doubt about His willingness. God is talking of subduing all the enemies of His children. He is speaking of saving any who seek salvation in His Son, Jesus Christ. He is offering aid to all who apply for the priestly sacrifice presented by Christ to God. He is proclaiming His ability to keep all of His children. The force of this word "keep," used only here in the New Testament, is to prevent them from falling during their journey from earth to glory.

A child may wander from the protective care of a father and fall over a cliff to her death. The father was able but not willing to keep his child from falling. Our Father, on the other hand, holds each of His children in His hand and "no one is able to snatch them out of my Father's hand." Note the emphasis: "no one is able" to undo what God is able to do! We are "kept by the power of God," writes Peter.

Not one will be left behind. Not one will have fallen out by the way.

God is keeping each one of us in order to present us to Himself, to bring each to perfection. Not one will be left behind. Not one will have fallen out by the way. Not one will have sinned so grossly that it cannot be forgiven. Not one will fall out of the grace of God. Not one will wander so far from the path that the Father cannot keep him. Not one can break the bond connecting the Father to His children. Not one can be taken by anyone or anything out of the protective care of the One "who is able to keep."

What a day for God and for us when we are presented without spot or wrinkle before His presence, with glory and great joy. Could joy possibly fill the scene if several or even one was missing from the family of redeemed and justified saints? Sorrow would pervade the whole event and cast a pall over the very character of God and of Christ. He is able and willing to prevent us from falling!

ৡ ———————————— ଓ

*Father, the blessing of Your keeping power is an amazing comfort to me. I
trust Your power and willingness to prevent me from falling.*

April

GIFTS TO GIVE THANKS FOR!

". . . grow in the grace and knowledge of
our Lord and Savior Jesus Christ."

2 Peter 3:18

He giveth more grace when the burdens grow greater;
He sendeth more strength when the labors increase.
To added affliction He addeth His mercy;
To multiplied trials, His multiplied peace.
His love has no limit; His grace has no measure.
His power has no boundary known unto men.
For out of His infinite riches in Jesus,
He giveth, and giveth, and giveth, again!

Annie Johnson Flint

April

Vine and Branches

Sometimes I carry a drinking straw with me as an illustration of a simple truth. The text that it illustrates is John 15:5: "I am the vine, you are the branches." A branch is a sophisticated straw, a very amazing and complicated conveyer of the nutrients absorbed from the soil that are then transformed by the vine into life and fruit. The vine is the manufacturing plant for the resources necessary for the branches to bear fruit.

The branch cannot produce fruit of itself because it cannot generate the nutrients needed to develop fruit. It is interesting, as the Lord expands this metaphor, that the only parts of the whole process are the vine (which includes the roots), the branches, and the fruit. In other plants, such as trees, we speak of the roots, the trunk, and the branches. But the vine is the whole plant, which exists independent of the branches. In nature, the branch might be trimmed, but the vine remains and may in fact bear new branches each year.

The lesson for us is that the responsibility of bearing fruit rests solely in the branches, while the responsibility of producing nutritious fluids is solely that of the vine. As the branch begins the process of bearing fruit, the vine spontaneously offers food to each branch equally. As the fruit develops, the suction process continues, as each branch becomes the "straw" for transferring the resources that the vine produces and provides.

How exact the Lord is in choosing the vine and the branches as an illustration of our dependence on the Lord Jesus Christ. As we begin our God-given responsibility of bearing fruit, the resources of supply are all available in Christ. We need nothing other than what Christ provides to bring forth fruit that satisfies the desires of the Vine-dresser.

The picture of the vine goes further—a branch can only bear the kind of fruit which that vine is designed to produce. A vine branch cannot produce a pear or an apple, even though apples and pears grow on branches. The vine dictates the specific qualities of the fruit that the branch is to produce. These qualities include size, color, time of year, tartness, and, of course, the all-important flavor.

The Lord Jesus, by His very being, dictates the kind of fruit that we produce. Paul prays that the believers in Philippi would be "filled with the fruits of righteousness which are by Jesus Christ." If we are filled with the nutrients of the Vine, it overflows in "much fruit." The familiar verses on fruit from Galatians 5:22-23 offer a full display of the fruit of the Spirit, which are the glorious graces of Christ Jesus Himself.

The special responsibility for the believer is to abide in the vine who is Christ The danger is seeking the nutrients for fruit from some other source, or even trying to produce fruit by ourselves. It is possible for a branch trailing on the ground to find moist soil as an alternative source of food for fruit. A trailing branch can attempt to send down its own roots and have no further need for the Vine. The Vine-dresser then comes along and, as verse 2 says, "takes it away" or "lifts it up," as the word may be translated accurately.

A further problem to the branch is attacks by bugs, parasites, or diseases. These attacks sap the food that is destined for producing fruit. Again, the Vine-dresser is attentive to this serious condition by cleaning the branch. The text also reflects this activity by using a word translated "clean" in verse 3. What is not often revealed is that the word usually translated "prunes" in verse 2 is the same word as "clean" in verse 3. It is more accurately translated in verses 2-3, "He cleans it that it may bear more fruit."

Take a straw and poke a small hole in the side, then place it in a glass of juice and suck as you would normally. The result is a flow of juice with added bubbles, introduced from the hole in the side. The effectiveness of the straw is impaired by the hole. For the believer, a "hole" forms an alternative source of supply which reduces his usefulness. A straw with a hole in the side is of little use.

What a marvelous provision for our development of fruit by both the Father and His Son. The Vine-dresser deals with anything outward that would inhibit full production of fruit. The Son, as the Vine, is the source of all necessary supply for lasting fruit which glorifies the Father. Our task is to obey Christ's counsel, "Abide in Me." The spontaneous production of fruit will take place because of our submission and the supply from the Vine. Abide in Him!

Genuine Service

Not with eye service, as men pleasers, but as servants
of Christ, doing the will of God from the heart.

Ephesians 6:6

Although the New Testament realistically acknowledged the existence of slavery, everywhere the gospel has gone slavery has been abolished, only to create a multitude of believers who have pledged allegiance to a divine Master. Being a "slave" to the One who gave His life in loving devotion is a concept the world has never been able to comprehend.

We who have received Christ as Savior need to be reminded that we have been redeemed from the slave market of sin where we stood hopelessly inadequate to pay the price of our own release. Into this market the Lord Jesus came, demonstrating the infinite love of His Father for all. The price of release was not silver or gold, but His own precious blood. Willingly and with deep love, He laid down His life and gave all that He had to obtain our release from this insidious slavery to which we became entangled as sinners.

As we grew in our understanding of this glorious demonstration of self-sacrifice, we turned to Christ and said, "I willingly hand over all I am and have to serve You forever." He accepted our commitment and we became His willing slaves. We are no longer our own, because we were bought with such a staggering price. To be a slave to the Son who loved us so much changes the whole perspective of our relationship with Him. The price of our redemption was paid while we were still enslaved to sin and self. But being bought with such a price sets us free to be lovingly committed to another Master. Since I have no power or resources to repay the debt, I owe Him all I am and all I possess.

> *We are no longer our own, because we were bought with such a staggering price.*

In Paul's day, slavery of human beings was rife and slaves would tend to only serve usefully when the master was watching. When the owner was gone, the level of output greatly diminished. Even though we have offered ourselves to Christ as our Master, the temptation is still to only serve effectively when we think He is watching or when people are observing us. Genuine service is rendered when we have no concern about the opinions of others, about whether or not the lights are on, or whether we are on display. This is the test of true devotion to duty and to the Lord Himself.

༄ ———————————————— ৪

Father, thank you for saving me from slavery to sin and setting me free to serve You. I will never be able to repay all You have given me. Today again I give my life to You in honest service.

Christ, Our Adequate Advocate

*My little children, these things I write to you, that you
may not sin. And if anyone sins, we have an Advocate
with the Father, Jesus Christ the righteous.*

1 John 2:1

An advocate is another name for a lawyer, but the poor reputation that has grown up around that profession should not in any way discolor our impression of having Jesus Christ as our Lawyer. He is not only faithful, honest, and impartial, but He also is the only Son of the righteous Judge before whom we must stand and the very One who died so our sin could be forgiven.

The book of Romans has been called a courtroom drama in which the case being argued is against us as sinful human beings. We stand before God, the impartial Judge, and must confess that we are sinners by habit and nature, deserving the full punishment which God established before sin came into the world.

This heartfelt confession of sin was what the Judge was waiting for from us. He could then turn to His Son, assess the adequacy of His substitutionary sacrifice for our sin, and pronounce Himself righteous in forgiving our sin when we place our faith in Christ's work. The Judge, now our Father, views us standing in Christ's righteousness and says we are no longer condemned; we are in Christ, set free from sin's penalty of eternal death. The judge might be heard to say the words of Christ: "Go, and sin no more."

But as we leave the courtroom with justice met and condemnation removed, we find another law in our members warring against the law of our mind. I am doing things I do not want to do and realize that I'm being brought under the very power from which I was freed when I was forgiven. I respond with a cry: "O wretched man that I am . . . who shall deliver me?" I thank God for my forgiveness through Jesus Christ who is my Advocate in the face of the enemy's prosecution.

Are sins brought against me after I have been discharged from the punishment of sin? Am I again under condemnation? As the charges are leveled against me either by the enemy, my conscience, or my mind, I am rushed back to court and stand before the Judge where my Lawyer represents me against these charges. "Paid in full," answers my Advocate. "I paid it in full," Christ says. No one can condemn. No one can charge. Free indeed from all charges!

ဆ ——————————— ໕

Father, thank you for establishing Your Son as my Advocate against all charges laid against me. Although I am still prone to sin, I rejoice in the adequacy of my Advocate's sacrifice.

The Bible Stands

For which I suffer trouble as an evildoer, even to the
point of chains; but the word of God is not chained.
2 Timothy 2:9

The universal freedom of God's Word to accomplish His will is a constant blessing. No one can limit the Word of God. Nothing has more effect on the life and activities of a person, family, community, or nation. God's Word is free and cannot be contained, even though for generations man has tried to chain it, destroy it, and prove it false. Yet each succeeding wave of hostility is met by a sword that cannot be dulled. The Bible will not lose its power or be rendered lifeless.

Today's Scripture challenges people who pray for the Word to be blessed, to work, to spread, to be powerful, and not to return empty. All these things will take place because of the character of the Word of God in and of itself. Can we have water that is not wet? Can we have a sun that is not light? Can we have a God who is not love? Can we have the Word of God which is not powerful and free? Certainly not.

Then why is such a powerful force seemingly so powerless in people's lives? The Word is preached, taught, shared, and quoted, and still we see such little results even in our own lives. Perhaps it is not so much the ineffectiveness of the Word we should consider, but our unwillingness to receive it. Since the Word of God is free, what is *not* free?

Since the Word of God is free, what is not free?

When we look into our own lives, do we see a heart chained or imprisoned by things and ideas that render the Word ineffective? Have we closed our hearts to the Sword of the Spirit, the water and bread of life, the honey out of the rock, the purifying fire of God's Word? Have we shut our doors to its blessing and power? Has it become a common message we no longer choose to hear? We want music, but not the Word. Fellowship, but not the Word. Entertainment, but not the Word!

We need not pray for God's Word to be "blessed" or to spread or to be powerful. We are not to pray that it will accomplish its goal. We must submit our lives to its truth and power, enabling its life-giving spirit to change us. God is waiting for us to receive with meekness the implanted Word which is able to save, sanctify, satisfy, and subdue all aspects of our lives. The Word is certainly living and powerful!

Father, thank you for giving us this unleashed power in Your Word. I submit my life to its living authority. I believe it will change me.

Accepted

To the praise of the glory of His grace, by which
He has made us accepted in the Beloved.

Ephesians 1:6

Prior to making this statement, Paul said we were chosen, predestined, and adopted as sons. He goes on to say we are redeemed, forgiven, enriched, and the recipients of many other blessings. No other section of the New Testament lists as many of our spiritual benefits in such a short portion as this first chapter of Ephesians. Soak your soul often in this bath of blessings. You will always come away refreshed in thanksgiving and appreciation. And in the midst of this madrigal of praise, Paul tells us that we are accepted by God. We are as welcome to God as Christ Himself in the circle of love that belongs to God. We are accepted into God's presence because of Christ. He accomplished an enormous amount of "work" to make this possible.

Many Christians struggle with thoughts about their acceptance by God. If failure comes, they tend to think they are no longer wanted in the holy climate that surrounds the throne. If they do not pray as often as they should, they wonder if He still wants them. Their own fear keeps them from coming to His throne. Their prayerlessness convinces them that they must do something good so that they are welcome again. Those thoughts are from the enemy, not the Father. No matter what we attempt, nothing can make us "more accepted." Regardless of what we make ourselves to be, our efforts will not make us accepted.

Nothing in us or done by us adds anything to our acceptability.

The only reason we are accepted in the light and love of God's presence is because God accepts Christ Jesus the Lord, the perfect Son of God, who is one with His Father. When we trusted Christ as our Savior, God wrapped us in the righteousness of His lovely Son. He enrobes us in Christ's pure, sinless garments. We are clothed with Christ Himself! When God sees Christ, He is accepted. Knowing we are in Him, we are accepted with Him! Nothing in us or done by us adds anything to our acceptability. Not only does Christ introduce us to the Father as belonging, but He also enfolds us in His robes making us presentable, welcome, acceptable, suitable, and qualified for access into His presence. Come often, stay long, rest, luxuriate, bask in, and savor every blessing He has given.

☜ ——————————————— ☞

Father, thank you for clothing me in Your Son, Jesus Christ. I bless Your name for making me Yours through Your Beloved. I am Yours.

Marvelous Mystery

. . . by which, when you read, you may understand my
knowledge in the mystery of Christ, which in other ages
was not made known to the sons of men, as it has now been
revealed by the Spirit to His holy apostles and prophets.
Ephesians 3:4-5

The word *mystery* conjures up all kinds of possible scenarios about how the story line will be played out. A skilled author keeps the focus moving from character to character until the final, unexpected revelation. But that is not the kind of mystery God unfolds for us in the Ephesian epistle.

The New Testament reveals many mysteries that relate to all believers united to Christ by the Holy Spirit. The specific details of this mystery are given in the next verse: that Gentiles are fellow heirs, with believing Jews, in the church of God. The importance of this revelation goes back to the blessing God gave Abraham in Genesis 12 when He promised that Abraham's descendants would receive blessings available to no other nation. The offspring of Abraham, Isaac, and Jacob firmly believed in the promises reserved for them through their coming Messiah.

But Israel rebelled and turned from God. As a result, He dispersed them throughout the world. Into the arena of this scattered nation came the Messiah, the Anointed One of Israel. But Israel continued in their rebellion, proclaiming, "We will not have this man to reign over us!" In the face of such rejection, Jehovah turned in grace to the Gentiles. The "dogs" of the nations were repugnant to the elect Jews, so the offer of grace and mercy to them was unthinkable to Abraham's progeny.

However, God had always planned to offer the blessings of Abraham to Gentiles who believe in Christ. The "mystery" was that God had covered His plan in a cloth of secrecy until the Holy Spirit led Paul to write about it. What was unthinkable to the Jews was welcomed by the Gentiles and, from that time to this, God has been gathering out of the nations a people for His name. God's plan designed one body of believers from every tribe, nation, kingdom, and tongue, all equally sharing in the blessings of oneness in Christ. The promises made to Abraham are being fulfilled spiritually in the lives and hearts of all who believe. The nation of Israel, now pushed to great jealousy by such divine love for Gentiles, are challenged to accept the Anointed One as their Messiah.

As Gentiles, we are united to the Anointed One and share in all the blessings of the body of Christ, where there is neither Jew nor Gentile.

☙ ——————————— ❧

Father, You have made me, a Gentile sinner, a fellow inheritor of the blessings You promised to Abraham. Thank you for such love.

The Spirit's Abiding Presence

*Do you not know that you are the temple of God
and that the Spirit of God dwells in you?*
1 Corinthians 3:16

The most elementary aspect of salvation is the fact that Christ lives in us, and that by His life He has translated us out of death into a state of life. Yet even though the Scriptures repeatedly remind us of this grand truth, we continue to ask the Lord to be "with us." Few requests in prayer are as obvious an indication of unbelief or misunderstanding as this. It is a habit that is hard to break, but we *can* break it with one of the great "3:16" verses in the Bible.

Although we have reminded ourselves of this truth before, we return to it because it is so much a part of our Christian culture. *God with us* is an Old Testament truth that was pressed on Israel before God chose to place His name in the midst of His people. Today's Scripture passage echoes back to the same issue in the rhetorical question it poses.

God is closer to every believer now than He was while Jesus was living on earth with His disciples.

Jehovah initially chose a tabernacle for a dwelling place, one that He designed and superintended building. The temple of Solomon replaced Moses' tabernacle, and the coming of Christ fulfilled them both: "The Word became flesh and dwelt [tabernacled] among us," writes John. But was that close enough for God to get to His people? No! By Christ's death and resurrection, He came the closest possible. He chose us to be His temple. God is closer to every believer now than He was while Jesus was living on earth with His disciples.

The specific means of God's residency is the Spirit of God dwelling in us. His occupancy of our body is guaranteed because of God's work in saving us. We cannot lose the Spirit of God. He will not leave us as He left Solomon's temple (recorded in Ezekiel 10). Christ said, "He will abide with you forever." It is an unholy thought to suggest that we have lost the person of God in our lives and need to ask Him again "to be with us." The life of faith begins with this first step: believing He is with me always, because He lives in me.

There may be no physical evidence of His residence, but He proclaims it and I respond—not by asking for "a sense of His presence" or "a feeling of being near," but in true faith: "Thank you for Your faithfulness, living in my body as Your temple."

ɞ ———————————— ϶

Father, thank you for saving me so Your Spirit could come and live in me. I confess I often ask to walk by sight and sense rather than by faith. I am eternally grateful that the Spirit of God lives in me!

Grow Up!

Finally, brethren, farewell. Become complete. Be
of good comfort, be of one mind, live in peace; and
the God of love and peace will be with you.

2 Corinthians 13:11

The goal of every parent for their child is full maturity—physical, social, emotional, mental, and (we would hope) spiritual. As long as children are provided with food, water, shelter, discipline, exercise, and rest, they will develop normally and eventually fully exercise all the body parts or members with which they were blessed at birth.

In 2 Corinthians 13:11, Paul gives his final farewell to the church in Corinth. He is aware that they are not spiritually mature. He wrote in his first epistle that many of them were like little children; they had not grown up, even though they did not lack any of their "body parts" and had been provided for spiritually by Paul himself. He had done all he could; the rest was up to them. Parents who die before their children are grown leave some lingering doubts about their further development. In this verse, Paul summarizes his hopes for these believers. He provides exhortation in four specific areas, and, in doing so, conveys that in Christ they have all the necessary resources to be mature and responsible members of God's family. It is not so much the commands that Paul gives with which we are concerned, as the assumptions he makes in giving the exhortations.

Using the words "become complete," Paul is saying that they already had the resources for full maturity and order of life. He desires them to employ those truths in their lives. By telling them to "be of good comfort," he reminds

> *The goal of God our Father is that we grow up to full spiritual maturity.*

them that the God of all comfort is theirs; it's the *acceptance* of the comfort from God that brings encouragement. The command to "be of one mind" suggests they were to think the same things and so manifest the oneness they had by virtue of the work of the Holy Spirit. And it was possible to "live in peace" because the God of peace was living in each one. All four exhortations assume that each Corinthian believer had the resources to obey these instructions. It is just like a father telling his children to "grow up!" The goal of God our Father is that we grow up to full spiritual maturity.

The last part of the verse is not conditional on following the guidelines. The God of love and peace is always with us. We cannot lose Him. But failure to grow up means we do not enjoy His love and peace.

Father, thank you for all the resources You gave so I can be brought to maturity. I commit my life to growing in Christ.

On Display

But we have this treasure in earthen vessels, that the
excellence of the power may be of God and not of us.

2 Corinthians 4:7

A treasure is something valuable enough that it is either put in a special place so all can observe it, or hidden away so none can enjoy it. Wealthy people put their jewelry and other treasures in locked boxes so no one will steal them. They live in fear of possible loss. How nice it is when national or personal treasures are put on display so all can appreciate their beauty and value.

The glory of God is a divine treasure that has been on display on many special occasions throughout history. Abraham saw it when God confirmed the Covenant with him. Jacob saw it from his stone pillow. Moses and Israel followed it from Egypt to Canaan. Peter, James, and John saw it on the Mount of Transfiguration.

The resurrection and glorification of the Lord Jesus Christ made it possible for every believer to partake of this divine treasure while still in their earthly bodies. When we first believed in Christ, we were given "the light of the knowledge of the glory of God in the face of Jesus Christ." This permanent personal possession is the glory of God imparted to us by the Holy Spirit. He reveals the excellence of the knowledge of Christ. What an amazing treasure to hold in our earthly bodies!

Just as Christ enveloped the glory of God in His earthly body, so we have that same treasure, because we have Him. Those who accompanied Christ on His earthly pilgrimage did not see the "brightness of His glory" in the way the disciples did on the Mount. Instead, they saw His glory displayed in His humble acts and by His gracious speech.

We have this treasure in our earthly bodies of clay, as our Lord said in John 17:22: "The glory which You gave me I have given them . . ." We have that glory! We choose if, when, and how it shines through our acts and words. Such a treasure should not be reserved for special occasions! It should be displayed in all we do.

As believers, we fail to fully reveal His glory when we sin or refuse to consecrate our bodies to God. A dirty glass in a display-case shadows the brightness of the treasure. As vessels of the Lord, we need to be clean. This treasure is for the entire world to see. The treasure is ours! What we do with it is our responsibility.

— ⟪ ———————————— ⟫ —

Father, thank you for the glorious treasure purchased at such a great price.
I determine that everyone I meet will see in my face and life something of the
glory of God.

When Good Is Best

*Every good gift and every perfect gift is from above,
and comes down from the Father of lights, with whom
there is no variation or shadow of turning.*

James 1:17

In our language "good" does not always mean the best, but God uses "good" as the premier estimate of anything. Christ said, "None is good but God alone." James 1:17 reminds us that the Father is the giver of good gifts which are also perfect gifts.

One of the underlying spiritual principles here is that everything comes from God the Father. He is the fountain from whom all blessings flow and the designer from whom all plans proceed. The Son made possible the distribution of the gifts. Through His death and resurrection He set God free to give gifts to all His children. The Holy Spirit is the channel through whom the gifts come. He applies the blessings to the children of God. Each member of the Trinity, therefore, is active in all that God gives.

Without a doubt, the primary gift that came down from the Father was the Lord Jesus Christ. "For God so loved the world that He gave His only begotten Son . . ." But with Christ's death and resurrection complete, God in turn gives His risen Son to us as an indwelling presence, the perfect gift containing all other gifts in this One. The living Word, in whom is fully resident all the blessings the Father chooses, is bestowed on all His children.

Among the other gifts the Father sends down to us are many that we would not necessarily choose for ourselves: times of suffering, periods of trial and tribulation, losses and sorrows. James is quick to tell us that we are to rejoice in the trials of our faith, knowing that they have either been sent by the Father or that the Father has permitted them for our growth. Nothing comes into the life of one of His children without the Father's knowledge and His unwillingness to veto the gift.

When such "gifts" come, we should be able to turn to the Father and say "thank you." The Father allows temptation, but He does not tempt. The Father ordains trials, but He does not wish for our failure. The Father sends sorrows, but he pities His children. The Father guides us into trouble, but He never leaves us without a way through it. The Father watches us fall, but He is always there to lift us up. The Father sends us the impossible so we flee to Him for help.

› ———————————— ℃

Father, thank you for all Your gifts. I know all are good! I confess it is not always easy to understand Your blessings, but I surrender to Your wise care.

Mind Control

Let this mind be in you which was also in Christ Jesus.

Philippians 2:5

It is unthinkable that God would impart the person of Christ to us without imparting Christ's mind. Christ is not a power without personality. All the ingredients of personality belong to Him. Therefore, because we have Christ, all His personal capabilities belong to us.

The mind of Christ is not something we pray for or seek by imitation. It is part-and-parcel of the fullness of Christ who is our life. We should give thanks for the gift of a fully functioning Christ who has mind, emotions, and will, and turn over the direction of our lives to His capacity to determine how we are to act, feel, and decide.

The specific area of life referred to in Philippians 2:5 is that of being a servant. Most people consider serving to be a loathsome activity. We accept service without comment, and often with no word of thanks. Christ's condescension is paraded before us both as an example and as a call to follow Him on the downward path from the heights of glory to death on the cross. We say a hearty "amen" to the idea of His power, love, and grace to fallen men, but we hold back on agreeing to the pilgrimage that includes "being made conformable to His death."

> *Allow the mind of Christ to determine our choice to descend rather than to ascend.*

This verse is a call to allow the mind of Christ to activate and determine our choice to descend rather than to ascend, to humble rather than to exalt, to sit low rather than to sit high, to wash rather than to be washed, to choose a lowly position rather than to be forced to assume one, to eat with publicans and sinners rather than to recline in the fine soft clothes of princes. The Lord didn't do this just for show or only to be an example. It was His very nature which sprang to action in His life as the God-Man. He never looked at His service as a drudgery lasting for a few days after which He would return to the glory of His Father. He willingly accepted the lowest role for any human being and did so in loving care for man and loyal obedience to His Father.

Christ is waiting for us to surrender our minds and wills to His. If we do, our lives and activities will resemble His when He was on earth. The mind of Christ will be displayed in harmony with how He lived in Galilee. It becomes a joy to live as He lived because He is living through us.

჻

Father, thank you for giving me the mind of Christ. Today I surrender my thoughts, my choices, and my feelings to Him.

Alive in Christ

Even when we were dead in trespasses, [God] made us alive
together with Christ (by grace you have been saved).
Ephesians 2:5

The primary work of God in salvation is to give life. The penalty for sin is death, according to Romans 6:23, but God made the reversal of that condition possible: "the gift of God is eternal life." Death does not mean annihilation, but alienation and separation. When Adam sinned, He was alienated and separated from God. When unbelievers die, they are irrevocably separated from God. The work of saving us included restoring our nearness and access to God.

In the course of Christ's relationship with people, He gave life to some who were dead without giving them *His* life. Lazarus had been dead for four days before Christ called him out of the grave. But Lazarus died again. He did not receive eternal life when he reappeared from the grave. He was again subject to death.

The life of Christ in us is not resuscitation (as was Lazarus's experience) but the life of God, which is eternal. Christ was raised out from among the dead to die no more. That kind and quality of life is imparted to every believer. Although we are promised that we will not die, that does not mean we will not pass through death. We will never, however, abide in a state of being separated from God.

The life imparted to us is not independent of Christ.

Before receiving the gift of God, we were living in a state of spiritual death. We were separated from the life of God and practicing behavior characteristic of those who are devoid of God's life. We lived "according to the course of this world," in a culture where death reigned and true life was absent.

Of particular importance is the fact that the life imparted to us is not independent of Christ. "When Christ who is our life . . ." (Colossians 3:4) clearly declares that the gift of life is Christ Himself. It is impossible for God to give us life independent of Christ. We live because we have Christ.

Some people believe you can lose your salvation through sin and careless living. But eternal life is life without beginning or end. That life can only be described as God's life. If we have the gift of God, we are united to Him by His Son in a union that can never be broken. Christ is alive and so am I! My body may pass away, but Christ's life in me never will.

  ∮ ———————————— ∛

Father, You gave me the most precious gift You could give: Your Son. I am blessed eternally because Your gift is eternal. I bless Your name for lavishing on me the life that is Christ.

The Keeping Power of God

Who are kept by the power of God through faith for
salvation ready to be revealed in the last time.

1 Peter 1:5

John chapter 17 is a record of the Lord's prayer to His Father in the hearing of His disciples. One of His primary requests was, "Holy Father, keep through Your name those You have given Me, that they may be one as We are." God answered that prayer.

Peter must have been confused when he heard Christ asking the Father to "keep" these eleven men. The Lord was now at the end of His ministry and was speaking of going away, of leaving, of dying. Surely many questions were on Peter's mind. Later he would draw his sword to protect Christ and was rebuked for doing so. Then he would run, only to return to deny Christ three times and to leave, weeping bitterly. No one had so strongly declared his loyalty for Christ in His last hours as Peter. And no one fell so low as to deny he knew the Master. Would he be kept? Would he fall too far? Would the Father answer Jesus' prayer for the eleven?

> *There is no question of God's ability to keep or of His willingness to keep.*

Now, thirty years later, Peter was writing to believers who needed as strong an encouraging word as possible, because they were suffering for their faith. He began his letter by affirming that the Father had kept him, and that He would therefore keep all His children. There is no question of God's ability to keep or of His willingness to keep. But Peter also confesses that the keeping power and the divine contract to preserve His children must be accepted by faith. We have no signed contract other than the Word of God. We do not have a feeling. We do not have a vision. What we do have is an earnest or pledge given to us by the permanent indwelling of the Holy Spirit. All the work of God in salvation would have to be undone for us to be released from God's keeping power. The power demonstrated in saving Israel from Egypt and in raising Christ from the dead is behind His promise. No one can challenge that power.

But for how long? Until the day we are in His presence. Face to face with Christ will be the final day, when all things will be brought to consummation. We do not pray or plead for this. Christ did, and as a result, I am *kept!*

℘ ——————————— ℘

Father, thank you for making me Your child. I rest in Your power. I rejoice in Your promise. I look for that last day!

God's Revealed Will

In everything give thanks; for this is the will
of God in Christ Jesus for you.

1 Thessalonians 5:18

Many Christians talk about the difficulty of "finding God's will." It is interesting how a mundane thing like giving thanks is put in juxtaposition with such a profound and seemingly complicated issue as the will of God. But maybe thanksgiving is not so mundane, and knowing the will of God is not so complex. Perhaps the two are part of the normal Christian life. Certainly 1 Thessalonians 5:18 does not suggest that the will of God is so hard to find or so difficult to follow.

Should God have such a difficult time making His will known when it is plainly revealed in this verse? Ephesians 1:9 also reminds us, "Having made known to us the mystery of His will . . ." Many think knowing the will of God is limited to knowing who to marry, whether to be an engineer, or whether or not to go to Africa and live in a mud hut. Those are issues that demand the knowledge of God's will, we say. But if we were obedient to *this* revelation of His will, maybe He would not need to hit us with a 2 x 4 board to reveal the "bigger" issues. It just may be harder to do what this verse says than to go to Africa!

God says it is His will that we give thanks in everything. Elsewhere He says, "Give thanks for all things." These are similar responsibilities. Here we are to give thanks in everything. There is no circumstance in my life for which I cannot bow my head and say to my Father, "I give thanks in this particular situation." It may be sickness, financial problems, loss of a family member, or failure to advance in my job. "Everything" may be my fault or someone else's. It may be one who is against me. It may be a result of my testimony, or company, a failure, a natural disaster, a broken friendship, or whatever I am going through at the moment. It is the will of God to lift my heart to the Father and say, "I do not understand why this has happened, but I trust Your wisdom and I sincerely say thank you!" Part of growing spiritually mature is to say thank you in every circumstance, climate, and condition.

> *Say thank you in every circumstance, climate, and condition.*

Father, I trust Your choices for my life. I recognize that everything in my life comes because You sent it or permitted it. I accept it and say thank you!

The Indwelling Spirit

And what agreement has the temple of God with idols?
For you are the temple of the living God. As God has
said: "I will dwell in them and walk among them. I
will be their God, and they shall be My people."

2 Corinthians 6:16

The presence of Christ in every believer is one of the most difficult aspects of the Christian experience to habitually exercise. Many books have been written promoting the theme of "practicing the presence of Christ," and if it were not such a hard concept to appropriate, God Himself would not have repeated it so many times.

What strikes us reading this text now is that Paul's inspired reference to God's promise in Exodus is not related to the presence of the Holy Spirit in every believer. Rather, the verse relates to God's presence among the Israelites in the form of the pillar of fire and cloud—1,500 years before. Christ promised His followers that the Holy Spirit would "abide with you forever."

The first meditation of this book was purposely taken from the earliest biblical reference to the Lord's presence with His people (Genesis 28:15). In speaking to Jacob, God made this statement before the Holy Spirit was given to us. Consequently, how can anyone living on this side of the resurrection question God's presence with them?

In 2 Corinthians 6:16, God tells the Christians in Corinth, "You are the temple" where I dwell. God could not say it more plainly. God dwells in you! It is impossible for darkness and light to occupy the same space. The enemy and the Lord cannot be in the same temple. Yet one of the most common prayers from the lips of believers is "Lord, be with us." Those words escape the lips of pastors, leaders, elders, evangelists, and most who claim to possess the Lord. It is a habit that promotes unbelief, vain repetition, and thoughtless mechanical routine. It is an affront to the person of God who dwells in every believer. It is an insult to the Word of God which from antiquity repeats God's promise to His people, whether Israel wandering in the desert or a believer today permanently indwelt by Christ through the Holy Spirit. How amazing, that this promise came from so far back in antiquity.

Today, as in Corinth, the people of God fail to live in the knowledge of the Lord's presence. Yet most who pray for the Lord to be with them would also readily assert, "I know He is in me." We must more faithfully live in that knowledge.

☙ ─────────────── ❧

Father, thank you for indwelling my body as Your temple. I choose to believe You are in me permanently.

Living in Unison

There is neither Jew nor Greek, there is neither slave nor free,
there is neither male nor female; for you are all one in Christ Jesus.
Galatians 3:28

One of the most elusive elements of the Christian life is unity with others in God's family. Pride leads to individualism, which eventually leads to a rejection of dependence on one another. But our Lord prayed before He went to the cross that we would all "be one" (John 17:21), and Paul reminded the Galatian believers that they belonged to one another.

After the church was founded, Paul complained to the Corinthian church that they should not boast in their human leaders: "I am of Paul, I am of Apollos . . ." (1 Corinthians 1:12). Such isolation leads to separation and independence of one another. Paul also chastened that church by telling them that the eye cannot do without the hand. The basis of unity in Christ is the unique sharing of all the ingredients of His life. Just as a body shares the same nervous system, digestive system, and circulatory system, so in Christ every believer shares all that He is.

Although this fact should eliminate our pride, the temptation to boast remains strong. Men assert themselves even in the church. The Jew holds preeminence over the Gentile, and the free man is superior to the slave. But in Christ every believer, regardless of language, heritage, color, education, spiritual gift, and accomplishment, shares exactly the same blessings in Christ. We have different responsibilities in the body of Christ but share the same life. We are called to various ministries but share the same salvation, forgiveness, Father, and future. None is better than the other. Yet the Greek and Jew both think they are the better race. How prone we are to pride ourselves in a culture we did little to establish!

Has this particular prayer of Christ in John 17 been answered? Not yet. It is our responsibility to fulfill that prayer in this life based on the truth of our oneness in spiritual life. One of the great successes of the enemy is to divide us outwardly so the world thinks we are divided spiritually. *We are one!* But the only way the world is going to know it is if we show that identity in our life and through our lips.

What a miracle it would be if we all conveyed the same message of salvation, sanctification, and service. Determine to display and declare your oneness with another believer today as an answer to the prayer of our Lord Jesus Christ.

ಬ ———————————— ಛ

Father, thank you for making me one with every member of Your family. I renounce my superior attitude and actions, and acknowledge that I am no different than any other child of Yours.

Guaranteed for Life

*But of Him you are in Christ Jesus, who became for us wisdom
from God—and righteousness and sanctification and redemption.*
1 Corinthians 1:30

You are in Christ! This principle truth is followed by four of the greatest needs of mankind. The two words *in Christ* found here must be comprehended and appropriated. We have explored these words before and will do so again because God repeats them to us in a variety of contexts. They are given as the explanation of salvation. They show our association with Christ. They reveal the basis of sanctification. They expound the foundation of our security. They inform us of our unity. They reveal the reason for service. Here in 1 Corinthians 1:30, we are reminded that Christ is the fountain from which these four resources are given.

Since we have Christ, all of these assets are a believer's permanent property for life. The order in which these assets are given may seem unusual, but perhaps examining them will help us understand why the Spirit inspired Paul to put them in the order he did.

"Christ, the wisdom of God" (1 Corinthians 1:24), is from above and is pure, peaceable, gentle, willing to yield, and full of mercy and good fruits (James 3:17). This is the One we received when we believed the gospel. In His life on earth recorded in the Gospels, we see His purity, peace, and good works. Christ embodies the true wisdom of God. *Believe it!*

The righteousness of Christ is bestowed on us when we receive Him. God looks at us *in Christ.* He is pleased with the righteousness He sees (Christ's righteousness) and accepts us because of Him. We cannot stand on our own righteous acts, which are as filthy rags. In giving us Christ, God gives us a perfect standing in His righteousness. *Celebrate it!*

The third word used here is sanctification. We may stand accepted in Christ's righteousness, but in practice our behavior is far from perfect. Sanctification of and through Christ is a work begun at spiritual birth, and one which continues until we are with Him and perfectly like Him. This sanctifying work continues each day as we yield to God and His Word—the means by which He shapes us into the likeness of Christ. *Surrender it!*

Redemption here most likely relates to the redemption of our bodies at the end of our physical lives. The final aspect of our salvation will be when our bodies are changed to be like Christ's own body of glory. *Anticipate it!*

Rejoice in these wonderful provisions that are ours in Christ!

— ❧ ———————————— ❧ —

Father, thank you for Christ. The more I know Him, the more His resources are revealed. I bless You for all You have given me in Him.

Faithful Promises

*For all the promises of God in Him are Yes, and in
Him Amen, to the glory of God through us.*
2 Corinthians 1:20

We often make promises without regard to how we will fulfill them. Children make naïve promises; adults make unrealistic promises; countries make political promises. The truth of the Bible relies heavily on the many promises made by God. In 2 Corinthians 1:20, God reminds believers that all His promises are guaranteed by His unchanging character.

Why do we break our promises? Maybe it's an issue over which we have no control. Because God is in absolute control, there is no variation in His ability to keep His word. We say, "I feel differently about the issue now, so I've changed my mind." God doesn't change, so His promises are irrevocable. God doesn't say "yes" today and "no" tomorrow, changing His mind because He found a certain promise too costly or inconvenient. The issues of chance, change, choice, and cost are irrelevant.

> *The unchanging Son of God is the guarantee of the fulfillment of each promise.*

Notice that God's promises are centered "in Him," that is, in Christ. Here again the sum and substance of God's promises are eternally linked to (and find their fulfillment in) His eternal Son. This encourages us to go to Christ in search of the promises of God. This reminds us that the unchanging Son of God is the guarantee of the fulfillment of each promise. Because of the resurrection of Christ and His insusceptibility to death, all the promises are *amen*, meaning, "so it will be."

At the end of a prayer, people sometimes say "Amen" as evidence that they agree with what has been said or because they endorse its coming to pass. It is impossible to list all the promises of God given to us in Christ, but why not take a blank sheet and start a list of your own? At the end of each promise you can say a hearty "Amen" and offer your confidence that each promise will be fulfilled. Although Abraham waited many years for some of God's promises to be fulfilled, that did not cause him to waver in his confidence that God would prove faithful. You, too, may have to await God's timing for His promises. Just remember that He has been faithful and will continue to be so. Live each day in the blessing of His promises.

❀ ———————————— ❀

Father, thank you for all Your promises to me as Your child. I confess I do not know most of them, but I commit myself to live in the light of the ones I know and to learn more each day.

18

APRIL

Fathoming Forgiveness

Bearing with one another, and forgiving one another,
if anyone has a complaint against another; even
as Christ forgave you, so you also must do.

Colossians 3:13

Several attempts have been made to list in order of prominence the many aspects that comprise salvation. Surely high on such a list would be forgiveness of our sins. Even this glorious blessing, though, is not always grasped early in the Christian pilgrimage.

Some who have trusted the Lord as Savior never, until death, believe that all their sins has been forgiven. The instruction to forgive in today's Scripture is often dependent on how much we sense forgiveness. Some immature believers think that forgiveness of a sin is dependent on regular confession of sin. If that is a biblical view of forgiveness, then we must spend a lot of time digging into our past, both recent and forgotten, searching for any unconfessed sin. Given our proclivity to forget so many things, is it possible to remember every single sin? This reasoning continues to teach that if a sin is not confessed (and therefore not forgiven), it is held against us. This would mean that if a sin is charged against us, we are unforgiven, and if we are unforgiven, we are therefore lost.

It is clearly declared in Colossians 2:13 that we have been "forgiven all our trespasses." This is the most definitive statement of the fullness of our forgiveness. Why does God forgive? We recall that the penalty for sin is death. Christ paid the penalty for our sin by dying in our place, setting God free to forgive all who believe. As each person places their faith in Christ as Savior, God acts in grace by forgiving all sin—past, present, and future.

God chooses not to remember the sin He has forgiven.

Although I stand forgiven by God through Christ, what does the acceptance of my full forgiveness mean for me? Perhaps one of the most influential results is the peace God gives when we believe what He says. If we are not sure that all our sins are forgiven, then life is filled with a host of fears, not the least of which is, "Have we remembered all our sins and confessed them?" God chooses not to remember the sins He has forgiven. Only the enemy would have us try to dredge up past failures to ask for special forgiveness. Forgiveness is based on faith in Christ once for all. "God forgave my sins in Jesus' Name . . ."

꙰ ———————————— ꙰

Father, thank you for forgiving and sending away all my sin. I accept Christ's sacrificial payment once and for all. I accept peace of mind, setting me free to serve You with confidence.

Three Little Words

And the grace of our Lord was exceedingly abundant,
with faith and love which are in Christ Jesus.

1 Timothy 1:14

In these three common words—grace, faith, and love—Paul explains his conversion to believing in Christ. Let's consider them in the order they appear in today's text, which is also the order in which we encounter them in our spiritual pilgrimage.

Grace is the unmerited favor of God extended to all mankind. "The grace of God has appeared . . ." writes Paul to Titus in Titus 2:11. The fullness of grace is evidenced and explained there in terms of the incarnation and crucifixion of Christ. But since the word "grace" is also translated "gift" in other places, we can take the principle in this verse and see that His gifts are revealed to those who will receive Him as well.

When we began to understand the grace of God, we expressed faith in the Lord Jesus and came into possession of the life of God. This transformed Paul and each person who places his or her faith in Christ. Faith is to accept as true the facts that are presented. God reveals His grace through the good news of Jesus Christ. Our faith in this truth brings God's Son in all of His fullness into our lives. It is then that we begin to understand the extent of His grace and His gifts.

One of the primary revelations of God in Christ is His love. Love cannot be truly known without a personal relationship with God in Christ. John writes in 1 John 4:8 and 16 that "God is love." Many seek an understanding of love outside of the knowledge of God Himself. But it is only when these seekers are ready to accept God's grace that the love of God comes flooding over their souls. To believe in Christ as Savior is a rudimentary action which opens the floodgates of God's full revelation of Himself.

Imagine opening a boxed gift only to find there are many more gifts packaged inside, each one containing a greater treasure that makes up the fullness of the original gift. Only when opening God's gift does the greatness and vast extent of His blessings become a reality. To open the first box is to enquire about His grace. Choosing to open this first box is an exercise of faith. To continue opening others is to engage in learning about the greatness of His love. All are found in Christ. What abundance there is in all these blessings!

    ℬ ———————————— ℭ

Father, thank you for revealing Your grace to me. I accepted it, not knowing all You had in store for me. In faith I claim His love for today.

Christ, the Head

*But, speaking the truth in love, [we] may grow up in all things
into Him who is the head—Christ—whom the whole body,
joined and knit together by what every joint supplies, according
to the effective working by which every part does its share,
causes growth of the body for the edifying of itself in love.*

Ephesians 4:15-16

The head is the source of all the motor skills and senses in the human body. With the exception of the sense of touch, all the others are exclusively resident in the head. (Of course the head can also feel, but the sense of touch is not limited to it.) The sense of sight informs a person of what is going on around him. The sense of smell makes us cognizant of a woman's perfume. Countless taste-buds make us aware of the multitude of flavors in a simple hamburger. Our ears catch a thunderclap as well as a whisper. Each of these senses contributes to the well-being of the body. They act as appreciators of various inputs, as well as sensitive, early-warning systems that can preserve our lives.

> *Christ is the Head of His body called the church.*

Christ is the Head of His body called the church. It is through the head that the entire body receives all the input needed for its health and welfare. There is other natural way for food to get to every body part except via the head. The hand cannot feed the body except through the head. The foot cannot respond to information from the ear without the head processing it. It is possible to do without a large number of members of the body, but none can live without the head.

We grow and mature based on what every joint and member supplies to the overall plan. The lungs send oxygen to every living cell. The heart pumps blood to the same cells. The nerves act and react in every cell. But none of these can function without the precise coordination of them all through the brain.

God created both the human body and the body of Christ, one being designed to illustrate the other. It was in God's divine plan that we should see a picture of this truth, no matter where we are. Yet we so easily lose sight of the importance of each member of the body of Christ to the body as a whole. We fail to remember that Christ, as the Head of the body, must be revered and acknowledged for all He does. This will enable the body to function effectively in its entirety.

ಬಂ ———————————— ೞ

Father, thank you for giving Christ as my head. I acknowledge I could not function without His superintendence of all my activities.

Perfected by Christ's Sacrifice

For by one offering He has perfected forever
those who are being sanctified.

Hebrews 10:14

Looking back once again to the sacrifice of the Lord Jesus on the cross, the author of Hebrews addresses the truth of the sufficiency of the work of Christ as our substitute for sin. The contrast, also often repeated in this book, is that the Jewish priests not only had to offer sacrifices time and time again, but also had to first bring an offering on the Day of Atonement for their own sins. This they did before they could do so for the sin of the people. God accepted those sacrifices because they pointed continually to the death of Christ on the cross for all sin.

But the point the author makes here is that Christ's offering effectively perfected all who believe in Him for salvation. We see this truth illustrated in other Scriptures as well. When Christ died, we died with Him. When Christ was buried, all believers were buried with Him. When Christ arose, we as believers rose with Him. We ascended and sat down when He sat down.

Only those who are robed in perfect righteousness can enter the gates of glory. We must be perfect to be seated with Christ! Nothing I have done makes me acceptable. The sacrifice of Christ, in which I share, makes me acceptable to God. Christ took my sin and paid the penalty for it. On the basis of my faith in Him, God declared me righteous and clothes me in His righteousness. I sit perfected in God's sight.

Does that mean my behavior is perfect here on earth? No! The author is also saying we "are being sanctified" day by day as we surrender to the activity of the Holy Spirit impacting our lives by the Word. I sit perfected, but I walk imperfectly. God is still working in my life, bringing it into conformity to Christ. The goal of God in saving me is to produce likeness to Christ in my behavior. He wants my position in glory to be reflected and radiated in my walk on earth. Christ lives in me to bring this to reality.

> *I sit perfected, but*
> *I walk imperfectly.*

When I see Christ face to face I shall be like Him, for I will "see Him as He is." Then and forever I will be fully sanctified and will have put away all sin and the desire to sin. I will be perfected, completely sanctified, and forever with and like the Lord Jesus Christ. Oh what glory that will be!

&⁊ ———————————————— ☌

Father, thank you for clothing me in the righteousness of Your Son. I claim no merit but accept it as a gift from You.

Gifts from the Spirit

But one and the same Spirit works all these things,
distributing to each one individually as He wills.

1 Corinthians 12:11

In the midst of a comprehensive description of the many gifts given to the church, Paul states that the Spirit has the special responsibility of communicating gifts to each believer. This is a confirmation of the various actions of the Godhead to carry out the work of God. The Father is always the source of every activity God accomplishes. The Word of God came from the Father. The Lord Jesus is the one who accomplishes God's acts. The Holy Spirit is the Person of the Trinity who applies the activity of God. The Word of God was produced and is applied by the Holy Spirit to every reader.

The same pattern is seen with regard to the spiritual gifts given for the blessing of the church. The source of these gifts is the Father. "Every good gift and every perfect gift is from above and comes down from the Father . . ." The Father is the giver. The Son by His sacrifice, resurrection, and glorification obtained these gifts for distribution to believers. Christ opened the channel to God's reservoir of spiritual blessings. The Holy Spirit according to His will directs each gift to the one of His choosing. The Spirit applies the gifts to the children of God.

Thus the spiritual capacities entrusted to me are mine by the distribution of the Spirit. Christ also unlocked all the gifts of the Spirit, and the same Spirit chose among them a specific spiritual gift for my use to contribute to the overall welfare of the body of Christ.

Some believers are discontented with the gift the Spirit has given them. They pray and seek another of their own choosing. How can a sinful, frail, unwise child of God think he or she knows better than the infinite Spirit of God who is the embodiment of all wisdom? We see the same ignorance of a child asking her parents if she can play with fire, or a sharp knife. Should He entrust us with the choice of what gifts we should have? The question is preposterous! The only wise God has executed the wisdom of His plan for our good and the blessing of the church. The statement: "Be content with such things as you have," includes your spiritual gift.

What is your gift? Seek that knowledge from God and exercise your ability, thanking Him for His choice through the Spirit. Most of us do not use our gifts to their full potential because of our dissatisfaction with His choice. Lay aside such quarreling with God. Rejoice with a thankful heart for His choice and serve in the place He has put you.

℆ ———————————————— ℅

Father, thank you for giving me a spiritual gift fitting for my place in the body of Christ. I commit my life to use it for Your glory.

Walking in a Cleansing Flood

But if we walk in the light as He is in the light, we
have fellowship with one another, and the blood of
Jesus Christ His Son cleanses us from all sin.

1 John 1:7

The Scriptures repeatedly give us delightful uses of present tense activities that relate to our union with Christ: He forgives, He satisfies, He redeems, He gives, and—here in today's text—He cleanses from all sin.

On the night that signaled the completion of His earthly mission, the Lord Jesus washed the disciples' feet before He dined at the table with them. In doing so, He made a distinction between the bath each one would have taken before they set out for this important fellowship with their Master, and the washing they needed after they arrived. The defilement was confined to their feet, that kicked up dust that landed between the straps of their sandals and stuck to their sweating feet.

Eastern culture demanded that a service of washing such foul feet be performed before a meal was served. Foot washing was as frequent as the offering of a cup of tea or coffee is in today's western homes. Christ explained this action as the need for removing filth on a habitual basis. As often as the defilement took place, cleansing was necessary. The stain of sin is a constant problem, even for those who seek holiness.

When we trusted Christ, we were bathed from our sin. We know it as forgiveness. That cleansing is a once-for-all action of God for all our sin. But the taint of sin continues as we entertain an evil thought or commit a sinful act. It is at this point that the blood of Christ is applied, cleansing us at that moment from sin.

The tear water flowing from the lachrymal gland continually washes over the eye, removing the smallest particle of dust. The flow increases to cope with a larger speck, and occasionally a "beam" is lodged that needs to be removed by the sensitive attention of another person. The continual cleansing of sin is as automatic as is the washing of the eye.

The blessing of being continually cleansed from sin is described as taking place when we walk in the light. As we walk in the sphere of Christ's presence, we are drawing by faith on the constant washing from sin. No need to stop and sit for the cleansing to be administered. As we walk, the blood of His Son cleanses us.

꒰ ──────────────── ꒱

Father, thank you for giving me the blood of Christ to provide continuing
washing from my frequent defilement. I accept this action by faith.

Appropriate, Don't Ask!

I can do all things through Christ who strengthens me.
Philippians 4:13

" "Strength for today and bright hope for tomorrow" precedes the hymn line, "Blessings all mine, with ten thousand beside," which lends itself to the title of this book. Perhaps the composer had Philippians 4:13 in mind when he penned "Great is Thy Faithfulness." Certainly, both the Word and the hymn urge us to believe that an adequate supply of power or strength for service is found in Christ Himself.

Yet in spite of these and other texts repeatedly attesting to the fact that Christ is our strength, many Christians continue pray that the Lord give them additional or special strength to meet a particular need. Such prayer suggests that Christ has a storehouse of strength which is under His control to release, but that it is in addition to or separate from the power found in Him.

A number of Bible verses confirm the truth of the personal sufficiency of Christ for all things. "All power is given unto me . . . Lo I am with you always;" "Strengthened with all might through His Spirit in the inner man;" "Strengthened with all might according to His glorious power;" "God has not given us the spirit of fear but of power." Each of these statements or prayers encourages us to *appropriate* the strength that God has given us *in* Christ. We must accept the fact that strength for us is resident in Christ through His indwelling Spirit.

> *Asking for more than He has given is an exercise in unbelief.*

Since all resurrection power is resident in Christ and He is in us, then I possess all the necessary strength for the daily activities of the Christian life. Instead of pleading to the Father for more strength, we should instead adopt the practice of thanking Him for the strength that He *is*. It is Christ who Himself strengthens us. Asking for more than He has given is an exercise in unbelief. Thanking Him in faith for the resources He has given trains my faith to grow. We have Him. We have His strength!

ઇ ———————————— ଓଷ

Father, thank you for giving Christ to me. I accept the fact that all strength is in Him. I agree that I have all His resurrection power to live on earth as Your representative. I believe He is all I need.

Gifted to Give

As each one has received a gift, minister it to one another,
as good stewards of the manifold grace of God.

1 Peter 4:10

Many Christians offer fervent prayers asking God for different gifts. In today's Scripture Peter asserts that "each one has received a gift." But what gift is he talking about?

As the eleven disciples spent the last night with their Master, He unfolded to them a number of gifts He was giving them. Several of these gifts would not be truly appreciated or appropriated until they received the Holy Spirit— Himself, one of the gifts—whom they needed to comprehend the significance of the other gifts. The others were a perfect example, a new commandment, peace, eternal life, the Word of God, and His own glory. The purpose of each of these gifts was to equip the disciples to be effective ministers of the gospel and to preach to every nation.

> This gift is for serving others.

It is possible that Peter was referring to the spiritual gift every believer receives the moment he trusts in the finished work of Christ. Paul wrote that the Spirit gives each one various gifts as He wills. Each of us can count on the Spirit who gave us a spiritual gift when we believed. We assume many gifts we receive are for our own enjoyment and use. Yet, these gifts, given to members of the body of Christ, are specifically for ministering to the other members of the body. It is clear from this text that this gift is for serving others. The word used here as "minister" is the common word for deacon. We are called to serve others with the spiritual ability the Lord has given to us.

What is striking in Peter's words is that he uses the same Greek root word for both gift and grace. This usage is common and helps us understand the intention of God in giving us such wonderful gifts. We cannot complain to God that we do not have enough gifts to do His work. Sadly, some of the gifts received by believers are being prostituted in service to the world. The blessings are all resident in the church, but believers many times are unfaithful stewards of those gifts, with the result that some of the work we are called to do is left undone. You have a gift! Yours is one of the many committed *to* the church *for* the church. Be sure you are a faithful steward of your gift.

&) ———————————————— (&

Father, thank you for giving me a special spiritual gift. I choose to accept the one You gave me and commit my life to using it in service to Your people.

26 | APRIL

God's Building Plan

*You also as living stones, are being built up as a
spiritual house, a holy priesthood, to offer up spiritual
sacrifices acceptable to God through Jesus Christ.*

1 Peter 2:5

How do you make a dead stone live? Peter had just presented Christ as a living stone Who had been set aside by the "builders"—that is, the leaders—of the nation of Israel. They and their people had rejected the very stone God presented to them. They had singularly refused Him and set Him aside, not knowing that He will one day be placed in the most prominent position by the One who sent Him to the builders.

God continued His building program, not with stones of the nation of Israel, but with the Gentiles. He brought a host of stones from the quarry of humanity and, as they touched the Living Stone, each partook of that Stone's life. They thus became a building fit for God to inhabit. That glorious plan continues to this day. God, by His Spirit, adds to the spiritual building as each one is made alive by God's precious, elect, Living Stone.

In the middle of explaining the metaphor, Peter says that such a temple must have priests who offer sacrifices in this spiritual house. Who will these priests be? Will they be drawn from the tribe of Levi? No! The same ones who are designated "living stones" by their union with the Living Stone are now charged with the responsibility of serving as priests. They must carry out their duties by offering spiritual sacrifices to God by Jesus Christ.

Every believer is a priest sanctified (set apart) in the spiritual temple to present sacrifices to God, its Resident. Not one of us can escape the calling and commissioning of the priesthood.

What was so precious to these Jewish believers was the establishment of a priesthood in a spiritual temple. They had left behind the temple in Jerusalem when they believed in Christ. They elected to follow Christ instead of the temple in Jerusalem with its sacrifices, offerings, and vestments. In place of all the offerings and ordinances, they had Christ. In place of the vestments, they had the robes of the righteousness of Christ. In place of the sacrifices of animals, they brought themselves as living sacrifices to God by Christ. God was making the spiritual blessings and responsibilities of these new believers a more glorious temple than the one they had left behind in Jerusalem. As priests, we too must offer spiritual sacrifices to God.

Father, thank you for installing me as a priest in Your spiritual temple. I gladly bring my daily sacrifices of thanks, worship, and praise.

No Ordinary Man

Which He will manifest in His own time, He who is the blessed and only Potentate, the King of kings and Lord of lords, who alone has immortality, dwelling in unapproachable light, whom no man has seen or can see, to whom be honor and everlasting power. Amen.

1 Timothy 6:15-16

This benediction from the pen of Paul draws us to the presence of God in the person of Jesus Christ. It is all too easy for us, after reading the Gospels, to think of Christ as an ordinary man. Our mediocre perspective of Him needs to be shaken by the kind of magnificent description that we read in these two verses.

Paul is talking about the One who entered this world humbly, walked honorably, lived simply, suffered silently, died vicariously, rose victoriously, ascended modestly, and will return gloriously. This One is our Redeemer, the uniqueness of whose being will be evident in a day to come when every knee will bow and every tongue confess that He is also Lord of all. Let us consider Him portrayed from several perspectives.

He who entered His earthly pilgrimage as a baby is the only sovereign Lord God. The One who took up children in His arms and blessed them is the only One who is fully blessed. The One who was seen in the temple teaching the Scribes and Pharisees is the One whom no man has seen or can see. The One who was criticized and contradicted for His words of wisdom will one day be called "The Amen." The one who wore a crown of thorns and a purple robe is the King of kings. The One who was rejected by Israel as their Lord is the Lord of lords. The One who suffered alone in the darkness surrounding the cross is He who dwells in unapproachable light. The One who received shame from His creatures while hanging between heaven and earth will receive honor from both heaven and earth. The One who spoke pathetic words of weakness from the cross—"I thirst"—has everlasting power. The One who died on the cross for our sin is the only One who possesses immortality.

How can our simple minds draw the two contrasting pictures together? It behooves us to keep our intellectual capacities exercised as we contemplate Christ's lordly ways in Matthew, His lowly works in Mark, His lovely walk in Luke, and His lofty words in John. This background is for our instruction as we ponder the fact that God also has highly exalted Him and we own Him as our Savior. How can we continue to consider the One whom God has exalted as common and ordinary?

⅒ ———————————— ∛

Father, thank you for such an exquisite explanation of our majestic Savior. We worship in awe at His breathtaking magnificence.

28 APRIL

Reconciled to God

*And not only that, but we also rejoice in God
through our Lord Jesus Christ, through whom
we have now received the reconciliation.*

Romans 5:11

The doctrine of salvation rests on three great words—reconciliation, redemption, and propitiation—one of which is found in Romans 5:11. *Redemption* means to make a payment and set free. Christ's work on the cross was entirely adequate to pay the price—that of eternal death—for our sin. Redemption is directed toward the sin of mankind. *Propitiation* means to be satisfied: Christ's sacrifice satisfied the just and righteous standard of God. Propitiation is, therefore, toward God: God is propitiated. *Reconciliation* means that God completely changed the situation of mankind because of the substitutionary death of Christ on the cross. Without the death of Christ, mankind could never have escaped the judgment of God. But because Christ made the acceptable, redemptive payment for our sin, God withdrew the charges against sin—with the exception of the sin of unbelief in His own beloved Son.

> *God reconciled the world to Himself when Christ died.*

Consider this question: Why does mankind stand condemned? Many will answer that it is because we are sinners. Yet those who have believed are not free from sinning. Others will say it is because we have a sin nature. However, God does not remove our sin nature when we believe the gospel. The answer to the question resides in John 3:18: ". . . because he has not believed in the name of the only begotten Son of God." God withholds judgment against all of man's sin except that of refusing to believe in Christ as Savior.

God holds the sin of man in abeyance until the final moment of physical life. Should a person pass from this life as an unbeliever in Christ, God holds him responsible for all sin and lack of likeness to the perfection of God Himself. If a person chooses to believe the good news that Christ died for his or her sin and was raised again, God withdraws all charges against that person and blesses him or her in Christ with the salvation He accomplished at the cross.

The responsibility of each believer is to proclaim the offer of salvation, and pray that man will change his mind about the person and work of Christ. God reconciled the world to Himself when Christ died. We are challenged to follow Paul's example and plead with people, "Be reconciled to God!" We who believe rejoice in the adequacy of the work of Christ on the cross.

80 ———————— CB

Father, thank you for the blessing of reconciliation made available to me by Christ. I rejoice in the adequacy of that sacrifice for me.

A Botanical Lesson

Now may the God of hope fill you with all joy
and peace in believing, that you may abound in
hope by the power of the Holy Spirit.

Romans 15:13

This wonderful verse holds a key that will open our hearts to many other truths. Paul is coming to the close of his great treatise on the doctrine of salvation. Having set forth man's sinful condition, his need of a Savior, and God's provision for salvation and sanctification, the apostle outlines in the final chapters the service believers are to render to one another, and how we are to communicate the impact our Savior has on our lives.

In this verse, two of the many graces of Christ are singled out. Both joy and peace are listed in Galatians 5:22 as fruit of the Spirit, but in no other verse is the means of generating these divine characteristics presented so simply as in Romans15:13. The term "fruit" helps us understand the spontaneous production of joy and peace, as well as the other seven manifestations of it. In botany, nutrients are absorbed and transformed into flower, fragrance, and fruit. It is an instinctive process. The development and display of "joy and peace" are not mechanical, no matter how methodical our efforts. Nor are they the result of activity, however diligent we may be, or by legalism, no matter how much obedience we claim, or by imitation, no matter how many skills we learn. These graces of Christ are resident in Him and given to us in His person and work.

Paul prays that these believers, who have partaken of the heavenly Gift (having placed their faith in Him), are provided with all the resources for displaying joy and peace. The God of hope is the source of each gift made available by the work of Christ, and the gift itself is communicated "by the power of the Holy Spirit."

The key phrase is *"in believing."* The one ingredient God waits on us to employ is faith. We must believe for salvation, as Romans 10:9 so clearly states. The continual application of that same faith in God's Word results in lives of joy, peace, and the long list of other graces. Do I believe Christ is the only source of joy and peace? If I do, the acceptance and utilization of those gifts will spontaneously develop in my life and be visible in the way I live and serve the Lord in a wicked world.

> *Do I believe Christ is the only source of joy and peace?*

Father, thank you for providing in Christ all Your joy and all Your peace. I confess that I sometimes doubt that I possess them. I now choose to employ them in my mind, my life, and my words.

Rightful Worship

You are worthy, O Lord, to receive glory and
honor and power; For You created all things, And
by Your will they exist and were created.

Revelation 4:11

To create means to make something out of nothing. The God of creation began with nothing, and by His word the universe was brought into being. The worship of all created beings is properly directed toward the only One who by will and word brought into existence that which previously was nonexistent. He deserves all the "glory and honor and power" for His creative and sustaining acts. The designation of ascribing to the Lord these three marvelous traits is consistent with the superintendence of our sovereign God.

The *glory* of His pre-existence is His as bestowed by the Father in answer to His Son's prayer in John 17. The glory of the cross belongs to Him, as that event was the premier opportunity to display God's qualities as never before. He is due glory because of His original designs, His unique identifying marks for each member of creation, the dependency of every member of each segment of creation, and the interaction of all aspects of His creation. Glory to the Son.

The *honor* belongs to Him for the lofty position He gave to every strata of creation. The uniqueness of the mineral world with nutrients for every other aspect of creation is His design. The plant kingdom feeds the animal kingdom. The animal kingdom provides for the sustenance and survival of the human society. Mankind is responsible for superintending the kingdoms below him. The inability of any kingdom to lift itself to the next level without condescension from another kingdom is the divine order. Christ, as God, condescended Himself to the human kingdom in order to lift us up to sit "in the heavenly places" with Him. To Him be all honor.

The *power* belongs to the Lord because no one is able to stand in the way of all He intends to do. He could say at the end of His creative acts, "It is very good." And so it is! His purpose will not be overturned and no one will stand against Him. One day He will be all in all, and all kingdoms will have been put under His feet. He alone is the essence of all power.

In the King James translation of this verse we read, "For thy pleasure they are and were created." This adds the delightful thought that God made all of this for Himself. It all belongs to Him and exists by His will and for His enjoyment. We are stewards of all that is His.

ও ——————————— ঙ

Father, thank you for the creation of everything I enjoy today. Most of all I delight in being made a new creature in Christ Jesus.

May

IN THE SPRING OF LIFE,
NEW GIFTS SEEM MIRACULOUS

"That I may know Him . . ."
Philippians 3:10

Jesus, source of every blessing,
From the cross ascended high.
There to give us every dressing,
Clothed with beauty from the sky.

Here on earth put on the new man.
Lay aside the clothes of old.
Loaded daily from His full hand,
Found in Him in robes of gold.

Seen by all in Christ victorious,
He has won the war for me.
Nothing in myself is glorious,
Like the Savior now to be.

F. L. K.

May

A Seed

The seed is one of God's greatest preachers. It speaks every language. It always tells the truth. It travels to every country. It reproduces, so there is always plenty. It costs nothing to support. Every person on earth has heard one preach.

Most often, when I am in the bush or forest looking for an illustration to communicate some biblical truths, I ask for a seed. Many times I use a coconut, since it is the largest seed and can be seen by most in the audience.

The Lord Jesus introduced this metaphor in John 12:24 to the Greeks who wanted to see Him. His first statement in verse 23 to them was, "The hour has come that the Son of Man should be glorified." What followed was the profound explanation of the mysterious metaphor of a seed: ". . . unless a grain of wheat falls into the ground and dies . . ." Death is the road to glory. This is a principle of life that has been functioning in nature from Genesis 1, and it is displayed in the lives of victorious believers.

The seed teaches us that, whatever you plant, you will receive the same again. Whatever seed falls into the ground will produce exactly the same seed in due season. There can be no variation or violation in this law of the harvest.

The Lord is clear that the word "seed" is used of the Word of God. Seed is also used for those who are "sons of the Kingdom." As believers in Christ, we are those sons—we are the offspring of God by virtue of His Son. But what kind of seeds are we? The parable in Matthew 13:38 says that ". . . the good seeds are the sons of the kingdom . . ."

The seed teaches us profound lessons about the believer's life and lifestyle. We could look at any one of millions of kinds of seeds and ask where they came from and how they got there. The answer is given in Genesis 1:11: the seed came from a plant that produces the same kind of kernel.

Christ is the seed that fell into the ground and died, as John 12:24 says. We are the "much fruit" that has come from His death and resurrection. But what kind of seed are we? Exactly the same as the One that died to give us His life.

The qualities of the seed that died are reproduced in every seed that comes from that "plant of renown." In botany, the zygote that is borne is the same size, shape, color, weight, and flavor as the plant that bore it, and it has the same capacity for reproducing.

What is glorious is that the whole process is spontaneous. The seed does not try, work, pray, fight, or study, but simply surrenders to a divine principle placed in it by the Creator. Through death, life springs forth.

The parallel is remarkable. The Creator, by our regeneration, places in us His Seed which has the capabilities of reproducing Himself in me. The goal of Christ-likeness takes place spontaneously just as it happens in the seed.

It is true that we have the seed of Adam as well, which also wants to reproduce itself in us. But the Seed of Christ, placed in us, has the capacity to make the Seed that died visible in our life. First John 3:9 reminds us that "His seed remains in him . . ." The seed of Christ dwells in us, and it can only reproduce Himself as we allow His life to flow through us. This is glorifying Christ.

An acorn can only produce an oak; so, too, the Lord, as the Seed, has been planted in us to produce His own unique likeness in and through our being. This happens spontaneously as we submit to the divine principle of fruit and seed-bearing. The seed of Christ can only produce Christ-likeness; He can only produce "fruit that will last."

Peter concludes his second epistle with these words: "Grow in the grace and knowledge of our Lord and Savior Jesus Christ." A plant does not grow because we tell it to grow. It grows because we provide the nutrients necessary to allow the principle, lodged in the seed, to do what the Creator designed it to do. Christ lives in us, reproducing His likeness, as we apply the food of knowledge, the fertilizer of faith, and the moisture of obedience to the truth.

Let us feed the life principle waiting for its expression in our lives. All nourishment necessary for growth is labeled in the Scriptures, so we know where it comes from. Each has a reference, so its inventory can be counted. The resources are unlimited, since the Father gave us His Son and, with Him, He "freely give us all things" (Romans 8:32).

Sealed with God's Ownership

And do not grieve the Holy Spirit of God, by whom
you were sealed for the day of redemption.

Ephesians 4:30

One of the greatest needs of mankind is to belong. God created Adam and Eve with this need and bound them to Himself with care, devotion, provision, and fellowship in the cool of the evening. Sin destroyed this satisfaction with God's provision, and man went his own way in search of fulfilling his own needs. Satan also was quick to offer an alternative which gave a false sense of security. Much of what the world offers in unions, clubs, and fraternities are the enemy's attempt to misdirect man's need to belong.

Only in the church does God give the full extent of His provision for us. God bought us back and, by regeneration, sealed us as His own through the person and agency of the Holy Spirit. The work of Christ is the basis of this ministry, and the Spirit is continually active in making known this truth to us.

Ownership and security are two of God's works in sealing us and satisfying our needs. A seal on a document indicates who sent it or who wrote it. The name on the document tells us who it belongs to. We write our name in a book or on a possession so that all will know that we are the owners. God has placed His name on us by His Spirit. His signature is not a brand mark, but the character of Christ developed by the Holy Spirit. As others see Christ in us, the world will know that we belong to Him. How we live and the daily use of our body is a stage on which Christ is seen.

> *The presence of the Holy Spirit guarantees that we will never be removed from God.*

Security is the second purpose of sealing us by the Holy Spirit. Scrolls in Paul's day were secured with hot wax in which a seal was impressed. No one could open a document without breaking the hardened wax seal. The presence of the Holy Spirit guarantees that we will never be removed from God. We are placed in God by Christ through the Holy Spirit, never to be separated from the love of Christ. We will then be fully redeemed, completely changed, and forever with and like Christ Himself.

Christians are tempted to think that sin or sorrow will break our relationship with God. The Holy Spirit is in us to bear witness that we are God's and His forever. What a blessed union!

ℝ ———————————————— ℞

Father, thank you for sealing me so that I can rest in Your ownership and security. I confess that my fears are the result of my own unbelief. I glory in the fact that nothing can separate me from You.

Christ is Praying

Therefore He is also able to save to the uttermost
those who come to God through Him, since He
ever lives to make intercession for them.

Hebrews 7:25

C hrist is praying for you! None prays more faithfully for the children of God than Christ. Most of the prayers of the New Testament are prayers of intercession. We are commanded to pray for one another; Christ prays perfectly for each believer.

A few probing questions about this statement will help open our eyes to its deeper truths. Perhaps a most revealing question is, "What is He praying?" There is no doubt that His prayers are perfect and maintain the highest level of interest and devotion to us. Most of us pray that the Lord will deliver us from some difficulty. In our trials, we ask friends and family to intercede for us, expecting that they will pray for deliverance from the struggle. What we believe is that the more who pray, the greater the probability of our escape. Yet is Christ praying for our deliverance? Even the question helps us focus on the difference between what we want and what the Lord Jesus might pray.

Obviously, His prayer for us would be in harmony with the Father's will and according to His Word. The Lord did not keep His own disciples from many trials and tests, and we should not think that He would pray differently for us.

What did He pray for His disciples? In John 17:15, He prayed that the Father would not take them out of the world. That is the opposite of many of our prayers for ourselves. "Get me out of this mess" summarizes our feelings, if not our words. "Keep them from the evil one," He prayed. But He did not pray that the evil one would be taken away or fenced out. He expected that conflict would continue in their lives.

> *Christ is praying that we will become like Him.*

Christ prayed that Peter's faith would not fail. Again, it is clear that the Lord did not pray that Satan would not attack, but that Peter would be strong in faith to defeat the enemy. This is especially instructive as we ask what Christ is praying for us. Christ prays that we will draw on the resources that He has made available to us by His death and resurrection. He is praying that our faith will grow as we face the trials of life. Christ is praying that we will become like Him!

— ❧ ——————————————— ❧ —

Father, You have given me all that I need to live. I rest in Christ, who is praying for me that I will grow into His fullness and likeness. Today I walk in faith, strengthened by my Savior's intercession.

Living in Wisdom and Prudence

In Him we have redemption through His blood, the forgiveness
of sins, according to the riches of His grace which He made
to abound toward us in all wisdom and prudence.

Ephesians 1:7-8

The term "riches of His grace" seems highly spiritual but hardly practical. We count our accumulation of money, but wonder about the reservoir of Christ's riches. Paul reminds us that all our resources for life are found in Christ. All we need to do is to accept His provision. In Philippians 4:19, Paul states it another way: "My God shall supply all your need."

Paul first said that the forgiveness of sin is based on the riches of His grace. Our Lord's riches are infinite, and so is His forgiveness. Believers sometimes think that certain sins are beyond the forgiveness of God. We look back to a particular sin and wonder whether it was really forgiven. We ask, "Was full fellowship restored?"

Yes, God says that His Son paid the debt for all sin, and no sin is beyond His forgiveness. The enemy continually badgers us with thoughts of sin and the idea that we have done something that is greater than His grace. Paul confirms God's blessing by writing in Romans 5:20, "But where sin abounded, grace abounded much more." The grace of forgiveness is made to overflow or abound—it is totally adequate. So, because the sacrifice of Christ covers every sin, does this give us the liberty to continue in sin? Paul responds, "God forbid!" Instead, the greatness of forgiveness should motivate us to please the One who forgave us.

This forgiveness is understood through the "wisdom and prudence" which is supplied with His grace. His wisdom teaches that we cannot appreciate His grace and still continue in sin. Wisdom is the proper use of knowledge. Knowledge tells me that I am forgiven of all sin. Wisdom tells me that this forgiveness is not simply a license to continue in sin.

His prudence says unequivocally that the sin we commit presumptuously is covered but not countenanced by God. Prudence says that, if you "continue in sin that grace may abound," maybe you have not been forgiven at all. John tells us that, if anyone sins, we have an Advocate.

Do you know "the riches of His grace?" These blessings are like a river of grace which overflows its banks without inundating those living nearby. Absolute adequacy!

ᏅᎥ ———————————— ᏨᎧ

Father, thank you for Your all-encompassing grace. I accept that forgiveness
and choose to listen to Your wisdom and prudence, as they counsel me not
to continue in sin.

Training in Patience

My brethren, count it all joy when you fall into various
trials, knowing that the testing of your faith produces
patience. But let patience have its perfect work, that
you may be perfect and complete, lacking nothing.

James 1:2-4

James gives us an important message concerning the trials and tests in our lives. Every trial comes to the believer with the permission of God. Nothing escapes His knowledge. In addition, we must accept the principle that the Lord Himself may in fact send trials or tests, just as He did to most of His people throughout the Bible.

In the above Scripture, James seems to be asking us to do the impossible: rejoice in the trials that come to our lives. Joy and trials seem incongruous. We often think that if we have joy we are not experiencing trials. But God more than once states that both can be present at the same time in the same life.

When we accept God's superintendence over our lives, it releases us from fear and uncertainty and encourages us to "count it all joy." This is a command, not just advice. The context also reminds us that we are to know the purpose or outcome that God has planned. The trials are sent for specific reasons. The plan of God is well defined even before trials arrive in our lives. We must recognize that purpose and work to bring the desired fulfillment in our lives.

God's goal in these trials is for us to become perfect and complete. The words do not suggest sinless perfection, but rather full maturity. The Lord Jesus is perfect! His life develops in me as I learn from trials and tests that come my way. Can I say "thank you" to God for sending each particular trial? If I remember that He allows them to bring maturity to my life, I will be able to do so. I must understand and trust that His plan is perfect and involves a number of tests, which He will use to complete my development. The end result should be that I find all my resources in Christ and thereby lack nothing.

My duty is to allow patience to work in me to produce full growth. A child is not born with patience but develops it as parents provide discipline and training. Only then will he demonstrate true patience. God my Father is seeking to train me through tests and trials. As I accept them and employ them toward patience, I become mature, accomplished, and like the Lord Jesus Christ.

ଓ ———————————— ଓଷ

Father, thank you for overseeing every aspect of my life. I trust You with my training, and so rejoice in Your choices for me.

The Lord Knows Me

Nevertheless the solid foundation of God stands, having this seal: "The Lord knows those who are His," and, "Let everyone who names the name of Christ depart from iniquity."
2 Timothy 2:19

We know that the Lord Jesus is omniscient, yet this truth is often forgotten in our everyday lives.

The Lord knows that we belong to Him, but can we stretch it further to include "the Lord knows *all about* those who are His?" What a blessing for sheep to understand that the Shepherd knows they are His. It is comforting for sheep to realize that the Shepherd knows its name, its age, its natural tendencies, its scars from falls, its temperament, its history, and its special desires. Our Lord knows all this and more—He also knows our future.

"The Lord knows" is a favorite phrase of many in the Scripture. Peter says, "The Lord knows how to deliver the righteous." Paul writes, "The Lord knows the thoughts." David proclaims, "For the Lord knows the way of the righteous." Job states, "He [the Lord] knows the way that I take."

Even when we try to hide our activities and thoughts from Him, He knows. This pressures us to correct our lives, even as we are comforted in the midst of trials that the Lord may send our way. He knows how much we can bear and in what area of life we need to grow. He knew the pride of Peter, the unbelief of Thomas, the sectarianism of James and John, the background of Matthew, the purity of Nathaniel, the need of Zaccheaus, the fear of Nicodemus, and the devotion of Joseph of Arimathea.

David says in Psalm 139:2, "You know my sitting down and my rising up; You understand my thought afar off. You comprehend my path and my lying down, And are acquainted with all my ways." Before we were ever formed in the womb, the Lord knew every aspect of our developing personality and DNA. He designed the mix of personality traits from my parents that was exactly according to His plan. I am an original like no other!

Why are we filled with fear, worry, and anxiety when the Lord, who knows us best, loves us most? Marinate your mind in this truth. Soak your soul in this blessing. Wash your will in this fact. Ameliorate your attitudes in this reality. Memorize this proverb. Gaze on this glorious Person. What rest and peace is mine because He knows me!

 hown ———————————————— cg

Father, You know me better than any. Forgive me for trying to hide my life and thoughts from You. I realize that I am completely transparent to Your mind. I surrender my life afresh each and every day.

A Perfect Substitute

Who gave Himself for our sins, that He might deliver us from this present evil age, according to the will of our God and Father.

Galatians 1:4

The concept of substitution goes all the way back to Genesis 3, where an animal had to die in order that its skin might be fashioned by the Lord to cover Adam and Eve's nakedness. Life had to be sacrificed for the sin of man. Abraham took a ram from a thorn bush as an offering instead of his son Isaac. The Passover lamb died in place of the firstborn son before the exodus from Egypt. Christ, by His death, fulfilled all the types and pictures as the paragon of substitution.

> *The substitutionary work of Christ was not limited to paying the price of sin.*

The phrase "for our sins" carries the impact of "instead of us," as in the case of Isaac. Romans 5:6 states so powerfully, "Christ died for the ungodly." This is a specific characteristic of all who are away from God and living in sin. If we understand the power of these two statements, we see the comprehensive nature of Christ's substitution. He gave Himself for what I was doing—sinning. He died for what I am—ungodly. Put them together and you have an apt description of mankind without God: an ungodly sinner.

God gives a reason for this wonderful provision: that He might deliver us from the sinful life that we were embroiled in before Christ saved us. Many people suggest that God saves us from hell and leaves us to live on earth as we like. Nothing could be further from the truth of the Word. Christ, our substitute, bore our sin away and gives us power to overcome the influences of evil around us.

Today's society is ruled by the god of this age and is responsible for opposition to the rule of Christ. Our Savior's victory over sin *was* a victory over *this* world system and its ruler—the god of this world.

It is God's desire that we employ that victory in the power of a risen Christ. The substitutionary work of Christ was not limited to paying the price of sin; He also gave Himself to us in His resurrected life. The risen Christ is, therefore, the source of power over continuing sin. We have an adequate substitute for the sin of the whole world—Christ Himself.

Father, thank you for Christ as the personal substitute for all my sin.

Sanctified and Justified

*And such were some of you. But you were washed, but
you were sanctified, but you were justified in the name
of the Lord Jesus and by the Spirit of our God.*

1 Corinthians 6:11

The term salvation is a summary of all the specific blessings of God in making me His own. This miracle of spiritual birth has a past, present, and future aspect. In 1 Corinthians 6:11, God reminds us of our present condition by using three specific words to describe the fullness of His work in us.

Each phrase in this verse describes an action of God doing His work in the name of the Lord Jesus and accomplishing it by the Holy Spirit. Each is a permanent work that does not need to be repeated. None can be undone by us, nullified by the enemy, or reversed by our Father. This is an act of God demonstrating His faithfulness.

"Washed" does not refer to the foot-washing that the Lord Jesus performed on His disciples, but to the bathing that He spoke of as taking place once— symbolized by baptism. Washed refers to the defilement of sin which needed to be forgiven once for all. It refers to the stain of sin which is present in every person, with the exception of Christ Jesus. When we believed in Christ, we were washed and fully cleansed in the blood of the Lamb.

"Sanctified" simply means to be set apart. We use it in reference to being set apart from sin, and that is the practical out-working of God's full effort of sanctification. The book of Hebrews reminds us that we are sanctified as believers once and for all. God set us apart for Himself the moment that we confessed Christ as our Savior. This did not stop us from sinning, but meant that we were forever separated from condemnation, death, destruction, and the punishment that we deserved.

"Justified" is our position, because God declares us righteous in His sight. This does not make us righteous, but declares that we are in a right standing before a holy God. We still have a tendency to sin, but God looks at us in Christ and sees His righteousness, and so has the authority to declare us righteous. He wants us to live up to that statement and behave righteously until we are with Christ forever.

These three aspects of God's work are the act of a moment, and are finished and finalized by His salvation. God moved us from filth to washed, from being slaves of sin to being set apart to God, from standing under God's condemnation to standing in the righteousness of Christ!

�’ ———————————— ଔ

*Father, thank you for saving me and for finishing Your work in me. I confess
that there is much for me to do in working that out in my life.*

Spirit of Faith

*But since we have the same spirit of faith, according
to what is written, "I believed and therefore I
spoke," we also believe and therefore speak.*

2 Corinthians 4:13

All people are born with the ability to exercise faith. Adam used faith as he partook of every tree of the garden except the tree of the Knowledge of Good and Evil. Adam and Eve had the capacity to place their faith in either the lie of the serpent or the Truth of God, and eventually their faith was placed in the lie of the serpent.

This faith was not unique or different from what we all possess. Does God demand a special kind of faith for salvation? Is it necessary for God to "give faith" to a select few so that they can believe? Certainly not! Man is lost "because he will not believe in the name of the only begotten Son of God." God holds man responsible for whom he places his faith in.

"We have the same spirit of faith" and are given the opportunity of exercising it in the only worthy object of faith—the Lord Jesus Christ. The psalmist says, "I believed," and Paul responds, "we also believed." He acknowledges that the act of placing faith in Christ is not something that God did for him. Paul did not wait for God to do any more than offer the knowledge of salvation by presenting the person and work of Christ to him.

The challenge is to place your faith in the only worthy object— Christ alone.

The issue is this: which object do we place our faith in? Some have faith in the church, or baptism, or keeping the Ten Commandments—which is tantamount to having faith in yourself. The challenge is to place your faith in the only worthy object—Christ alone.

The person of Christ saves; our faith does not save. God responds to my faith, placed firmly in Christ, and is set free to bestow all of His blessings in Salvation. That faith continues to work day by day as I learn more of the gifts that God has given me in Christ.

I believe God for those things as well. The exercise of a "special faith" does not bring Christ closer, does not make me more saved, does not lift me in preeminence over others who have placed "simple faith" in Christ. We all have the same faith. The object of our faith differs. Christ alone saves through our faith.

☙ ——————————— ❧

Father, thank you for giving me faith as a common ingredient of all human beings. Thank you for drawing me to Christ for salvation.

Grace for the Race

*Therefore gird up the loins of your mind, be sober,
and rest your hope fully upon the grace that is to be
brought to you at the revelation of Jesus Christ.*

1 Peter 1:13

G race is one of the great themes of God's Word. We read elsewhere of the many forms of grace which "abound" to us here and now. But in this verse, Peter teaches us that grace is also awaiting us at the end of the journey. He is writing to believers who are suffering for their faith. He says that their present hope rests in the gifts which lie ahead of them. These gifts are safe and secure in the keeping of God.

"God gives grace for the race 'til we see His face!" The word "grace" is also translated "gifts" elsewhere in the New Testament. The race of the runner is not a pleasant thing, as he marks mile after mile. But the hope at the end spurs him on with patience and perseverance. For the believer, as for the runner, the need to "gird up" is essential to keeping up the pace and finishing the race. "Gird up" suggests removing any encumbrances that would impede progress.

I have often said, "God gives grace for the race 'til we see His face!" Our hope will be satisfied as we make the final turn and see the glorious Person who has called us to partake of His grace every step of the race. It is the end of the run that urges the athlete forward, putting one foot in front of the other for the final grueling miles. It is not competition but completion that is viewed here. We find a sense of confidence that, at the end of the race, the finish line is there and a trophy awarded. The gifts of God will be fully revealed in all their glory as we look unto Jesus, who successfully completed His race.

The added worry of never finishing would make a marathon all that much more difficult. But the runner knows its exact length and the terrain of the final leg of the journey. Hope is based on having seen the race course. Because we do not know when the race will end or the terrain of the final leg, our hope is set on the Person and His grace awaiting us at the end of our journey. So, fellow runners, "gird up" and run the race set before you, and set your heart on the gifts awaiting you when you see His face. There is adequate grace for each step of the race including the last one, which takes us across the finish line to see Him face to face.

Father, thank you for all the resources afforded me to run my race with patience. I accept these blessings and carry them to the finish, where I will see Him.

His Workmanship

To this end I also labor, striving according to
His working which works in me mightily.

Colossians 1:29

God is working in all believers, and He is doing so with great power and might. Yet, when Christ comes to live in us, what exactly is He doing in there?

First, we ought to consider Paul's statement from Colossians 1:29. The apostle's desire is for every believer to become perfect or mature in Christ. Paul's stated goal is for all saints to grow into the likeness of Christ.

God is the primary worker, and we are to work in harmony with His efforts which we know to be according to His will. Elsewhere it says, "It is God who works in you" and "working in you that which is well pleasing in His sight" and "according to the power that works in us." God is in us as a worker! He is not just energy or a force, but a Person who wields tremendous power to mold and shape us into the likeness of His Son.

Note that Paul uses the present tense, "works." God is at work now in our minds, teaching us by His Holy Spirit to know the things given by God. He ministers to our emotions, prodding us to enjoy the mysteries of the faith. God works in our will to empower us to do His good pleasure. It is astonishing that the One who created the world in six days and then rested from all His labors is still working in our lives. The Creator who hung the worlds in space has stepped into my heart, making it His workshop.

We are His workmanship. The tools that He uses are the circumstances and trials of life. He may use our plans that do not work as we would like. He may use our failed dreams or designs. He may use friends, family, or even those opposed to us to work in us. When we become angry at someone who irritates or disturbs

> *The Creator who hung the worlds in space has stepped into my heart, making it His workshop.*

us, we fail to realize that that person was sent by God to work in us. We mistake the messenger and respond in anger to him. It is not the fault of the messenger. He or she was sent by God to work in us mightily.

Remember that God is working. A piece of clay does not know its ultimate end, but we know the goal of God for each of us: to draw ever closer to Christ-likeness. As God is working toward that end, we need to work with Him. Happy harmony comes when we know His plan and submit to it.

૪૦ ———————————— ૯૪

Father, thank you for working in me. I present my life to You to remodel, until it is like that of Christ.

Both Faithful and Just

*If we confess our sins, He is faithful and just to forgive us
our sins and to cleanse us from all unrighteousness.*

1 John 1:9

Today's meditation is on a familiar verse dealing with our fellowship with God. Note the words "faithful and just." Without these words put together, we end up with an unbalanced view of God's activity. He is faithful because of His personal commitment to the work of Christ on the cross. He is just in character. He can forgive because He is just. He demanded an adequate sacrifice so that He could remain just and also justify all who believe in His Son.

Unfortunately, some people find little comfort in this verse. They tend to read it backwards: "If we do not confess our sins, He does not forgive us or cleanse us from all unrighteousness." It might seem at first glance to be true both ways, but that is a trap which can produce error and cause a host of fears to overcome us. Some people add another phrase, "and forgive all my sins," to every prayer to ensure that they will not lose their salvation. This verse is not referring to obtaining or losing salvation.

> *Confession is to take sides with God against any action or attitude which is sin.*

We must understand that the issue John is writing about is the continuation of fellowship with our Father and His Son. Fellowship is a much different concept than relationship. Relationship is established when we trust Christ for our salvation, which includes the forgiveness of all of our sin. This makes us a child of God and creates an unchangeable and unchallengeable union with God.

But if we sin, our fellowship is injured and broken. This does not break our eternal connection to God which is through the life of His Son. How is our fellowship restored? The simple answer given here is confession of sin. Confession is to take sides with God against any action or attitude which is sin. My confession opens the path that has been clogged by sin. God has already overcome my sin in the death of Christ. But fellowship is restored as the path is cleansed, and we again enjoy the healing of our communion with Him. The path has been there from the beginning of our salvation.

This verse does not command us to "ask for forgiveness," but to confess. If we do our part, God is faithful to restore our fellowship, because His Son paid the sacrifice for all our sin. I confess, and God has forgiven. We both enjoy the restoration of fellowship.

₧ ———————————— ₧

Father, thank you for forgiving my sin and restoring our fellowship when I honestly confess my sin. I rejoice in Your restoration.

No Condemnation

*There is therefore now no condemnation
to those who are in Christ Jesus.*

Romans 8:1

We were all born into the world under the condemnation of God because of our sin. Now Paul announces that a huge change has taken place between God and the believer. For seven chapters, God has revealed His righteous judgment against every person, regardless of who he is, where he lives, how he was raised, what type of job he has, how little education he has, or how deprived he may be. All are under the judgment of God.

What brought that change? From God's standpoint, the gift of His Son on the cross has satisfied God's demands against our sin. The penalty that God imposed back in Genesis 3 was death. There was no lesser penalty for any sin. All sin deserved the same punishment. Christ died on the cross and met the standard of punishment that man deserved and the benchmark of justice that God demanded.

Because God was satisfied with the sacrificial death of Christ, He was set free to receive anyone who would believe in Jesus Christ. One by one, people are coming to God through Christ and accepting His sacrifice for their sin. When they do so, God immediately removes all condemnation that hung over the head of each one.

What is the condemnation which was justly ours from a holy God? The most serious condemnation was eternal separation from God's presence, which the Bible terms eternal death. That condition was reversed by God giving us His life—eternal life. A second judgment is permanent existence in a place of total darkness. Outside of God's presence is absolute darkness. God dealt with this aspect of judgment by giving us His Son as the Light. A third punishment is slavery to enemies, including the world, the flesh, sin, death, and the devil. God gained victory for us and releases us from that slavery by giving us the person of Christ, who sets us free from bondage to all these enemies. A fourth charge that was laid against us is punishment for sin. God provided forgiveness because Christ shed His blood for our sin. A fifth condition which I was deserving of was banishment from God's home forever. God in His grace has promised me a home with Him in glory forever. A sixth penalty for my sinfulness is conflict in life. God has given me His peace in exchange for my conflict. He has made peace for me through Christ. There are many more aspects which deserve condemnation, but in Christ they have all been banished. No judgment can be lodged against me.

☙ ——————————————— ❧

Father, thank you for receiving me in Christ and justly setting aside all condemnation which was due to me. I bless Your amazing grace.

God's Greatest Gift

For by grace you have been saved through faith,
and that not of yourselves; it is the gift of God,
not of works, lest anyone should boast.

Ephesians 2:8-9

We all enjoy receiving gifts. God is a giving God and makes Himself known through His gifts. Today's Scripture has an interesting distinction in that it summarizes the basic act of God; imparting His salvation to all who place their faith in Christ (grace). We repeat it over and over as the simplest and most succinct description of how we are saved.

The gift is salvation! All it entails in the mind of God and all that we learn of its ingredients causes us to grow in grace. The most important feature of this gift is Christ Himself, communicated to us by the Holy Spirit. In Him, we partake of forgiveness through redemption. We receive the life of God through regeneration. We are sanctified, reconciled, adopted, received, justified, and blessed with all blessings by Christ. We inherit God's love, joy, and peace. We are promised a home in glory, a reward for service, and likeness to Christ. We are given a spiritual gift, a place of service, and a stewardship of grace. This and much more is bestowed in God's grace to all who believe.

> *We are sanctified, reconciled, adopted, received, justified, and blessed with all blessings by Christ.*

A gift is not a reward for performance, nor can it be purchased. It is not payment for service, or fruit of labor, or wages for activity, or promotion to position. Salvation is strictly a gift open to all who will receive Christ by faith. This faith is not a special kind of faith or a faith that is selectively given to a few. Faith is a common commodity, inherent in all human beings. We exercise faith when we eat food that we did not prepare, ride in a car that we do not drive, sit in a chair that we did not make, take medicine that we did not formulate. All of these are evidences of faith in the common activities of life. Some trust baptism for salvation or expect church membership to take them to heaven.

But does faith in the church save? The Scriptures are clear: only faith in Christ can save. God is waiting for each one to move his faith from that which does *not* save to the One who *does* save. What a blessing that salvation is a free gift and available to all who believe. There can be no pride for accomplishment, just thanks to God for placing His gift of salvation in my outstretched hand of faith. God is the giver of all that we receive.

❧ ———————————— ☙

Father, thank you for making my salvation free and without merit. I could never have earned such abundant blessings.

Everlasting and Eternal Life

He who has the Son has life; He who does not
have the Son of God does not have life.

1 John 5:12

D o you have the Son of God? The answer to this question is the only means of determining salvation. Those who are bent on arguing come to this verse and want to challenge God's demand that we possess His Son. Many want to come with their own good works, their attempt to keep the law, church membership, baptism, and a host of other accomplishments that they think will open the door for receiving the Son. Sinful man is not satisfied with Christ alone. He wants to add to His work by his own attempt to please God. But God rejects all human efforts, and accepts only faith in the gift of His Son.

Elsewhere in John's writings we are told that whoever believes on the Son has life, while he who does not believe the Son shall not see life. Possession of the Son is exclusively dependent on our faith in the person and work of the Son of God, as John says in the next verse.

By the term "life," God is referring to His own life, centered in His Son and available to all who believe that Christ died for their sin. The terms are exclusive but the offer is universal, as John again says, "Whoever believes."

In the English texts dealing with this life, two different words are used. We are told that we have eternal life. The word eternal refers to the extent of life which has no beginning and no ending. This is the life of God exclusively. God had no beginning and will have no ending of life. When we receive Christ, we have the life of God—eternal life.

We live eternally and everlastingly from the date of our salvation.

But another text, John 3:16, says that we have "everlasting life." Everlasting by definition declares that this life has a beginning but no ending. So the moment we believed in the name of the Son of God, we began to live in the divine sense. His life began in us. We were dead in sin, and the entrance of Christ into our lives began everlasting life in our being. Will we die? We may physically, but our death is not a permanent event. We may well pass through death, but death cannot hold us because we have true life. A seed that possesses life cannot stay in death because, as it passes into death, it springs to life and continues on and on through the seeds produced on its branches. Our body may be sown in death, but we live eternally and everlastingly from the date of our salvation. I am alive forever!

෨ ———————————————— ෬

Father, You have given me Your most precious possession, Your only Son. I live because Your Son lives in me.

MAY
15

Christ's Poverty, My Riches

For you know the grace of our Lord Jesus Christ, that
though He was rich, yet for your sakes He became poor,
that you through His poverty might become rich.

2 Corinthians 8:9

God uses grace as the primary word to explain the character of His salvation. We are saved by grace, justified by grace, grow in grace, have the Spirit of grace, receive grace, learn grace, stand in grace, abound in grace, experience grace, are under grace, have a throne of grace, and are heirs of grace. Imagine such abundance!

To know Christ is to know the grace of God. He is the personification of all the graces of God. He is the sum and substance and the center and circumference of grace. The Greek word for "grace" is also translated "gift" in many passages. Our word "charismatic" comes from this Greek word, *charis*. It refers to those who are occupied with the gifts of God.

We could also read this verse, "you know the *gifts* of our Lord Jesus Christ." Christ is the one through whom all the gifts of God are given. God's goal was to endow all His people with His riches, and the only way possible was through the death, resurrection, and glorification of Christ Jesus.

The incarnation and death of Jesus Christ are described in the words "He became poor." Not until we see Him face to face will we understand the riches of Christ before He came into the world. The Lord Jesus prayed in John 17 that we would be able to behold those riches. We cannot fathom the riches that Christ enjoyed with the Father before being born in Bethlehem. Yet he gave them up voluntarily and became fully man that we might be rich!

The List of riches is infinte and can only be learned by knowing Christ.

Poverty was not financial for Christ, nor are our riches financial. Daniel 9:26 says that He would die and "have nothing" (NASB). We were poor spiritually and had nothing of value to offer God. He wanted to enrich us, and that could only come through Jesus Christ freely by His grace.

Death and resurrection were the channel that God chose for His Son. That same channel became the avenue through which all the graces of God could flow to us. Christ died and lives to communicate the same qualities in all for whom He died. All the riches of His grace are ours. The list of riches is infinite and can only be learned by knowing Christ, since in Him are hid all these riches. What poverty for Christ, but what riches for me.

ЂꙨ ──────────── **ᯓ**

Father, thank you for the riches that I have in Christ. I acknowledge that Christ became poor so that I could be rich.

Children of God

To redeem those who were under the law, that we might receive the adoption as sons. And because you are sons, God has sent forth the Spirit of His Son into your hearts, crying out, "Abba, Father!"
Galatians 4:5-6

Adoption is a word full of emotion as well as glorious truth for every child who has experienced it. In our society, adoption is the choice of the prospective parents. The child has little input unless he is older. Most adopted babies are carried away from an orphanage or from parents who do not want the responsibility of care and provision.

Adjusting the mind and heart of an adopted child is often traumatic, as he grows up learning that he was not wanted by his birth parents. Other children can be mean-spirited with ugly words when they learn that the child has been adopted.

However, there are several ways that our western idea of adoption falls short of the biblical metaphor. In fact, the Bible adds to the western idea of adoption by inserting the Roman practices. The Romans took the firstborn son and, at maturity, placed him before his peers and superiors and assigned him full-fledged privileges and responsibilities in what might, more accurately, be called "son placing." This is what God will one day do for all His children.

The role that the Holy Spirit plays in us as adopted children is important in this context. God, as our adoptive parent, takes us from the authority and superintendence of the enemy and places us in His own loving, protective custody.

The Holy Spirit within helps us learn and adjust in the transition from children of disobedience to children of the living God. When we disobey, we become fearful of being disowned. When we fail, we wonder how disappointed our Father might be. When we fall and get our clothes dirty, we are concerned how our Father will react. When we sin, we are anxious about the chastisement that is our due. When we doubt, we may be seized with anxiety about our future as a child.

The Spirit, however, teaches and trains us to say the simple and profound words, "Father, Father." He will continue to teach us of the eternal love of the Father, our permanent union with our Father, the unvarying provision from our Father, the unchanging forgiveness of our Father, and the unending devotion of our Father to all His children. This is not because of what we do, but because of who we are. We are the children of God our Father.

ൠ ———————————————— ൪

Father, thank you for making me Your child. I confess that I do not fully accept this blessing. I choose to listen and learn from the Spirit.

Faithfulness and Fellowship

God is faithful, by whom you were called into the
fellowship of His Son, Jesus Christ our Lord.

1 Corinthians 1:9

The hymn, from which the title of these meditations comes, reiterates the words of this important verse: "Great is Thy Faithfulness." One of the purposes of Scripture is to teach the faithfulness of God. Each biblical story is a reminder that He can be trusted by anyone, in every circumstance of life.

The specific area of faithfulness in this verse is the "fellowship of His Son." Two great words are put together: faithfulness and fellowship. Faithfulness has to do with dependability, integrity, and reliability. But the faithfulness of God is not measured by the scale of our expectations. We might entertain the idea that God will always do what we want. We may pray that we would never get sick and feel that God is unfaithful when we are ill because He could have prevented it and did not.

But God's faithfulness relates primarily to His promises. They are fully and openly declared in His Word. We may easily misread or misunderstand them, but they remain the fountain from which blessings come to us. God's faithfulness does not mean that He will do all that we ask, because we do ask for wrong things and for wrong purposes. We may challenge the faithfulness of God by our unsound judgment of His actions.

The second word of importance is the beautiful word "fellowship." This is the Greek word *koinonia* which is translated different ways to deliver the precious meanings of sharing, giving, and receiving. The "fellowship of His Son" is the abundant sharing of the Son of God with all in the Family of God. It is natural for a child to say of some special toy, "It's mine and you can't have it." But all that belongs to Christ is freely shared with every believer equally.

Fellowship is broken when one person is unfaithful to the other. A marriage bond is not broken by unfaithfulness, but the fellowship and enjoyment of that relationship is destroyed. Sin breaks fellowship, but not our relationship. God is faithful to hold our relationship together by giving His life to us. God is faithful in keeping His fellowship unbroken because His Son does not break the connection. What joy to know that the fellowship of His Son cannot be spoiled by Christ. That, of course, means that if fellowship is hurt, it is something that I must mend and repair through confession and recommitment. It's not God's fault—He is Faithful.

ဟ ———————————— ဪ

Father, thank you for giving an unbreakable relationship. Thank you for being faithful and wanting fellowship with me.

Holy Spirit in Residence

Who also has sealed us and given us the
Spirit in our hearts as a deposit.

2 Corinthians 1:22

God must have known that we need to be repeatedly reminded that the Holy Spirit has been given to every believer. What Paul adds in 2 Corinthians 1:22 is that He is in our heart. Some people mistakenly believe that the Spirit leaves us whenever we fail, only to return to us when we ask for forgiveness.

This Scripture is a powerful reminder that the Spirit is a *permanent* possession of every believer as a guarantee of all the blessings included in the gift of Christ. Sealing is a reminder of security and ownership by God. A seal was put on the grave of our Lord, but that did not impede His departure from the tomb. Only God can apply a seal which cannot be broken or defaced.

The Spirit is not given as an accompanying angel hovering nearby along our pilgrim journey. He is not given as a parent who can be called on by a child with a cry of alarm. He is not an employee that shows up for duty at appointed times, only to depart at another time. Nor is He a master sergeant, a servant, a captain, a lucky charm, a power, or a host of other images created by our carnal mind.

Since He dwells in our being, the Holy Spirit is there to inspire the activities of our thinking.

This Person is a resident in our heart. The heart in the Scriptures refers to the core of our being. Perhaps we can understand it by reminding ourselves that we are a soul with capacities for thinking (our mind), for deciding (our will), and for feeling (our emotions). The heart is usually considered to include all three of these aspects of our personality. It is inconceivable that any person can be closer and more intimately involved in our life than to dwell in our soul or heart.

Since He dwells in our being, the Holy Spirit is there to inspire the activities of our thinking, encourage our deciding, and stimulate our feelings. As a person, the Holy Spirit also has mind, will, and emotions, because He is the eternal Spirit of God. The harmony of my mind with that of the Spirit, the surrender of my will and my emotions to His, brings a personal guarantee of the display of Christ-likeness. God has given us His Spirit as a seal of ownership and a guarantee of all the other blessings found in Christ.

ଚ —————————————— ଓ

Father, thank you for the gift of Your Spirit as a permanent, personal possession dwelling in my heart. I choose to obey Him.

The Abiding Truth

Because of the truth which abides in us and will be with us forever.

2 John 2

No one else could rightly be called the *Truth* other than our Lord Jesus Christ, who said, "I am the way, the truth, and the life" (John 14:6). Truth is one of the primary controversies that John was called upon to deal with in his writings. Over and over again he pleaded for the truth against the lie of the enemy. He campaigned for truth from the mouths of his disciples. He wanted a true life, true behavior, true words, and a true message. During the days of John, the temptation was to tarnish the message, to take away from the person of Christ, or to add something to the work of Christ.

John begins by laying the foundation of all spiritual arguments. Truth is the issue. He was well aware that "truth will allow no error, but error will allow some truth." The enemy's deception is so effective because he allows subtle truth to cover his lies. A layer of truth is like a candy coating that makes the deadly lie acceptable to many. The coating of candy must be cracked and the compound inside carefully examined in the laboratory of truth.

John is not urging us to pray for the truth. He says categorically that the truth abides in us.

We have the Scriptures which stand as the judge and jury in any courtroom where truth is being challenged. What does the Bible say? If it is inconsistent with or contrary to the Word of God, it must be dismissed, even if it has some truth in it. Both the written Word and the living Word are Truth.

The special blessing that John announces to us is "the truth which abides in us." That is a profound statement, and one that should be a source of great blessing and security. But the fact that the Truth lives in us does not guarantee that we give Him the freedom to work in our lives and words. Christ came into our being the moment that we believed the gospel, but we bear the responsibility of allowing Him full authority to determine what we say. Is it the truth? How do we live? Do we walk in the truth? Have we brought every thought into obedience to the truth?

John is not urging us to pray for the truth. He says categorically that the truth abides in us. Can we lose the truth through sin or disobedience or unbelief? No! It will be with us forever. The truth is there. Let us learn it, listen to it, love it, lean on it, and live the truth. In a day to come, controversy will depart as the Truth reigns supreme.

Father, thank you for the absolute standard of truth placed in my life. I confess that I have not given it free reign in my life as I should. I submit to it today.

Christ-like Through Suffering

For it was fitting for Him, for whom are all things and by whom are all things, in bringing many sons to glory, to make the author of their salvation perfect through sufferings.

Hebrews 2:10

The goal of God in saving us is to populate heaven with people who resemble His Son, Jesus Christ. But most of us behave far differently than He wants of His children. The long term program is to save and transform us by His grace. In the beginning, God created a son in Adam. But Adam's sin ruined that relationship for himself and for his children.

God's desire for His sons is for them to live in harmony with the overall aspect of His sovereignty. In fact, it defines a significant dimension of His purpose. All things are designed for His delight. All things came into being for Him. Fallen man must be regenerated by His intervention into humanity. He gave permission for sin to come into His creation in order to allow a part of His being to be radiated which we would have missed in a perfect society.

The roadblock to bringing Adam's sons into glory was their own sinfulness. God dealt with that by the sacrifice of His only begotten Son. Our sonship is accomplished when we receive God's life made possible through the resurrection and glorification of Christ. Had we not received the life of God, we could not be called the sons of God. The qualifying characteristic of any son is that he possesses his father's life, imparted through conception and birth. Without the life of God, we are children of the flesh and not the Spirit. The gift of the Holy Spirit is the transaction that imparts the life of God, giving me the authority and power to become a child of God.

> *"He learned obedience by the things which He suffered."*

But calling every believer a son of God does not innately change the behavior of His children. Had God been satisfied with a label of sonship, there would be no need for discipline and learning Christ-likeness through suffering. Christ was fulfilled and complete because He experienced suffering as a finalizing aspect of His training. We cannot share in Christ's vicarious suffering for sin, but we can share in the suffering that He went through as a learning experience. "He learned obedience by the things which He suffered" (Hebrews 5:8). Through discipline and training, we become more like Christ. Likeness is possible because we have His life. Likeness is fulfilled as we surrender to the sufferings that our Father allows in our life.

ЯО ———————————— СЯ

Father, thank you for making me Your son by giving me Your life. I celebrate being brought into glory as a full and perfect son.

Angels are Watching

And to make all people see what is the fellowship of the mystery,
which from the beginning of the ages has been hidden in God
who created all things through Jesus Christ; to the intent that
now the manifold wisdom of God might be made known by the
church to the principalities and powers in the heavenly places.

Ephesians 3:9-10

Angels desire to understand those things that are of vital importance to the church. Several times in Scripture, we are reminded that the angelic host is watching and wanting to know the ramifications of Christ's redemptive program to fallen humans. Peter says that the angels desire to look into the complexities of salvation as it has played out in God's plan over the centuries. Paul says in 1 Corinthians 11 that the angels watch the gatherings of the church as it meets for the Lord's Supper. Again, he says that we will judge the angels.

Angels yearn to see that oneness in the body of Christ displayed by the church.

God withheld from us several mysteries and waited until His chosen time for their unveiling. The great mystery referred to is the fact that Jews and Gentiles were to accept the same salvation by faith and enjoy the same blessings in Christ. For so long, the Jews thought that they were exclusively the people of God. They believed that God could not give any of their blessings to anybody else, particularly to the nations of the world.

But the Jews had refused the good news that Christ preached. They rejected Christ by crucifying Him. In the book of Acts, a number of Jews came to faith in Christ and began to see that the blessings of Abraham could be enjoyed and appreciated by them solely through Christ, the risen Messiah. Some believing Jews felt that these blessings should not overflow to the Gentiles, even if they believed in Christ. The Holy Spirit stopped them and said that both the Jews and the Gentiles receive the same blessings, enjoy the same promises, and have the same position in Christ. No difference exists. One group is not better than the other. All are the same in redemption, sonship, sanctification, position, privilege, and all the other blessings that come to believers. Angels yearn to see that oneness in the body of Christ displayed by the church.

The angels are listening and learning. They are informed and interested. They are watching and wondering. They are observing us. What wisdom are we making known by our life and lips?

———— ❧ ———————————————— ❧ ————

Father, we stand amazed that the unseen angelic host is interested in how we live out Your salvation. I offer my life to You for them to see.

The Privilege of Suffering

For to you it has been granted on behalf of Christ, not
only to believe in him, but also to suffer for His sake.

Philippians 1:29

The opportunity to believe in Christ is a special gift that God has given to the world. No one can come to the Father but by Christ, and no one can come except the Father Himself draws them. Because salvation is available only through Christ, our response as believers should always be a grateful and thankful heart for the opportunity to become a member of God's family. Give thanks today for that wonderful blessing.

We may walk through the valley of the shadow of death for a time, but we will dwell in the house of the Lord forever.

Philippians 1:29 reminds us that the opportunity to suffer is given to every believer. For such suffering, it is much harder to give an honest and full thanksgiving. This remarkable statement comes from the pen of Paul who, in Philippi, went through suffering which included being in prison. Paul's response from the jail in Rome was to praise and glorify God. It is recorded in Acts that the apostles gave thanks that they were counted worthy to suffer for the Lord.

We must first remind ourselves that everything that comes into the life of a believer is allowed by God or is sent by Him. Nothing happens to us without the Father's permission. In that truth, we find a basis to say "thank you" to the Father for such a blessing. He trusts me to suffer.

Believers suffer for many reasons. One is a refining process, which is God's way of purging out the dross of selfishness. Placing a seed in the soil produces fruit in a new life. We, too, are put into the soil in order to die to self, that we might rise in resurrection power and live, not to ourselves, but to Him who raised me. The grape must be crushed in order to release the juice produced over the 90 days of growth. Only then can it be processed to bring forth wine for those of a heavy heart. The clay must not only be pressed and squeezed for a vessel to be pleasing to the potter; it must also be put in the furnace to harden the shape of the clay. The rock from the mine must be crushed and the powder mixed with acids before being heated seven times over. Only then can gold be poured out 99-percent pure. The school desk is hard, the lessons cheerless, the tests arduous, the rules rigorous, but the end of all these is glorious. We may walk through the valley of the shadow of death for a time, but we will dwell in the house of the Lord forever.

— ∞ ———————————— ∞ —

Father, thank you for giving me suffering. I realize that believing does not insulate me from the suffering that You bring into my life.

Members of the Body of Christ

But now God has set the members, each one of
them, in the body just as He pleased.

1 Corinthians 12:18

Every believer has an important function within the body of Christ. God has put you exactly where He wants you—yet not all believers are happy with where God has placed them. Some of us think that we have an important function in the body. We imagine that, if we had a more visible ministry, we would be more effective. If only we had a more vocal position, so much more would be accomplished. If only God did what pleases me instead of what pleases Him!

We are placed as members in the body as only a perfect Designer would do. It is for us to accept the place of His choosing. Some are on beds of sickness for a lifetime and may never be "visible." One may be hidden on the other side of the globe and may never be heard from. A few are placed in the midst of suffering which results in a short life. Another may be caring for children and never stand behind a pulpit. Some may sit at a computer; others may cook or clean.

Some sisters thrust themselves into public ministry, when God has not placed them in the body for that purpose. Such a circumstance is like trying to drive a nail with a fine, long-stemmed goblet. It just doesn't work. Instead, we are to serve where God has put us!

God does not scatter us like seed in the earth, but places us as a chosen plant in His garden. Each one of us has been carefully designed for his place in the body. An elbow does not make a good lung. A toenail does not make a useful ear. An intestine would make a foul mouth! Many of our members, if not most, are found inside the body, providing non-visible and non-vocal service to the rest of the members. Few of our members are truly pleasing to the eye.

Can we accept the wisdom of God, who has put us in the place of His choosing, without complaining and seeking a different position? We should seek to be as useful as possible in doing our part for the smooth functioning of the body. Fighting among members in the body seriously impairs our usefulness. As the poem says, "Do what you can, being what you are. Glow as a glow worm if you can't be a star." God has put you where He wants you.

ℰ ———————————— ℭ

Father, thank you for placing me in the body of Christ according to Your
wisdom and design. I confess my desire to be more prominent. I trust You to
use me so that the body will function for Your glory.

God, the Rewarder

*But without faith it is impossible to please Him, for he
who comes to God must believe that He is, and that He
is a rewarder of those who diligently seek Him.*

Hebrews 11:6

Take four words of this text and feed on them all day: "He is a rewarder."
Like cutting a rose from your garden and making it a centerpiece on
your table, some words can be cut out of a text and provide fragrance
to the entire house. Gaze on it, observe it, enjoy its perfume, stop each time
you walk by it, and extol its richness. At the end of the day, you have feasted
your eyes on its colors, your nostrils have absorbed its aroma, your hands
have touched the delicate tapestry. You have made that one rose your own.

Do that today with this wonderful phrase. In doing so, the glory of its truth
will flood your soul. It will not fade as a flower, because it is more gloriously
real than any rose. It is new today, still fresh tonight, and in the morning its
fragrance and loveliness are unchanged.

The long list of saints and sinners who have proven this truth will only be
revealed in glory, as each one tells the story of His rewards: the faithful
steward who is now ruler over ten cities; Abraham, who walked up the hill
called Moriah with his only son Isaac; Noah, who floated for a year in his
own boat with God as his captain; Moses, who dared to confront Pharaoh;
Elijah, who believed that fire comes from heaven; Peter, who concluded that
"trust and obey" were stepping stones in the storm on
Galilee; Nicodemus, who with little faith came by
night; the wise men, who rode long and bowed low;
the shepherds, who listened and left their sheep to
see the Savior.

*Is it safe to
trust God?
Yes, He is the
only safe one
to trust.*

God rewards faith. The records in the Bible are
primarily written to disclose God and to inform us
that the One who is revealed is a rewarder of any
who place their faith in Him. Is it safe to trust God?
Yes, He is the only safe one *to* trust. He rewarded the paralytic who came
for healing by forgiving his sin. He fed, with miraculous bread, the hungry
multitude that came to Him. He gave sight to the blind who called to Him for
mercy. He cleansed nine unthankful lepers. He gave salvation to a little man
sitting in a sycamore tree. He gave discipleship to a man that He saw under a
fig tree. He gave paradise to a lone sinner hanging on a cross.

છ —————————————— ૪

*Father, we believe that one day all who have placed faith in You will be
fully rewarded. We trust Your Word and obey its truth, counting on Your
faithfulness to reward such confidence.*

Dying to Live

*To them God willed to make known what are the
riches of the glory of this mystery among the Gentiles:
which is Christ in you, the hope of glory.*

Colossians 1:27

The risen Christ dwells in every believer. The resurrection of Christ is the reason that He can take up residence in us. A dead person cannot live in another, but one who has been raised from the dead has the ability to live in all who were "in Him" at death and resurrection.

Romans 6 tells us that, when Christ died and rose, all who would believe were in fact "in Christ." Because of His resurrection, He gives all that He is to those who receive His life. As a seed gives its life, so in resurrection all seeds borne by that tree share all the qualities of the seed that died. The same color, size, flavor, weight, fragrance, and, above all, the same life, is given to every seed.

Because Christ dwells in all believers, we have the prospect of glory in a hope that is as sure as the resurrection of Christ Himself. To understand the riches of this glory, we must accept the same path that our Lord took. To know resurrection, we must first die to self. Our Lord died, not for Himself but for us, and so we follow in His footsteps. We die to ourselves in order that we might live unto "Him who died for us and rose again."

This, of course, is not a goal or struggle but a pattern and principle that we see every day in the garden. We die, not to obtain salvation, but because we follow the glorious path of our Savior. Is it safe to die? Ask the seed! It will say, "It is the only safe thing *to* do." If we live to ourselves, we will die alone. But if we die to self, we will live. That is the principle of the risen Christ carrying on His life in us. Which is more glorious in resurrection, the seed or the plant? Surely the plant is more glorious, displaying new life through death and resurrection.

> *. . . that Christ
> may show forth the
> exceeding riches of
> His grace to all.*

What a display is worked out in every believer who chooses to die, that Christ may show forth the exceeding riches of His grace to all. If we refuse to die, we will remain by ourselves and never become what God intended. If we die to self, His principle of life takes over and shapes our ends, causing us to live to the praise of His glory.

☏ ———————————— ❧

Father, thank you for giving the risen Christ to live in me. I acknowledge that I often choose not to live in the light of His presence. Today I die to my own plans and surrender to Your life in me.

Resurrection—With or Without Death

Our Lord Jesus Christ . . . died for us, that whether we
wake or sleep, we should live together with Him.

1 Thessalonians 5:9-10

The death of Christ did far more than provide a fire escape from eternal judgment. A number of profound and practical accomplishments are results of the death and resurrection of our Savior. Redemption from sin is a most important aspect of Christ's death. Propitiation of a holy God is His satisfaction from the death of Christ. Reconciliation is a great accomplishment of God in the substitution of Christ for us. All of these benefits hung in the balance until Christ was raised from the dead.

Paul reminds us that, if Christ is not raised from the dead, we are still in our sin and the most miserable of men. But this statement was made in the greatest passage defending the resurrection of Christ—1 Corinthians 15. If Christ is not raised, we are consigned to death and eternal separation from God. The risen Christ reminds us that our own resurrection was secured by His visible resurrection.

Part of the return of Christ will be the announcement of His appearance by trumpet, a loud shout, the voice of the archangel, and other events of our joining Christ in glorified bodies. The dead will be raised from the grave first, and those who are alive at the coming of Christ will be caught away to join the transformed bodies of the believers who were in the grave. What a glorious reunion of friends and family who know Christ. Yet how much greater it will be to see our Savior face to face!

His death and resurrection are such grand events that Christ's spectacular victory over death is communicated to all who believe. Those who have passed through death have the promise of resurrection. Those who are alive have the promise of escape from the very door of death itself.

The basis of this shared victory with all His saints is the death of Christ for us. "He died for us" is Paul's grand proclamation at the end of his defense of our union with Christ. Two glorious prospects are laid before us: to be with Christ and to be like Him. The only way for those two things to take place is for Christ to die for us and for us to die with Him. We share His death. Christ was raised, and we have been raised with Him. There is no consignment to the wrath of God since we have been delivered by the death and resurrection of the Lord Jesus Christ.

„ ———————————— ‘‘

Father, thank you for delivering me from Your wrath by Christ's death. I am not anxious about how or when I will meet Christ. I await my union with Him, whether by death or translation.

Looking Like Our Father

Behold what manner of love the Father has bestowed on
us, that we should be called children of God! Therefore the
world does not know us, because it did not know Him.

1 John 3:1

The word "children" is used most often to describe those who belong to God. He does not tire of repeating this exquisite picture by reminding His children where they received their life. Where we came from, what we brought with us, our beginning, birth, baptism, and blessings—all are inscribed on God's family crest.

We bear the family likeness because of training received from the Father and modeled by His Son.

The family connection began before the foundation of the world, when we were chosen in Christ. A "chosen child" seems to be a display of favoritism, which our Father repudiates in 1 Peter 1:17. But God gave His Son to die for us and the motive was love. His love is higher than any other. "Greater love has no one than this, than to lay down one's life for his friends" (John 15:13). His is a love which is greater in its length and breadth and height and depth than any other love. It is unfathomable love.

The primary characteristic of a child is that he possesses the life of his parents. God also uses that distinction to set us apart from those in the world who are without God and therefore without His life. He who has the Son has life. God has lavished His life and love on us by implanting His Son in us. This life cannot be taken away for, to do so, His love would have to be removed as well. How can a perfect Father cease to love? The love of my Father has taken up residence in my heart and soul, because God is love.

His life is able to reproduce the family traits in our conduct and behavior. If we walk like our Savior, it is largely because Christ is walking through us. If we talk like Christ, it is chiefly because He is using our mouth to speak His words. We bear the family likeness because of training received from the Father and modeled by His Son. Perfect imitation is not possible and will not bring glory to our Father. As we surrender to the life of Christ within, He will produce His love through us. The characteristics of God are revealed, with the result that the world does not recognize us or want to be identified with us. The world did not know Christ. So as much as we are like Him, the world will give us the same disapproval.

——— ———

Father, thank you for loving me before I could even love You. Your love was first, and my response is only because of Your love to me.

28 MAY

Two Sacrificial Goats

*And you know that He was manifested to take
away our sins, and in Him there is no sin.*

1 John 3:5

God sent Christ into the world for a specific purpose: to take away our sins. At His incarnation it was announced, "He shall save His people from their sins." It is true that He gave a perfect example of obedience and dependence on His Father, but a perfect example would not atone for any sin. Sin must be carried away. The fact that they are carried suggests getting under the load of sin and bearing them far from the person who has sinned.

That picture was drawn by God Himself in Leviticus 16 when He instituted the Day of Atonement for the nation of Israel. The instructions for the High Priest were to take two goats from the people, one of which was to live as a sin bearer. As this goat stood before the High Priest, God's representative would place his hand on the head of the goat and confess all the sins of Israel on that animal. The goat was then taken to a deserted place and let loose to live in isolation from the nation of Israel.

The second goat was killed before the altar in the tabernacle courtyard. The blood was caught in a basin, carried into the Most Holy Place, and sprinkled on the mercy seat. When God saw the blood of the substitute on the mercy seat, He considered the sins of Israel covered.

Covering sin was adequate for a time, but it could not atone for the sins of the world forever. The Day of Atonement was repeated each year because the sacrifice of the blood of the goat was inadequate for all time.

> *Covering sin was adequate for a time, but it could not atone for the sin of the world forever.*

The work of Christ on the cross fulfills the picture of both of these goats. He died to pay the full sacrifice for our sins. He said, "It is finished." Christ, who took on the load of our sins and carried them as far as the east is from the west, is pictured by the other goat. He took them away, never to be brought against us again.

How did He do this? He is sinless. His own people affirmed, "This man has done nothing amiss." "This was a righteous man." "I have betrayed innocent blood." He needed no sacrifice for His own sin, for in Him there was no sin, "who Himself bore our sins in His own body on the tree" (1 Peter 2:24). Our sins are forever gone.

₭ ———————————— ℋ

Father, thank you for fully and completely taking away all my sins. I know that I stand in Christ forgiven because He died in my place.

Crucifying the Old Man

Knowing this, that our old man was crucified with
Him, that the body of sin might be done away with,
that we should no longer be slaves of sin.

Romans 6:6

Jesus died on the cross—but only physically. The words "death" and "died" almost always suggest the end or cessation of life. That is true physically, but it is by no means true spiritually. The Lord Jesus was crucified, but He did not cease to exist. For a time, He was separated from God for our sin. "He gave up His spirit" suggests that living was changed from a physical realm to a spiritual one. That is also true for all believers when we are brought to the door of death. Passing through that door ushers us into a capacity of life much richer and more expansive than we can imagine.

So when Romans 6:6 says that "our old man was crucified with Him," it does not mean that the "old man" ceases to exist, or that he no longer has any hungers, lusts, desires, or drives. Rather, our old man was put to death in the sense that he was separated from his position of dominion to a place of submission to the new life of Christ that dwells in each believer.

Before we trusted Christ and possessed the indwelling Son, the sin nature had free rein. No controls were in place and no outside force could curb or shut down the sinful desires. That does not mean that all of us were as sinful as we could be; rather, it means that we did not have any ability to depose the old man off the throne from which he ruled our lives.

It is easy for the flesh to think that we must continually deny the desires of the body with all the energy that we can muster. Martin Luther attempted to do this by punishing his body. He learned from the Scriptures that the old man cannot be corrected or trained to be better. There is nothing good in my flesh (Romans 7:18).

When Christ controls,
we are no longer
slaves of sin,
but of Christ.

Paul reminds us that we know what took place at the cross, yet many believers still do not understand. They attempt through legalism, license, or modification of behavior to bring good out of what is fully evil. The answer to this conflict is to remember that our old man was removed from the throne of our life and Christ was established as Lord. It is true that we can invite the flesh to sit as king again, but the result is separation from the blessings that God wishes to impart through Christ's control. When Christ controls, we are no longer slaves of sin, but of Christ.

Father, thank you for the power of Christ to subdue the old man.

30
MAY

Spiritual Healing

Who Himself bore our sins in His own body on the
tree, that we, having died to sins, might live for
righteousness—by whose stripes you were healed.
                                                    1 Peter 2:24

L oud voices have preached this verse, teaching that true believers should not be sick. The main theme of this idea is that, if you have enough faith, God will heal all your diseases. The one who remains sick obviously does not have enough faith and so returns to a darker future and deeper frustration with his spiritual and physical sickness. The Lord is not the author of such nonsense. The sufferings in our present body may be sent by the same Lord who "healed all our diseases."

Jesus died for us so that our spiritual healing will be full and complete. His suffering in body and soul is satisfactory to the Father, who will make all things new—including our physical body. The sufferings of this present time in this body of humiliation are not worthy to be compared with the body that is not made with hands and awaiting us in glory.

A note rung by all New Testament authors is the identification of every believer with Christ in His death. When Christ died *for* our sin, we died with Him *to* our sin. Does this mean that we no longer have a problem with sin or sickness? Obviously not. The word "death" does not suggest that the desires of sin have been annihilated or cease to exist. Rather, the hungers of sin have been separated from the very things that sin wants to feed on. Sin is not annihilated. The lusts of the sinful nature have been set apart from the food that it so desperately seeks.

This victory over sin is made possible by the indwelling Christ, who has presented the believer with a host of new desires which are contrary to the flesh. As believers, we now hunger for spiritual food and spiritual fulfillment which overwhelms the cravings that ruled our life before Christ came to dwell inside.

The lifestyle of every believer can be characterized by righteousness, empowered by faith, dominated by the truth, and directed by the Holy Spirit. The work of God in and through that life will begin to manifest the spiritual healing power of a transformed life. The changed behavior is a powerful message of spiritual healing from within, even in the midst of physical sickness.

ઇ ———————————————— ଔ

Father, thank you for the substitutionary sacrifice of the Lord Jesus Christ,
my Savior. I am set free from the tyranny of sin and choose to live in the
power of Christ, who gives me victory over indwelling sin.

The Big Lie

I have not written to you because you do not know the truth,
but because you know it, and that no lie is of the truth.

1 John 2:21

An insightful saying states, "Truth will allow no error, but error will allow some truth." Christ announced to the disciples in the upper room, "I am the truth."

A group of Bible students were asked, "If you could change anything in the world, what would you change?" A number of answers were offered: eliminate AIDS, remove sickness, take everyone to heaven, eradicate poverty, etc. The answer that the professor had hoped to hear was that everyone would tell the truth.

Only the Lord Jesus always told the truth. Dishonesty is a disease that affects all human beings. It is not something that we learn from the previous generation. All of us know how to lie and do it without thinking. Lying is set apart from other sins when God says, "and all liars shall have their part in the lake that burns with fire and brimstone" (Revelation 21:8).

> *To know Christ*
> *is to know*
> *the Truth.*

Akin to lying is deception, a specialty of Satan. The level of deception in our world is beyond comprehension. It is impossible to pass a day without being faced with some kind of deception, whether it be a politician talking, a magazine advertisement, a TV commercial, or a radio promotion. The enemy of our souls is the biggest deceiver, and he allows some truth to creep into his deception.

The Lord Jesus says that the devil is a liar. He only tells the truth when he is talking to God. From the garden to the present, this enemy has fashioned error in such a contorted way that most are willing to receive it as truth. *The lie* is that man can be God without God, just as the serpent construed God's words: "You shall be as gods." It was his way of urging unfallen Eve to surrender her dependence on God and live independently, just as he had done in seeking to be like God. Today, his lie is the same in content, even if different in import. "You can be God without Christ" is his invitation through philosophy and empty religions. Most eastern religions offer a form of divinity by self effort without any reference to the sacrifice of the Lord Jesus Christ.

Christ Himself is the Truth, made known through the Word of God. To know Christ is to know the Truth. In Him is no deception at all.

ॐ ———————————— ☙

Father, thank you for giving me the truth without any error. I choose to read, learn, and obey Your Word.

June

SPECIFIC GIFTS GIVEN TO YOU LONG BEFORE YOU KNEW THEM

". . . filled with the fruits of righteousness
which are by Jesus Christ . . ."

Philippians 1:11

Great is Thy faithfulness.
Great is Thy faithfulness.
Morning by morning new mercies I see;
All I have needed Thy hand hath provided.
Great is Thy faithfulness, Lord, unto me!

Thomas O Chisholm

June

The Potter and the Clay

Pottery is one of the oldest forms of manufacturing, yet the process has not changed over the millennia. Making pottery requires three ingredients, one complex and the other two very simple. The simple ingredients are the piece of clay taken from the earth and a potter's wheel. The complex ingredient is the potter, who is necessary to turn an inert piece of clay into a useful vessel.

The sovereignty of the potter is the essential ingredient in this metaphor. If we go to the potter's house, we would not think to challenge his right to make what he wants with his piece of clay. A potter can do as he chooses with his clay. He bought or dug the clay, and it is his. Interestingly enough , God asks in Romans 9:20 whether the piece of clay will ask the potter, "Why have you made me like this?"

In God's illustration, the wheel is the only thing without personality. God suggests personality in the clay which we might realistically question. But

God will answer us, reminding us that we are more closely related to the clay than to the Potter, since there is infinite distance between God and man, and only a finite distance between clay and man. Remember, we were made of the dust of the earth initially.

It is not always easy to see our similarity to clay. But what is important is that the clay will only experience the ultimate design of the potter through submission to the potter's hands. Jeremiah reminds us in chapter 18 that Israel refused to submit to God's plans and was destined to be made a different vessel. Can we conclude that the same may happen to us? If we refuse to abide by the plan and will of the Potter, will He choose to use us in another way? We would then only know His second best.

We are not without some idea of what the Potter has in mind for us. As a spectator observes what the potter is doing, he can guess the ultimate result. But we who have the mind of Christ have perfect guidance regarding where the Potter is headed with us as His clay.

In order to learn the design of the Potter and His will, we must be submissive. But we are also given the delight of inquiring of the Potter regarding His final design. His hands are the primary tools of His trade, but there are other tools that He may use to shape and mold us as He chooses. Potters use sharp knives, thin wires, smooth spatulas, pointed rods, rough cloths, and hardened chards to produce the desired effect. As we study the Word, we learn about those tools in His hands and how they were used in the lives of other vessels, such as Job, Abraham, Joseph, Moses, David, Jeremiah, and Paul. We also learn the results in each of these lives if they resisted the will of the Potter as in the life of Jonah.

The Potter is willing to give us insights into His plan and purpose. But we must accept the parameters of our involvement and allow God the limitless rights of His prerogative. Part of our learning is to try to grasp all that God has given us. He bought us through the precious blood of His Son.

Many of the aspects of His proficiency are laid out in the Word of God. As I appropriate the blessing of this relationship, God will do His work in me for His own good pleasure. We must not interrupt the Potter by asking, "Why are you making me like this?" His wheel may, on occasion, move very fast, or it may move too slowly for my plans. Loving hands mold, while a devoted foot controls the wheel and unswerving eyes focus on His piece of clay. His hands never seem to leave the clay. Of course, the vessel must be fired in order to be really useful, as Peter writes in 1 Peter 1:7: "That the trial of your faith . . . tried with fire" (KJV).

The whole process is in the mind of the Potter. Submission is my primary response. All the ingredients are embraced when the piece of clay is "thrown" on the wheel. Rest in the love and intelligent design of your Potter. Accept the fact of His sovereign control over every aspect of His fashioning. Appropriate His every intervention in the procedures to make you like His Son. Thank Him for His superintendence over every detail of your development.

Our Father's Guidance

Having made known to us the mystery of His will, according to His good pleasure which He purposed in Himself.

Ephesians 1:9

Knowing the will of God is a big hurdle for many believers. Many people ask, "How can I know the will of God?" or "What does God want me to do?" But God's will has been made known. The verb tense in Ephesians 1:9 declares that it is an accomplished fact. This simple concept, expressed by the Spirit, is hard to accept because we have been subtly taught that God is waiting for us to pray and plead with Him to show us what He is reluctant to reveal. God has, however, with special pleasure, chosen to disclose His will to us.

The truth is, God is more eager for us to know His will than we are to accomplish it. This verse, as well as others, opens to us the treasury of God's dealings with man. God has not put a maze before us that we must search through; rather, He has handed us a book that is available. The Holy Spirit, its Author, is in us to teach and guide us. The Lord Jesus, as the central character of the book, lives in us to define our path and to be the source of all truth. God gives His will through His Word. His Word is truth! We must expect that, as we read it, He will guide us moment by moment. Our problem is that we often do not open the book for guidance. Instead, we sit back, wishing that God would speak to us audibly or give some circumstance that is unusual or miraculous.

When Israel entered Canaan, God ceased to guide them by the visible pillar of fire and cloud; instead, He guided them by His written law (Joshua 1:9). Cloud guidance is for wilderness wandering, not for possessing Canaan. Ephesians is the New Testament exposition of entering and enjoying Canaan— our blessings in Christ, "in whom are hid all the treasures of wisdom and knowledge" (Colossians 2:3). It is in exploring the book that God says, "This is the way; walk in it." We walk by faith, not by seeing the cloud or hearing the sound of the trumpet. As we know Him better, we shall know His will more fully. Knowing God is the key to knowing His will.

Have we done what we know His book says? God has made known His will. It is no longer in mystery form but in clear, readable, reasonable responsibilities.

We have far more than the cloud that guided Moses. We have Christ and His Word. How blessed we are!

⟶ ❧ ⟶

Father, thank you for giving the full revelation of Your will in Your glorious Word. I commit my life to do what I learn from its pages.

The Word of God

For this reason we also thank God without ceasing, because
when you received the word of God which you heard from us,
you welcomed it not as the word of men, but as it is in truth, the
word of God, which also effectively works in you who believe.

1 Thessalonians 2:13

What does your Bible look like? Does it have a soft binding, gilt edging, smooth paper, and a nice marker or two so that you can find your place? There's nothing wrong with owning a beautiful-looking Bible, but most other books like that are for show, not work. Tools don't have to look good; they must do a job. The living Word of God in the hand of God Himself is a worker. It excavates a heart like a shovel, slashes thinking like a bush axe, cuts feelings like a weed-eater, and attacks false teaching like a chain saw. It *works!*

The people in Thessalonica received the Word of God, and it began its powerful work in them. When the soil receives a seed, the life of the seed begins its work of sending a shoot up and a root down. These folk experienced the work of God by the Word of God, described in 1 Peter 1:23. They had been "born again . . . through the word of God which lives." The amazing thing is that this lovely book is a powerful, living force, able to change the hardest heart. It is a hammer, a sword, a light, fire, oil, water, and seed, depending on the work that God sends it to do.

> The Word of God works in us to the degree that we welcome it.

The word "received" is the key to its working in us. Some shield themselves from its work the same way that fair-skinned people shield themselves from the sun. The Word of God works in us to the degree that we welcome it. Many receive it as the word of man, and in doing so they neutralize its message. To receive it is to open our heart, expose our emotions, and surrender our will, just as the soil does to a seed.

The word "believe" is a similar key to its power in our life. We must accept the truth of the Word and act in faith upon its message. Let it cut, dig, clean, pull, rake, sift, tear, and shift our behavior and practices. Dare we set it free in the garden of life to do its effective work? What a change it will work in our life!

───────── ❧ ─────────

Father, thank you for giving the living Word to work in my life. I surrender and allow it to change me as You choose. I believe in its power to bring my life into conformity to Your will.

High Priest

We have such a High Priest, who is seated at the right hand of the throne of the Majesty in the heavens, a Minister of the sanctuary and of the true tabernacle which the Lord erected, and not man.

Hebrews 8:1-2

Most religions have some person or persons who represent their people to their god, usually by offering sacrifices to appease the god's anger at their wrongdoing. No matter where anthropologists have gone, they have found some means, conceived by the people, to atone for their sin. In almost every case there has also been a special person responsible to perform these rites for the people.

God Himself set in motion a plan by which Israel would be represented to Him through a high priest. This servant was from the tribe of Levi, the office being passed down from father to son. The high priest's official duties included offering the sacrifice on the Day of Atonement and carrying the blood into the Most Holy Place as an atoning sacrifice. This ceremony was to be repeated annually.

The high priest was not always an honorable person or one who felt keenly the sinners' sense of sin. Some misused the office, as in the case of the two who were high priests when our Lord was accused, condemned, and crucified. Little did the people, the priests, or the high priest know that, in the very act of crucifying Christ, they fulfilled every type and picture carried out by the high priest since the time of Aaron, the first to hold the office.

Christ, as God, has perfect sympathy for all sinners who come to God for compassion and forgiveness. As man, He can feel the pain of man in his desire to overcome sin. Christ was raised from the dead, and He continues to serve in the office of Great High Priest forever (having been appointed after the order of Melchizedek, not Aaron, since He was of the tribe of Judah, not Levi).

No seats were in the tabernacle or the temple in Jerusalem. But Christ sits, because His sacrifice was satisfactory and complete. As the Great High Priest for all who believe, Christ continues as a minister of the heavenly tabernacle. As our Great High Priest, He has finished the work of redemption given Him by the Father—satisfactory and sufficient, final and eternal, once and forever done! Christ stated it clearly: "It is finished." He now sits as the interceding High Priest for His people.

❧ ———————————————— ☙

Father, thank you for giving me a perfect High Priest. I am satisfied with His sacrifice and His availability to feel my pain and desire to overcome evil habits. I draw near with a tender heart.

Riches

*That their hearts may be encouraged, being knit
together in love, and attaining to all riches of the full
assurance of understanding, to the knowledge of the
mystery of God, both of the Father and of Christ.*

Colossians 2:2

For a manufacturing company to prosper, it is vital that its inventory be handled wisely. What do we have? How many do we have? Where can we get more? How much will they cost? How long will it take to get them? Not knowing what you have on hand might lead to ordering things that you may not need. That would tie up financial capital and cost you dearly when you run out of some other item. Balancing inventory is crucial to success in business.

The same principle is true in the Christian life. What spiritual riches has God given us in Christ that all believers need to live useful lives? The answer to this important question is the focus of this devotional book. *Blessings All Mine With 10,000 Besides!* is a compilation of some of the riches that belong to us. We need assurance that we have them and a full understanding of their use.

We do not attain these riches by earning them or praying for them; they are given to every believer when he or she receives Christ as Savior. All these riches are in Christ. The problem we face is the same as the ignorant businessman. Because he does not know his inventory, he buys more, only to find out that he has plenty. Many believers think that God has not given them enough blessings, so they pray for more—only to discover in their Bible reading that they indeed have those blessings already.

Paul's concern is that we face the need for this spiritual wealth and that we get to know these blessings and use these riches. The problem is not a lack of possessions, but a lack of the knowledge of those resources. If we know that we have them, we can employ them in our lives, just as a good businessman employs what he has in stock to his best advantage.

Verse 3 goes on to state that Christ is the one "in whom are hid all the treasures of wisdom and knowledge." It is my responsibility to find out what God has given me in Christ. As I read the Scriptures, they tell me of my wealth in Christ. When I know these riches, I can understand and employ them. I learn of them, appreciate them, appropriate them, and grow into Christ-likeness. My response to all of this is the "thank you" of faith.

ಶಿ ——————————— ೞ

Father, thank you for giving to me Christ and all the riches hidden in Him. I accept those blessings by faith and seek to know and use them.

Access and Fellowship

*In whom we have boldness and access with
confidence through faith in Him.*

Ephesians 2:12

Access and nearness were lost to humanity when Adam brought sin into the world through his disobedience. The personal relationship between God and His creature had been perfect. God was available to the man and the woman, and they both enjoyed intimate communion in the cool of the day. As we seek to understand Adam's fellowship with God, it seems that the description Paul gives us of our relationship with God is all that Adam lost through sin. Much of the New Testament is devoted to God's plan of redemption and its execution to bring back the blessed union and communion of God and man.

The price to restore access was infinite, since the distance between God and man was immeasurable. Man had fled in sin and entered darkness and death. Adam and Eve were driven from the garden and from God's presence. Boldness was replaced by fear. Confidence was exchanged for dread. Even as God developed the plan in picture-form in the Old Testament, man demonstrated an apprehension and fear of God's presence, as demonstrated by the children of Israel at Mount Sinai.

God's desire was to return to man the access and nearness that He so missed. The program involved God becoming man and suffering for our sin. God could then forgive man's sin when he puts his faith in Christ. He would open the door to His throne room for every believer to approach Him. What a wonderful provision! How beautiful that God has restored to us all that Adam lost, *and much more.*

The psalmist says of Christ in Psalm 69:4, "Though I have stolen nothing, I still must restore it." Man forced God to remove access and nearness. Christ's work on the cross and His resurrection gave God the liberty to return to man access and nearness, and also to add personal intimate fellowship through the Holy Spirit and the indwelling Christ. In Christ, God is much nearer than He was to Moses, Noah, or even Adam. God can now be *in* man. A previously sinful man has available, near, accessible, and unrestricted fellowship with a holy God.

In addition, this access is so abundant that we can come boldly and confidently to Him. God desires our fellowship. Of course, our continuing sin makes that access less attractive, but God waits for us to confess any sin and enjoy restored fellowship.

❧ ─────────────── ❧

Father, You have opened wide the avenue of Your presence. I have Christ near to me always. Thank you for Christ.

Knowledge of Christ

But indeed I also count all things loss for the excellence of the knowledge of Christ Jesus my Lord, for whom I have suffered the loss of all things, and count them as rubbish, that I may gain Christ.
Philippians 3:8

God has revealed through the Scriptures all that we need to know to live the Christian life. Sometimes we are tempted to ask the Father to unveil new knowledge of Him to meet some special need. That desire and effort should be directed toward personally knowing Christ Jesus.

> *We are responsible to get the information, understand it, and employ it.*

Paul was willing to offer up everything of human value in order to appreciate the excellence of the knowledge of Christ. In Philippians 3, he is not asking God to reveal *more* of Christ to him. We are often more comfortable waiting for God to reveal Christ than to realize that God is waiting for me to set aside everything else of human value and, in diligence and discipline, get to know my Lord myself.

We are like a child who asks his father to explain why a light bulb glows when he turns on a switch. The father can choose to give a long explanation and details from his training as an electrical engineer or he can say, "Go to your computer, open the encyclopedia, and learn the wonderful properties of electricity and a bulb." The father provides access to an abundance of information by giving his son a computer and a link to all the detailed drawings and descriptions to answer his question. Like the son, we are responsible to get the information, understand it, and employ it. God has revealed the totality of His person in His Son by and through the Word. With the revelation available, God is waiting for us to set aside things of temporal value in order to obtain knowledge that has eternal value. The choice is ours.

Yet how often we would rather pray for a revelation from God than change our life of spiritual indolence and confess our lethargy in these matters. A few minutes reading a short meditation like this will not suffice for a person who, like Paul, changed his entire value system in order to gain an intimate knowledge of Christ. We tend to assess eternal and temporal things on the same value scale. The alternatives for us are clear. The issue is not so much having "things" as putting the world's stuff so far up the scale that Christ does not have the preeminence in our lives. Christ must be first!

ॐ ─────────── ☙

Father, thank you for giving the full revelation of Your Son to us. I confess that I do not value the knowledge of Him as I should.

Union

But he who is joined to the Lord is one spirit with Him.

1 Corinthians 6:17

The closest union known in human relations is the bond that a baby shares with his parents. As the child grows, those who know the parents observe the parents' likeness radiated and reflected in him. A certain oneness of body exists because they share genes and DNA.

Another fusion designed by the Creator is the union of husband and wife in physical relations. God chose this intimacy as a means of demonstrating the oneness of spirit that the Lord made possible by implanting His life in us by His Holy Spirit. And from 1 Timothy 3:16 we see that this mystery is a miracle comparable to the implanted life in the virgin Mary for the birth of Jesus Christ. "Without controversy, great is the mystery of godliness: God was manifested in the flesh."

The birth of Jesus demonstrated the closest union of God and man ever revealed to human perception. The resulting individual was not a split personality or a man with multiple personalities. Instead, the Lord Jesus Christ is the perfect revelation as the God-Man—absolutely God and totally man. The exception is that Jesus did not have a sinful nature and could not sin. He exists as one person, now glorified both spiritual and physically.

Our union to the Lord is the result of the fulfillment of Christ's work on the cross, celebrated in His resurrection, capped by His ascension, and finalized by His seated position in heaven today. My faith in the person of Christ sets God free to create in me a union with Himself that is much more than a joining together in marriage. It is a union that is as eternal as God Himself, since we both possess the same life—the life of God Himself. "This life is in His Son" (1 John 5:11).

This relationship makes me a spiritual person and guarantees my transcendence beyond time and space when I see the Lord Himself in glory. God has given us the glorious promise of union that is beyond any conception of man's intellect. The amazing union of human flesh with God's Spirit correlates the miracle of the virgin birth with our spiritual birth. Second only to the mystery of God manifested in Jesus' flesh is the life of God manifested in my mortal flesh. The daily activities that order my behavior give me opportunity to make this spiritual union known where I live. What possibilities! What responsibilities!

— ∞ ——————————— ∞

Father, thank you for sending the Lord Jesus to die for us, rise because of us, ascend without us, and be united to us in the Holy Spirit.

Reveal Christ

*. . . It pleased God, who separated me from my mother's
womb and called me through His grace, to reveal His Son
in me, that I might preach Him among the Gentiles . . .*

Galatians 1:15-16

Paul never lost sight of his calling and commission, given by God on the road to Damascus. It lit the roadway of his life's journey, at the end of which he could say that he had not disobeyed that heavenly vision.

We don't all have the same calling and commission as Paul, but we do share one of the important drives of his life: that God's Son be revealed in him. This responsibility did not depend on his calling as an apostle, his gift as a preacher, his travels as an evangelist, his vocation as a master builder, his suffering as a prisoner, or his writings as an author. It was dependent on the indwelling Christ in his life.

This is the challenge to everyone who trusts Christ as Savior. The moment we believe the gospel and experience God's salvation, His goal is to write the message of Christ's life in our life. We are God's book for the world. For those who cannot read the Word, we are a picture-book of Christ's life. We are called to display the graces of Christ in the way that we live. We are God's mouth-piece in the same way that Christ was the mouth-piece of the Father.

> *We are called to
> make an invisible
> Christ visible.*

The Lord Jesus came into the world to make the invisible God visible. That was the first and only perfect revelation of the Father in visible form. We as believers are called to make an invisible Christ visible. And, despite the fact that we fail time and again to portray Him as we should, we are still responsible to reveal Him in our flesh. "No one has seen God at any time"—Christ revealed Him. No one sees Christ today—we are called to reveal Him.

This revelation of Christ is not a result of imitation. We do not try to live as Jesus lived. If we were successful in that imitation, we would get glory for our artistic skills. Instead, God sent Jesus Christ to dwell in every believer to live His life through our body and soul. For that reason, we offer Him our being to control as He chooses. As Christ lives His life through us, the world sees the reality of a living Christ in our good works and glorifies our Father who is in heaven.

⁎ —————————————— ℃

Father, thank you for giving Christ to live in me. I confess that the world often sees so much of me. I choose to decrease so that He may increase. I give my life to You today to reveal Your Son in me.

Resurrection

Knowing that He who raised up the Lord Jesus will also
raise us up with Jesus, and will present us with you.

2 Corinthians 4:14

The resurrection of the Lord Jesus is the greatest event in history. Repeatedly, it is declared to be the most important link in the events that brought us salvation. In 1 Corinthians 15, Paul reminds his readers that if Christ is not raised we have no basis for faith, for preaching, for forgiveness, or for joy. But because Christ *is* alive, we have reason for all of these and much more.

In 2 Corinthians 4:14, Paul expounds a short, pithy statement that Christ made to His disciples just before He went to the cross: "Because I live, you will live also" (John 14:19). He is predicting His resurrection. Since Christ is life, He could not be held by death, and there was no question about His resurrection. Is there a question, then, about *our* resurrection?

The guarantee of our own resurrection is Christ's resurrection. God, at the moment of our salvation, gave Christ to live in us as a permanent possession. This indwelling is repeatedly declared to be "His life." The life of God resides in the Son and, because we have the Son, we have God's life. In giving us His life, God obligates Himself to raise us up from the dead.

The past guarantees the future. We will be raised.

Why does a seed come to life after planting? Because it has life. But if you plant a stone the same size and color as a seed, it will not grow. It does not have life. The sole ingredient necessary to be raised is life. All who have the life of God will be raised. All who exist in death without God will remain in the grave until the end of all things. They will not be resurrected as we understand the word, referring to the change in Christ and in us. They will "exist" forever but not "live" in the true sense of the word.

In a spiritual sense, the resurrection is already past. We are told that, when Christ died, we who have believed in Him died. When He was buried, we were buried. When He was raised, we all were, too. We ascended with Him. We are seated with Him, because we share His resurrection. The past guarantees the future. We will be raised. The day will come when we will be like Him, in resurrection, when we see Him as He is.

ಬಿ ———————————— ಜ

Father, thank you for raising Your Son from the dead. I look forward to my own resurrection shared with Jesus. I choose to live in the power of a resurrected and living Lord Jesus Christ.

Judgment

But we know that the judgment of God is according
to truth against those who practice such things.

Romans 2:2

We live in a world of injustice. The news regularly reports of someone who, either literally or figuratively, "got away with murder." Some lawyers and unjust judges let the guilty go free, causing others to rise up in righteous anger, wondering why the Lord allows such things to slip by His notice. The rich live in opulence and the poor exist in squalor. The wealthy often choose to get rich at the expense of the poor. A segment of the population rails against inequity and wants to redistribute the wealth of the world. Many, including David, the psalmist of old, have asked why the wicked prosper and the righteous seem to suffer.

In the Scriptures, we read of Abraham asking the rhetorical question, "Shall not the Judge of all the earth do right?" (Genesis 18:25), and in Hebrews 4:13 we read that "all things are naked and open to the eyes of Him to whom we must give account." It is comforting to know that the day will come when the Judge *of* all will dispense righteous judgment *for* all.

Judgment in our mind is giving a review of a person's behavior, measuring what he does or what we think is right. But true judgment from the mind of God is to review and measure our actions against the perfect standard of either His written Word or Christ the living Word. Christ is the standard of behavior for all men, whether they believe or not.

Judgment in the Scriptures is always a review of works. The Judgment Seat of Christ will not be an assessment of unforgiven sin, but a review of motives and accountability of our stewardship of the possessions and blessings that the Lord gave us. The Great White Throne will be a judgment of works, recorded from the beginning of time. Every person at that judgment will be one who rejected divine light, whether the gospel or God's revelation in nature. They will all be sentenced to the lake of fire, and the degree of punishment will be according to their works.

It is not our responsibility to judge others or to set ourselves as the standard of holiness and devotion. The duty pressed on us is to live in the light of the truth and thereby make Christ known to others.

God shall bring all under His review. That judgment will be according to the Truth, which is found in Christ and personified by Christ. No one will escape this righteous Judge.

„ ———————————— ⅓

Father, thank you for the promise that one day the righteous Judge will preside over all mankind. I do not escape His eye.

Living Stones

*You also, as living stones, are being built up a spiritual
house, a holy priesthood, to offer up spiritual sacrifices
acceptable to God through Jesus Christ.*

1 Peter 2:5

When I was a boy, a preacher used to speak at our church, often bringing with him a collection of rocks. They all looked the same until, with all the lights turned off, he would switch on an ultraviolet "black light." Suddenly, all the living colors in those stones would be illuminated in the darkness, each unique in color and configuration. Included in the demonstration were some stones which failed to respond with any color to his special black light. The preacher taught that the living stones reflected light, while dead stones projected no color. We were asked, "Are you a 'living stone' or a 'dead stone'?" It was a powerful gospel message.

That demonstration still colors my understanding that all believers are "living stones." Obviously, the stones used in the gospel message fell short in revealing the profound truth that Peter declares. The "living stones" in the illustration were painted by the Creator with special variations of minerals that respond to ultraviolet light in red, blue, green, orange, and yellow. The colors were only visible under that special light. Without that light, no one could see the colors hidden in the minerals. Christ, as the Light of the world, knew and exposed the glory of God for all to see.

As believers, we were once in the quarry of the human race. Isaiah 51:1 reminds us of "the hole of the pit" from which we were "dug." Christ came to our quarry and saved us out of the quagmire of death and darkness that characterizes the mass of humanity. He touched us in response to our faith and moved us from death to life, from darkness to light. We became living stones, not because a light caused us to reflect light, but because Christ, who is alive from the dead, gave us His life. Upon our receiving Christ as our light, He gives us the light of God to radiate. And, because He is the "Light of Life," we will never be in darkness or separated from God. Rather, we will live brilliantly and eternally in His presence.

The living stones demonstration was a vivid picture of the difference between the living and dead. Though all looked alike under normal light, the living stones offered an amazing kaleidoscope of color that glorified the Creator of each mineral placed in those rocks. We believers, like stones, can display the light of Christ as we walk in the light, just as He is in the light. We are the living stones of the house where the Light lives!

₭ ———————————— ℨ

Father, thank you for making me as a living stone by Your living Son.

Our Father's Forgiveness

*And be kind to one another, tenderhearted, forgiving
one another, just as God in Christ forgave you.*

Ephesians 4:32

The knowledge of forgiveness sets us free from fear. Our world has the capacity to inject fear into our lives from every quarter. Fear is a powerful tool of the enemy, but faith in the Word of God delivers us from it.

Some of the sweetest words in the Word of God regarding our salvation are, "God in Christ forgave you." This fact is based on Christ's substitutionary work on the cross and His glorious resurrection. A living Christ gives us assurance of forgiveness. Without this guarantee, we would all wonder what more was necessary to convince us that our sin has been paid for and that we have been reconciled to God. The sufficiency of Christ's redemptive payment made it possible for God to accept and forgive us.

> *A living Christ gives us assurance of forgiveness.*

For the rest of the believer's life, the enemy does not want us to hear, accept, or rest in these comforting words. He blinds the mind of unbelievers to this message. But *our* eyes have been opened by the Holy Spirit, so that this truth stands like 30-foot letters on a skyscraper. Some see the writing from the street and believe. Others need to stand on the rooftop and be dwarfed by the message. Yet the message does not change. It declares the truth, no matter where we are standing. If we believe, we rest in that peace. If we find it hard to accept, we may need to stand closer.

Some see it once and are satisfied. Others need to repeatedly read it until their mind comprehends, their emotions are thrilled, and their will chooses not to be filled with fear. This grand work is a finished one; there is no need for any additional exercise on your part. If your faith fails, your forgiveness does not depart. You are still forgiven!

Scripture declares that this forgiveness is for past, present, and future sin. Does this mean that we are free to go on sinning and to live carelessly? *No!* It means that we can rest in the wonderful gift of forgiveness and seek God's grace to cease from sin. One of those issues is resting in Christ's finished work. Nothing we do can undo the forgiveness registered for us with the Father. Sing the chorus, "God forgave my sin in Jesus' name, I've been born again in Jesus' name."

ೞ ──────────────── ೞ

Father, You sent the Lord Jesus Christ to die for me so that You, as God, can forgive all my sin. I thank You for Your gift of forgiveness. I choose to rest in this truth and confidently live in victory over sin through Your strength.

Restraining Lawlessness

For the mystery of lawlessness is already at work; only He who now restrains will do so until He is taken out of the way.

2 Thessalonians 2:7

Regarding present spiritual conditions, John writes in his first epistle, "We know that we are of God, and the whole world lies under the sway of the wicked one" (5:19). The "lawless one" is another descriptive term for the devil. Few would challenge the statement that wickedness and lawlessness abound in our world. Some would suggest that the situation is so grave that God has lost control. A significant number of popular teachers of the Word have concluded that Satan, as a powerful influence in our world, is unleashed and free to operate without hindrance. This position tends to put the power of the enemy on a higher level than that of our Lord Jesus Christ. There are plenty who think that Christ is powerless to set the limits of activity for the lawless one.

"He who has been born of God keeps himself, and the wicked one does not touch him."

Today's Scripture, as well as various others, gives us no room for such a conclusion. To suggest that there are no restraints on the enemy is to teach that he is stronger and more powerful than God Himself. That cannot be the truth! In the account of the conflict between God and Satan (going back to the time of Job), Satan could not touch Job's animals without God's permission. The same truth is also written by John in 1 John 5:18, "He who has been born of God keeps himself, and the wicked one does not touch him."

2 Thessalonians 2:7 has not always been easy to understand, largely because of changes in the English language. In the KJV, the word "restrains" was translated "letteth." Back in 1611, the word "let" meant the opposite of what it does today; it meant "to hinder," and now it means "to permit."

The question has been raised many times: "Who is the 'He' who is doing the restraining?" Most scholars conclude that this is a reference to the person and ministry of the Holy Spirit in and through the church. As believers live in our world and pray about conditions in our society, the conflagration of wickedness is held back. A few godly men and women feel called to influence their nations by running for official positions in government. Their influence by the Holy Spirit also restrains the activity of the wicked one.

One day the Holy Spirit will be removed when the church is taken, and "all hell will break loose." The Holy Spirit does indeed restrain evil.

☙ ——————————— ❧

Father, thank you for the ministry of the Holy Spirit in my life. I accept the challenge in Christ to help hold back the advance of lawlessness.

Brothers

No longer as a slave but more than a slave—a
beloved brother, especially to me but how much
more to you, both in the flesh and in the Lord.

Philemon 16

There was a time when Paul, Philemon, and Onesimus were brothers. Paul was the first of the three to become a part of God's family. On the road to Damascus, he met the Lord and began a pilgrimage that took him from being a hater of the "brethren" to a lover of them. That word—"brother"—became an important and meaningful term in his life and letters. It was, in fact, the first word that he heard from a fellow believer after he surrendered his heart to the Lord Jesus Christ. Ananias came to him and said, "Brother Saul." That was tantamount to saying, "Welcome to the family."

Philemon was a slave owner who probably trusted Christ as a result of Paul's preaching. It is easy to imagine Paul at one time saying to him, "Welcome to the family, brother Philemon." Now, as Paul writes this little letter to Philemon, he states again the preciousness of this relationship which he had nurtured for so many years. However, he now also has a special request of his long-time friend and brother.

A new addition to the family had been made while Paul was in prison. Onesimus, one of Philemon's slaves, had made his way to Rome while running from his master. He had somehow wronged Philemon, stolen some goods, and made his escape. God providentially brought the fugitive into Paul's circle in Rome. The gospel hit the heart of Onesimus, and he was soundly converted. His salvation brought with it the blessing of entrance into the family of God. He was now a brother to Paul *and* Philemon.

In those days, a slave owner was free to mistreat a slave as a piece of property. This particular "piece of property" was now a brother of the slave owner and of Paul. Paul entreated his friend to receive the runaway slave back—not as a slave, but as a beloved brother in Christ. To do this meant a change in relationship and position: receive him into the church and into his household as a true brother. What a privilege for Onesimus. What responsibility for Philemon. What blessing to Paul. What glory to God!

Brothers and sisters in the Lord make up the family of our Father. Because we share the same Father and the same life with every other believer, we are brothers (and sisters) in the Lord.

ಬಿ ———————————————— ೞ

Father, thank you for the great joy of being one of so many in Your family. You welcomed me after I had run away for so long. What a blessing to know You as my Father and to know Your family as my brothers and sisters.

Sonship

Therefore you are no longer a slave but a son, and
if a son, then an heir of God through Christ.

Galatians 4:7

An heir is someone who is waiting for his benefactor to die so that he can receive the inheritance granted to him by that person. In Galatians 4, we are reminded that we, as believers, were once slaves of sin and the world, but now we have been brought into the family of God as full-fledged sons. The transaction of making a slave a son is a miracle that only God can accomplish, because a slave does not have the life of the master in him. The slave must be adopted into the master's household if he is to inherit his master's estate at some point.

But that is only part of the story. The rest of the story is that we received the life of God through Christ at our spiritual birth. The two concepts are not contradictory; they are complementary, like two sides of a coin. Because we were slaves, we needed to be released from slavery by redemption. We were born again into God's family by the Holy Spirit. He gave us life by birth, making us God's children. On both counts, we are eligible for the inheritance. God has made us His heirs, and Romans 8:17 adds to this truth by saying that we are "joint heirs with Christ."

> *The transaction of making a slave a son is a miracle that only God can accomplish.*

The transformation from slave to son was unimaginable in their thinking. We have come to look on the transition as commonplace and accept the change without excitement. Yet any slave who went through such redemption would never have lost sight of where he had been and where he was now. To move from the slave house to the father's house in itself would be astonishing to the former slave.

Because every believer has experienced this transition, it should prompt a daily round of excitement. We moved from being slaves of the world, with no future, to becoming sons in the household of God. We shifted from being slaves to the god of this world to being mature sons of the God of heaven. Can we accept this and believe it without some degree of celebration affecting every facet of our thinking and living? Could a slave ever be the same? Will a new son not change every phase of his behavior because he is now an heir? You were a slave, but are now a son. Celebrate!

⁎ ——————————— ⅓

Father, thank you for my sonship. I could not buy it. I did not deserve it, but You have given it to me by faith in Your Son Jesus Christ.

His Possession

And you are Christ's, and Christ is God's.
1 Corinthians 3:23

The church is God the Father's gift to His Son. The Lord Jesus referred a number of times to "those You have given me" in His prayer in John 17. Christ reckoned believers, individually and collectively, as His own possession.

The New Testament gives several reasons why it is reasonable that we belong to Christ. Perhaps the most important is that He bought us with His own precious blood. The value of His death, expressed in terms of His blood, is the way that God prefers to explain the price that was paid. Purchasing something is the best evidence of ownership. We may buy an item as a gift, but before we give it, it belongs to us. Christ bought us for Himself.

When you buy something, your vested interest almost guarantees that you will take good care of it. Are we more careful with our own car or with a rented car? God has purchased us, and we are now His personal property. But we were bought with the express intention of God giving us to His Son to be His bride. This whole concept adds to the special care that the bride receives from a faithful bridegroom.

A further reason that we are special possessions of Christ is that He has taken up His residence in us. Christ lives in us, He occupies us, and His occupation is a specific reason for claiming us as His own. It is also a significant reason for His caring for us. Again, we can ask a simple question: Do we take better care of the house that we live in or one that we rent from others? When we receive Christ as our Savior, He comes to dwell in us by His Holy Spirit. He will abide forever. He takes care of His own house.

Elsewhere, we are reminded that the Holy Spirit is the seal of God's ownership. God put Christ's name on us, indicating that His ownership was made possible by the purchase price. How does the world know that we belong to Christ? The seal is the name and nature of God, manifested by the ministry of the Holy Spirit.

Ownership also bolsters our security as His possession. As if it were not enough to say that we are Christ's, the inspired writer adds that "Christ is God's." The Lord Jesus gave Himself to the Father in ministry to procure our salvation, which included His incarnation, substitution, and resurrection. And even now, by His ministry of owning and keeping us, we are secure in Christ who belongs to God in a wonderfully mysterious way. We are Christ's!

ഇ ———————————— ര

Father, thank you for redeeming me through the sacrifice of Your Son on the cross. I praise Your divine plan for my security.

Victory and Triumph

Now thanks be to God who always leads us in
triumph in Christ, and through us diffuses the
fragrance of His knowledge in every place.
2 Corinthians 2:14

The victory of Christ on the cross and in resurrection is fully shared with all who possess Christ as personal Savior. At the heart of this triumph is our full identification with Christ. In Romans 6, we are reminded that, when Christ died, I died; when Christ was buried, I was buried; when Christ rose, I rose with Him; when Christ ascended, I ascended; when Christ sat down at the right hand of God, I too sat down in a position of finality, completion, rest, and even triumph.

The fact that the triumph is always available to us is crucial to our diffusing the fragrance of Christ everywhere. There should be no doubt about Christ's triumph over the world, the devil, the flesh, sin, death, and the grave. His resurrection, ascension, and seated position are proof that victory and triumph are permanent and can never be reversed.

What a stench comes from our lives and lips if we doubt Christ's victory and triumph. What a smell if we question whether the resurrection was the full evidence of His victory. What an odor if we wonder if He really ascended into heaven. If we doubt that Christ is seated in glory, our lives will reek of defeat, and we will tend to employ every fiber of our being to accomplish a victory that Christ has already won. Our striving will give a lie to the finality of Christ's work. Our doubts will cause others to turn away from such an unsatisfactory religion. We will drive men and women to do their own thing in hope of better results than are available in Christ. We will give credence to the lie of the enemy that we can earn our own salvation.

The Father accepted the Son's sacrifice as full and final. There is nothing else for anyone to do. God now leads His family in celebrating the magnificent triumph of our blessed, glorious Savior. Our heart's response is a perfume of thanksgiving for that victory. This is an aroma that wafts through every place that believers celebrate the triumph of Christ.

God leads and we must follow. The Father promotes the celebration, and all His children enter by faith into the grand announcement that "Christ died and rose and is seated at the right hand of God." Repeat it! Publish it! Sing it! Say it! Because I am in Christ, I partake of all these victories. I too can triumph over sin, the devil, and the world and therein release the fragrance of Christ wherever I go.

Ꙙ ———————————— ꞔ

Father, thank you for leading us to triumph in Christ. I choose to believe
these truths and have them shape my words and life.

Heirs

And if children, then heirs—heirs of God and joint
heirs with Christ, if indeed we suffer with Him,
that we may also be glorified together.

Romans 8:17

Receiving Christ gives us the authority to be called the children of God, and Paul was writing to some of God's children, the saints who were in Rome, as well as to believers today. The statement in Romans 8 concerning the wealth of blessing is one of the most profound descriptions that God makes of His children. In it, Paul sets out in legal terms the glorious provision for every one of them.

An heir is one who usually receives an inheritance because of a blood relationship. The life of God is implanted in us, thereby making us members of His family. The blood of Christ purchases a relationship for believers into this family. So, whether the concept is adoption or birth, the blessings are the same since the relationship is expanded and is not impaired by the two ideas.

If a man has a thousand acres and leaves them to his four sons equally as his heirs, each would receive a quarter of the property when the father dies. If another man had a thousand acres and four sons and left his property to his sons equally as "joint heirs," the story would be very different. After the judge read the will to the four sons, they would come out of the courtroom with an interesting story. Ask the oldest, "How much did your father leave you?" and his answer would be, "A thousand acres." The second, third, and youngest would all say confidently, "My dad left me a thousand acres!" They would be *"joint* heirs," so each of the four would fully own all the property that their father had left. What wealth!

All the resources that God released to His children in Christ are mine.

We are joint heirs with Christ. What belongs to Christ, because of who He is and what He has done on the cross, belongs to us. That abundance belongs to me as a joint heir with Him. That does not make me God. I own all the wealth that is Christ's because I possess the life of my Father. I inherit all the riches of divine grace because God designated all His children as joint heirs with His blessed Son. All the resources that God released to His children in Christ are mine. But being a joint heir does not insulate us from suffering, as Romans 8:17 notes. Spiritual riches and physical suffering are a normal part of His children's experience.

Father, thank you for designating me as a joint heir with Your Son. I confess that I do not deserve or comprehend all the wealth that You gave me.

Works of Art

We are His workmanship.

Ephesians 1:10

In six days, God created His kaleidoscopic array of colorful flowers, an almost infinite variation of fragrances, and a comical collection of animals. Yet His crowning work was man and woman, whom He made "fearfully and wonderfully" in His image (Psalm 139:14).

God took the dust of the earth, shaped it, molded it, squeezed it, and pinched it until that dust became a body. He placed an eye in the special socket. He touched the heart to compel it to pump. He loosed the string holding the tongue. He blew into the prone form through the nose and filled the lungs, forcing air in and out. He stroked the spinal cord as one does a harp string, sending nerves echoing throughout the body. He called the stomach to dinner to enjoy hunger for food from a perfect garden. He spoke the words, "Get up! Come. We will walk together in the cool of this evening."

Adam and Eve *were* His workmanship, beauty that none of us has ever seen, whether in a mirror or the unreflected gaze of our eye. But that workmanship was defiled and defaced by sin. The hearing dulled, the eyes dimmed, the lungs struggled, the hunger waned, the muscles shriveled, the nerves died, the cord broke, and man returned to dust because of sin. What demise!

What will God do with His work of art which was marred in the hands of the Potter? He will make it another vessel, one that pleases Him. Does He get input from the vessel? *No.* Once again, re-creative genius is free in making us grow into the stature of the fullness of Christ. We are being redesigned—not like Adam, but like Christ.

> *We are being redesigned —not like Adam, but like Christ.*

He remakes our eye so that "we see Jesus, who was made a little lower than the angels." He restores our ear so that we will "hear what the Spirit says to the churches." He reworks our lungs so that we can breathe life eternal. He touches our silver cord so that we respond to His commands. He loosens the string of our tongue so that we all say and sing, "Blessing and honor and glory and power be to Him who sits on the throne, and to the Lamb, forever and ever." What re-creation!

We *are* His work of art, and that work begun in us and through us continues until the day of Jesus Christ. At that time, we will behold how glorious His art work is. It is now—and it will be then—to the praise of His glory.

❧ ——————————— ☙

Father, You have chosen mankind as the final medium of displaying Your workmanship. Thank you for beginning that work in me. I surrender to the Artist's mind and hand.

Redeemed by His Precious Blood

*Knowing that you were not redeemed with corruptible
things, like silver or gold, from your aimless conduct
received by tradition from your fathers.*

1 Peter 1:18

T he story of the little boy who carved a boat with the help of his father is well known. The boat was carefully worked and then finished with a coat of bright red paint. The boy took his little craft to the lake and, controlling it by the attached string, would let the wind take it far from shore.

One day the wind pulled the string from his little hand and the boat sailed out of sight. The boy was heart-sick. He longed for his boat. Months later, father and son were walking the streets of a town on the other side of the lake. As they passed a second-hand shop, the boy spied his boat in the window. They went in and asked the shop keeper about it. The price was given; it was much more than the boy had in his pocket. The boy complained that he had made the boat; it was rightly his. But the shopkeeper stuck to his price. The lad looked up to his father and asked about buying it back. The willing father took from his pocket the required money, and father and son left the shop with the somewhat battered little boat. The boy looked lovingly at his creation and said to it, "You are twice mine now. First I made you, then I bought you!" The father smiled in approval at the profound lesson that his son had learned.

So it is with humanity. We were formed by God for His glory and enjoyment. The winds of sin and disobedience drew us away from Him. We went our own way and became slaves of sin and disobedience, far from God and out of control. Into this market the Son of God came. He found us there among the collection of lost humanity. The price to set us free from this bondage was enormous. Yet the Father and the Son worked out a plan by which the Son would give His life and pay for the release of those whom He had made. Not all come, but the ones who do come by faith are set free from bondage to liberty.

Under the Mosaic Law, silver and gold could redeem an animal. But the just requirements of God's plan of salvation required the price of the precious blood of Christ. To redeem means to pay the price for something and set it free. We have been bought with the blood of Christ and set free into the glorious liberty of the children of God.

ဆ ———————————— င凄

*Father, thank you for purchasing my redemption so that I am free to serve
You with all my heart. You paid a debt that I could not pay. I am redeemed!*

The Body of Christ

Now you are the body of Christ, and members individually.
1 Corinthians 12:27

The body of Christ, the church, is made up of all believers from the Day of Pentecost until the rapture. In the New Testament, we read of the church's beginning, how it was born, who make up the members, how to determine who belongs, the relation of the members to the Head of the body, the connection of the members to each other, and many other practical and spiritual issues.

In writing to the believers in Corinth, Paul states in unequivocal terms, "You are the body of Christ." This is not a prayer or a position to be earned or sought after; it is a statement of fact. It is interesting to note that Paul does not say that the body is comprised of just the more spiritual ones in Corinth, or those who follow a certain leader, or just the leaders, or ones with special spiritual gifts. In that local church were people given to division, to sin, and to misusing spiritual gifts. Some held questionable doctrines, and others were misbehaving at the Lord's Supper and the love feast. In fact, the church at Corinth was one of the *least* spiritual churches in New Testament times in practice and doctrine. Still, all the believers in Corinth were part of the body of Christ and individual members of it.

We also learn that the body was not limited to the church in Corinth. Other passages tell us that all believers everywhere are members. Paul taught in 1 Corinthians 12:13 that all believers were baptized spiritually into the body of Christ by the Holy Spirit, some at Pentecost when the church was born, and others as they believed the gospel.

With membership of the body comes privilege as well as responsibility. Since the physical body of Jesus Christ is in glory with the Father, His body on earth is the physical evidence of both oneness and His resurrection power. Each member, functioning by the direction of the Head, produces a vital demonstration of the reality of a living Christ. The spiritual union of all believers is worldwide. How else could He be known around the globe?

With membership of the body comes privilege as well as responsibility.

What, then, is my place? Should I pray for a special position? How do I earn more influence? Will I be given a more visible activity if I am faithful? Who decides where I function in the body? The Holy Spirit places me in the body as He chooses. I accept that truth, along with the fact that I am indeed in the body permanently to glorify the Head.

⮚ ———————————————— ∛

Father, thank you for placing me in the body of Christ. I accept my role and seek to glorify Christ through my life in Him.

Chastening

For whom the Lord loves He chastens, and scourges every son whom He receives. If you endure chastening, God deals with you as with sons; for what son is there whom a father does not chasten? But if you are without chastening, of which all have become partakers, then you are illegitimate and not sons.

Hebrews 12:6-8

A child finds it hard to believe his father when he says, "I am spanking you because I love you." It's difficult to understand that love and deliberate infliction of pain can dwell in the same heart. Even mature believers struggle with this concept.

We tend to have a common reaction to any suffering: "What did I do to deserve this?" One thing that we must remember is that the punishment for our sin was borne by Christ at the cross. Any pain that we endure cannot, therefore, be seen as a further payment on the bill that has already been paid by Christ in full. Our discomfort or sorrows, then, must be seen in the light of the Father's instruction and training of His children and not as punitive. Our earthly fathers *do* punish with pain so that we will remember and change our behavior. God, as our Father, does not inflict pain as punishment. His chastening and scourging is done to correct and discipline with a desire to bring His child to maturity.

The word *chasten* conjures up the image of a child learning, of being trained by a father. A child can sit at a table and be told to eat everything that his mother puts on his plate. But, if the child dislikes one item, he might ask, "What did I do wrong to be forced to eat this?" The answer is—nothing! The parents are training their child about good nutrition, not to waste food, to be obedient, or to learn social graces. Similarly, God allows or brings pain and suffering into the lives of His children so that they will learn obedience, dependence, and many other characteristics that we seem only capable of learning in the context of suffering.

In addition, the Father "scourges" every one of His children. This word refers to flogging. That is a strong term in our culture and prompts visions of "child abuse." But, in the case of God, the flogging or spanking is under His careful eye and administered by His loving hand. It will not be more than we can bear, for longer than we need, or without specific purpose. This learning experience is for our development and spiritual growth. God, as my Father, chastens me as His child for my good. He loves me!

⊰ ———————————— ⊱

Father, thank you for the way that You discipline me. I need it and want to learn to be grateful for each experience.

Hidden in Christ

For you died, and your life is hidden with Christ in God.
Colossians 3:3

Physical death is, for most of us, a fearful prospect, something that we do not really look forward to experiencing. But the phrase "death with Christ" has some of the most profound and practical ramifications of any truth dealing with the Christian life. Paul's teaching on the subject gives us a categorical statement which none can refute. It is especially helpful for those who are fighting the activity of the "self-life" along their Christian pilgrimage.

The context helps us put this important event into perspective. When did you die? The chapter begins by stating, "You were raised with Christ." But we cannot be raised if we did not die. It is sometimes suggested that we can live *like* Christ without dying *with* Christ. But that is as impossible as it is for a seed to produce a lovely tree without being planted. The first thing that must happen is that the seed must fall to the ground and die. Only then will it spring to life in germination and rise as a tree, to fill the air with beauty and fragrance and offer the owner its fruit in season. Its death is necessary.

> *He was raised, and we are raised with Him to walk in the newness of His life.*

What is in a seed? Hidden life—life that cannot be seen under a microscope or be identified by dissection. Yet its presence is proven by planting, death, and patience. The life is divinely placed there, as the new seed emerges from the bud through the flower, protected by the fleshy fruit of apple or pear. It cannot be duplicated by man. He might make a facsimile of the color and weight of a seed to deceive his fellow scientists, but he cannot place life in it. That is proved by planting anything that man makes: just see if planting a ball produces a tree with flowers and fruit. Impossible!

Our life is hidden in Christ, just as life is hidden in every seed. Since Christ was the seed that fell into the ground and died, all who would receive life from Him died also. If He was not raised, neither were we. But He *was* raised, and we *are* raised with Him to walk in the newness of *His* life. My old life was condemned and crucified when Christ was condemned and crucified. My old man was buried when Christ was buried. My new life was revealed when Christ rose from the dead. God hid me with Christ from the beginning so that I might share in all that my Savior experienced.

ॐ ———————————— 03

Father, thank you for securing me in Christ. I claim His death, His resurrection, and His life.

Love of God

*Now hope does not disappoint, because the love of God has been
poured out in our hearts by the Holy Spirit who was given to us.*

Romans 5:5

Today's Scripture is the last of five verses that describe God's plan for our salvation. One of the major issues discussed here is that, although we have been justified and now enjoy peace with God through faith in Christ, the prospect of tribulation still remains. We are often urged to accept the message that—if we have enough faith—problems, trials, and sickness will not be able to touch us. Yet, here and elsewhere, we are reminded that salvation does not insulate us from tribulation. God's love still allows us to endure suffering.

Two wonderful blessings are reiterated in this verse: the love of God has been poured out, and the Holy Spirit has been given to us. We must not separate these two primary blessings. In our meditations, we have repeatedly focused on the truth of the presence of the Holy Spirit in every believer. It is essential that we never forget this fact. Since the Holy Spirit has been given permanently and personally to every believer, we now have the presence of God and Christ by the Holy Spirit. He will never leave us nor forsake us. He is the foundation on whom our security rests, the fountain from whom all blessings flow, and the river from whom our resources are appropriated.

The cross of Christ is the prism that radiates God's love.

The heavens declare the glory of God. The mountains show God's handiwork; the water, His power; the wind, His sovereignty. Every part of His creation displays some aspect of His creative genius. But what about His love? Only the cross of Christ is the prism that radiates God's love and all the attending displays of love's spectrum of blessings.

We must not look beyond the cross for a fuller knowledge of the love of God. The Holy Spirit has been given to us in order that He might take the things of Christ and dispense them to us. As we gather before the cross and learn its glory, we will see the love of God poured from that bottomless reservoir. We need not ask for a further fountain of love. We need not pray for a deeper well of love from which to draw. God's full and complete revelation of His love has been poured out in each of our hearts. Believe that it has been done. Drink deeply. Soak your soul in that fountain. Marinate your mind in His love. Bask in that blessing!

ဢ ——————————— ଓ

Father, thank you for the full revelation of Your love to me and to the world. I bless its bounty. I gaze on its glory. I delight in its depth.

His Attention

"For the eyes of the Lord are on the righteous, and
His ears are open to their prayers; But the face
of the Lord is against those who do evil."

1 Peter 3:12

The above verse is a quotation from the Old Testament, where the Lord regularly reminded His people of His superintendence. The reference comes from Psalm 34, but the concept is implied in other places. The nation of Israel had no excuse for not knowing it. They were God's chosen people; His eyes would never be taken off them and their circumstances, and His ears were continually attuned to their call.

Of course, we know that God is spirit and does not have eyes, ears, or a face. However, He has chosen to describe His personal activities using human characteristics so that we can comprehend what He is doing. God is infinite; He cannot describe Himself in finite terms and still communicate His infiniteness. We learn of God in terms that we can understand, such as having eyes, ears, and a face.

God revealed Himself to the nation of Israel by His name, "the Lord," or Jehovah, meaning the "covenant-keeping God." This is the most frequently used name that the Holy Spirit inspired the human authors to use for Him, and it is the name that appears in Psalm 34 and Peter's quotation. Jehovah continually reminded His people of His faithfulness, greatness, goodness, and grace by this name. He is the One who is so personally involved with His people that His eyes and ears are constantly directed toward them. His eye is on a sparrow, we hear the Lord instructing His disciples. He sees the sparrow fall; how much more does He see the righteous, whom He has redeemed by His precious blood? The prayers of His people are always welcome to His ears. How He longs to have those He loves speak to Him! It was true for His covenant people Israel, and it is true for the church, His New Testament people.

It is our responsibility to focus on Him so that our eyes may meet His. He can then guide us with His eyes. Our voice must be directed to Him, since His ears are waiting for our prayers. Nothing can change God's being attuned to His people. If we do not look to or speak with Him, we lose the blessing of His intimacy. He is waiting for us to realize our need for communion that includes eyes and ears exchanging looks and words.

— ಬಿ ——————————— ಛಿ —

Father, thank you for the personal attention that You have promised me
because You redeemed me for Your own glory. I choose to focus on Your
eyes. I offer the fruit of my lips as praise and prayer to You.

Propitiation

*And He Himself is the propitiation for our sins, and
not for ours only but also for the whole world.*

1 John 2:2

The comprehensive work that Christ completed on the cross is wrapped up in three great words. *Redemption* is the payment of a price, allowing the one redeemed to be set free (Ephesians 1:7). *Reconciliation* suggests a thorough change (2 Corinthians 5:19). The word in 1 John 2:2 is *propitiation,* which means complete and full satisfaction.

Throughout the Old Testament, God required a sacrifice to appease His anger against man's sin. That sacrifice was primarily a lamb, as is seen in the Passover in Exodus 12. But God was never satisfied by the death of an animal. The blood of those sacrifices covered sin but did not actually take sin away.

Then God sent His Son, who "was manifested to take away our sins" (1 John 3:5). He was declared to be "the Lamb of God who takes away the sin of the world" (John 1:29). The Lord Jesus accepted that responsibility and went to the cross, where He died for all human beings as their substitute. God was fully satisfied with the redemptive payment that Christ made for sin, and declared His pleasure by raising Him from the dead and seating Him at His own right hand in the heavens. Christ sat down! The work of salvation was finished. God was now set free to act in mercy, love, and grace to all who believe.

The word "propitiation" is also translated "mercy seat" in several places. Annually, the high priest would sprinkle the blood of a sacrificed goat on the mercy seat (the lid for the ark of God) in the Holy of Holies of the tabernacle. For one year, God accepted the death and blood of an animal as a suitable covering for the sin of the nation of Israel. But that blood never took their sin away.

Only one offering could take sin away—the blood of Christ. The publican, in his prayer in Luke 18:13, pleaded, "God be merciful [or, propitious] to me a sinner!" In admitting his sin, the man begged God to be satisfied with the blood on the mercy seat and to show His mercy to him. Because of Christ's finished work on the cross, God is as merciful as He can be. There is now no need to plead for God's mercy. The cross stands as the greatest evidence that He *is* propitious. God is full of mercy and offers it to all because of the cross.

❧ ———————————————— ☙

Father, thank you for the wonderful sacrifice of Christ on the cross. I am grateful that You are satisfied with that offering.

Washed In His Blood

*And from Jesus Christ, the faithful witness, the firstborn from
the dead, and the ruler over the kings of the earth. To Him who
loved us and washed us from our sins in His own blood.*

Revelation 1:5

The book of Revelation aptly begins with this song of praise about the one whom God unveils for all to adore. The entire book is an exposition of the worth, worship, wrath, wars, work, and witness of the Lord Jesus Christ. The reason that we are to listen as it speaks of Him is that Christ is faithful in all that He has done and all that He says, unlike any other man. He is trustworthy. Silence every voice but His!

Three glorious statements are given in divine and practical order. Jesus Christ is the only one who always told the truth, because He is the Truth. He is the faithful witness. All that came from His mouth was true, and Israel's leaders could only conclude, "No man ever spoke like this Man!" The words that fell from His lips were true, whether in condemnation or compassion, pain or power, rebuke or rejoicing, of law or love.

He is the chief, the first in the order of all who will rise to die no more. He took on a glorious display of life, resumed in a sphere that no other man had experienced. His is a quality and quantity of life which all believers share. Never again will He enter the kingdom of death. Having died once, He dies no more. Nor shall any of us who partake of His life remain in death, even though we may pass through it momentarily. Death no longer has dominion over Him or us, His redeemed ones. He is free from the clutches of death, and so are we.

The future for Jesus Christ is to be the King of kings and the Lord of lords. He is the King of the Jewish nation and will sit on the throne of His father, David. No one will depose Him and none will succeed Him. He is the Lord of the church, and no other religion can proffer a "lord" to equal Him and His spiritual dominion.

Such an Exalted One "loved me and gave Himself for me."

Such an Exalted One "loved me and gave Himself for me." The sacrifice of His blood set up a fountain that has flooded from His side, washing away every sin from all who confess their inadequacy before Him.

⸭ ———————————— ⸬

*Father, how glorious a description of the One who personally loved me
enough to die for me. I stand amazed at His exalted position and His loving
condescension for me. I worship and adore Him!*

Prophets

Of this salvation the prophets have inquired and searched carefully, who prophesied of the grace that would come to you.
1 Peter 1:10

If we, on this side of Calvary, cannot take in the length and breath and depth and height of the love of God which passes knowledge, how can we expect the Old Testament prophets to have comprehended it? Yet they were the ones who were chosen to deliver the initial revelation. God's salvation is like a mosaic of truth, delivered by a myriad of spokesmen to a limited number of listeners. God gave the message to a small number of individuals who then proclaimed it to a generation that lived in the dawn of revelation. That extended society searched, compared, and considered. They concluded that the only reasonable place for faith was in the Word of God.

Those who believed looked through a glass darkly, and even with blurry comprehension accepted all that the prophets spoke. They stood out as a small remnant who, through faith, accomplished all kinds of astonishing feats. As a result, they may be found among the portraits of the faithful. Each holy man of God—with a special view, and speaking in a different voice—contributed to the full-orbed volume inspired by the Holy Spirit. These words were written for our learning and edification. It is inspiring to meet those who knew so little but rose to such heights of boldness in their faith in God.

Part of the problem that faced each writing prophet and his readers was the seeming contradiction between the glory and suffering promised to the Messiah. How could those two very different experiences be attributed to the same person? The high and lofty glory was easier to accept than the suffering and sorrow that they so graphically prophesied. Even Peter had problems with the juxtaposition of these contradictory descriptions. Only after Christ's resurrection and ascension and the descent of the Spirit did he accurately conclude that the proper order was "the suffering of Christ and the glories that would follow" (1 Peter 1:11). The New Testament preachers were better able to comprehend the blessings that would be poured out *as a result* of Christ's sufferings.

The prophets also told their generation that one day the grace of God would be fully poured out on other people whom they did not know. We are that generation, says Peter. We, by the cross, have the entirety of God's grace made available to us. The prophets may be excused for being confused, but we have no excuse for misunderstanding God's amazing grace.

Father, thank you for the prophecies that validate other words from the pens of holy men. I take Your grace poured out on me in Christ.

The Father's Love

Behold what manner of love the Father has bestowed on us, that we should be called children of God! Therefore the world does not know us, because it did not know Him.

1 John 3:1

It often seems impossible for brothers and sisters to live together in harmony and love. Most children usually get a large and early dose of conflict with others in the family, particularly siblings. It is only as they begin to understand the love that the parents have equally for each child that they begin to dwell together in unity.

Repeatedly, we read the Lord and His apostle John commanding believers to "love one another." In today's Scripture, John uses the infinite love of the Father for each child to promote love between children in His family.

John's readers are urged—if not commanded—to take their eyes off themselves and one another and focus solely on the love that the Father has for all of us. The Lord Jesus told His disciples that they needed to abide in His love. That abiding is the responsibility of each child of God. If we were to choose to obey this counsel and be so occupied with the love of the Father, we would leave our grudging and carping attitudes behind and instead drench our differences in the ocean of His love.

> *Our appreciation of the Father's love sets us apart from the world.*

But let's remember that not all are called the children of God. Many think that, because they are doing expected duties, God will somehow call them His children. They establish a pattern that must be followed in hopes that the Father will designate them as His child. Man is to confess his sin to receive forgiveness and acceptance into the Father's family. God bestows His life and His love on everyone who accepts His Son. That position of a child in His family is a relationship with the Father which is without preference or respect of persons.

We should also remember that the Father's love is without measure. In His prayer to His Father, the Lord Jesus states that the love the Father has for the Son is the same as He has for the rest of His children. That love is not dependent on our obedience or our love for Him. The Father's love is unchangeable and unaffected by our behavior. His love is for His perfect Son. We are in His Son, so we are loved as much as He is. Our appreciation of the Father's love sets us apart from the world.

— ❧ ————————————— ❧ —

Father, thank you for the abundance of Your love. I confess that I do not know its greatness, but I bathe in its blessing and seek, by the strength of Christ, to declare to the world the wealth of Your love.

Creator

And He is before all things, and in Him all things consist.
Colossians 1:17

This verse is found in the middle of one of the most glorious statements about Christ's exalted position. A graphic view of His past is produced for our admiration. His present ministry to the church is reviewed for our encouragement. The prospect of His future glory and blessing is a source of hope for all who believe.

For centuries, scholars have debated about the timeline regarding the choices and decisions that God dictated before He made "all things." Accusations fly, and some are belittled if they do not ascribe the proper role of God in decreeing all things. Not a few hold their stipulated positions as the basis of fellowship in the family of God. Much love is lost between fellow students if there is not complete agreement in all the factors that make up the process by which the infinite God elected to do His work. Yet not one is able to comprehend, let alone explain, the infinite mind of the God who existed before them and the things that He made. How little we all are when standing in front of such a comprehensive statement about our Creator.

The "all things" of God is a far-reaching definition of the extent of activity and dimension of materials used by Him to set in motion what we see, as well as what we do not see. Each gaze into a bigger and better telescope only causes the viewer to exclaim, "It is much bigger than we previously thought."

The structure of our universe causes even the most skeptical to privately have doubts about how it all "happened." Even those who reject this simple statement of Scripture for a "deeper" meaning have second thoughts about their authoritative declaration based on their puny scientific discoveries. Many of these people close their minds to the inspired Word of God in favor of "progressive science." The finality of the Word in simple terms confounds their foolishness and forces them to change their position regularly. Time itself will direct these "scientists" back to the simple but profound Word of God.

Not only are many confused by how it all got here, but they face their own consternation about how it stays together. The most godless student of our world has questions in the recesses of his mind about why evolution does not work and entropy does. One day, he will have to face the Creator and be accountable to His revelation and authority. "All things" point to the Creator—Jesus Christ our Lord.

ဆ ———————————— ⟂

Father, thank you for setting out in so few words Your superintendence of all that You created and sustain. I am thankful that I am included!

July

DISCOVERING A COLLECTION OF GIFTS PREVIOUSLY HIDDEN

"In whom are hidden all the treasures
of wisdom and knowledge."

Colossians 2:3

Oh! What a Treasure He has given me.
All I have needed just to set me free.
Hidden in the Savior who lives in me,
I have the Treasure and I have the key.

All He has given I have needed here,
In every trial I am called to bear.
Even when there falls a painful tear,
Everything in Him is free and clear.

F. L. K.

July

A Drop of Rain

A ll of us have thrilled at seeing God's rainbow in the sky. We have wondered how it got there, where it ended, and if we could, in fact, run or drive till we found where it touched the earth. What lessons can we learn personally from this glorious sign in the sky?

Scientists tell us that light is invisible. It is hard for us to accept that fact since we can see what we think is light or its reflection. But the invisibility of light offers us a wonderful illustration of the person of God, when He says "no one has seen God at any time" (John 1:18). If God is invisible, how is He to be known by mankind? How are we to understand the revelation of God in Christ, who is now at the right hand of God and invisible to humans on earth? Has God left Himself a witness of His reality and personality? The resounding answer is, yes. He has given the responsibility of His revelation to a special group of people called the church.

The church has the enormous task of making the invisible God visible. That is a staggering undertaking, to be responsible to make God "known and read by all men."

This revelation of Christ to all men has been made possible only by Christ's resurrection from the dead and His ascension into glory. We are to display a risen Christ. So to start with, we do not help people to see that Christ died for their sins by dragging out a corpse and showing it around. There is more to the gospel than a dead Christ; it is the risen Christ who must be revealed so that all may know that, "Because I live, you shall live also."

How is this to be done? Christ has been raised from the dead as the living God and He chooses to live in everyone who believes on Him for salvation. Over and over again, the apostle Paul reminds us that Christ dwells in every believer fully, completely, personally, and permanently. We must accept that truth by faith.

The second step in revealing Christ to the world is to believe that Christ takes up residence in us. As Christ lives His life through us, others who see our behavior will know that Christ is alive. In this way, we make an invisible Christ visible in terms of our personality, our being, our body, and our behavior.

The lowly drop of rain is a glorious illustration of this responsibility. What makes a rainbow visible to us? Two things: a drop of rain and light. We have learned that light is invisible and so, because "God is light," the imagery is almost perfect. God and light are both invisible.

Consider how ineffective a mirror would be in making invisible light visible. A mirror does not give off a rainbow. Why? A mirror reflects light, but it does not refract or radiate light. In order for the rainbow to be seen, the light must enter into the drop of rain and find its way out. So what happens to the invisible light once it is inside the drop of rain? It is reflected like a mirror. It is refracted (broken up by bending) by the prism into its various colors seen by the naked eye. And it must be radiated (scattered) into an orderly orb called a bow.

So the humble drop of rain receives the invisible light, then reflects it, refracts it, and radiates it across a darkened sky for the world to see. (In reality, it is a circle of color from the drop, but we normally only see an arc.) The invisible light is visible in terms of the glorious colors of the rainbow.

As believers, we receive a risen, living Christ into our lives. We then reflect, refract, and radiate His person as we exhibit the graces of Christ such as love, joy, peace, longsuffering, gentleness, goodness, faithfulness, meekness, and self control. We do not add anything to the Light but take in all that the Light is and make it visible. If we do add something to the Light, we distort the revelation.

Each believer has the capacity and responsibility to radiate the beauties of Christ just as one drop of rain gives off a small rainbow. But the church gathered has the amazing ability to provide a bow strung across life just as a storm of drops produces a huge display of light across the sky.

Our blessing and responsibility is to receive all the resources of Christ and reveal all the graces of Christ. He does not hold back any to those who offer themselves to reveal and radiate His invisible person, making Him visible in their life. This month, appropriate more of the graces of Christ for display.

Christ, Our Benefactor

In Him also we have obtained an inheritance, being
predestined according to the purpose of Him who works
all things according to the counsel of His will.

Ephesians 1:11

Most people wish for a big inheritance. The idea has a certain attraction because it means a lot of money without any work. Secretly we hope for a windfall of riches. The very idea of the lottery's enticement is summed up in three words: wealth without work!

The intricacies of receiving an inheritance are rather simple. A person amasses wealth. He writes a "last will and testament" in which he designates how he wants it distributed—that is, according to his will. In Hebrews 9:16, we are reminded that the testator must die for the will to be active. When the person dies, the wealth is distributed according to the will, although sometimes a lawyer is called in to see if the will can be altered and the distribution changed. Such is man's method of scattering an inheritance.

God's plan for the distribution of His wealth follows a similar pattern. The Lord Jesus amassed His wealth because of who He is, as well as what He has done. The Lord wrote His will during His life and ministry: "I give to them eternal life." He died to make His will active, but He rose from the dead so that He could be the executor of His own will. There should be no confusion about the tenets of His will. Not only is He alive, but the Holy Spirit has been sent to live in every believer "so that we might know the things that have been freely given to us by God."

Today, for the believer, the inheritance is being distributed by the risen Christ through the Holy Spirit. We have obtained an inheritance that is incorruptible and undefiled and will not pass away. In this life, some people wait for a relative to die so that they can enjoy the inheritance. Christ has died, has been raised, and has even now opened the storehouse of His wealth for all believers to receive a continual supply of needed blessings.

Paul writes that this inheritance is "in Him." The wealth is not bestowed apart from Christ. If a rich uncle dies leaving us riches in his will, we are sad that he must leave this life but happy that we receive an inheritance. How wonderful if the rich uncle were still with us and we could enjoy him and his wealth. God supplies every need because He has infinite wealth in Christ and gives lavishly to all His children according to His will. I have Christ and His wealth!

୨୦ ———————————— ଓଷ

Father, thank you for giving Christ to me with all His wealth. I receive His
power, His peace, and His patience for today.

Strengthened from Within

*That He would grant you, according to the riches of His glory, to
be strengthened with might through His Spirit in the inner man.*

Ephesians 3:16

God's work most often is done from the inside out. Change and
empower the inner man, and it will be apparent that a work of glory
is being done. Even the Old Testament law was summarized by the
command to love God from the heart, followed by loving your neighbor as
yourself. With the indwelling Holy Spirit at work, His goal is to reveal the
new man through our personal behavior.

This verse is part of one of the prayers for believers which not only guides us
in our prayer life, but also helps us see the process that God uses to develop
Christ-likeness in His people. We must not construe from this request that
Paul was asking God to give the Ephesians more than He had given them in
Christ. The specific desire in Paul's mind was for the saints to be strengthened
with "the riches of His glory;" those are the resources that are hidden in
Christ Jesus.

One of the most common prayers from our lips is "give me strength" to cope
with some special effort or to resist some temptation. Paul reminds the church
several times that their strength is in Christ who indwells them. So again here
he acknowledges that the strength they need is in them by "His Spirit." Because
the Spirit who raised Christ from the dead dwells in us, the demonstration
of that power also permanently resides in us. It is the consciousness of our
weakness and of His strength that produces a dependence on what God has
given us by His Spirit.

The "riches of His glory" are the complete resources held in reserve for us to
appropriate by faith. We are not infused with additional strength in answer to
prayer; rather, we are to claim this strength from the storehouse of His person.

*We must learn
to relinquish
our own efforts
to His might.*

What an opulent supply is available to any believer
who acknowledges his weakness and confesses this to
God! Faith placed in Christ Himself empowers us to
do all things according to His will.

God places the responsibility firmly in our control,
whether we use our own strength or appropriate His.
We must learn to relinquish our own efforts to His might. By His strength
we make an invisible Christ visible in our lives. He is then glorified in my
weakness.

ଓ ──────────── ଔ

*Father, thank you for empowering me in Christ and through Your Spirit. I
confess my weakness and claim Your might. My inner man is refreshed and
strengthened by Your Spirit to obey Your Word.*

Grace, Full and Free

But He gives more grace. Therefore He says: "God
resists the proud, but gives grace to the humble."

James 4:6

Twice in the course of one verse we are told that God gives grace. What an all-encompassing expression of the provision of God! The word "grace" is the translation of the Greek *charis* and is translated in different ways, including "grace," "gifts," and "thanks." The Scriptures are clear in telling us that God's adequate grace is available to fulfill our on-going needs. John says in the first chapter of his gospel, "Of His fullness we have all received, and grace for grace." And Paul writes in 2 Corinthians, "God is able to make all grace abound toward you."

God gives more grace than I can use. Although we might deceive ourselves into thinking that we can use up the gifts He gives, we cannot. Rather, we should take enough for today, knowing that His river of grace will flow tomorrow for that day's supply. We should dip our daily cup without asking what the level of flow is or from where it is supplied. We should freely take of the water of grace.

God gives more grace than I need. In explaining God's provision for our salvation, Paul reminds us, "But where sin abounded, grace abounded much more." There is no lack in God's saving grace for any sinner who comes to God. There is no lack in sanctifying grace for the daily work of the Spirit of God through the Word of God.

He gives more grace than I expect. We live in a society that gives as little as possible for the most money, and it is hard to adjust to God's overwhelming provision. Many expect God to give grace for salvation but not enough for living. Yet the same river that flowed for our salvation flows for our sanctification and our service. Draw all you will. "He gives more grace."

He gives more grace than I ask for. There are people who approach God thinking that they are imposing on Him, as if they are interrupting Him by asking Him for grace. Perhaps the Lord will answer them, "Fill your cup yourself! I have given you all my grace." His river of grace is for your every need, every day, every trial, every sorrow, every problem, every joy, and every service.

Only the proud choose to live without the resources of the river flowing past their door. But the humble bow, dipping as big a cup as they desire into the river's abundant supply.

೮೦ ———————————————— ೞ

Father, thank you for the overwhelming adequacy of Your grace, given to me
in Christ. I draw deeply for the burdens of today.

Deliverance, Soon and Certain

*And to wait for His Son from heaven, whom He raised from the
dead, even Jesus who delivers us from the wrath to come.*
1 Thessalonians 1:10

E very society has its prophets of doom. Both religious and social
activists proclaim the end of the world in one form or another. War, the
alignment of planets, change in the weather, the end of a millennium,
and a host of other reasons prompt people to warn everyone of the end. What
is a person to do? Some people build homes with bomb shelters. Others move
from the city to a farm where they can subsist without much interaction with
the rest of society. Some move to another country that is more attuned to
preserving our beautiful earth.

From whatever philosophy these prophets draw their message of doom, there
is some truth in each one. But the warning from the Bible is to flee from the
wrath to come—God's wrath. There is no question that it is coming. The
world should be wondering how and by what means escape is possible.

God's calendar includes a cataclysmic judgment of the world and our
society as we know it. It will come suddenly and without any reasonable
escape. It will engulf the globe and affect the entire world by changing the
ecological balance, economic division, sociological distinctions, and religious
allegiances. It will usher in a new world economy, governed by God, in and
through the Lord Jesus Christ.

The event which is next on God's schedule may take place at any moment.
After Christ comes from heaven to take the believers out of the world, He will
plunge the remaining crowds and their society into gloom and doom. Those
who have refused to accept Christ as Savior will be left to experience the
manifold calamities of the tribulation.

The salvation that God has provided in
Christ through the work of the cross includes
forgiveness of sin, entrance into the family
of God, eternal life, and a home in glory, as
well as deliverance from this wrath to come.
It is unthinkable that the work of Christ was

> *Jesus is the One who
> delivers us from God's
> awful judgment.*

sufficient to pay the penalty for all our sin but inadequate to deliver us from
"the wrath to come." 1 Thessalonians 1:10 gives rest to the faint of heart that
Jesus, who was raised from the dead, is the One who delivers us from God's
awful judgment on a world that has rejected His Son as Savior.

⁕ ———————————————— ℋ

*Father, thank you for the resurrection of Jesus, who has promised to deliver
us from the wrath to come. I eagerly await His coming and live accordingly.*

The Spirit Flows

Whom [that is, the Holy Spirit] He poured out on us
abundantly through Jesus Christ our Savior.

Titus 3:6

D o we have the Holy Spirit in us? The repetition of this great truth throughout the New Testament would lead any believer to say yes. Yet when was the last time that we even acknowledged that the Holy Spirit of God is indwelling us? In the midst of our busy schedules and activities, we are prone to leave Him out of our plans. The habit of making decisions without consulting Him is proof that we do not consider His presence or His wisdom necessary for life. We need to be reminded many times over that the Spirit has been given to be a source of guidance and direction.

Every believer is given all of the Spirit.

This gift from God was as costly as the salvation of our souls. Our Lord came to save us from sin and to empower us to live in a perverse and perishing world. It took His resurrection and subsequent ascension to set God free to send His Holy Spirit to dwell in the heart and life of everyone who believes in Jesus Christ.

The picture of abundance referred to in today's text is not hard to imagine. An overflowing cup is reason to get a towel and clean up the mess. However, in Psalm 23, the gracious abundance of God's provision encourages us to lift the cup to our face and pour out its abundance all over us. And what is more glorious is that the cup continues to flow, just like the cruse of oil that filled the pots and would have continued to do so had not the widow and her sons run out of vessels to fill (see 2 Kings 4). Paul adds elsewhere that the Holy Spirit is not given by measure. We could just as soon measure the exact flow of water over Niagara Falls as to limit the abundance of the Holy Spirit, poured out on each believer through Christ.

But one will say, "I have more of the Holy Spirit than you." No! The Holy Spirit cannot be given in parts or pieces. Every believer is given all of the Spirit, but not everyone employs the abundance and allows Him to fill and flood their hearts to the point of overflow, demonstrating the fruit of the Spirit to all who will behold. The abundance of the Holy Spirit produces "much fruit" that pleases the Father. Limited fruit points to a failure to appropriate the power and provision of the Spirit. The Holy Spirit has been poured out abundantly. "Be filled!"

ൠ ——————————————— ♋

Father, thank you for Your Holy Spirit. I confess that I have lived days without consulting Him and receiving His wisdom for daily life.

Minding the Mind of Christ

*For "who has known the mind of the Lord that he may
instruct Him?" But we have the mind of Christ.*

1 Corinthians 2:16

This is one of the simplest statements of God's great salvation gifts to believers. For many of us, it is a long, hard road learning about all the blessings that God has poured out in us through Christ Jesus. The Old Testament quotation reminds the readers that there is an infinite distance between the seeker and that which he seeks. Puny man simply cannot know the mind of God. Added to that, he certainly cannot consider the prospect of instructing or teaching God anything.

> *Christ is speaking and waiting for us to listen.*

In spite of this, the temptation is to think that we, even this side of the resurrection, have a better grip on our lives than does the Lord Himself. How many times do we question the Lord's decisions? In most cases we would choose differently from how He chooses. It is human nature to see things only from our perspective; we do not have the big picture that God has at His disposal.

With the advent of the Holy Spirit, God has endowed every believer with more than the Old Testament saints ever had. It is only because of the resurrection and ascension of Christ that God was set free to bestow the person of Christ in each believer. We can sum up our spiritual condition: Christ crucified, Christ raised, Christ glorified, the Spirit sent, and every believer endowed with all the blessings of salvation that are found in Christ

Paul's authoritative statement is not based on experience but on the unity of the risen Christ. Because the Holy Spirit is not given by measure, the person of Christ cannot be given partially. We either have all of Christ or none. If we do "not have the Spirit of Christ," writes Paul, "we do not belong to Him." We have not been given a piece of the mind of Christ as though we only received certain profound statements of truth for occasional consideration. We have Christ! We have a living person indwelling us whose wisdom and knowledge springs from His divine mind.

The fountain of all "wisdom, righteousness, sanctification, and redemption," and a host of other aspects of His gracious mind, is ours. Is the problem that Christ will not speak His mind? Of course not! The problem is that we do not listen to the Word or His Spirit. Christ is speaking and waiting for us to listen and learn His mind.

ॐ ———————————— ᘯ

Father, thank you for giving Christ with all His infinite mind, emotion, and will. I tune my heart to listen and learn of Him today.

Under New Ownership

Or do you not know that your body is the temple
of the Holy Spirit who is in you, whom you have
from God, and you are not your own?

1 Corinthians 6:19

It is hard to give up ownership of something that we greatly value. To acknowledge that we do not belong to ourselves challenges our sense of ownership, because most of us think highly of who and what we are. How many people who come to Christ for salvation are told that in doing so they are giving away ownership of themselves? Not many. How many realize that believers are soldiers in Christ's army, His stewards, slaves, students, and sons? Very few. Maybe we should be more careful to let those seeking salvation know more of these details—and, in particular, that all believers are God's property.

I suppose that some prospective Christians would reconsider if we gave all the details about what it means to receive Christ into their life. Even some seasoned believers have difficulty turning their life over to the new owner because they are His possession. It comes down to our willingness to trust God for some things, but not others. We can trust Him for the forgiveness of sin because that is a once-for-all transaction. We can trust Him to take us to heaven because the alternative is pretty bad. But to trust Him with the direction of our life, the daily decisions, the use of our abilities, and ownership of all our possessions becomes a lot harder. It's as if we are saying to Him, "Take care of my past, and take care of my ultimate future, but don't monkey with my present plans." One reason that this struggle exists is a failure to really know our Owner.

> *It comes down to our willingness to trust God for some things, but not others.*

Yet, whether we like it or not, the plain fact remains—"you are not your own." We belong to God. He bought us and can do with us as He wishes. But think of it this way: we have a lifetime coming to understand Him and His plans for our life. We hope that it does not include any huge problems, major sickness, or great losses, but the more we know Him, the easier it is to trust Him with His property. We cannot change ownership, but we can change our trust in the One to whom we belong. We are owned by God! He is far more trustworthy than we are to order our life. We cannot change ownership, but we can change our objection to His ownership.

Father, thank you for making me Your own property. I know that I can trust You every day and in every way. I confess my fear when I think of what You might allow in my life today. I choose to trust You.

Free to Live

*For the law of the Spirit of life in Christ Jesus has
made me free from the law of sin and death.*

Romans 8:2

W hen the children of Israel placed themselves under the Mosaic Law, the people said, "All that the Lord says we will do." But they did not know all that the law would require, regulating every detail of their life with its 613 commandments. Nor did they understand its effects on their lives, how its very presence would provoke in them a desire to break it, or that they would be punished for disobedience. What a mess they got themselves in.

Into that mess came the Lord Jesus as a perfect man, born to live under the law and to redeem those burdened by its heavy requirements. Not only did He live a perfect life, fulfilling all the law's requirements, but He also upheld it before all as a perfect standard. Since not a single person could profess to having equaled that standard, all were summarily condemned as having "fallen short of the glory of God." This law silenced every mouth and declared everyone guilty and incapable of keeping it or of extricating themselves from its bondage.

More than a perfect life, however, was needed to deliver the oppressed world from the judgment of God's holy law. The further provision of God was the death of His beloved Son on the cross. Among the huge accomplishments of the finished work of Christ are redemption from sin, reconciliation of man, and propitiation of God. In addition, Christ took away obedience to the law as a rule of life. He delivered man from the curse of the law by hanging on a tree under God's judgment. God was satisfied with Christ; He cancelled our debt to the law by nailing that debt to His cross. All this so that no one would confuse His way of salvation or the means of sanctification (Colossians 2:14).

In freeing us from the law that provoked sin and brought death, God set forth His Son as the only source of salvation. To believe that Christ died for my sin is to be set free from the principle of law, from bondage to sin, from eternal death, and from a host of other influences that condemn me. In place of a law that results in sin and death, I have been given "the law of the Spirit of life." This Spirit sets forth Christ's perfect life before me and strengthens me to walk in the power of that Spirit—in Christ-likeness.

⁊○ ——————————————— ○⳩

Father, thank you for nailing my debt to the law to Christ's cross. I confess that the principle of law awakens in me a desire to disobey. I now celebrate the law of the Spirit of life working in me.

Outward Death, Inward Life

*Therefore we do not lose heart. Even though our outward man
is perishing, yet the inward man is being renewed day by day.*
2 Corinthians 4:16

Most of the prayers that we offer are for the health of the body, yet the Lord still allows the faithful to be as sick as the sinful. The aging process that began because of sin will continue until we die. Death itself is part of the outward man perishing, and being a believer does not insulate us from the tragic ravages of disease and a declining body. But, as beings bound to the outward man, we are often more occupied with it than with the inward man which is progressing and renewing.

The soul of man does not age. This fundamental truth lies like gold in a mine. The body, the brain, the eyes, the nerves, the muscles, the digestion—all tend to become less effective as we age. They decay. But the spirit is given life at spiritual birth like a fully mature Adam when he was created. Sure, the soul must be trained and disciplined as the body matures, but the new man is an entity that does not wear out from use.

Into this debilitating equation comes the gift of eternal life, an inheritance that adds a dimension to the being of man not previously present. Before we received Christ (who is our life), the prospect of an aging body was all-consuming. With the addition of an "inward man," the prospect is delightful. As believers, we have a choice that the unbeliever does not have. The unbeliever is driven by a crumbling body. The believer has a choice of whether to follow the old ruler, the body, or to be fully occupied with the renewing of his inner man. What a choice! Yet most believers have a hard time shaking the practice of unsaved days when they were fully absorbed with the body and had no knowledge or consciousness of the inner man.

As believers, we can and must dwell on renewing the spiritually alive inward man rather than our collapsing house. The renewing man must be fed, enriched, and directed so that it will remain healthy and lively, growing in faith, hope, love, joy, and peace. The inward man is capable of vital fellowship with God, though the outer man's functions decrease.

Who will control? The decaying body with its failing eyesight, declining hearing, loss of taste, sleepless nights, and poor digestion? Or the inward man who is growing in faith, expanding in love, celebrating truth, enjoying peace, developing in patience, and growing up into the stature of the fullness of Christ?

ಬ —————————————— ೞ

*Father, I am aware that my body is decaying. Thank you for the new man
which is renewed day by day as I grow in truth from Your Word.*

A Helper for the Helpless

And I will pray the Father, and He will give you another
Helper, that He may abide with you forever.

John 14:16

I s the fulfillment of this promise contingent on anything or anyone but the faithfulness of God? The answer is obvious. God can be depended on to fulfill the Son's prayer for the gift of the Holy Spirit. He will never leave us nor forsake us, since He will abide in us forever. The residence of the Spirit in the life of every believer is one of the foundational gifts in the great bundle called salvation.

It is a blessing to know of the Spirit's presence, but so much more important to be aware of His ministry in us. His is not only an abiding power, but a person who is all powerful. He is here as an anointing that is never withdrawn. He is in us as a resource for the fruit of the Spirit, the embodiment of the fruit itself as manifested in the Lord Jesus. He is not only our help in time of need, but the Helper who is with us always.

It is important to be aware of the Spirit's ministry in us.

So often we appeal to God for "special help" when "the Helper" is abiding in us. Why have we not learned the simple lesson that the Holy Spirit is in us as the Helper? If we will simply acknowledge that the burden is heavy, He will not stand by and let us struggle with the burden of the day.

Do I think that my prayer is more effective than the Lord's own prayer to the Father that I be given the Holy Spirit? No! Christ was raised from the dead in order that that victory might set God free to bestow all blessings proceeding from the cross. The Lord ascended so that the Holy Spirit would be set free to indwell every believer and be the Helper to everyone on the road from earth to glory. Since God in Christ did all that for every believer, do you suppose that the self-same Spirit, sent from the Father, would indwell a believer without "helping" him? Of course not. The Helper is given to help a believer, not because he asks, but because he acknowledges his weakness.

What is the difference between my asking for help and my acknowledging my weakness? Asking for help suggests that outside of Christ and His Spirit is something not given to me *in* Christ. Acknowledging my weakness is to confess that there are things that I cannot do myself, but which can be done in the power of the Spirit.

ℝ ———————————— ℭ

Father, I confess my weakness and inadequacy and rely on Your help. Thank you for giving me my Helper.

Our Hope in Heaven

Because of the hope which is laid up for you in heaven, of
which you heard before in the word of the truth of the gospel.
Colossians 1:5

Our world is often described as a hopeless place. The moral fiber of the world is decaying. The spiritual climate is being contaminated. The intellectual strata are filled with deception. The family structure is being destroyed. Integrity is missing in important relationships. Love is defined as lust. Peace is destroyed by anger. Treaties and vows are broken with no pang of conscience. Man hopes that things will change, but in this world there can be no hope apart from the knowledge of Christ and His gospel of salvation.

When we heard the gospel, none of us knew of the full scope of blessings that are available as a result of being saved. No one verse gives a full and complete summary of all that God offers in Christ. It takes a lifetime of study to gather all the blessings of the gospel. The ones that we tend to think of most often are forgiveness, heaven, and eternal life, but we will never know the fullness of these blessings until we are like Christ and with Him in heaven.

So what is this hope? The consideration could be explained in terms of a lot of things that we hope *for* in glory. Many believers hope for a large mansion in the Father's house. Others are hopeful of receiving a big collection of rewards. Others are hoping that they will have important responsibilities in the heavenly kingdom. Maybe we hope for these desires as a way of focusing our minds and hearts on heaven, but are such things in the mind of God? Are these hopes sure?

Perhaps closer to the meaning of this verse is the understanding that the hope that is laid up in heaven for us is Christ Himself. We are prone to think only in terms of having *things* in heaven. The Bible does not say much about heaven or our occupation and activities there. Rather, the emphasis is on the Person that we will be with when we are in heaven. Surely the fullness of "the hope" is not in having some things in heaven, but in being with our Lord Jesus Christ.

We are encouraged to desire to be with Him. It is not so important what we have, as who we are with. The hope of the believer is to see Christ as He is in glory. What anticipation is awakened in our heart when we think of seeing Him face to face!

───── ༄ ──────────────── ༒ ─────

Father, thank you for presenting Your Son as my hope. I fill my heart today
with the anticipation of seeing Him. Perhaps that will happen even today!

Father Knows Best

*Then the Lord knows how to deliver the godly out of temptations
and to reserve the unjust under punishment for the day of judgment.*
2 Peter 2:9

If our child were facing a problem that we could easily solve, or one that we could keep him from experiencing, most of us would be tempted to intervene. But God our Father obviously does not always do that with His children. Sometimes we earnestly pray and plead for God to intervene, but He stands by and watches us handle the situation. He is, of course, wiser than we are.

Peter wrote his two epistles to encourage believers who were suffering for their faith. Most were Jews who were experiencing severe persecution. Many had lost their homes and possessions and had been driven from their land, finding themselves in what we know today as Turkey. There they continued to suffer because of their testimony for Christ. Peter was guided by the Holy Spirit to write to them in the midst of their trials and persecution.

Did the Lord deliver these suffering believers from the temptations that they were facing? The answer is no, both for them and for many who endure similar experiences. He will deliver us *through* the trial, but not necessarily *from* facing it.

It is encouraging to know that the Lord is a righteous judge, and that He will consign the unjust to the final punishment reserved by God for the wicked. But it is also clear that He does not commit these unjustified ones to the place of punishment as soon as their injustice is recognized. The Lord is longsuffering and waits patiently for even the most ungodly to change their behavior. Seldom is there immediate judgment by a righteous God. Nor is there normally instant release for the godly from every trial and problem by a compassionate God.

What encouraged these believers was that the Lord was in control. Nothing is beyond the supervision of our sovereign Lord. He is working behind the scenes for His glory and our good. And, if we are patient enough to observe it, even our own lives reveal the hand of the Lord working all things for our good and His glory.

Most of us, however, impatiently plead and maybe even command the Lord to immediately deliver us from every trial. Instead, He preserves us in the trial so that we will grow by appropriating His graces. The fact that the Lord knows how to deliver us does not mean that He will—no matter how much or how long we pray. Father knows best!

⁎ ———————————————— ℙ

Father, thank you for Your superintendence in my life. I submit my will to Yours and await Your action in my life, because You know best.

We Shine

For you were once darkness, but now you are
light in the Lord. Walk as children of light.

Ephesians 5:8

The light most often used in Bible times was a candle or torch. This kind of light was not intended to be turned on and off repeatedly in the course of a few minutes. One of the advantages of a flashlight is the ability to push a button and have light for as long as needed. When the switch is released, the light goes off. That's why it's called a *flash*light. But Christians are not called to be flashing lights. God has declared in His Word that we *are* light. This light is not something that we decide to reveal or not. We are revealing our light every moment of our earthly journey. Walk like Christ who is the Light!

Many believers, however, could better be described as flashlights, in that they "push a button" to reveal their Christian life when they want people to see the light. Their life is flashed before the world at their discretion. But today's Scripture says that "we are light," having been "switched on" by God when we believed. There is no off button. We are not flashlights, but lights.

We cannot stop our light from shining.

Where our walk takes us is our decision. The Lord condemns putting a light under a bushel or bed, yet many believers think that the light is displayed according to their prerogative. Some lights are in a closet, and no one other than themselves knows that the light is on. By cutting themselves off from the world, they cut their light off from the world. A light is best set on a table, a post, or a hill, so that its radiance can be diffused where it is needed. Light is needed in the darkest part of the house, street, or town. When we are in the market, our light shines. In the office, at home, at school, to our neighbors, within the church—our light is on. Our light is needed in the darkest place.

We cannot stop our light from shining, but we can decide where it will shine based on where we "walk." We may put shades around our life to change the color or brightness, or we may even diffuse our light in a certain direction. But our light is to be fully displayed and unencumbered by any artificial filters that display only certain parts in certain directions. We need to remove all obstructions and filters and keep the globe clean. We are "light in the Lord" to the world. This is a divine calling, a practical challenge, and a personal responsibility.

Father, thank you for making me a light in a dark world. I commit my life and light to go into the darkest part of my world.

Death, Defied and Defeated

Inasmuch then as the children have partaken of flesh and blood,
He Himself likewise shared in the same, that through death He
might destroy him who had the power of death, that is, the devil.
Hebrews 2:14

T he victory of our Lord Jesus over the devil was complete and final. No future conflict is in question. God the Father could have sent Satan to the bottomless pit when He raised Christ from the dead, but, instead of chaining him at that time, He sentenced him to future banishment from His presence—and from ours as well.

Many Christians think that Christ's victory would have been greater and more glorious if the devil had not been allowed to roam. Had he been sent to the lake of fire at that time, we would not face our current conflicts with this enemy and his army. But God chose to defeat the devil at the cross and to postpone his final sentencing. At God's appointed time, Satan will be bound in the bottomless pit for most of Christ's thousand-year reign. Then he will be released for a season to challenge Christ's authority one final time, after which he will be banished to the lake of fire forever.

Hebrews 2:14 tells us that the devil "had the power of death." But, in Christ's victory on the cross, the keys of death were snatched from his grasp and now hang prominently at Christ's side, next to the key of hell. We have in the Scriptures a graphic picture of this conflict in David's confrontation with Goliath. David hit him in the head with a stone, knocking him down flat, then ran, took Goliath's sword, and killed him by cutting off his head (1 Samuel 17:51). David kept the sword and the head as symbols of victory. Goliath's power was now in the hands of the man who killed him.

> *Christ entered into death with the full assurance that even death could not defeat Him.*

Christ entered into death with the full assurance that even death could not defeat Him. Rather, it was the means of snatching the power of death from the enemy and returning it to Christ Himself. Because of this, believers do not need to fear death. Christ secured the victory and shares it with us, just as David shared His victory with all Israel. The fruits of victory have been fully distributed. We have been set free from the fear of death and await the day when the enemy's sentence will be fully executed. Satan is a defeated enemy!

ಬಲ ──────────────── ೞ

Father, thank you for Christ's victory over the devil. I enjoy the fruits of that victory and am at peace because of it.

Faith from Start to Finish

*As you have therefore received Christ
Jesus the Lord, so walk in Him.*

Colossians 2:6

The walk of faith does not change from the one step that put us on the journey in the first place. The step which Paul calls "the obedience of faith" in another text is but the beginning of the life-long pilgrimage. The command from Paul's pen in Colossians 2:6 is to walk in Christ. The initial step was taken when we understood our sinfulness and received Christ as the Way, the Truth, and the Life. The resurrected Savior came to indwell us permanently for the entire journey. His presence is applied to us by the Holy Spirit, who abides with us forever.

The children of Israel began their journey to Canaan by a step of faith in the blood of the lamb on that Passover night. God wanted them to take every continuing step in the same faith. But, as the record shows, they believed that God could take them out of

> *The true walk
> is by faith
> and faith alone.*

Egypt, but refused to believe that He could take them into the land of Canaan. How sad to miss God's ultimate blessing of victorious living by refusing to trust the One who delivered them from bondage and slavery. They were "unbelieving believers." They took the first step of faith and a few more, but then at the door of the land of rest they said no.

They are not alone. We too can face the same temptation and fall into a life of unbelief. Our journey should be characterized by walking by faith, not by sight. Yet we wish and even pray for a walk directed by sight, sound, feeling, and touch. The true walk is by faith and faith alone. God may give an occasional confirmation to our senses but, as we grow, those will become less and less frequent. We often wish that we could see the end of the journey or know the climate and conditions of a month or a year ahead. That attitude falls into the same category of unbelief as with Israel. To that disposition our faithful Lord says, "I will care for you, walk with you, direct your steps, provide for you, and bring you to the Father's house. Walk in me."

Many people think that only the first step is by faith and that subsequent steps are dependent on physical effort, human wisdom, or personal arrangement. But, from the first step to the last, the exercise is to be one of faith in Him. He will light the path step by step as we walk in Him.

ℬ ──────────── ℭ

Father, thank you for Christ. I choose to walk in harmony with Him. I will follow His path, enjoy His care, and rest in His wisdom today.

Our Eternal Savings Bank

Now may He who supplies seed to the sower, and bread
for food, supply and multiply the seed you have sown
and increase the fruits of your righteousness.

2 Corinthians 9:10

Money! There is much written about it in the Scriptures, yet it is one of the most misused commodities that we handle. Like time, it comes and goes. As with time, God has made us stewards of it. Time is a blessing that is given to everyone equally. No one gets more and none less. It cannot be retrieved or used again. Money, on the other hand, is not given to everyone equally. Many in our world have only a few coins in their pockets, whereas others have bulging bank accounts. Yet every person is accountable for the use of what is entrusted to him.

God takes responsibility to repay all who engage in buying, selling, and giving seed and money. The farmer is conscious of his dependence on the Creator for the increase of his seed. Everyone in the agricultural sector knows that if you do not sow seed you will not reap an increase. Laws of the harvest are universally accepted. Sow, and you will reap the same kind. The harvest always takes place in a different season than sowing. You reap more than you sow. What great laws of the harvest!

Paul teaches that the one who regulates the harvest also controls the multiplication of money from our hands. The comparison of seed with money is amazing. Why do we accept the laws of the harvest and so easily reject the laws of giving? Many Christians are more convinced of the profit of investing money in a secular context than of investing in spiritual values and eternal issues. Yet the fruits of righteousness are reaped by the one who places his resources at the disposal of the Lord of the harvest—guaranteed! Let's remember that we will give account of where we invested our "seed."

> *Knowing this, why do we trust the stock market more than the Master?*

We have a glorious promise that the gift that we sacrificially invest in eternity will be multiplied many times over in the hands of the God of creation. There is no question of the superintendence of God over our resources. Knowing this, why do we trust the stock market more than the Master?

ഇ ———————————— ൭

Father, thank you for the wealth that You have entrusted to me. I know that You have given me what I can handle. I confess that I have squandered much that could have been invested in eternal things.

People of Title

*To the church of God which is at Corinth, to those
who are sanctified in Christ Jesus, called to be
saints, with all who in every place call on the name
of Jesus Christ our Lord, both theirs and ours.*

1 Corinthians 1:2

The apostle Paul gives the lofty designation of "saints" to believers in most of the letters that he writes to the churches. And, although we tend to use the word as a description rather than a grand title, the designation is not dependent on behavior; rather it is bestowed by the Lord Himself.

We often do not use the word "church" in the correct sense, either. What is a church? To most people, the term commonly refers to a building frequently topped by a steeple or a cross. Yet, in the Scriptures, the term is reserved for people—a group of people who have gathered for the specific purposes of worship, fellowship, and edification.

Who makes up the church? Here again confusion reigns, not from Scripture but from common use. A Baptist church is a building where Baptists gather. The same idea pertains to every denomination. But, in the New Testament, a church is simply a group of people who have believed on the Lord Jesus and who gather out of the world for spiritual activities. Common English usage of "local church" refers to both saved and lost alike, but the church in the Scriptures is limited exclusively to those belonging to Christ by regeneration. Not only that, but the word is used in the Bible for the local church (such as the one in Corinth), and also for the universal (or "catholic") church, which is made up of all believers from the Day of Pentecost to the present day. Although every believer can and should choose to belong to a local church, believing on Christ automatically makes one a member of the universal church.

Church members are called saints—that is, by designation they are saints. Most people use the word for those who have lived a life of piety and so deserve the title of saint. But Paul is saying that every believer of this local church was a saint. That does not mean that they lived what we would call a saintly life. But still the title is valid, because each believer has been set apart to Christ the moment that he or she believed.

This is a high calling, one to which we should all aspire to live. I must ask myself, "Do I live up to my name of 'saint'?"

୨୦ ──────────── ୧୪

Father, thank you for making me a saint. I confess that I do not always live a saintly life, but I know that You have given me the resources to live a life of piety and holiness. I commit myself to live like that today.

18 JULY

Blessed Because We Belong

*So then, brethren, we are not children of
the bondwoman but of the free.*

Galatians 4:31

The allegory of this chapter is a remarkable revelation of the blessing and inheritance belonging to those related to Christ by faith. The two mothers referred to here were Hagar and Sarah. The two sons were Ishmael and Isaac. There were two covenants: law and grace; two identities: flesh and promise; two mountains: Sinai and Jerusalem; two conditions: works and faith; two results: rejection and acceptance; two consequences: the one was thrown out, and the other inherited the blessings.

Paul used those striking comparisons to teach the Galatian believers that keeping rules and regulations was useless for salvation and sanctification. These readers were hoping that obedience to the law would make them acceptable to God. The inspired Word, however, states that no amount of obedience to commandments can obtain the blessing of salvation. In the same way, Hagar and Ishmael were cast out, and the heir according to promise remained in the household of faith.

Today, many believers are of the impression that the blessing of God in their life is guaranteed only if they keep restrictions and obligations imposed by themselves or their mentors. Many people think that if they do not go to church then God is displeased and will not act favorably toward them. Long lists of laws that include tithing, baptism, church membership, and prayers describe a program of righteousness that people think will entice God to "bless" them.

The powerful point made in Galatians 4:31 is that believers have been given salvation that is in Christ alone, without regard to our works. We are heirs because we are related to God by faith in Christ. We do not earn anything spiritual, but we are accorded all the blessings of Christ by faith in Christ. We are under the promises by which we are free from bondage.

We are not related to Christ by the law or the bondwoman. We are united to the promises found in Christ by faith alone. Isaac did nothing to obtain the promises. He was born into that position. The blessing of his father Abraham was based solely on his birthright. He could not earn it, buy it, pray for it, seek it, or beg for it.

All the blessings of salvation are ours by faith. We cannot earn them, buy them, pray for them, seek them, or beg for them. All the blessings of Christ are our permanent personal possession. Live in the light of that provision!

₞ ———————————— ∛

Father, thank you for the blessings of my salvation, provided to me because of my faith in Your Son. In Your strength, I cast out all legalism from my life.

Fight the Good Fight

For the flesh lusts against the Spirit and the Spirit
against the flesh; and these are contrary to one another,
so that you do not do the things that you wish.

Galatians 5:17

A few Bible students argue that the old sin nature is eradicated when we believe. If God did so much, they say, would He not go all the way and dispose of the old nature (the flesh) when He comes to dwell in each of us? Of course, God *could* have done away with the sin nature—but He didn't. This verse clearly says that a conflict is going on in the life of the believer, between the Holy Spirit and the flesh. It is instructive that God has left "the flesh," knowing that a battle would take place continuously in our lives. It is also enlightening that the Spirit is as active in the conflict as is the flesh. It is a continuing struggle.

The message here is that we have a significant role in the victory of the Spirit over the flesh. We decide who is going to win control. By nature, the flesh rules, since we were born under its control. When we were born again and the Holy Spirit came to indwell, a conflict was created that was not there before.

Even as believers, we can fail to give the Spirit His place of authority in our lives, thereby yielding to the flesh. We must vigilantly choose victory over the flesh by consciously yielding to His control. Since the old man is not annihilated in our being, this conflict in the body will continue until we see Christ's face.

In some old English homes the kitchen was carved out of the soil below the house. The ground was so damp that the earth oozed a kind of mold that could be swept up daily. The only way to keep the kitchen mold-free was to keep a fire burning in the hearth so that the room was warm and dry. If the fire was neglected, the mold grew. If the fire burned continually, the mold was defeated. It was a daily battle.

> *God could have done away with the sin nature—but He didn't.*

The "old man" is not going away, but the fire of the Holy Spirit in our new nature, fed by Bible study and prayer, will keep the flesh in check. Should we fail to keep the fire burning, the flesh will get the advantage in our lives and we will lose a few fights. The battle is in our hands.

₨ ———————————— ₳

Father, I know by this battle that You are seeking victory in my life. I commit my will to join in harmony with Your Spirit for daily victory.

Transformed by Tests

He who calls you is faithful, who also will do it.
1 Thessalonians 5:24

What good is faithfulness without a test? The test of faithfulness is actually doing what I promised. Peter boasted that he would never deny Christ, but shortly afterwards the Lord gave him three tests. He subsequently wept bitterly at his three failures.

We sit in a church service, challenged to dedicate more of our time to spiritual matters. We might vow to eat less or to read the Bible and pray more. The proof of our commitment comes as we sit to eat, or when morning dawns and we are faced with the opportunity to spend more time with the Lord. Do we rise from our bed?

In verse 23, Paul has just said, "May the God of peace Himself sanctify you completely" and preserve you for the coming of Christ. The use of "may" suggests that it is a prayer or a request of Paul for the Thessalonian believers: "May God sanctify," "May God preserve." In our vocabulary, the word "may" suggests areas of doubt. Paul wants God to do it; we may want it to be done; but will it in fact be accomplished? Here the Holy Spirit leads Paul to add, "He is faithful, who also will do it."

God is faithful in His goal, His process, His provision, His methods, and in reminding us that no tests come without His permission.

If God does not operate as we think He ought, we are tempted to question His faithfulness. But God's faithfulness does not change, only our perception of it. The Bible is laced with stories and biographies of men and women whom God was seeking to mature and perfect as they walked this pilgrim journey. Their roads were perforated with daily testing. God's goal was to perfect them. He shaped and molded their lives without their permission, and He is doing the same in our lives.

God is faithful in His goal, His process, His provision, His methods, and above all in reminding us that none of these tests come to us without His permission. One day we will be like Christ, when we see Him as He is. He will do it! We can allow Him to do His work on the final day, or we can respond every day by accepting each test and, little by little, becoming more like Christ.

— ❧ ——————————— ❧ —

Father, thank you for Your faithfulness, recorded for our learning. I trust Your work in me, shaping me through Your tests and trials.

Considering Our Conception

Having been born again, not of corruptible seed but incorruptible,
through the word of God which lives and abides forever.
1 Peter 1:23

By definition, birth is a once-for-all experience which has continuing results that flow from that event. This is true physically and spiritually. A birth is marked by a specific date and time. It is reasonable to assume that God has also set aside a day and time when each of His children is born into His family. Now, not every child knows the date or time of his birth. We have talked to young people in Africa and India who have no idea when they came into this world—but the issue of their birth cannot be challenged. They may not be able to celebrate the actual day when they were born, but they can and do celebrate their obvious life.

> *The Word of God is living, holds life, bears life, and sustains life.*

Every child comes from the union of a man and a woman. That union creates the relationship between child and parents which cannot be broken. We are related to our parents by a physical connection that began at conception, is borne out in life, and makes itself evident in the similarities that we share.

The seed in today's Scripture is the Word of God which is living, holds life, bears life, and sustains life. God acts by placing His Seed in us, thereby uniting us with Himself in a bond that cannot be broken. By placing Christ in us, He gives us His own life. This transaction takes place on a day and in a moment that may only be known to our Father. His record is vital and may not be revealed to us until we are in glory. Whether or not we know the exact moment or even the day is irrelevant to the possession of spiritual life, brought about by the new birth.

In 1 John 3:9 we are reminded of the enduring nature of this life: "His seed remains in him." The life of Christ is called "His seed;" the presence of this seed in every child of God is the guarantee that we are God's children, just as the DNA of our physical parents is present in each of their children and guarantees that we are their offspring. It is only by spiritual birth, or the implantation of God's seed, that we are born again. No imitating or mimicking of Christ can produce this glorious display of the life of God in His children.

₧ ———————————————— ℃

Father, thank you for giving me Your life when I trusted Your Son for salvation. Show Your seed through me as I surrender my body and soul to Your control.

Dead to the World

If then you were raised with Christ, seek those things which are above, where Christ is, sitting at the right hand of God.

Colossians 3:1

The word "if" as used here is an already-concluded condition. To get the full force of the thought, it helps to translate it, "*Since* then you were raised with Christ." When Christ was raised, we were raised with Him. Obviously, our resurrection is not dependent on us, but on God. Whether or not we exercise faith in Christ on a daily basis does not affect our heavenly position, but it does affect our enjoyment of the wonderful blessing of living out that resurrection life. This truth relates to our being chosen in Christ, to our death with Him, to our burial, resurrection, and ascension, and to our being seated with Christ.

Going into the baptismal waters graphically pictures death, burial, and resurrection.

Romans chapter 6 reminds us of the permanence of this condition, but the daily blessing is dependent on living out our identification with Christ. Since we were given new life in Christ, a new kind of walk is possible. The picture of baptism in Romans 6 helps us understand it. Going into the baptismal waters graphically pictures death, burial, and resurrection. We did not go into death alone but with Christ or, more accurately, "in Christ." When Christ died, I died. When Christ was buried, the old "me" was buried. When Christ was raised, I was raised—but raised to live out *His* life, not mine. Had He not been raised, I would still be dead and I would have no new life to live.

A person who is baptized comes out of the water all wet. Of course, he dries off, but his first steps drip with the "waters of death." We died with Christ and were raised with Him but, in contrast to the physical illustration, all our steps should continue to drip with the evidence of having gone into death with Him. We are raised to walk in a new way, by a new rule, for a new purpose. Because of that, we now seek things that are above, where Christ is seated. We no longer live for the world but for the things above, which are eternal. This is a new walk which is clear to all who see us "dripping with death to this world," but alive to the things that please the Lord Jesus. We chose to be united to Christ when we believed. We choose to live His life by faith.

ಙ ———————————— ಚ

Father, thank you for uniting me to Christ so that each of His experiences is mine as well. I declare that I died to this world, and I commit to seek the things that are eternal, where Christ is seated.

Our Waning World

And the world is passing away, and the lust of it; but
he who does the will of God abides forever.

1 John 2:17

What kinds of things are going to last, and which will pass away? Many of the activities that we invest our time in will have to be done again and again. Clothes get dirty and must be cleaned. We repeatedly have to fill the car with gas. We eat at lunch time and need to eat again a few hours later. Night comes and, once more, we need to rest.

The world is the best advertisement for its own lack of permanence.

Is there anything that we do that lasts forever? The answer is simple. To trust Jesus Christ as Savior is a once-for-all action that never needs to be repeated and has results that last for eternity. A challenge for the believer is to invest time, effort, and money in what will last forever. The Lord Jesus said plainly that laying up treasures on earth is fruitless as far as eternity is concerned. Although we are encouraged to lay up for specific expected needs, our goal should be to lay up as little as possible of that which will pass away, and as much as possible of that which will endure forever.

The term "world" in 1 John 2:17 comes from the Greek word *cosmos*, which is the root of cosmogony, cosmology, cosmetics, and cosmopolitan. In our changing world, perhaps the best reminder of the teaching in our text is the contents of magazines such as the one actually entitled *Cosmopolitan*. Articles and advertised commodities all testify that the world is passing away. A hundred ads in each issue reinforce the fact that fragrances dissipate, color fades, skin sags, wrinkles deepen, vitality deflates, fads change, fashions go out of style, lusts flourish, and bulges balloon. The endless reminder is mostly limited to the wearing out of the body, but it also applies to things that we use, such as our car, house, and possessions—all these will pass away .

Such magazines, however, are incessantly pressing on us the lie of the world that these things will *not* pass away—yet they continually need to be replaced, repaired, reconditioned, re-colored, restructured, and redone. The world is the best advertisement for its own lack of permanence.

Nothing can change this effect of sin begun in the garden. The world is not going to last forever. Instead, the believer is urged to make every effort to do the will of God, which means investing in that which will last as long as our soul.

--- ✂ ---

Father, thank you for preserving me forever. I forsake the world.

Enriched to Enjoy

Command those who are rich in this present age not to be haughty, nor to trust in uncertain riches but in the living God, who gives us richly all things to enjoy.

1 Timothy 6:17

Some Christians think that neither they nor other believers should have any fun in life. They go around with long faces, transmitting the idea that God is looking down watching them, and if He sees so much as a bit of fun in His children He leans over the banister of heaven and says gruffly, "Cut it out, you're a Christian!" Their singing proclaims the truth that their Lord was raised for them, yet you would think that He was still in the grave. Their worship services resemble funerals rather than festivals. No games may be played, and sports are not considered respectable enough for believers.

The last few words of today's Scripture are left for us to expand, since we are not given a list of activities that we should not engage in as believers. The context of these few words is the place of riches in the life of those who follow the Lord Jesus. Riches are all too often condemned as out of character for the Christian. Financial prosperity is viewed as inconsistent with those who are committed to the lordship of Christ and His endeavors. Those who may not have much of this world's goods find it easy to criticize those who do, even if both are believers. Covetousness (which is idolatry), envy, and jealousy stand like armed servants of our mind to challenge and condemn the rich, who seem to be taking pleasure in all the things that God has given them. Our tendency is to focus on their riches, their possessions, their pleasures, and all the things that they enjoy.

> *We should focus more on what God has given us than on what He has given others.*

Perhaps we should focus more on what God has given us than on what He has given others. A spiritual conclusion is the wonderful truth that God has made us stewards of the possessions that He knows we can handle. If you have little, perhaps it is because He cannot trust you with much. If you have much, perhaps He cannot trust you with little. He is certainly wise in the distribution of "all things," giving each exactly what he can handle. He does not give *all* of us all things to enjoy. That idea would drive us to a kind of Christian socialism. Rather, He has given to each of us what we can faithfully be good stewards of, and He encourages us to enjoy those things.

ဪ ———————————— ⳋ

Father, thank you for the spiritual and material blessings that You deem are good for me. I choose to enjoy and employ them.

Bound Together by Blood

But now in Christ Jesus you who once were far off
have been brought near by the blood of Christ.

Ephesians 1:13

One of God's great goals in saving us is to bring all believers together. He never intended us to live solitary lives, doing our own thing, only becoming "one" when we get to glory. Pictures such as the body of Christ, the building of God, and His bride are a few of many that the Divine Artist draws in the Scriptures to testify to our oneness.

When the New Testament Scriptures were written, there existed a great distinction between the Jews and the Gentiles, a division of great antiquity. They had no dealings with each other. As the gospel spread, the gap between the Jews and Gentiles was not closed, practically speaking. Of the many problems that we see recorded in the book of Acts, one was the rigid gulf that the Jews wanted to keep between themselves and believing Gentiles.

The problem was that, although some Gentiles were now fellow-believers, the Jews still viewed them as the "off-scouring of the earth." They likened them to wild dogs and pigs. Being saved, in and of itself, was not enough of a change to allow the Jewish believers to accept Gentiles as spiritually equal. Conflict appeared as the Spirit of God dealt with this issue of bringing the two together.

As Gentiles, we understand that our existence would have been abhorrent to the Jewish mind. The Jews were God's chosen people. Gentiles were outside the circle of God's favor. No other nation had such privileges, possessions, priesthood, prophets, promises, and protection. Gentiles were therefore thought to be rejected by God. With this in mind, the Jews went about their worship and service to God, setting aside all other nations.

Yet, as Gentiles, we believed in the same Lord, received the same salvation, experienced the same redemption, partook of the same reconciliation, enjoyed the same propitiation, and, by God's declaration, become recipients of the same blessings as Jewish believers. We do not have less because we were Gentiles before we believed. They do not have more because they were Jews before they trusted in Christ.

It is sad and divisive when believers with a Jewish background continue to think that they are better than those who were Gentiles before they were saved. Completed Jews, Messianic Jews, and any other titles only promote the divisions that God was destroying by the blood of Christ. We all have the same Father, forgiveness, family, favor, freedom, fortune, and future.

„ ———————————— ℣

Father, thank you for taking me into the one church where there is neither
Jew nor Gentile. I declare to the world that there is only one body.

Acceptable on Account of Christ

And be found in Him, not having my own righteousness,
which is from the law, but that which is through faith in
Christ, the righteousness which is from God by faith.

Philippians 3:9

God has always demanded righteousness in order to be acceptable to Him. The Law of Moses was given, not only to declare the righteousness of God, but also to prove that no one is capable of attaining His righteous standard. What's more, as Paul writes elsewhere, if righteousness came by keeping the law, then Christ died in vain. Paul's testimony to the believers in Philippi was that his union with the Lord Jesus Christ was the reason that he was accepted by God. The same can be said of all believers in Christ.

Every human being falls short of the perfect standard of the glory of God. No one has, or can, attain the absolute perfection seen in Christ. Many are still tempted to do good and be good, hoping that their good works will be enough to be acceptable as "righteousness." Sometimes a person will say, "Only perfect people go to heaven," but that statement eliminates all but Christ. Because we are all less than perfect, we are condemned to judgment—unless there is someone who has righteousness adequate enough to make up for deficiencies in others.

> *We are accepted in Christ and so share His death, life, and righteousness.*

The glorious message is that the Lord Jesus, as the Righteous One, went to the cross to die for the unrighteous. The more profound teaching, found here and elsewhere, is that those who are "in Christ" are accorded the righteousness of Christ Himself. We must then ask the important question, "How does a person get in Christ?"

The plan of God to bring many sons to glory is sealed in the simple principle of a living seed and its capacity for multiplication. Christ is the seed, and the life of the seed is communicated to every seed that grows from that original seed. But, in order for that seed to multiply its life in other seeds, it must first die, then spring to life. Since Christ has perfect righteousness, we can partake of His righteousness and person. We are accepted in Christ and so share His death, life, and righteousness. It has nothing to do with our keeping the law or living a good life. It is given by God! We are perfect "in Him," and so are welcome in heaven.

    ଅ ———————————————— ଔ

Father, thank you for placing me in Christ because of my faith in Him. I confess that I have nothing in myself that is pleasing to You. I claim His righteousness as the reason that I am acceptable to You.

No Mediocre Mediator!

But now He has obtained a more excellent ministry,
inasmuch as He is also Mediator of a better covenant,
which was established on better promises.

Hebrews 8:6

Job was the first person recorded in Scripture as longing for a mediator to stand between God and himself. Consciousness of sin and distance from God makes any sensitive heart cry out for someone who understands both God and man. Jesus is that Mediator. He is the one who fully understood the position and passion of both God and man.

One of the great messages of the book of Hebrews is the multitude of qualifications that the Lord Jesus possessed as Mediator. In 1 Timothy 2:5, we are reminded that "there is one God and one Mediator between God and men, the Man Christ Jesus." In the Old Testament, we see Moses as a mediator of the Old Covenant. He stood in the gap for the nation of Israel and spoke to God about the rebellion and disobedience of His people. Moses was also called at the burning bush to be the spokesman *for* God *to* His people. But, in refusing that task, God divided the responsibility, making his brother Aaron the high priest and Moses His prophet.

Christ fulfilled both those roles, roles in relation to a better covenant which is eternal and unconditional. Christ's qualifications began with the absolute fact that He was and is the eternal God. As God, He knew and understood God's anger against sin. He also possessed the divine heart of compassion for sinful man who had forfeited fellowship with God. Christ comprehended the awful punishment for sin that would require His voluntary suffering at the hands of both God and wicked men.

But Christ was also fully man—except without sin. He took the nature of man and lived a perfect life in the midst of His wicked and rebellious people. He offered Himself as a full and satisfactory sacrifice, which ratified the unconditional covenant defined as the New Covenant. Three times Christ is described as the Mediator of the New Covenant. This New Covenant is presented in Jeremiah 31, and its terms are explained to believers in Hebrews 8.

This covenant is established by the death of Christ, not by the obedience of man. The promises include the forgiveness of Israel's sin. As believers, we enter into the spiritual blessings of this same covenant, through the work of Christ on the cross and His glorious resurrection. This covenant will be continually effective because He lives forever.

〜 ───────────────── ∽

Father, thank you for the perfect God-man who, as my Mediator, served both in death and life to minister all the blessings of the covenant.

Gracious Gifts

But by the grace of God I am what I am, and His grace toward
me was not in vain; but I labored more abundantly than they
all, yet not I, but the grace of God which was with me.

1 Corinthians 15:10

We have reminded ourselves in other meditations that the words "grace" and "gift" are renderings of the same Greek term. In each case, the word choice depends on the context—though it does not always make a lot of difference, as is the case here.

The gifts of God to each believer make him what he is. Paul is saying here that what he is, he is by the grace, or gifts, of God. The initial deposit of God in each of His children is the cumulative resources or blessings that are found in Christ.

> *God has given each of us an infusion of Christ's life.*

Paul does not point to his education, his training, his heritage, his effort, or his spiritual diligence to declare who he is. His only source of spiritual being is due to the grace of God. And, although God used Paul's previous training and talents to fashion him into a useful tool, many of those natural characteristics had to be conformed to Christ's image or counted as loss in order to win Christ-likeness.

God has given each of us an infusion of Christ's life. It is that reservoir from which we draw resources that enable us to say, "I am what I am." The alternative is to be proud of our own accomplishments, to point to ourselves and say, "I am what I am because of what I have done." This is the world's philosophy, and it puts pride and prestige at the center of attention. In a "Christian" context, the legalist is one who, in keeping the law, has reason to boast in himself while condemning others for failing to live up to his standard. He has little need of the grace of God.

Paul drank deeply from these God-given resources, and the result was a graphic depiction of the life of Christ in Paul's flesh. His attitude was no passive resignation; he actively and energetically applied himself to bring about the reality of Christ in his life. Even the energy to do that was not his own; it was the power of Christ in him. Paul actively denied all his own desires so that Christ might be all in all in him. He could not earn or claim credit for who he was. It was all of Christ in him.

❧ ———————————— ☙

Father, thank you for the abundant grace that You gave me when you placed Christ in my life. I willingly surrender all that I am and have so that Christ might be manifested in my flesh.

Insightful Intercession

Who is he who condemns? It is Christ who died, and
furthermore is also risen, who is even at the right hand
of God, who also makes intercession for us.

Romans 8:34

Near the end of the eighth chapter of Romans, Paul refers to an important ministry of Christ which He exercises on our behalf, that of High Priest. It is comforting to know that the Lord Jesus, who died and rose again, is interceding for me. The fact almost overwhelms me. The Creator of the universe is seated in glory by the Father, and He is praying for me. The One who loved me unto death is pleading for me. The One who knows me best is asking His Father on my behalf. He who will come back for me is between the Father and me in prayer. Is such intercession even comprehendible?

But what does Christ pray? If you listen to Christians praying for fellow believers, you might not get much insight into His prayers for us. Can you hear Him asking the Father to be with us? Do you suppose that He asks God to bless us? Would He pray that we would have more strength than He has already given in Himself? Does He only pray for healing? Our continual repetitions seem trite when we consider what *He* prays.

So let's ask ourselves, "What did Christ pray when He was here on earth?" One answer comes from an incident recorded in Luke 22:31-32. The Lord Jesus knew that Peter was headed for an intense temptation and trial by Satan. Satan had requested permission to sift the disciples as wheat (the "you" in verse 31 is plural). But Christ said that He had prayed specifically for Peter. We might think that the best prayer would have been to remove the temptation, since that is what *we* usually pray. We ask that a trial or temptation will never happen, that the Lord will build a fence or a hedge around the one tempted, for strength against the tempter, for grace, for help, and so on.

Christ prayed that Peter's faith would not fail! Christ prayed that Peter would use the resources available to remain strong in faith, just as He had commanded Joshua and had seen in Abraham. He prayed that Peter would avail himself of the teaching and ministry that the Lord had given him over the previous three years. He prayed that he would be strong in faith!

> *It is comforting to know that the Lord Jesus, who died and rose again, is interceding for me.*

ဆ ─────────────── ☙

Father, thank you for the intercession of Christ for me. I confess that I do not understand it, but I choose to follow His pattern in praying for others.

L-O-V-E

In this is love, not that we loved God, but that He loved us
and sent His Son to be the propitiation for our sins.

1 John 4:10

I have difficulty singing songs—whether old hymns or contemporary choruses—which have lines that repeat over and over about my deep love for Jesus. Maybe you also find it hard to repeatedly sing the same few words about your great love for God.

Today's Scripture urges us to diminish how much we love God and instead focus on how much He loves us. Throughout the Scriptures, we are reminded of God's love for the lost world and Christ's love for the family of believers; so I get the idea that God is asking us to realize that, compared to His love for us, our love for Him is next to nothing.

It is true that we are commanded to love the Lord our God with all our heart, but the way that we demonstrate our love is so pitiful that it is bragging to call it love, just because we sing it.

> *Compared to His love for us, our love for Him is next to nothing.*

The apostle John described himself as the "disciple whom Jesus loved." It is comforting to know that he was inspired by the Holy Spirit to write this. It was not John, however, but Peter who reversed the description of devotion in answer to the Master's question, "Do you love me?" John was very familiar with the exchange of the risen Christ with His impetuous disciple on the beach. That is all the more reason for John to remind us that our love for God is best not proclaimed, let alone compared with His love for us. Our love is variable, measurable, and often confused with infatuation with His gifts, rather than unchangeable devotion to the person of Christ.

On the other end of the scale, God's love for us is demonstrated by the ultimate gift—His Son. The Lord Himself said to the disciples, including John and Peter, "Greater love has no one than this, than to lay down one's life for his friends" (John 15:13). From the very place that He stated this truth, He made His way to the cross and proved that His love was greater than any of His boastful disciples.

The Father demonstrated His love by sending His Son for all, and the Son demonstrated His love by giving His life for all. That is love! Repeat it often, and bask in the glory of God's love for you.

ᛒ ———————————— ᛤ

Father, thank you for loving me and sending Your Son to die as my substitute.
I claim Your satisfaction for my sin in the sacrifice of Christ.

Because He Lives

*When Christ who is our life appears, then you
also will appear with Him in glory.*

Colossians 3:4

The promise of the Lord's second coming has comforted the church since it was born. Confidence in His return permeates the New Testament, but the particular emphasis in Colossians 3:4 is that the promise rests in the fact that He has been raised from the dead and is alive today.

This most salient event is often relegated to one significant date in the third or fourth month of the year. It appears to be regarded as an almost obscure event, because the church in general does not celebrate it more regularly. It should, however, be recognized every Lord's Day, since that day is itself a celebration of the day Christ was raised from the dead. His day should not be concluded without a reminder that He is no longer on the cross or in the tomb, but alive forever! Not only that, but if He is not raised, then we are still in our sin, our preaching is in vain, our faith is useless, we are of all people most miserable, and we have no hope in this world or that which is to come (see 1 Corinthians 15).

Colossians 3:4 states another important truth on which the Christian life rests. We use the phrase "the Christian life" without stopping to realize that it is indeed the only *life!* We have become accustomed to hearing of "life" in so many connotations that we miss the impact and meaning of the designation. Eternal life, Spirit of life, newness of life, endless life, crown of life, and many others can be added to such a listing.

> *"He who
> has the Son
> has life."*

Few more profound descriptions are given in the many discourses on our salvation than the fact that Christ is our life. The gift of salvation is not eternal life without Christ. It *is* Christ! Being saved is not everlasting life without Christ. It *is* Christ. Christ is life because He is God. Existence without Christ is death. To be separated from God is death. Just as John writes, "He who has the Son has life."

Because Christ is our life, His indwelling allows us to walk in this world in the power of His life. "It is no longer I who live, but Christ who lives in me," is Paul's testimony. It is not my peace, joy, strength, love, patience, kindness, or gentleness, but the graces of Christ who is living in me that await manifestation. What Jesus Christ gives, He is! And He is *life*.

℘ ———————————— ℃

Father, thank you for giving me Your life in Your Son. I realize that if I did not have Christ I would exist in death. I now live because He lives!

August

OLD TRUTHS BRINGING NEW VITALITY!

". . . that we might know the things that
have been freely given to us by God."
1 Corinthians 2:12

Blessed be God, our God,
Who gave for us His well-beloved Son.
The gift of gifts, all other gifts in one;
Blessed be God, our God!

What will He not bestow,
Who freely gave this mighty gift, unbought.
Unmerited, unheeded, and unsought.
What will He not bestow?

Horatius Bonar

August

Butterfly

A little child with eyes filled with wonder may ask, "Where does a butterfly come from?" That is a difficult question to answer apart from the glorious creation of God which comes to parade its beauty before us, both literally and metaphorically.

The mysterious acts of God through nature give us a beautiful picture of the work of God in making us come "to a perfect man, to the measure of the stature of the fullness of Christ." Paul's counsel in Romans 12:2 is not to be conformed to this world "but be transformed by the renewing of your mind."

"Conformed" assumes an outward force. In this case, it is the world that wants to press us into its mold. The word "transformed" presupposes an inward force that works spontaneously. It is this word "transformed" that gives rise to our picture of metamorphosis. In fact, we get our English word metamorphosis from the Greek word translated here "transformed." The illustration of this great idea springs from the four stages of a caterpillar becoming a butterfly.

The caterpillar must die to all that it knows and has learned in its short life. The process seems simple to me, as I have been fascinated with the process since I saw my first butterfly. The difficult explanation by my parents of where it came from was the beginning of my understanding of the spontaneous life of a victorious believer.

We, like they, were born with certain natural

instincts, passed from Adam through our parents—instincts which were not learned but were a part of our life as unbelievers. We lived those actions that sprang from a sin nature. We were not capable of changing ourselves to better behavior. We were condemned to a very earthly life, like the lowly caterpillar.

God's plan for us in the new creation is pictured beautifully by the ascendancy of the caterpillar from a worm-like creature to a flying creature. The transformation is accomplished by the instinct that God built into the caterpillar. It gives up all the activities and habits that bound it to the earth. The choice for the caterpillar is spontaneous. For believers, it is a very real choice, coming from our mind and will, to allow the new life of Christ to live through us. This surrender, which is often a fight with the old man, sets free the life of Christ to live in and through our being, personality, and body.

For the caterpillar the change is dramatic, as it moves from a crawling instinct to a flying instinct, from chewing to sucking, from fur or hair to scales, from green leaves to flower nectar as food, from slow progress to flitting from place to place.

The change for the believer should be just as dramatic: from selfishness to sacrifice, from anger to self-control, from taking to giving, from competition to unity, from fear to faith, from antagonism to peace, from hate to love, from self to Christ! In this way we are being "transformed into the same image from glory to glory" (2 Corinthians 3:18).

What is important to remember is that the change is spontaneous. The caterpillar does not attain the glory of a butterfly by effort, but by death. So the believer, by death to self and all its desires, is transformed into Christ-likeness. Paul makes this clear by saying that the change is by the "renewing of your mind." The key is not what I try to do, but what I think. The activity of the mind is the key to transformation. We have been given the "mind of Christ," and it is His mind that is to shape our thinking. As Philippians 2:5 says, "Let this mind be in you." The mind of Christ is the example, as well as the force, that shapes our lives.

In Philippians 2, Christ, like the caterpillar, submitted to a program so humbling that it culminated in death. But such a program was followed by resurrection, just as the caterpillar also receives a totally new life in a new sphere, with new possibilities, new fulfillment, and a new purpose. The believer who submits by death to self will realize a new principle of life. "Christ's life" will take over and shape his or her ends with a new sphere of life, new possibilities, new fulfillment, and a new purpose. The result is the multiplication of Christ in the life of the children of God.

How challenging to see old things pass away and all things become new because we have allowed the new creation to transform our lives from inside. All we need to become what the Lord wants is to be willing to die to our plans so that we can come alive to His. We cannot be a caterpillar and a butterfly at the same time! A choice is before us all.

Filling Our Minds

For this reason we . . . do not cease to pray for you, and
to ask that you may be filled with the knowledge of His
will in all wisdom and spiritual understanding.

Colossians 1:9

O ne of the great themes of Scripture is that God reveals Himself to any whose spiritual eyes are open. Even in a physical sense there are several occasions that the eyes of some were "restrained" so that they did not comprehend His revelation. In a metaphorical sense, the Lord spoke of those who could see with physical eyes but were spiritually blinded.

With the coming of the Holy Spirit and the completion of the Scriptures as God's full revelation, Paul's prayer for the Colossians is not for a revelation of additional truth. He is interceding for believers to open their hearts to the truth available to all in the Bible. It is common to hear believers plead with God to reveal some aspect of His will that is more direct, more plain, or more acceptable to their mind and will.

The specific prayer is that we might be filled with the revelation that has already been made known by God. This kind of discovery of the will of God is not as "exciting" as the Lord using some miraculous intervention in our lives. It is faith that quietly accepts the Scriptural mandate as the Lord's will. If we applied our hearts to what we already know is His direct command to us, we would find other questions of direction easily answered. But, when we refuse the simple directive in favor of our own will, "His will" seems less desirable and less urgent. Our mind, filled with the Scriptures, will reveal the knowledge of God and His will to our hearts.

The more we get to know the Lord, the less dramatic the guidance must be. A small child does not know his father's will without strong statements and forceful "intervention." But an adult child knows the father's will because they have lived together for so long. The mature believer, filled with the knowledge of the Father, knows his Father's will. The Lord perfectly knew the Father and said, "I always do those things that please the Father." He said, "I know the Father."

In Colossians 1:9, Paul prays that we would apply our heart to the understanding of the truth of the Word because it spontaneously reveals God's desires. His revelation is living and powerful for all who will read or hear its statements. Open the book and fill your mind today.

ဢ ──────────── ℃

Father, thank you for the complete revelation of Your mind, Your pleasure, and Your will for me. I choose to fill my mind with Your Word and to do what pleases You.

God's Omnivision

And there is no creature hidden from His sight, but all things are naked and open to the eyes of Him to whom we must give account.

Hebrews 4:13

Many false gods are reputed to be able to see all creatures, shown by giving the "god" many eyes or a central "all seeing eye." But only the One True God is able to see all things, and this "omnivision" is a source of special comfort to us as His children.

Most believers underestimate God's capacity to observe everything that is going on in His creation. Men love darkness rather than light because they think that God cannot see in the dark. The added responsibility is that we must give a report of all that goes on in our lives. It is easier to give an account if we are sure that the "accountant" knows. If we think that the accountant does not know, we are tempted to hedge on certain facts.

But Scripture is also clear that His eye is on His own in a special way. Our hairs are counted, not just numbered. Sparrows fall with our Father seeing each one. Our value is greater because He bought us by the blood of His Son. We value what we own, especially if we paid for it ourselves.

God's omnivision is a challenge to our behavior. We do things that we wish God did not see. All aspects of our thoughts are seen. All actions of our hands are viewed. All changes of our emotions are known. All places that our feet take us are traced. All things that our eyes focus on are also viewed by God.

God's capacity for seeing all things is a source of comfort in the darkest hour. No matter what we are going through, the Father knows and sees. The disciples did not know that the Lord saw them in the middle of the storm, but He came to them in the fourth watch of the night, revealing His knowledge of their position and problems.

All tears that our eyes shed are collected. All sleepless nights that we spend are observed. All cries from a broken heart are heard. All anxieties that our soul endures are open. All calluses from serving are felt. All steps following a wayward son are recorded. All stories of denial are counted. All attacks against my character are chronicled. Every fall is observed. Every slip is studied. Every weakness is known. This should be a comfort to buoy us up and a challenge to live transparently before Him.

> *No matter what we are going through, the Father knows and sees.*

Father, I am aware that You see all that I do and know all that I think. I am comforted and challenged by this special blessing.

The Rejected Cornerstone

Therefore it is also contained in the Scripture, "Behold, I lay in Zion a chief cornerstone, elect, precious, And he who believes on Him will by no means be put to shame."

1 Peter 2:6

Some of the stones in Solomon's temple weighed an astonishing forty tons. The length and breadth raise the question of how they were moved from the quarry to the temple site. This mystery adds a thoughtful dimension to how the Lord Jesus came from glory to the world where sinful men and women are being transformed into living stones.

The spectacle of a living temple being built alongside a material temple is explained here by Peter and by Paul in Ephesians. The spiritual building, not made with hands, is more permanent than the great temples to Diana and Zeus which lie in ruins today. That which is unseen is eternal.

F. B. Meyer describes the occasion of a huge stone being quarried during the building of Solomon's temple. When it arrived at the temple site, no place was found for it. The builders set it aside as unsuitable for the building. There it lay rejected for some years. Eventually, a void was found in a key corner of the building and, after measuring the space, they found the stone perfect for the chief cornerstone. This stone, previously rejected, was now moved to a place of prominence.

Jesus, infused with absolute deity, was sent by the Father from the quarry of humanity to be the Savior of the world. Though He came to His own people, His own builders refused Him, His place, and His position. He was chosen of God but rejected by men. He was precious to the Father and precious only to those who believe.

The believers in what we now call Turkey received these encouraging words from Peter. He reminded them that, though they were surrounded by many temples of stone, they themselves were part of an enormous spiritual temple being built of living stones. The Lord added daily each sinner who received the life of the Son. How thrilling to be added by the architect to the eternal temple—a habitation of God by the Holy Spirit.

Those who believe on Him will not be disappointed. The crumbling edifices of men point to the permanence of the chief cornerstone and to all the other stones made permanent by the implanted life of God. This guarantees our eternal union with Him.

         ও ———————————— ও

Father, thank you for sending Your precious Son to be the chief cornerstone. I align my life to Him today for Your glory.

Charges Dismissed!

My little children, these things I write to you, that you
may not sin. And if anyone sins, we have an Advocate
with the Father, Jesus Christ the righteous.

1 John 2:1

O ne of the many names given to our Lord Jesus is Advocate. It is also given to the Holy Spirit in His ministry to us as believers. The name itself simply means someone who comes alongside. *Paraclete* is the Greek word that describes this specific partnership. The first part of the word describes someone who works or serves alongside; paralegal and paramedic are terms that describe the relationships and locations of these helpers.

The goal of God for every believer is sinlessness. Certainly the practice of sin is inconsistent with a Christ-like life. And, although the resources for a life free from sin have been given to us in Christ, we still sin. We have another nature within that draws us into sin. Yet we are not left without a comforter in the midst of our failure. Christ is our personal Advocate.

The enemy accuses and condemns our behavior as unfitting for a follower of Jesus Christ. He points out the inconsistencies in our behavior that seem to contradict our profession of faith. We hear in our mind the charges of the enemy against us, and the voice of the enemy sounds so accurate and disturbing that we are further tempted to give up and say that it is impossible to live as we ought. But we are not alone in the courtroom.

On our side of the court is the Lord Jesus Christ, who "bore our sins in His own body on the tree." It is He who steps forward and closes the mouth of the accuser and says, "I paid for that sin. My blood was an adequate price for every sin of my client." The Judge, who is also our Father, declares loudly for the retreating advocate of evil to hear, "Paid in full!

> *The Judge, who is also our Father, declares loudly for the retreating advocate of evil to hear, "Charges dismissed!"*

Charges dismissed!" With the proceedings over, we return to the streets of the world with our Advocate at our side, providing all the resources for life in a wicked and perverse world. Our Father is for us, since He has given His life to us. His Son is on our side, having paid a debt that I could not pay. "Jesus paid it all! All to Him I owe!"

       ᔓ ───────────── ᔓ

Father, thank you that the death of Christ satisfied Your justice and holiness.
I receive the restoration of fellowship and take the resources from Your hand
to live in the likeness of Christ today.

Our Humdrum Sanctuaries

*Being filled with the fruits of righteousness which are
by Jesus Christ, to the glory and praise of God.*
Philippians 1:11

This phrase is the last line of Paul's prayer for the church in Philippi. They had sent him a financial gift by the hand of a faithful brother. Out of their deep poverty, their liberality became known around the world.

The prison where Paul was housed and received this gift became the sanctuary for all sorts of spiritual exercises. Here he preached to the soldiers that came to guard him. Here he encouraged the hearts of his visitors. In this place he preached to Onesimus and guided his thinking into salvation by Jesus Christ. Chained in this house of worship, he praised God for the expanding of the gospel into the court of the Emperor. In this prison, he wrote this lovely letter to the church at Philippi. In these cramped quarters, he manifested the fruits of righteousness that overflowed from his life and affected so many people.

It was a sanctuary without stained glass windows, carpeted floors, electric lights, robed choir, and many others things that we commonly associate with a sanctuary. That kind of a sanctuary is the easiest place for the fruits of righteousness to grow and flourish. It is a kind of greenhouse where the climate is controlled. All the "plants" seem spiritual and lively in their vigor and passion for Jesus Christ. Yet we cannot and should not stay in that kind of atmosphere all the time.

> *The prison became the sanctuary for all sorts of spiritual exercises.*

The miracle of the spontaneous fruit of righteousness is the lush, tasty, colorful, fragrant fruit that grows in a prison-like place. But we are neither in a prison nor a stained glass sanctuary. We are in the common humdrum of our own society. The Philippians in deep poverty had overflowed with this kind of fruit, demonstrated by the abundance of their liberality.

The word "fruit" reminds us of the spontaneity of production. Go into a garden and sit quietly as flowers make the path fragrant, trees expand their girth, grapes glisten in the light, leaves display their colorful foliage, and a drop of dew clings to a blade of grass, radiating a tiny rainbow across a fallen leaf. Even a butterfly flutters its way around, proclaiming that growth does not take effort but surrender to a principle of life placed in every living thing, including all the Father's children. With His children robed in the fruit of righteousness, the Father, like the gardener, is put in excellent display.

꿍 ──────────── ལ

Father, I believe that all the resources for the fruits of righteousness are available in your Son. I draw from Him for all that I will need today.

A Saved and Cleaned Home

*Not by works of righteousness which we have done, but
according to His mercy He saved us, through the washing
of regeneration and renewing of the Holy Spirit.*

Titus 3:5

Three words summarize the work of God on our behalf: "He saved us." Taken by themselves without including all the statements of God's work and man's responsibility, it would seem that God saved us as a gardener might pick up branches and, instead of throwing them into the fire, push them into the ground where they grow with new life. But this is not Paul's teaching.

> *Because the Holy Spirit cannot dwell in an unholy house, God washed us to prepare a habitation fit for him.*

Rather, it is a contrast between all the works that man wants to do to earn and merit the mercy of God, versus the gift of God. As A.P. Gibbs used to say, "A self-made man is a horrible example of unskilled labor." Such are our works. Yet the pillars of God's love, grace, peace, and mercy hold up an intricate and perfect plan for taking mankind out of death and bringing him into life.

Paul emphasizes the concept of mercy because no one can say that God has dealt with us in accordance with our sin. As David writes in Psalm 103, "so great is His mercy to us." Since "all of our righteous acts are as filthy rags," mankind was and is in desperate need of the unchanging mercy of a loving God. He reaches down and saves those who believe.

In addition to saving us, He purifies us. Because the Holy Spirit cannot dwell in an unholy house, God washed us to prepare a habitation fit for Him. He cleanses our lives and puts away the filthy garments of our good deeds, creating a place where His Holy Spirit can dwell. It is easy to see how we, too, would want to destroy the filthy, smelly, putrid garments that we have been wearing all our life. But man has no opportunity of washing or purifying his own garments. We were helpless to make our house and life suitable for this perfectly pure guest.

The guest, who becomes our host, is set free by our faith to clean house, wash the walls of our mind, scrub the floor of our conduct, disinfect the atmosphere of our thinking, and ready His new abode for His own enjoyment and control. This new resident is the very life of the God who saved us.

ඤ ———————————— ඣ

Father, what a plan of salvation! I am thankful that Your plan included me. I glory in your unchanging mercy.

Thanks Be To God

But thanks be to God, who gives us the victory
through our Lord Jesus Christ.

1 Corinthians 15:57

❝Say thank you!" As parents, we often repeated this exhortation and wondered whether our children would ever learn to respond spontaneously with the proper words, "Thank you." Eventually they did, and we felt satisfied that our insistence was rewarded. Our Father also reminds us frequently to say thank you for the blessings that He has given us in Christ.

Today's Scripture is at the end of a long chapter that celebrates two important events. The first is the resurrection of Christ, and the second is the reappearance of Christ. If there is no resurrection, then the work of Christ is incomplete and of little value. If Christ is not alive, then we are still in our sin, our faith is vain, our preaching is invalid, and we are miserable people. But Christ is alive! The greatest event in the history of the world is the resurrection of Christ.

This historical and spiritual event is the primary reason for a victorious celebration. Because of His resurrection, God is able to impart His new life to all who believe. The victory that Paul is primarily referring to is the victory over death. Death was destroyed by His death and resurrection. There is no victory without Christ going through death Himself. Everyone who has Christ shares in that conquest, and because Christ lives we also live. When Christ was raised, we were raised.

We may pass through death physically, but we cannot remain in death any more than Christ could remain in death. Death for Christ was the doorway to a new life which He shares with all who believe on Him. Death for us is the door to the full and eternal presence of our Lord.

Yet let us never forget that Christ is coming again and will raise the bodies of those who have already passed through death. He will change the bodies of all who are alive when He comes again. That is victory for every believer who has died and for those still alive at His coming. Either way, we share the victory of our Lord. He defeated death, the world, sin, and a host of other enemies. We participate in each of these victories without any personal conflict. He fought and won, and we are partakers of His success. This is not dependent on our devotion or prayers. He did it all and offers it to all who will believe.

ೞ ───────────── ೮

Father, thank you for the resurrection of Your Son. You have given me all the fruits of this victory. I celebrate His triumph today and choose to live in an attitude of thanksgiving and joy.

Liberated from the Law

*But this occurred because of false brethren secretly brought in
(who came in by stealth to spy out our liberty which we have
in Christ Jesus, that they might bring us into bondage).*

Galatians 2:4

Liberty. It is the cry of many nations, the longing of many hearts. The call for freedom by activists is for no restriction on behavior, speech, or anything else that curbs their dreams or rights. But liberty in the life of a believer is not freedom to do anything he wants.

The Lord Jesus cried out to the enslaved world of His day, "If the Son shall make you free, you will be free indeed." That freedom has many branches in its far-reaching impact. Freedom from sin is first and foremost—freedom from the penalty of sin, its power in our lives today, and its presence in the age to come.

But the freedom that Paul celebrates in Galatians is a freedom from the Law of Moses that was given more than a thousand years before Christ died. The believers who received this letter found it very difficult to set aside the divinely sanctioned legal system that had been in place for so long. How could it be swept away by the act of one Man on a cross in Jerusalem?

The message of Paul was that it is impossible to mix the Law of Moses with the grace of God. Does the antiquity of the law vouch for its authority and validate the faith of all the Old Testament saints? No, says Galatians: the law was set aside as incapable of saving or sanctifying anyone. Although the law was good, it cannot offer the power needed to obey its precepts. Christ, in contrast, is the doorway to God. Such a free gift negates any boasting that a law-keeper might offer as a means of coming to God. It cannot be Christ *and* the law.

But even after trusting Christ by faith, there was the danger of trying to keep the law as a means of staying in grace. Again, the Bible is clear that keeping the law cannot save and it cannot sanctify or secure. We are not made like Christ by relying on obedience to the law of Moses.

Religion in and of itself wants to add laws to grace and lead a liberated believer into bondage. Christ sets free all believers from keeping the law as a means of salvation and sanctification. This does not mean that we are free to be lawless. To be free in Christ is to be bound to the Savior in willing and loving service.

༐ ———————————————— ༒

Father, thank you for setting me free from the obligation of the law. I willingly offer my life to be obedient to You, my Liberator.

What Is Light Affliction?

For our light affliction, which is but for a moment, is working
for us a far more exceeding and eternal weight of glory.

2 Corinthians 4:17

Trials, suffering, burdens, and afflictions are seldom welcomed in the life of any believer. In fact, too often our prayer life consists of pleading for God to take away affliction.

Yet Scripture is full of stories of great men and women of faith who, in enduring afflictions, discovered that the trials were helpful in understanding themselves and God. David says that it was good for him to be afflicted. He learned the Word of God in the trials of life. The Bible is also sprinkled with texts that remind us of the value and purpose of suffering.

But what is a "light affliction?" My affliction may seem heavy to me, while your affliction may not burden me as much, because we tend to dwell on our own problems more than those of others. We were basically self-centered before we trusted Christ, and we fight that tendency even after we believe.

The similar question could be asked about how long a "moment" is. Scripture describes an hour as the experience of Christ during His crucifixion, while a day is measured as more like 1,000 years. Peter reminds his readers that the trial of their faith was for "a season." The comparison in this text is between the passing physical suffering and the eternal duration or weight of glory.

> *Pain, sorrow, and affliction all work for our greater blessing.*

The previous verse says that the outward man is perishing. For most of us, that is a period of years where we find our energy less and need more effort to do things. Our light afflictions are medicated and drugged, even as we attempt to pray them out of existence.

Think of the impact of four words: "is working for us." This statement of fact is a reminder of the Lord's working in us, both to will and to do His good pleasure. The perspective for the believer is that the eternal, which is not seen, is of much greater value than the physical that we daily struggle with.

If we did not have these afflictions, we would not want to go home. It is our body perishing under the weight of afflictions that cries out, "I want to go home!" While living in healthy bodies enjoying this life, we do not think much of arriving in glory. Our sorrow is working in us a desire to be absent from our body and present with the Lord. Pain, sorrow, and affliction all work for our greater blessing.

ॐ ──────────── ☘

Father, thank you that we do not live forever in this perishing body but will one day be like Christ. Thank you for today's afflictions.

Lord of Every Room

That Christ may dwell in your hearts through faith;
that you, being rooted and grounded in love.

Ephesians 3:17

Christ's presence in the life of every believer is one of God's greatest gifts. The most familiar verse in the Bible says, "For God so loved the world that He gave . . ." Most of us would automatically assume that this reference is to the cross, but the verse does not say that. God's gift is not limited to the cross, but blossoms out into all the other aspects of giving.

If Christ had gone to the cross without providing a way to get into the heart of each believer, His work would be of little value. The death of Christ makes it possible for God to forgive our sin, thereby cleaning our heart to make it a suitable residence for the living Christ. That transaction took place when we "received" Christ as our Savior. Because of that act of faith, Christ began His lifelong residence in our heart.

But residence and preeminence are two different things. Our heart is like a mansion in which we have many rooms—the library where we read, the family room for fellowship, bathroom where we cleanse ourselves, dining room where we feed our mind, closets where we store secrets, a board room where we make decisions, the bedroom where we rest in His Word, etc. The Lord wants to be welcome in every room.

The question is, "Is He Lord of every part of your heart?" The God of Israel chose to express His presence with His people in advancing intimacy. With Abraham, He talked on the plains of Canaan. To Jacob, He spoke face to face in Bethel. Moses had the most dramatic encounter at the bush. But for all Israel, His presence was by cloud and fiery pillar that guided and protected the migrating hoard from Egypt to Canaan. That presence settled down over the mercy seat for all to see when they arrived in the land.

> *The question is, "Is He Lord of every part of your heart?"*

Then God chose to dwell in human flesh in the body prepared by the Father, produced by the Holy Spirit, and possessed by the Son. He was raised from the grave so that He might dwell in the heart of every believer. "Christ in you" is the mystery of His lodging in my flesh, second only to the incarnation of God Himself in Jesus' body. This is permanent. It is not dependent on my continuing faith, but on the transaction of salvation.

—————— ❧ · ❧ ——————

Father, thank you for the gift of the risen Christ in my heart. Today I open all the doors and closets of my heart to the fullness of Christ. I give Christ preeminence over my life.

The Eternal Word

"But the word of the LORD endures forever." Now this is
the word which by the gospel was preached to you.

1 Peter 1:25

Books pass out of print and are lost to future generations. Despite all the marketing and promotional activities, few books survive longer than one edition. In stark contrast is the Word of God. It is guaranteed to survive the scorn of skeptics, the hostility of humanists, the anger of atheists, the rejection of revisionists, the condemnation of crowds, the aspersions of antagonists, the apathy of authorities, the passion of paraphrasers, the disapproval of doubters, the fights of feminists, and the suppositions of scientists.

But the point of Peter's message is not the endurance of the written Word of God. The term that Peter uses here is the word used of something spoken. We can understand how God has produced the Bible, protected its contents, preserved its accuracy, prepared its hearers, promoted its authority, prospered its printing, proved its endurance, and promised its preservation, but the words that flowed from the mouth of God seem like all other words that spill out of so many other mouths. When they fall silent, they are never to be gathered again.

Men have developed the ability of recording and preserving the word of any who wish to speak into a microphone. The electronic technology is so advanced that a recording of an entire book can be carried on a thin CD or keychain-sized flash drive. But the words spoken by God were not set free into a climate where they could be technologically caught, preserved, and duplicated for future generations.

The same term is used in Hebrews 11: "the worlds were framed by the *Word of God.*" Is it possible that the sounds articulated by the mouth of God are as infinite as the God who spoke them? Do the words that come from His mouth continue to reverberate in our hearing, even though we do not have the capability of hearing them?

These are the words of the Lord, who is the Jehovah of the Hebrew people: the covenant-keeping God who created all things and causes things to appear out of nothing, who wills that things which are not seen continue eternally. This gospel was spoken to these believers, and it will endure for all eternity. The suffering that they were enduring was only for a moment of time, but the words of God will endure forever. We can learn them, lean on them, love them, and live them.

℘ ──────────────── ☙

Father, thank you for the continuing effect of Your word in our world. I choose
to rest in its message and rejoice in its truth.

He Chose Us

Knowing, beloved brethren, your election by God.
1 Thessalonians 1:4

One of the major battlefields of the Christian church has been the doctrine of election. So much acrimony has been stirred up for so long that it is difficult to see the Son for the clouds of dust that have been scattered and blown into our spiritual eyes. Although we can't reconcile the differences that exist, we can accept this statement of the Word of God. To know that something exists is different from comprehending how it works or why it functions the way it does.

As we walk this pilgrim journey from earth to glory, we need to accept the fact that is stated here. "He chose us," says Paul (Ephesians 1:4). "Elect," writes Peter (1 Peter 1:2). Paul comforted these Thessalonian believers

> *We should be blessed by the knowledge that God made a choice, and that choice included us.*

who were concerned about the coming of the Lord and the misconception that they might be left behind. Peter encouraged the believers who were facing persecution and suffering for their faith. Paul gave instruction to the Ephesians, who were learning the complex nature of the spiritual mystery of the Church and their part in that organism.

We, too, should be blessed by the knowledge that God made a choice, and that choice included us. Let us bask in the blessing, soak our soul in the joy of His choice, and mold our mind by this amazing truth. If we were responsible for the choice, we would be led to boast about our capacities, abilities, or value. But, because He chose us, we are humbled. Bill Gaither sings, "He who knows me best, loves me most." Paul calls his readers "beloved brethren." It is the knowledge of this truth that buoys up our spirits even if we concede that it "is too wonderful for us."

Knowledge of God's election gives us a significant reason for faith, an adequate reason for joy, a profound reason for hope, an enduring reason for peace, and a suitable reason for love. Our life should overflow with gratefulness of this knowledge, even though our mind struggles to fully comprehend it. We adore the choice that God made and marinate our mind it its message. We will understand it better by and by, but until then let us glory in the One who chose us. Glory in what you know; don't grapple with what cannot be fully known. Our election is of God. That is enough for abundant wonder and worship!

☙ ——————————————— ❧

Father, thank you for choosing me. I envelop my emotions in this blessing so that I can show forth Your love, joy, and peace by my faith and hope.

No Fear of Death

And release those who through fear of death
were all their lifetime subject to bondage.

Hebrews 2:15

The fear of death dates back to the effects of sin in the Garden of Eden. Hebrews states that "it is appointed for men once to die but after this the judgment." Perhaps it is as much the fear of facing God, knowing that He knows the details of your life, as it is of dying itself. The book of Genesis repeats the words "and he died" to remind all readers of the truth that sin brings death.

But the previous verse of today's Scripture reminds us that Christ by His "death destroyed him that had the power of death." One of the primary victories of Christ's work on the cross was to snatch the keys of death from the enemy's grasp and take control of the punishment for sin. We can celebrate the victory of Christ and His release from fear for all who believe.

This blessing, like others made possible by the death of Christ, can only be enjoyed by faith. In 1 Thessalonians 4:14 we read that, "if we believe that Christ died and rose again, even so God will bring with Him those who sleep in Jesus." The validation of Christ's victory is His resurrection from the dead.

Those who have never received Christ as their Savior will be hounded by the terrors of death. All who spurn Christ will appear before the throne of the God for condemnation. With the conscience awakened by sin and the certainty of pending judgment, most fear the doorway of death and the events on the other side.

The resurrection of Christ is the basis of our faith; therefore, we need not fear death.

Believers may fear the process of dying, yet not death itself. Most of us would like to put our head down in a good old age and wake up in His presence. For some, however, the doorway is a long fight with cancer, a debilitating disease like Alzheimer's, or even a traumatic car crash.

The resurrection of Christ and His victory over "him that had the power of death" is the basis of our faith; therefore, we need not fear death. Christ asked Martha, "Do you believe this?" We may be uneasy about the way that we die, but not about death itself. We pass through death, but need not fear staying there. Christ has set us free from fear's bondage. What release and freedom to live with no fear of death.

☙ ———————————————————— ❧

Father, thank you for the victory of Christ over death. I confess that I am uneasy about meeting death, but claim victory in Christ over fear.

Much More Than We Think

Now to Him who is able to do exceedingly abundantly above all that we ask or think, according to the power that works in us.
Ephesians 3:20

This wonderful line from the pen of Paul seems like a blank check, a debit card without limit, or a credit card that someone else pays. Paul concludes the doctrinal section of his letter with a prayer and a Christ-exalting tribute of praise about God's amazing capacity to answer our requests. If we seriously consider its meaning, it will cause us to stand in awe of the One who knows our thoughts and hears our prayers.

It is interesting that Paul wrote the word "ask" before he wrote "think." Our thoughts are often unspoken or unsaid, for we are sometimes hesitant to verbalize requests. We are convinced that our thoughts are ours and ours alone. But they are read by the One who knew our thoughts before they were formed in our mind. To ask is to express thoughts that have been rolling around the halls of our mind. But what we think includes dreams and fears, wishes and wants, loves and hates, hungers and hopes, riches and poverty, and a multitude of other ideas. God reads them all. He is able to sort, satisfy, fulfill, refuse, and surprise us by bringing to fruition our very thoughts. "Be careful little mind what you think!"

The two words "in us" narrow the landscape where He is at work. We were dreaming of all that we wanted God to do by adjusting our circumstances, only to realize that He wants to work "in me" more than in people around me. God is in the business of changing me more than changing those around me for my benefit. God wants to work in us and through us. The power of the risen Christ is working. We need not ask Him to work, for He is already working. As we think about Christ and meditate on His person and work, His power is transforming us. He will do things in us that we do not even think possible.

> *As we think about Christ and meditate on His person, His power is transforming us.*

How can we come away from this stimulating description of our Lord by continuing to say, "Lord be with, bless, guide, direct, and protect us"? That is a thoughtless prayer that must disappoint our great God who wants to do in us more than we can ever ask or think.

☞ ———————————————— ☜

Father, I choose to bring every thought into obedience to Christ, setting you free to transform my being and actions.

Thank you!

Thanks be to God for His indescribable gift!
2 Corinthians 9:15

Thanksgiving is an attitude of gratitude. In Scripture, believers are frequently called on to "give thanks." We are told to give thanks *in* all things and to give thanks *for* all things. It should not be hard for each of us to develop and employ the habit of saying thanks for every blessing that God has given us in Christ. But we are so prone to rely on our own resources that we forget, "without Me you can do nothing" (John 15:5).

> *After we have said all we can, "the half has not been told.*

The emphasis in 2 Corinthians 9:15 is not so much on giving thanks as it is on the indescribable gift of God. There can be no argument that the gift referred to here is the Lord Jesus Christ. He is the one gift that encompasses all other gifts of divine blessing. Because He is beyond description, we may choose to not say anything about Him. That would be a fatal mistake, as He has called us to do what we can to "make known the unsearchable riches of Christ." He is the absolute expression of all that God is. He is the full revelation of all the attributes of an infinite God. His is a full salvation which is complete and available to all who will believe. He was crucified for our offences which were the epitome of all wickedness. He has been given to us through His resurrection from the dead.

This resurrection sealed our justification and made it possible for God to bestow His righteousness on each believer. The gift of the Holy Spirit applies all the glory of the Son into our hearts and causes us to declare with confidence, "Abba, Father!" This unspeakable gift has been bestowed without money and without price on all who place their faith in the risen Christ. At that moment, the unimaginable blessings in Christ are bestowed, and we begin to discover how vast those blessings are. At every new discovery, our lips part with joy in a burst of thanks for a further expression of God's generous supply. This exciting and thrilling discovery of the inventory of resources grows every day, producing our appreciation by saying "Thanks!"

After we have said all we can, "the half has not been told." If everything was written about this infinite person, "I suppose that even the world itself could not contain the books that would be written" (John 21:25). Let us talk of Him even though He is inexpressible, unfathomable, and ineffable!

ଚ —————————— ଷ

Father, how can I ever adequately express my appreciation for the wonderful and indescribable gift of Your Son? I commit my life to a habit of thanksgiving with each discovery, and a constant attitude of gratefulness.

Free Indeed

Stand fast therefore in the liberty by which Christ has made us free, and do not be entangled again with a yoke of bondage.

Galatians 5:1

S lavery is a tragic result of one person being stronger than another, and this is true both spiritually and materially. Spiritual slavery is just as debilitating, but it is often coated with attractive clothing by the world. Everyone brought into this world is born into slavery and bondage to sin. That bondage manifests itself in different ways. Every Israelite born in Egypt was the child of a slave and born into bondage to Pharaoh. They had no choice and no prospect of deliverance, except the promise given by God to Abraham.

That story helps us understand our release from slavery to sin, self, and the world. Most Israelites in Egypt did not know the state of the rest of the world or the complete history of their people. They did not fully know what freedom was. So also, those enslaved to the world cannot understand the climate of freedom offered them in Christ. It is foolishness to them.

The redemption and freedom of the Israelites was arranged by the Lord. A lamb was to be killed and the blood splashed on the doorposts and lintel of each home. Those who believed the good news responded in obedient faith on that fateful evening. Those who presented the blood received life for the firstborn and freedom for the family. A long procession

The danger is that the old life seems better to live in than the liberty found in Christ.

of freed slaves left Egypt with great hopes of a new life in Canaan. A rejoicing people reflected and reiterated their blessings in the song in Exodus 15.

Yet the prospect of freedom and a homeland was not enough to curb the murmuring and grumbling of the freed people who wanted to return to Egypt's bondage. Egypt was seen by murmurers as the good life. Even slavery was seen as better than the arduous journey to Canaan. For us, the danger is that the old life seems better to live than the liberty found in Christ. Each time we face the allure of the world or sin, we are tempted to become entangled in the yoke of bondage. The great truth here is that "Christ has made us free!" Live in the joy and blessing of that freedom. Fill your mind with the delights of freedom and separation from the influence of the world that enslaved you previously. Stand mentally and spiritually strong in your freedom.

        ℘ ———————————— ℘

Father, thank you for setting me free. I renounce the attraction of the world that enslaved me, and choose freedom by rejoicing in Christ and my release from bondage by His blood.

Purchased Slaves

*For you were bought at a price; therefore glorify God
in your body and in your spirit, which are God's.*

1 Corinthians 6:20

Seldom do we buy things that we do not want. Most of our purchases are carefully calculated. God made those same careful calculations when He bought us.

The price was high—the life of His only Son—but the purpose was clear: to gain additional children. The process was painful and the problems were enormous, but the pardon was complete.

The purchase of a slave did not involve any consideration of the slave's wishes. The market was open to any who could pay. The slaves were on display for all to see and handle. The purposes of a buyer were not questioned. Like an auction of machinery, the slave was not asked what he wanted. The lives of men and women were radically changed by the highest bidder.

This truth by itself seems to indicate that God did not consider our mind or will in the matter of our becoming His property. Faith is necessary for salvation, but purchase is a transaction between God and God.

The universal purchase is explained in 2 Peter 2, where even those who reject Christ are said to "deny the Lord who bought them." Our faith in Christ makes effective and personal the redemption provided for all. Our part in this transaction, our faith in Christ, helps us enter into the responsibility of glorifying the purchaser.

Few slaves knew what kind of life was ahead of them while chained in the slave market. Our understanding, though seen through clouded glass, is far clearer than a slave's. The Scriptures are open to any who will read of the privileges of belonging to God. The catalogue of benefits and blessings available to us "eye has not seen nor ear heard." Part of the purpose of our meditations is to remove the film from our spiritual eyes. The Lord is opening our eyes to the beauties of sonship.

Our duty in the ensuing relationship is to display the glory of God in both the physical and spiritual parts of our being. Our body is a stage for the world to see our appreciation and debt to the One who paid so high a price, so that we might be His children. Though we are primarily occupied with what blessings are ours, this verse declares that we are His! What does God get from this purchase? Our body is His. Does it show? Our spirit is His. Do people know?

❧ ———————————————— ☙

Father, thank you for making me Yours. Where would I be if You had not bought me? I choose to confess Your ownership today.

Living Epistles

You are manifestly an epistle of Christ, ministered by us,
written not with ink but by the Spirit of the living God, not on
tablets of stone but on tablets of flesh, that is, of the heart.

2 Corinthians 3:3

P ages and ink do not live, and books do not know what they were written for. But we, as people redeemed from the judgment of God, have not only been written but also informed by the Author that we are His epistle, "known and read by all men."

Every believer is *an* epistle of Christ, not *the* epistle of Christ. If a believer were the only book that the world had to read, so many pages of life would be clouded, confusing, and at times contradictory. It would be a sad revelation of Christ if a believer's narrative were the only story a non-Christian could read.

But we can appreciate the fact that we are epistles and therefore lined up on the shelf of society with many others who have taken Christ's name. The world, curious to read about the Savior, will read a few pages of our life, then pick up another volume for a few days, and another one for a chapter or two, and so on as they pass by our lives in this world

We cannot escape the fact that, as soon as we trust Christ as Savior, the pages begin to fill with our life, actions, attitudes, and activities. Our pages are open and available for all to read. The binding may be worn by much usage. We may want some chapters to be hidden or perhaps edited in a different way. But if we venture out among our family and friends, as well as our neighbors, they will see and hear about us and our story of Christ.

Your life reads like a book of what Christ is teaching you and how much you are learning of the Word of truth.

The Holy Spirit inspired Paul to write 2 Corinthians and to describe our Savior's abundant supply of grace and mercy. This grace and mercy should be evident in all of our activities. Out of the heart proceeds a long list of desires and actions. Can someone read your heart? Your life reads like a book of what Christ is teaching you and how much you are learning of the Word of truth. Learn well because it is being written down and read by the world.

૪૭ ─────────────── ർ૪

Father, thank you for writing in my heart the story of Your grace and mercy. I surrender my heart to the pen and ink of Your Spirit. I know that my life is an open book for the world to read of You.

Life Everlasting

*These things I have written to you who believe in the name of the
Son of God, that you may know that you have eternal life, and
that you may continue to believe in the name of the Son of God.*

1 John 5:13

L ife is one of the primary blessings of our salvation. The above
verse reminds us that the possession of Christ means possession of
life, because life is in the Son. This life is primarily spiritual and is
provided because the Lord Jesus died and rose again to communicate His life
to all who believe.

Today's Scripture teaches that this life is "eternal life."
In other passages, the words "everlasting life" describe
the provision of God. The need for life goes all the way
back to Adam who received death as the punishment for
his sin. The word death covers three different aspects
of death. Adam began to die physically as his body
started to deteriorate. But being dead does not mean to
cease to exist or respond. It means to be separated. In

> *The moment
> that we trust
> in Christ for
> the forgiveness
> of our sin, we
> begin to live.*

physical death, the soul and spirit are separated from the body, and the body
begins to rapidly decay. Spiritual death was also a result of Adam's sin, as
God drove him from the Garden of Eden. Man and God were separated from
each other. And, had God not provided a substitute who died in order that he
might be clothed, Adam would have experienced eternal death.

Eternal life has no beginning or ending. We receive it the moment we believe,
because Christ Himself comes in. We pass from death to possessing God's
life by that transaction. Everlasting life has a beginning but no ending. The
moment that we trust in Christ for the forgiveness of our sin, we begin to live.
We were dead in trespasses and sin, but are made alive by the gift of God's
Son. The day we believed, we began to live. So both characteristics of God's
life, eternal and everlasting, and their application to us are true at the point of
believing in the name of the Son of God.

The assurance that we have this life can be confirmed in two ways. First and
foremost is the faithfulness of God in giving the gift of life as He promised
in His Word. We believed, and He gave His life to us in His Son. The second
evidence of life is the behavior and conduct of each person. Evidence of
life is visible by a desire for food, exercise, and determination of action and
attitudes. Are you alive?

    ℝ ———————————————— ℳ

*Father, thank you for the life that You gave me in Your Son. I know that I have
that life because of Your faithfulness to Your promises.*

Filled with the Spirit

And do not be drunk with wine, in which is
dissipation; but be filled with the Spirit.

Ephesians 5:18

The fullness of the Spirit is a truth that is in danger of being lost in the evangelical church. This is in part because of the confusion that exists in teaching about the person and ministry of the Holy Spirit. A generation of teachers have stretched the meaning of words and dictated the effect of the work of the Spirit in believers. Others have misused biblical truth to demand certain evidences of the fruit of the Spirit in those who believe. There is certainly a need to return to the basic teaching about the person and work of the Holy Spirit, being careful to use only biblical terms to define His ministry.

The fullness of the Spirit should be the normal experience of believers. It is not a special endowment for unusual work. All believers are expected to appropriate the fullness of the Spirit for daily activities.

The Holy Spirit comes to indwell every believer at the point of salvation. Faith placed in Christ and His work on the cross and His resurrection is the foundation for all spiritual blessings. One of the most important aspects of the saving work of God is imparting the Holy Spirit. If any person does not have the Spirit, he does not belong to Christ, Paul writes in Romans 8:9.

A second act of the Holy Spirit is to baptize new believers into the body of Christ. This instantaneous work of the Spirit is universally accomplished at the point of conversion. The result is that each believer is united to the Lord Jesus in the body of Christ, and also to every other member of His body. When this work is accomplished, the believer is indwelt and sealed in salvation for sanctification and service in the family of God.

Once the Holy Spirit is in permanent residence in the believer, He can be allowed to control every aspect and act of that person. Fullness is a result of several actions on the part of the believer. First, it involves confession of all known sin. Second, there must be a consecration of all that I am and have to the Spirit's control. Third, I must acknowledge the response of the Spirit by thanking God for fulfilling all His promises. Fourth, I must act in faith, believing that my decisions and actions are directed by the Spirit who fills and controls me. The result is to do the work of God in the power and presence of Christ, who is within by the Holy Spirit.

છ ———————————— જી

Father, thank you for Your Holy Spirit and for the prospect of continually being filled with Him and His power for living today.

Passing from Death to Life

But has now been revealed by the appearing of our Savior
Jesus Christ, who has abolished death and brought
life and immortality to light through the gospel.

2 Timothy 1:10

The grace of God is the centerpiece of the work of Christ on the cross. Over and over again, the grace of God is described as the primary display of God's abundant blessing in working out man's salvation. Grace was fully displayed in the "appearing of our Savior Jesus Christ."

Three separate aspects of His grace are listed for our consideration and appreciation in today's passage. One was accomplished in the past and endures in the present. One is the blessing of the present with continuing effects, and the third is a prospect promised to all who believe.

First, He has abolished death. That, of course, does not mean that death no longer exists for all mankind. Rather, the striking announcement is that the work of Christ on the cross has reversed the effects of God's punishment for the sin of Adam. Death was facing Christ as He went to the cross—that is, physical death, spiritual death, and the second death. Death, meaning separation, is seen in all its ugliness as Christ endured the anger of both God and man. For the believer, death or separation from God will never be a threat or an experience. Christ has forever defeated death for the believer.

Second, the goal of God in the death of Christ was to produce life out of death. The resurrection is the foundation on which God offers life to all who believe. Life is found in fellowship with Christ, because of the presence of God Himself. The indwelling Holy Spirit makes us the residence of God, and brings to us all the blessings of salvation. No believer can say that God is not resident in him or that he is in any way separated from God.

> *The resurrection is the foundation on which God offers life to all who believe.*

The third blessing is the promise that we are immortal. That does not mean that we will never pass through death. It means, rather, that we will not remain in death. The unbeliever not only enters into death, but he also never passes out of death. Death is separation from God. Believers are immortal, even as we pass through the door of death. We are never separated from God, who is life.

These and many other blessings comprise the glorious message of the gospel of God. May we be careful to explain the blessings of the Good News so that more may believe in the name of the only Son of God.

  ✠ ──────────── ☙

Father, thank you for these three blessings that proceed from the cross and resurrection of Christ.

Prince of Peace

*For He Himself is our peace, who has made both one, and
has broken down the middle wall of division between us.*

Ephesians 2:14

The blessing of peace is recorded for us several times in the New Testament. The promise of Christ to His disciples in John 14:27 is a favorite for believers experiencing trials and afflictions: "Peace I leave with you, My peace I give to you." The disciples might well have asked how their friend was going to give them peace if He was leaving and, in fact, going to the cross. The answer is given in our text. He is our peace because He lives in every true believer.

From a theological perspective, peace is intimately related to the person of Christ. Romans 5 speaks of the doctrine of salvation and addresses the need for peace. "Therefore, having been justified by faith, we have peace with God through our Lord Jesus Christ." This announcement describes how the animosity was removed between God and man. Christ died and rose again for our sin to pay the penalty that removed God's anger toward sinful man. God was then free to act in peace toward all who believe. But the provision of peace is only available in and through Christ. He is our peace toward God.

Another source of comfort is the instruction of Paul in Philippians 4:6-7 regarding the lack of peace in a believer's life. The answer is a command for all the faithful Philippians to set aside anxieties by presenting their petitions to God, and "the peace of God which passes all understanding will guard your hearts and minds through Christ Jesus." The sanctifying work of Christ is provided by allaying fears and anxieties and making the petitioner aware that Christ is his peace.

It is instructive to note that the introduction of Christ brings peace. For those in a state of unbelief, trusting Christ brings peace with God. For the believer overwhelmed by worry and anxiety, the reminder of Christ's presence gives that person the opportunity of accepting and enjoying peace in Christ.

In our text, the great barrier between Jew and Gentile made peace a scarce commodity. The Jews had no dealing with Gentiles, whom they called "dogs." To this sad circumstance came the Lord Jesus, who died for all and, by resurrection, created the one body of Christ, made up of believing Jews and Gentiles. Each shares the same blessings and continues to do so in Christ, who is peace. Now harmony and peace is possible, as each finds satisfaction in the person of Jesus Christ.

೮౦ ———————————————— ೮౩

*Father, thank you for the peace that I have in Christ. I confess that I do not
always enjoy or appreciate it.*

Planning Our End

For whom He foreknew, He also predestined to be
conformed to the image of His Son, that He might
be the firstborn among many brethren.

Romans 8:29

F ew terms in Christian doctrine have been fought over more than the word predestination. Families have fought, churches have divided, and communities split because of conflicting definitions of God's work in predestination.

What is important is that God has a plan for every believer who was foreknown, and that is "to be conformed to the image of His Son." God plans the end of the one who is foreknown. Simply put, predestination means "to plan the end."

This glorious truth is that the final condition of every believer is Christ-likeness. In practical terms, this verse establishes the final presentation of each one who began the journey when he trusted Christ as Savior. Our first step toward the divine goal is to "believe in our heart that God raised Him [Christ] from the dead." What we understood of our first step was very limited. It may have included going to heaven when we die, the forgiveness of all our sin, a Father to love, a special plan for our life, or other aspects of God's work of salvation.

Few of us thought that the first step would eventually bring a final step of being like the One who died for us and rose again. God wants to populate His home with children just like His perfect Son. He made that possible by sending the Lord Jesus to the cross to die for our sin. Sin was one of the primary reasons that we could not be like Christ. In addition, divine life needed to be put in everyone who would ultimately be like Christ. The resurrection of Christ made divine life possible. The coming of the Holy Spirit made God's plan effective.

When God gave us the life of His Son, we began a lifelong pilgrimage of training, testing, and developing the life of Christ in and through our mortal flesh. Our responsibility is to learn through the sufferings, to grow by feeding on the Word, to accept the chastening of God, to keep my life clean, to exercise my abilities, to obey every command, to follow all directions, and to live in total dependence on the Lord Jesus. As we do this, the image of Christ will spontaneously develop in and through us. If we do not do these things, God will wait until we see Christ to accomplish His predestined plan.

                                             — ❧ ———————————————— ☙ —

Father, thank you for the glorious plan for my life, both here on earth and in Your presence. I confess to being lazy and thoughtless about Your conforming me to the image of your Son. I choose Christ-likeness.

Raised by the Spirit

But if the Spirit of Him who raised Jesus from the dead dwells
in you, He who raised Christ from the dead will also give life
to your mortal bodies through His Spirit who dwells in you.
Romans 8:11

This portion of Romans communicates the characteristic that sets believers apart from all others. That characteristic is the presence of the Holy Spirit in everyone who believes. Yet, we do not always consider the importance of the third person of the Trinity as a resident in our lives.

One of God's primary goals in His plan of salvation was to become an abiding presence in all who believe in Jesus Christ. Man was driven from the presence of God in the Garden of Eden when sin entered the world. God chose to restore that relationship by forgiving and cleansing each one at the point of believing. (The word "if" in this verse has the force of "since.") Once cleansed, the house becomes a proper residence for the Holy Spirit.

Who is this Holy Spirit? Our text tells us that the Holy Spirit raised Jesus from the dead. But what about the references that say that the Father raised Him from the dead? And how do we harmonize the words of the Lord Jesus who said, "I have power to lay [my life] down, and I have power to take it again?"

As with all that God does, the Father is the source or the architect of His work. The Lord Jesus accomplishes it in and through His finished work, and the Holy Spirit applies the work day by day in our lives. Here the application of the resurrection of Jesus is credited to the Holy Spirit. No greater event has taken place in the history of man than the resurrection of Jesus.

All the blessings of our salvation are possible because Jesus Christ is alive. The fact that Jesus came out from among the dead puts the seal of God on His suffering and death. We are told, "It is appointed for man to die once" (Hebrews 9:27). All questions about our own mortal bodies being raised from the dead are erased by this statement. Christ was the first to be truly resurrected, and that makes it stand alone in the works of God. The Holy Spirit raised Jesus as the first fruit of those who slept, and our resurrections are an extension of that act performed so many years ago. There can be no doubt that the living Christ in us guarantees our own resurrection. Our mortal bodies will be fashioned like His own body of glory by that same Spirit when we see Christ as He is.

ଓ ───────────── ଔ

Father, thank you for the Holy Spirit who raised Jesus from the dead, guaranteeing that He will raise me from the dead on that coming day. "Even so, come, Lord Jesus!"

Deeply Rooted

Rooted and built up in Him and established in the faith, as
you have been taught, abounding in it with thanksgiving.

Colossians 2:7

The purpose of roots is to take the nutrients of the soil and transfer them to the branches that produce fruit. When a botanist investigates a diseased plant, he first checks the condition of the soil that the roots are living in.

Similarly, when we consider our spiritual health, we need to examine our own foundation. Although we are rooted in the excellent soil of Christ, this does not always guarantee fruitfulness. There are other issues that must be considered. Many believers are rooted in and devoted to other things besides Christ. Throughout Scripture, we are repeatedly warned to set our affection solely on Christ and not on the things of this world. The concept of rooting suggests that our roots are actually in that which we love, adore, or spend a lot of our money, time, and resources on.

The main point of Colossians 2:7 is that the person and work of Christ is available for our roots. There are many other metaphors used to express our spiritual relation to Christ. Walking, feeding, growing as a child, studying, and running all teach about our dependence on Christ. The relationship between the branches and the vine is one of the most profound in all of Christ's teachings.

Paul's teaching here is an exposition of Christ's message in the upper room. The root is a straw which moves the minerals and moisture from the ground to the flower and fruit. We are simply straws to take the resources of Christ and lift them by faith into our behavior, displaying them as the fruit of the Spirit.

An important habit that we should establish is that of thanksgiving. All the resources of Christ are available to us. Begin by learning what those vital ingredients are and habitually giving thanks to God for providing them. If we do not know these blessings, we cannot give thanks. If we do not believe that we have them, we will not be grateful for them. If we do neither of these things, we will not produce real fruit, but just an imitation which will result in pride of our own abilities. It is all of Christ. These meditations are a summary of what we have received. Believe that these blessings are in Christ and by faith appropriate them, just as a straw draws liquid from a glass. Roots lift the food from the soil. As branches, we produce fruit, drawing the resources from Christ. Begin by saying thank you.

80 ———————————— C03

Father, thank you for all the resources available in Christ. I choose to believe
that they are mine, and I draw enough for the moment.

Love the Unlovable

But concerning brotherly love you have no need that I should write
to you, for you yourselves are taught by God to love one another.
1 Thessalonians 4:9

What part of "love one another" do we not understand? This oft-repeated injunction, given by Christ in the upper room, continues to challenge believers today.

The amazing makeup of the universal church adds to the difficulty. The languages, cultures, locations, denominations, skin colors, backgrounds, practices, functions, and beliefs tend to set us apart from one another, instead of binding us in love and appreciation.

We are often asked, "What is the biggest problem on the mission field?" We usually answer with the question, "What is the biggest problem in the church?" The answer, of course, is that the church has trouble getting along with the church—that is, loving one another.

Division within the church is one of the greatest successes of the enemy. The unbeliever sees and hears the fighting and arguing that pervades almost every segment of the church. He concludes that he does not need a community that cannot live in peace and love. His own world is often as harmonious as the Christian society.

These same people, who cannot get along with each other, often strive to cram their heads with knowledge—knowledge that ironically tends to further divide them. Each group seeks a greater accumulation of facts and ideas that enhance their intellectual achievements, and arm themselves with reasons why they are more spiritually astute than the group down the road.

Paul writes that he does not need to remind his readers to be obedient to this command because God has already given them clear teaching. He does not need to repeat it again because it is so often repeated.

This teaching about loving one another is inborn in every believer when we receive Christ as Savior. The renewed conscience, the indwelling Holy Spirit, and the person of Christ remind us that we are commanded to love every other member of the body of Christ. When we say that this is hard, we acknowledge the need for the resources of Christ who loves every member of His body equally. The Holy Spirit in us will love other believers if we allow Him to minister through us. The fruit of the Spirit is love. He is waiting for us to appropriate the love of Christ toward that unlovely Christian who is a living member with me in the body of Christ.

ൽ ────────────── ന

Father, thank you for the command to love every other believer. I confess my
failure. I choose to love an unlovely Christian today.

Abundantly Living Water

And He said to me, "It is done! I am the Alpha and the Omega, the Beginning and the End. I will give of the fountain of the water of life freely to him who thirsts."

Revelation 21:6

The Father is the source of the fountain of living water. The Lord Jesus, by His death and resurrection, broke the gates so that the river of the water of life could flow freely through Himself. The Holy Spirit leads us to that flow and invites all to drink deeply and be satisfied.

Jesus Christ invites all who thirst to come, and He will generously give of Himself as a river. Some bring a cup once a week and gently dip up a few drops and go on their way. Others take bucket after bucket from its flow, and a well-worn path to the river becomes evident. A few come to the river and dive right in. They immerse themselves in all its abundance and invite the timid to enjoy the fullness.

The intention of the Lord Jesus was to provide a reservoir of riches, a fountain whose adequacy would never be independent of Him. A river is fed from the springs of water that lie deep in the recesses of the earth. An underground stream pushes its way up through the heart of the mountain to burst forth and flow through the towns on its way to the sea.

> *The resources in our Savior are sufficient for the few, adequate for the many, and abundant for the multitude.*

Any and all can come to drink of its abundance, but few do. The rush of the creek is abundant enough for the handful of people near the source. As it descends, the volume increases so that all on the gentle slope of the mountain can take of its opulence. And when it finally arrives in the plain, this same river is full and wide, and the multitude of people there can take as much as they will for all their needs. So the resources in our Savior are sufficient for the few, adequate for the many, and abundant for the multitude.

Men and women of this world seek to satisfy their thirst from the world's cisterns. The reservoirs of pleasure, wealth, and knowledge are populated with a host of spiritually thirsty souls. All come away empty and disappointed. The One who said on the cross, "It is finished," invites all to leave the stagnant ponds of the world and instead be satisfied in Him, the fountain of living water.

—————— ⊘ ——————

Father, thank you for the resurrection by which you loosed the torrent of spiritual riches locked in the bosom of Your Son. Thank you for His flow into my life. I dip my soul and satisfy my heart in His abundance.

No Further Revelation Is Needed

That I may know Him and the power of His resurrection, and the fellowship of His sufferings, being conformed to His death.
Philippians 3:10

Do I really want to know Him? This oft-quoted text is a continual reminder of the responsibility that we have to employ our mind and activate our will to develop the characteristics of Christ.

The fulfillment of this desire lies fully in our own hands. We sometimes think that our desire is all that is required of us to set the Lord free to begin His work in us. The point is clearly made by the Lord Jesus to Philip, "Have I been with you so long and yet you have not known me, Philip?" For three years the Lord Jesus had walked, taught, served, and lived the life that revealed His Father, but still the disciples asked for more. We, too, cry out in prayer or song to our Lord, "I want to know you," expecting some new dramatic revelation. His response may very well be, "I have fully revealed myself to you in my life, death, and present ministry. It is your responsibility to get to know me, not mine to reveal more to you!"

> *Have we studied His sufferings and death as much as we have His power?*

Many believers plead with God for more power in this life—power for service, for victory, and for living. Again the Lord reminds us that He has fully demonstrated His power by His resurrection and has communicated that power by His life in every believer. No greater source is available to us than the resurrected Christ who dwells within us.

Knowing this, we cringe at the prospect of such fellowship. We know that we should aspire to the last two characteristics in this verse as we do the first two, but our heart is faint and our soul unwilling. The suffering and death of Christ is just as available to us as the knowledge of Christ and His powerful resurrection. Have we studied His sufferings and death as much as we have His power? Are we as diligent learning the pain, sorrow, and anguish of the cross as we are in studying His miracles? All of these truths fully reveal the Lord whom we claim to want to know. We need not ask for a further fresh revelation of the Father or the Son. The Holy Spirit is waiting for us to devote our mind and our will to knowing Him. He will reveal all the glories of Christ to the mind and heart that passionately seeks Him.

ಬ ──────────── ೞ

Father, thank you for the full revelation of Yourself in Your Son. I confess the laziness of my soul and my desire for an easy way to be like Christ. I commit to know His life, His sufferings, and His death.

Priests and Kings

And have made us kings and priests to our
God; And we shall reign on the earth.

Revelation 5:10

When Israel was under the law, no man was allowed to be both a king and a priest. The priests were to come from the tribe of Levi and the family of Aaron. The kings were to come from the tribe of Judah. A king who acted as a priest or in a priestly way was severely punished by the Lord.

The exception to this is, of course, the Lord Jesus Christ, who sits as both the King of kings and as High Priest, both for the nation of Israel and the church.

The book of Hebrews tells us that Jesus Christ is especially called to be a high priest after the order of Melchizedek. Christ could not be a priest after the order of Aaron, since He came from the tribe of Judah. He must have a different order of priesthood. That was made official by His ordination in the line of Melchizedek. He then offered Himself as the adequate priestly sacrifice. But death was not enough for a priesthood which was going to endure "after the order of Melchizedek." The resurrection of Christ made it possible for Him to serve forever in an endless priesthood. He is the King-Priest who will rule and serve forever.

Because of the union that we have with Christ, all believers are united to Christ as kings and priests. We have been given His life and are identified with Him in His death, burial, and resurrection, as well as His ascension and His seated position. We did not earn these positions because of our heritage or our service, but because we are uniquely united to Christ in all that He does on behalf of His people.

> *We have no sacrifice*
> *to offer but that of*
> *Christ Himself.*

In Revelation 5:10, we are reminded that we will reign with Christ on earth. Who are the ones selected to serve in this auspicious position? Elsewhere we are told, "If we suffer with Him we shall also reign with Him." As priests, we can offer "the praise to Him who called us out of darkness into His marvelous light." We have no sacrifice to offer but that of Christ Himself. God is pleased as we present the praise of the One who died for us and rose again. As priests, we are called to offer the sacrifice of praise continually.

ℬ ———————————— ℭ

Father, thank you for making me a priest and a king. I confess that I do not serve in either role faithfully. I offer my praise to You as my God and am grateful that You accept the sacrifice of my lips in worship to Your Son.

Stewards of Our Gifts

As each one has received a gift, minister it to one another,
as good stewards of the manifold grace of God.

1 Peter 4:10

The relationship of believers in the church is not the primary propose of Peter's letters, but he does give some practical teaching and encouragement to suffering saints. As best we can understand, the early believers he wrote to were not as spiritually mature as others. It would seem that the church in Ephesus, Rome, and Corinth was instructed far more about the interdependence of each member on the others. Now Peter writes to believers in what is today known as Turkey, reminding them of their responsibilities.

In 1 Peter 4:10, Peter focuses on three main ideas. He begins by assuming that every believer has received a spiritual gift. These gifts were to be used to enrich and support other believers. Furthermore, every believer should employ the gift because they are not ours but God's.

It is helpful to understand that the words translated "gift" and "grace" are from the same root word, *charis*. This word is also translated "thanks" in many places, and hence we ask someone to "say grace" before a meal.

When we accept that every believer has received a gift from God, this should result in a proper "thank you." Although many in the church cannot specifically say what their spiritual gift is, they are in active service to God and the church. Some do not know their gift and so do nothing in the church. Some would go so far as to say that they do not have a spiritual gift, contradicting this verse and others. If you are a believer, you have a gift given by God.

Much confusion circulates in the body of Christ because many reject the premise that each gift is for the blessing and service of others in the church. A number of people seem satisfied in hiding their gift without any consideration for the rest of the family of God. Your gift is to complement others who are using their gift. Your gift serves others in the Church.

"As good stewards" indicates that, though God has given each a gift, He reserves that property as still His own. We are stewards, not owners, of the grace or gift of God. He gives to us so that we can use the talent or ability for the good of the whole church. As stewards, we also must give an account to God of what we did with the grace He gave. Say thank you for the gift. It is an exercise in faith.

ഈ ─────────────── ര

Father, you have given me a spiritual gift. I realize that it is a permanent personal blessing to be used for the enriching of the church.

Gone, Gone, Gone!

And you know that He was manifested to take
away our sins, and in Him there is no sin.

1 John 3:5

Sin divides, destroys, defiles, demeans, deadens, and deceives. It drives a wedge between God and man. It undoes the relationship that God had with man. It dirties the mind and heart of every member of the human family. It brings man down from the lofty purpose for which he was created. It cauterizes the sensitivity that God built into man's heart.

The gospel began in the thoughts of God long before the foundation of the world. The plan of God was not an intervention which was forced on Him by the unexpected disobedience of His creatures. "Plan A" was not set aside because of an unforeseen circumstance which surprised the omniscient Creator.

Sin was allowed by God to give Him the glorious opportunity to reveal aspects of His nature and person that could only be known by His loving sacrifice for our sin. Throughout the Old Testament, God opened His picture book with page after page of illustrations, forecasting how He would deal with sin. Those who study these presentations of the divine Artist know why Christ was revealed. They know that a goat, a bullock, a handful of meal, a ram, a dove, or even a lamb could never take away sin. Something or someone else must be unveiled to fully and finally remove sin.

The greatest mystery in the world's history was unraveled when Jesus was born in Bethlehem of Judea. But why did He come? The announcement was made before His feet touched the earth that He created. "He shall save His people from their sins."

For generations, sin was only covered by the sprinkled blood on the mercy seat and the annual reminders of the wickedness of every Israelite. The blood of bulls and goats never took sin away. The Lamb of God was specifically designated to remove the sin of the world. No one who read the earlier record of John can say, "We do not know why He came!" He came, lived, died, and rose for one primary purpose: to take away our sin.

No greater work could be done than to remove our sin "as far as the east is from the west." The sinless Lamb of God took the world's sin and, by death and resurrection, carried it to a desolate place from which it cannot be retrieved. Since it cannot be recovered, why do we bring back past sin and worry about their forgiveness? They are gone, gone, gone!

Father, thank you for casting away my sin. I choose the freedom of forgiveness today!

September

JEWELS TO DEVELOP FAMILY LIKENESS

". . . we shall be like Him . . ."

1 John 3:2

My desire, to be like Jesus,
My desire to be like Him.
His Spirit fill me,
His love o'erwhelm me
In deed and word
To be like Him.

Lillian Plankenhorne

September

The Lilies of the Field

L uke 12:27 says, "Consider the lilies, how they grow: they neither toil nor spin; and yet I say to you, even Solomon in all his glory was not arrayed like one of these."

Lilies of the field are a common plant that very few would stop to look at for more than a moment. Only the botanist would stoop down and begin to examine the complex structure of their existence, the amazing process of development, or the mysterious diffusion of color and fragrance. But it is this mundane plant that the Lord used as one of His illustrations of how the life of faith is lived. When a believer stops and reflects on the care of the Creator for this prolific plant of the meadow, meditating on the relationship of the Creator to one of the most uninspiring plants of the field, he must stand in awe of how much greater is the relationship and dependence of his own life to that same Creator.

It would seem that the Savior chose two objects of care from extreme ends of the spectrum of divine indulgence. On one end is the lily, created with a word and seemingly set on His field with little thought and predestination. On the other end is man, whom God made in His own image and toward whom His whole being is devoted. This array of wisdom is in His redemptive plan, conceived before we were created or fell to such depths of sin. It is in His plan for our restoration that the greatest display of wisdom is defined, and the glorious measure to which He has carried it out that astounds us as we stand beside the little lily.

The lily does not toil in its daily round of activity, which is hidden to the casual observer. For this little plant must draw up from the soil a daily supply of resources necessary to keep its stalk upright and its leaves full, green, and flexible. Each leaf must function as a manufacturing mechanism in the constant process of photosynthesis. The leaf must absorb carbon dioxide and give off oxygen, as ordained by the Creator, so that the superior being for whom His Son died can draw on that oxygen and glorify God. This same lily does not "spin," says the One who made it. To toil suggests the duties for survival. To spin directs us to the need for clothing. The Creator has provided for the "clothing" covering the field, as He has each individual stitch for every lily. That covering is made up of a kaleidoscopic display of color, fiber, fragrance, design, and a host of other differences, unseen except from the underside of the weaving.

That single plant is adorned with a beautiful flower, which is but one stitch in the fabric. But, as it is examined, it provides a host of details, leading us to the Creator and His intricate provision. What glorious implications from common plants.

We, who are the result of the most complex creative process, called to the highest divine responsibility, are to learn from one of the lowliest of His expressions. We who were created and redeemed to be "to the praise of His glory" are to understand that we, too, do not need to toil or spin, since the same Creator is also our Redeemer. To toil is to provide for our needs in our own strength. To spin is to seek to weave our own righteousness for a garment. The Redeemer has done it all. He toiled at the cross to guarantee us life. He rose from the dead to provide His own righteousness as our covering for all eternity. What a glorious tapestry!

The lily has only to draw from the resources that the Creator has put at its roots in order to be dressed in the most exquisite cloth of the field. It must accept the provision of the Creator so that it can offer the casual visitor a whiff of its fragrance. There is no toil, no spinning—yet it is clothed by the Creator.

As believers redeemed by Christ's precious blood, we are arrayed in more glory than Solomon because God's greater Son has, by the cross and resurrection, provided the resources for us to be clothed in glorious robes. God offers the riches of Christ, in whom we are rooted, in order to present radiance to all who will stop and gaze and then glorify our Father, who is in the heavens.

My dear brothers and sisters, draw deeply on the infinite blessings made available to you in and through the Lord Jesus Christ, from whom all our needs are supplied. Bloom where you are planted. Adorn the doctrine. Make the path fragrant. Brighten your corner.

Soldiers in Training

You therefore must endure hardship as a
good soldier of Jesus Christ.

2 Timothy 2:3

When you trusted Christ as your Savior, did He ask you if you wanted to be a soldier? Was there a choice of whether you wanted to be a baker, a teacher, a preacher, or a secretary? No, when you realized that you needed a Redeemer, you did not think much about what would be demanded of you. Our hearts were so full of spiritual blessings that the thought never crossed our mind what service we might want to render to the One who saved us.

The followers of Christ fill many different roles. As students, we are to study. As disciples, we must learn. As stewards, we are required to be faithful. As sons and daughters, we should radiate His likeness. As saints, we are to display holiness. As soldiers, we are to endure hardships.

This concept may come as a surprise when we consider the lifestyle that awaits followers of Christ. Most new believers think that an easier life is ahead of them. Yet many, early in their pilgrimage, find that the enemies of Christ come against them with ferocity. They are surprised that there are enemies who wish to impede their spiritual growth.

> *A study of war helps us understand the battles that await all who accept Christ for salvation.*

The long learning experience begins with the first step in the Christian life. Many are surprised at the condition of the road and the lack of comforts. Others discover that the road quickly becomes a full-fledged battlefield.

A simple study of war helps us more fully understand the battles that await all who accept Christ for salvation. Perhaps we should be more careful to describe the conflicts that lie ahead for any who consider joining the sojourners from earth to glory. The feeling of loneliness may become irksome. The lack of comfort or rest from battle is wearisome. Many sojourners seek refuge from such difficulties, but war demands discipline, obedience, endurance, and even poverty. All of this we were unprepared for when we said "yes" to Christ. Every son is a soldier, every believer a battler, every follower a warrior. Every Christian is in conflict! Although many want to retire, there is no discharge from this war, writes Solomon in Ecclesiastes. Endure, knowing that you are a soldier until the day we lay aside this perishing body.

ः ———————————— ॰

Father, thank you for all the resources, equipment, and armor that you have provided so that I can be an effective combatant against the enemies. I train today to be a good soldier of Jesus Christ in the army of the faithful.

Paid with Imperishable Coin

In Him we have redemption through His blood, the
forgiveness of sins, according to the riches of His grace.

Ephesians 1:7

If God were unable to forgive our sin, He would not be free to pour out the blessings of His grace. The cleansing of our sin made it possible for Christ Himself to dwell in us. The redemption of God toward our sin also prepared us for the eternal enjoyment of God's presence in glory. If sin remained, Christ would not have come in, and we could not have entered God's holy presence.

The word "redemption" is one of the grandest words that God uses to explain the effective work of Christ in preparing us for salvation. Redemption means to "pay a price and set free." Peter reminds us that we were not redeemed by corruptible silver or gold, as the law required. The purchase of that which is imperishable must be bought or paid for with imperishable coin. The eternal sacrifice of Christ is the required "coin" for the eternal forgiveness of sin. That sacrifice is centered in the precious blood of Christ.

We can celebrate the possession of redemption as a permanent, personal possession.

The redemptive price was not paid with currencies separated from Christ Himself. A person buys back his pawned watch with money that he can part with, and he goes on his way enjoying his redeemed watch. But Christ paid the ransom price with His own blood. He paid with His soul; as Isaiah writes, "He poured out His soul unto death." It cost Christ His life to set us free from the penalty of sin, allowing God to forgive all our sin.

Because the currency of His life was adequate for our sin, we can celebrate the possession of redemption as a permanent, personal possession. It is irreversible and unchangeable. No further claim can be placed against me because the value received was not a down payment. *"Paid in full"* is categorically posted on my life, and I leave the prison of sin inseparably joined to my Redeemer, the risen Lord Jesus Christ. I am His property because He has redeemed me. I am voluntarily His, as well, because this redemption, made possible by Christ's death, is made personal by my faith in my Redeemer and His sacrifice.

What abundance is poured out on me because my Redeemer set God free to include the fullness of the blessing of Christ, which is drawn from the infinite riches of His grace.

Father, thank you for receiving full payment from Christ for my sin. I am free from that debt and rest in the richness of this gift!

One Faith for All People

*Therefore, having been justified by faith, we have
peace with God through our Lord Jesus Christ.*

Romans 5:1

The above verse stands as one of the greatest monuments to the finished work of the Lord Jesus Christ. The previous passages declare that faith is the only acceptable means of approach to God for sin—faith in the person and work of Jesus Christ. Because "all have sinned" and stand condemned, God waits for all to come to Him by faith to receive forgiveness of sin.

The frightened soul and the forthright come by the same faith. The child and the criminal come trusting the same Savior. The adolescent and the ancient must believe in the same work at the cross. The innocent and the intellectual must come the same way. Their faith, whether great or small, produces the same declaration from the mouth of a holy God. "I freely and fully declare you righteous in My sight!" At the point of salvation, this announcement of an offended God categorically sets aside the punishment due to any sinner who believes. I stand justified in the sight of God only because of Christ.

God looks at the sacrifice of His Son and accepts His suffering as adequate to satisfy His righteous demands. And, although I still have a sin nature and commit sinful acts, God sees in me the righteousness of Christ and declares me righteous.

This glorious judicial act is the basis on which I have peace with the God whom I have offended. In a world filled with unrest and perversity, the believer can live with peace of mind and heart. This peace is the gift of God in and through His Son. Before the cross, the Lord Jesus said to His troubled disciples, "Peace I leave with you, my peace I give to you." Little did they know then how that peace would come. Yet they, too, would be able to rest in the finished work of Christ and appropriate peace from the God of peace. The inspired writer declares in Ephesians, "He is our Peace."

Peace now dwells in us as one of the most glorious blessings of the resurrected Christ. Daily, as we gaze on the empty cross and the vacant tomb, we are reminded that the

In a world filled with unrest and perversity, the believer can live with peace of mind and heart.

finished work of Christ guarantees our justification and our peace. Whether we enjoy these twin blessings is up to us. They are ours by faith. We enjoy them by faith.

❧ ———————————— ☙

Father, You have said that I have peace through Jesus Christ. Today I set aside my fears and anxieties and rest in Your Son and the peace He offers.

Keep Looking Down!

And raised us up together, and made us sit together
in the heavenly places in Christ Jesus.

Ephesians 2:6

An old Bible teacher used to repeatedly say, "Keep looking down!" He was referring to the perspective which we have as we come to understand that we are already seated with Christ in the heavens, gazing down on our own day-to-day struggles. Our position in Christ identifies us so thoroughly with Him that, when He died, we died; when He rose, we rose; when He ascended, we ascended; and when He sat down, we sat down!

Christ being seated means that we are seated as well. Our Savior is in the heavenlies, sitting at the right hand of God, waiting for His enemies to be made His footstool. The conflict for Christ is over, and He is awaiting the glorious celebration of victory.

We, seated with Christ, are to celebrate that victory and reject the temptation of fighting *for* victory instead of fighting from the position *of* victory. The Colossian epistle dramatically describes the fact that Christ ascended through the domain of Satan, openly triumphing over his minions in that migration back to the Father.

Many times we are urged to fight *for* victory in these spiritual battles so that, having been victorious, we are then offered a seat because of our success. It is Christ who has died and been raised, and He is now seated because of His victory. He fought the fight and won the war against the enemy. He shares the fruits of that conflict with us.

We must remember that we have no input into the conflict. Even our spiritual conflict with the principalities and powers is to be fought from the position of Christ's success against the same enemies. This seat is not just for the devout and mature, but also for all who are in Christ. There is not even a thought that our war has not been won. There is no doubt: the enemy has been defeated.

Seated together with Christ, we are sitting in satisfaction, sitting in completion, sitting in enjoyment of the Father, sitting in the blazing light of the glory of His face, and sitting in celebration.

From that high and holy place, we look down on our day-to-day struggle and know that our light affliction of the moment is but a reminder of the glory that shall be revealed in that day when we are with the Lord. Then we will not be looking down but gazing on His face forever.

છ ———————————— ૪

Father, thank you for the victory of my Savior against my enemies. I claim that victory and celebrate my position of satisfaction in Christ.

Our Unchangeable High Priest

*But He, because He continues forever, has
an unchangeable priesthood.*

Hebrews 7:24

The priests of the Old Testament all died, and death always brought an end to their priesthood. The ravages of age and the decline of capacities brought death to the body. The continual offerings reminded each high priest that he could not continue forever. For all of us, the realization of declining health tells us, ever more loudly, that the day is approaching when we will lay aside our physical body.

The difference for the Lord Jesus was that, though He knew the day of His approaching death, He also knew of His victorious resurrection and His installation as our great High Priest. What's more, as our Advocate before the Father, His priesthood will continue forever without change.

> Our Lord is able to understand our temptations and passions.

Our High Priest continues forever because of His resurrection. The aged priest facing death might be greatly mourned by the people, because a younger priest may not be as compassionate or caring as the grey-haired one who had walked this weary road for such a long time. The comfort received from the old man was easily remembered, because he more fully understood the sin and sorrow of his people.

Similarly, our Lord was tempted in all points just as we are, yet He was without sin. Because He traveled the same road as we, He is able to understand our temptations and passions. We are tempted to be angry and sin. We are challenged to be dishonest. Each has faced the lust of the flesh. No one has escaped the desires of the mind. Both young and old know the reality of coveting and loving the world and the things in the world. Both men and women have fought the lust of the eyes. Who has fully controlled that flapping tongue in our mouth? Each of these temptations, and many more, appear before us so regularly that it becomes discouraging to seek triumph.

Yet we have a Priest who lives forever and is interceding for each of us. What does He pray as our High Priest? We might want Him to pray that all temptations will go away, but He does not permit this. As He prayed for Peter, surely He prays for us, "that your faith does not fail." If Peter did not escape temptation, why should we? As Christ prayed for Peter, so He will pray for us. He serves as an unchangeable priest.

Father, thank you for raising Christ from the dead to serve as our unchangeable High Priest. I claim the offering of His blood and His prayers!

Reconciling the Aliens

*And you, who once were alienated and enemies in your
mind by wicked works, yet now He has reconciled.*

Colossians 1:21

O ne of God's greatest works is to change mankind. God Himself is perfect and does not need to change. It was man who changed in the garden, from being perfect to being sinful, and on that day the Lord God set in motion a wonderful plan to change him back again. The Bible is clear that mankind cannot change from sinfulness to perfection on his own. What's worse, he does not want to change. Because of this, God intervened in human life by the cross to reconcile the world.

The word "reconcile" means to "thoroughly change." The Lord did not move away from man in the garden, but moved man away from Him. God's plan has always been to move mankind back into loving fellowship with Himself. The only way was through the blood of His Son. At the cross, God thoroughly changed man from a position where he could not be saved to a position where he can be saved. This change was for the entire world. Without the cross, the Lord could not have invited anyone to "be reconciled to God." But because of the cross, He "commands all men everywhere to repent" and to change their mind regarding Christ as Savior.

Separated from God because of sin, our mind produced wicked works that proved that we were enemies of God. For this reason, God sent Christ into our world to die for sin and to reconcile us to Himself. But this act of God in and of itself did not bring us into a loving relationship with God. It cleared the way and tore down the wall that made it impossible for us to approach Him.

It is at this point that God requires a response to His commands. The Colossians heard of the work of the cross, as Paul reminded them in his letter. Like them, we also realized the need to change our mind about the Lord Jesus Christ. We were enemies of Christ. We were separated from God, and our minds were antagonistic to His Word and His will. The conviction of the Holy Spirit, together with the power of the Word of Truth, came to our consciousness and there was a change of mind, manifested in faith toward God and the Lord Jesus Christ. God acted on our faith and personally and permanently reconciled us to Himself.

We now humbly bow in thanks that God orchestrated this plan to reclaim the relationship lost in the garden through sin.

ᛒ ——————————— ᛗ

Father, thank you for including me in the reconciliation of the world by the blood of Christ. I know that I could never be Your child if You had not acted in love toward me by Christ's death.

Baptized with the Spirit

For by one Spirit we were all baptized into one body—
whether Jews or Greeks, whether slaves or free—and
have all been made to drink into one Spirit.

1 Corinthians 12:13

The baptism of the Holy Spirit is unfolded in this key verse as an accomplished fact for everyone in Christ.

This is a blessing to be much appreciated as we consider the way in which God has dealt with us, bringing us into the closest union possible with Himself. The baptism of the Spirit is mentioned about eleven times in the New Testament—once in each of the Gospels (telling the disciples that He was coming) and twice in the book of Acts (the first promising it shortly and the second referring to it as already accomplished). We accept that this baptism was an initial outpouring of the Holy Spirit on the Day of Pentecost, in answer to the prayer of the Lord Jesus.

It was a once-for-all event for the church as a whole, creating the body of Christ. It is repeated for each believer who confesses Christ as Savior. We are not urged to pray for or seek this miraculous transaction of God. The Spirit makes us one with Christ and with all other believers.

What must be accepted is that this is one of the primary blessings of our salvation. The work of God in all believers is the same. This event places us in the one body of Christ, but the fact that it takes place must be accepted by faith, not by feelings. A person who has been baptized in water shows his identification by being wet; so also each believer is to show the ministry of the Holy Spirit in his life.

The work of the Holy Spirit continues to cause us to drink of Him. Drinking involves ingesting for satisfaction and growth. Drinking is the response to thirst. Drinking brings the vital meaning of Scriptures to bear on our life and behavior. For every believer, the work of the Holy Spirit brings us into contact with needed truth. The absorption of truth feeds the needs, hungers, and thirsts of a living, growing soul.

As believers, we are related spiritually, rather than nationally or ethnically. This blessing is universally applied to all, regardless of station or relation in life. We may think that our connection to our fellow countrymen is important, but the universal relationship to every believer is preeminent.

Father, thank you for joining me to Your Son and to every child in Your family. I accept the action of the Holy Spirit in my life. What a special blessing this union is in a broken, perishing world.

Grace, Love, and Communion

The grace of the Lord Jesus Christ, and the love of God, and the communion of the Holy Spirit be with you all. Amen.

2 Corinthians 13:14

A ll believers are able to say "amen" to this wonderful provision of our loving Lord for our every need. Note the three words that Paul has placed together in this passage: grace, love, and communion. (The little word "be" can be misleading, suggesting that His provision is not yet fulfilled. It could just as accurately be translated: "The grace of the Lord Jesus Christ . . . *is* with you all.")

Grace, as we often read in the New Testament, is the root word for gifts. All the gifts of God are wrapped up in His grace, and all the grace of God is found in the Lord Jesus Christ. What abundance is mine in Him!

> *The communion or fellowship of the Holy Spirit is also available because the Holy Spirit is living in me.*

The love of God is with me because the perfect expression of His love is mine. 1 John 4:16 tells us, "God is love, and he who abides in love abides in God, and God in him." We cannot be without the love of God since Christ lives in us. We would have to lose Christ to lose His love. With His love in us, the practical expression of that love in my life is possible as I surrender to this ever-present resource.

The communion or fellowship of the Holy Spirit is also available because the Holy Spirit is living in me. Fellowship speaks of our joint participation or sharing in the resources of Christ, dispensed by the Holy Spirit. Jesus reminded His disciples that the Holy Spirit would "take of what is Mine and declare it to you." We need only to "come boldly to the throne of grace" and receive all the resources administered by the Holy Spirit from the "riches in glory by Christ Jesus." A resounding "amen" comes from the pen of Paul, and should also come from our heart, if not our lips.

Our Savior's resources and blessings are not dependent on my asking, but on my appropriating this wealth. Grace in Christ, love centered in God, and fellowship of the Holy Spirit—all of this is mine, as much as Christ, God, and the Holy Spirit are mine. What a powerful conclusion to a book that often celebrates the blessings of God to His children.

࿇ ———————————— ࿇

Father, thank you for the abundant resources of grace, love, and fellowship. I do not always understand the lavishness or permanence of these blessings, but I receive ample supply for today.

Committed, Even Unto Death

Always carrying about in the body the dying of the Lord Jesus,
that the life of Jesus also may be manifested in our body. For
we who live are always delivered to death for Jesus' sake, that
the life of Jesus also may be manifested in our mortal flesh.

2 Corinthians 4:10-11

Every mortal being has a strong desire to survive. Many people who come to Christ for salvation consider that one of the most attractive aspects of God's gift is life—eternal life and everlasting life. Perhaps the most powerful blessing of salvation is the prospect of living in heaven with God forever. That promise is so joyous that few want to consider a much more difficult promise: that the life of a believer is likely to involve suffering, persecution, and perhaps even physical death.

If someone asked us if we wanted to be like Jesus, most of us would readily answer that we do. Our idea of our Savior's lifestyle would include doing good, helping the fallen, healing the sick, giving to the poor, defending the truth, ministering to the helpless, and keeping the ten commandments. Few would dwell much on the death of Christ or His suffering and sorrow from His fellow man. Maybe we should present a more balanced view of the gospel by including the hatred and persecution that Christ promised to His faithful followers.

It is clear from the words of both the Lord Jesus and the epistles that the normal Christian life is to be characterized by a commitment to Him, even to the point of death. This does not mean that we are to be suicide bombers, but rather that we are to live such a committed life that we have died to our own desires and hungers and live to please our Master. The Lord Jesus came to the earth to die, and by His death and resurrection He secured life for all who believe. He did not please Himself, but always did those things that pleased His Father. He died to His own glory, power, and satisfaction. We are to always bear in our body the same death to our own goals, pleasures, and possessions.

The normal Christian life is to be characterized by a commitment to Him, even to the point of death.

Since Christ is in us, we have both the death of Jesus and His life in us. We can give our lives wholly to Christ and allow His love to be revealed for all to see. In seeing our selfless and servant lifestyles, people will see the life of Jesus in our mortal flesh.

— ∞ —

Father, thank you for giving me not only an example of death but also giving Christ to reproduce His death in my behavior. I choose to follow Christ's example, even in suffering and trials.

10

Strength and Power

Finally, my brethren, be strong in the Lord
and in the power of His might.

Ephesians 6:10

This is one of more than two dozen times that the Word of God commands His people to be strong. It is striking that God repeats this injunction so many times in a host of different circumstances. Israel was the first to hear these words from the mouth of God through Moses. Joshua heard them more than any other. The church is challenged to obey this injunction in two different places, and Timothy is also charged to "be strong."

But as many times as the people of God read these words, we still do not seem to understand the meaning and importance of what God is saying. One of the most oft-repeated prayers is a request for more strength or power. Many different situations come to the child of God in which he responds, "Give me strength." But we are not commanded to ask for additional strength, but to employ the strength that we possess in the Lord Jesus.

Even before the Holy Spirit had been given to believers, the command was the same. Joshua lived in the dawn of God's revelation in and through His people. We can assume that he was empowered by the Holy Spirit for the work to which he was called. Samson and King Saul knew the coming and going of the Spirit in their lives.

But we on this side of the death, resurrection, and ascension of the Lord Jesus have been fully empowered by the presence of Christ and the power of His Spirit. We have been given the power of His resurrection. We have been endowed with the Spirit of Power. We "can do all things through Christ who strengthens" us. All power is given to Christ, and He is with us always.

The context of our verse is spiritual conflict with spiritual wickedness in heavenly places. This combat is not fought in physical strength by superhuman feats. The conflict is in the area of our faith. The display and deployment of the shield of faith is the source of victory. The sword of the Spirit is an authoritative weapon in our hands.

The Word of God is living and powerful when employed by someone who fully trusts and employs its truth. The Living Word and the written Word are the most powerful combination for spiritual conflict in the arena of faith. God commands us to acknowledge our weakness, claim His power, and "be strong."

ॐ ———————————— ଔ

Father, thank you for the power of Christ's might. You have adequately distributed and described all the resources that I have in the Lord. I choose to appropriate the blessings of His presence to empower me for victory.

11

I Surrender All

Now may the God of peace who brought up our Lord Jesus from the dead . . . make you complete in every good work to do His will, working in you what is well pleasing in His sight, through Jesus Christ, to whom be glory forever and ever. Amen.
Hebrews 13:20-21

God is working in us. Though we may hinder the work through unbelief, God is working because it is His will. The goal of God in this ministry is our growth to maturity. It is easy to lose sight of the fact that the work is internal, with the results being observable externally.

The metaphor of a baby in his birth and growth can help us understand this process. The child may have external change through discipline and training, but the development of physical characteristics is spontaneous from within. The life received from the parents controls that development. The life of God given through Christ controls the development of what is pleasing to the Father.

> *God is accomplishing His will and is only limited by my willingness to surrender all that I am and have.*

Many Christians attempt to duplicate the qualities of Christ-likeness by cosmetic behavior. It is not imitation that produces likeness, but allowing an internal power to develop change from within. A child has blond hair, brown eyes, light skin, or a certain height because his parents had similar qualities. We have the qualities of Christ who dwells in us. Our risen Lord is working in us to create His likeness, which will be visible through our human flesh.

Of course, we also have the life of Adam, which produces a fallen likeness to him. But it is our choice which of these identities we will display. The resurrection power of Christ is available to overwhelm the influence of the sinful nature, received from our parents and Adam. It is not our effort that gives victory over what is not pleasing in God's sight, but submission to the life principle in us. Do we allow Him to complete His plan in us, both to will and to work what is well pleasing to Him?

An imitator is praised for his excellent skill in replicating what he sees and hears. God receives the glory if Christ-likeness is reproduced in us from within by His life. God is accomplishing His will and is only limited by my willingness to surrender all that I am and have.

Father, thank you for taking my body, soul, and spirit to produce an image that pleases You. I know that Your plan for me is in perfect harmony with the living Christ. I reject my plan and accept Yours today.

The Waterfall of God's Mercy

However, for this reason I obtained mercy, that in me first
Jesus Christ might show all longsuffering, as a pattern to
those who are going to believe on Him for everlasting life.

1 Timothy 1:16

Paul was chosen by God to be one of the first in a long line of recipients of His mercy. What an amazing pattern God gave on that road from Jerusalem to Damascus. God's abundant mercy was poured out on the "chief of sinners."

Some suggest that, because of the seriousness of Paul's sin, he above all should have cried out on that fateful day, "God be merciful to me a sinner!" But there was no cry because the mercy of God was fully and profoundly displayed when Christ died on the cross. God made His mercy fully available to all who come to Him through Christ. He cannot be anything other than merciful because it is a demonstration of His character.

Paul, like all of us, stood under the waterfall of God's infinite mercy and bathed his soul in its cleansing flood. There is no thought of a sinner coming to God and pleading for Him to let loose the dam holding back the flow of His mercy. The dam was broken at the cross, it was washed away by the blood of Christ, never to be replaced, rebuilt, or restored. The flow of His mercy is not limited by anything! It is man who must come to the river of redeeming blood and realize that there is no sin too big, no fault too dirty, no failure so permanent, no transgression so wide that the mercy of God does not wash it completely away.

What a glorious provision for all mankind in every station of life, every land, every culture, and every language on the globe. The veil is rent from top to bottom. The mercy seat is red with His blood. The Savior is seated on the mercy seat from which flows the river, cleaning any who, by faith, dip themselves in its glorious flow.

> *We have been washed*
> *once and forever.*

Come, brothers and sisters, bathe your souls afresh in God's mercy, flowing unrestricted for all. Immerse your thoughts in its refreshing abundance. Soak your mind in its unrestrained fountain. Cleanse your conscience in its incalculable affluence. We have been washed once and forever, but we marvel in the fullness of this blessing every day. How glorious the effect when we celebrate His undeserved mercy.

Father, You have washed me and I am clean. Today I soak my soul in your
mercy, so abundantly poured out on me.

Inheritors In His Will

To an inheritance incorruptible and undefiled and that
does not fade away, reserved in heaven for you.

1 Peter 1:4

A n inheritance does not depend on the desires, prayers, or pleas of the inheritor. Usually the recipient of such riches is in line for the blessing solely because he is in the bloodline of the one who bestows the inheritance.

The rich more often are the ones who have the decision whom to leave their assets to. The person who is likely to inherit wealth will tend to view the one who is "remembering him" a little differently. If the rich relative is extravagant with his money, the inheritor may become concerned. Will the value of my share be diminished as time moves on? Is it possible to get an advance of the inheritance before the actual death of my rich relative? Will the "uncle" outlive the one he is "remembering?" These thoughts are self-evident in the heart of man.

The readers of Peter's letter were being persecuted for their faith. The loss of material possessions was tempting them to question the faithfulness and love of God for His children. Peter reminds them that an unseen eternal inheritance was reserved for them in a place where it could not be diminished, destroyed, or dissipated. The next verse tells us that God is also preserving an inheritance for us.

Our riches are reserved in the presence of our faithful Father.

But how do I become a recipient of this valuable, protected inheritance? God's answer is very exclusive: "You must be in the blood-line of my Son." The gospel declares God's great offer. "As many as receive Him, to them He gave the right to become the children of God" (John 1:12). To believe is to become an inheritor of the riches of divine grace. Have you believed?

The inheritor normally must wait for the death of the wealthy relative. But Christ has died and risen from the dead to be the distributor of all the riches of our inheritance. Our riches are reserved in the presence of our faithful Father. Although we currently enjoy a down-payment of this wealth to enjoy and employ in our daily lives, the fullness of the blessings will be imparted when we see our benefactor face to face. This wealth is ours, not because we are good or prayed for it, but because we are His children.

Father, thank you for the open invitation for all to come and receive Your life through Your Son. How amazing are Your riches to all who believe!

14 SEPTEMBER

Eyes of Faith

But we see Jesus, who was made a little lower than the angels,
for the suffering of death crowned with glory and honor, that
He, by the grace of God, might taste death for everyone.

Hebrews 2:9

The eye of faith is far more perceptive than the physical eye. With our spiritual eyes, we are able to look further into the past, more deeply into the present, and with greater clarity to penetrate the future. On the day that we received Christ as our Savior, the Creator opened our eyes which had been blinded by the god of this world. At that moment, our comprehension of truth was born of the Spirit who enlightened us.

The eye is the only sense that we can manually control. We can't stop ourselves from feeling, tasting, hearing, or smelling, but we can shut our eyes. It is an act of the will. Blindness is the state that God uses to describe the condition of those who choose not to believe.

> *The eye of faith, aided by the Word of God and the Holy Spirit, can look back to the cross.*

The eye of faith, aided by the Word of God and the Holy Spirit, can look back to the cross. In gazing on that spectacle, we see a Savior who died as a perfect substitute. Translators have paraphrased this verse in other versions to eliminate an important truth. The crowning of Jesus took place before the cross "in order that" He might taste death for everyone. Peter reminds us that His crowning took place when they "were with Him on the holy mountain" of His transfiguration (2 Peter 1:17). His glory is greater than that of Moses, and His honor is greater than that of Aaron, says the author of Hebrews.

We who have been given spiritual eyesight can look from the mount of transfiguration, where He was crowned by the Father, to the mountain of Calvary, where He hung on a cross. Our Savior tasted death for everyone.

We do not need to ask for our eyes to be opened again. They were opened once and for all, that we might behold the wonders of His mighty love poured out on the cross. Yes, we can take our eye off the Savior and focus on the things of this world. We can be tempted to gaze on our own efforts to earn His acceptance. We can think that we should return to our own sacrifice, as the Hebrews were tempted to do, and glory in what we have done. Or we can gaze continually with loving eyes on Him who died for us. The look saves, but the gaze sanctifies.

❧ ———————————— ☙

Father, thank you for unveiling all the glories of Your Son. You crowned Him to be a substitute for everyone. My life is changed as I gaze lovingly on the One who died and rose again for me.

Receiving Beggars and Kings

*Therefore receive one another, just as Christ
also received us, to the glory of God.*

Romans 15:7

Most of us would be thrilled to have a king visit our home. We would not be silent if we had powerful people as our personal friends. But the Lord received us when we were sinners. Though He has made us kings and priests to God, we were not in that position when He met us. Christ received us as sinners with no consideration of status or titles.

How blessed to know that it was all of God. He welcomed us into His family as ill-behaved children. He received us as His bride even though we had spots and wrinkles. He accepted us as stewards and committed to us the mysteries of His Father even though we had not proved faithful. He received us as ambassadors, even though we had not come up through the ranks of heavenly diplomatic service. He received us as followers even though we would rather lead than follow. He received us as servants even though we preferred to be served than to serve. He received us as disciples even though we would prefer to teach than to be taught. He welcomed us as brothers and sisters even though we did not always get along lovingly. He received us as saints even though our lives were not very saintly.

It is no glory to us that He received us. We tend to think that God should be pleased that we belong to Him. We act as if the Lord gained a lot when He received us. Many of our choruses teach that we have so much to give, as if God is lucky to have us on His team and in His family. What pride and arrogance we seem to muster up with our hands lifted high, our eyes half closed, our lips singing of our great commitment, and our hearts promising God all that we are and have. We have nothing to give except what He has given us to return back to Him!

We were filthy, but He received us. We were sinners and rebels going our own way, and He stopped us and invited us to come. We trusted Him and He received us. His blood cleansed us from all unrighteousness. That faith opened the door for us to walk into His love and blessing. He received us just as we are.

Faith opened the door for us to walk into His love and blessing. He received us just as we are.

∞ ———————————— ∝

Father, I stand amazed that Your Son would receive me into His circle of love and grace. I commit myself to receive others as I have been received. I know that it glorifies You when we love each other.

His Unfailing Promises

Therefore, having these promises, beloved, let us
cleanse ourselves from all filthiness of the flesh and
spirit, perfecting holiness in the fear of God.

2 Corinthians 7:1

God is faithful—His promises never fail. His Word is peppered from start to finish with promises to His people. An amazing aspect of those promises is that they are not dependent on us, but on God Himself. The Scriptures are laced with the failures of man, creating a contrast with the consistent faithfulness of the Lord.

It is often our disobedience or unbelief which causes us to think that God has the same tendency to inconsistency. It is important to our understanding of God's faithfulness that His promises are not at all dependent on us or necessarily on our faith. We do not change the attitude of God by our willingness to believe that He will do what He has promised.

Israel was promised blessing and prosperity when God first spoke to Abraham, yet this nation has failed in disobedience and unbelief time after time down through the centuries. Some Bible students tend to accept a distorted view of God, making man's faithfulness more important than God's promises. God will fulfill His promises to Israel in His own time and in His own way.

If we accept the idea that the fulfillment of the Lord's promises are dependent on us, then we have no reason to believe that God will be faithful to us as His children. Yet the "exceedingly great and precious promises" are revealed in the Word of God, not for our examination so much as a reason for our faith. God has repeatedly revealed in His Word many promises that will be fulfilled based on His faithfulness.

Our salvation in all its fullness is dependent on the faithfulness of God to apply His promises to each believer. Man's faith in the promises of God allows our Father to act in accordance with His promises. We take no credit for applying our faith to His Word, expecting Him to do what He has said He will do. Our faith appropriates the promises!

But do we know the promises of God? Here is our failure. We have poor study skills and poor memory of what God has promised to those who believe. We have the promises in His Word but do not know them. We need to apply our minds to learn the Word of God, and all His promises in particular. This will have a lasting affect on our worship and praise of the Father.

ℛ ———————————— ℘

Father, thank you for all Your promises to me. I confess that I do not remember many. I will apply my heart to learn and claim each one.

Heirs of Faith

*And if you are Christ's, then you are Abraham's
seed, and heirs according to the promise.*

Galatians 3:29

T he passage in Galatians 3:29 takes us back to the life of Abraham and his concern about who was going to be his heir. The problem of progeny was one of the primary issues in his life. Indeed, every family saw having children as a blessing from God, and to be childless bore the stigma of divine displeasure. For Abraham and Sarah, the birth of a son was according to promise, and a divine intervention long after the time of bearing children was past. To the promised child of Abraham went eternal blessing. No greater blessing was ever promised any child on earth.

As believers, we share in the blessing of the promises of God, as heirs of the father of the faithful.

In Galatians, God illustrates that the divine promise to Abraham had a far wider influence than just the nation of Israel or the descendants of Jacob. Christ was the ultimate fulfillment of the Abrahamic covenant. Christ is the sum and substance of God's divine intervention in humanity, and the primary theme of the New Testament.

When people believe in Jesus Christ as their Savior, God implants His life in them and they become His children. That impartation is a divine operation called regeneration. The result of that miracle is here stated as belonging to Christ. (The word "if" is an assumed condition and can be correctly translated, "Since you are Christ's . . .") Jesus, a descendent of the Virgin Mary becomes the source of our inheritance in Christ as the seed of Abraham.

The issue is not only life but also likeness. James and John were called the "Sons of Thunder," meaning that they possessed loud and unmanageable natures. So here, Abraham's seed have a likeness to Abraham in that they exercise faith, just as Abraham did. Not all of Abraham's seed believed. We who believe share a likeness to the patriarch Abraham.

As believers, we share in the blessing of the promises of God, as heirs of the father of the faithful—Abraham himself. All who are of faith are partakers of the blessings of God. Our Father's promises are as sure and valid as they were to Abraham, since they are all appropriated by faith.

ஐ ———————————— ௫

Father, thank you for giving me the blessing of Your promises, which You make available by faith in Your Son, Christ Jesus. We rejoice that You honor our faith as You did the faith of our father Abraham.

Already Revealed

But as it is written: "Eye has not seen, nor ear heard,
Nor have entered into the heart of man The things which
God has prepared for those who love Him." But God has
revealed them to us through His Spirit. For the Spirit
searches all things, yes, the deep things of God.

1 Corinthians 2:9-10

Although we would like to know many of the facts and details about what heaven is like, the Bible does not provide an extensive amount of information on the topic.

Instead of describing heaven, the Scriptures are filled with a complete revelation of the person of Christ. The reason that there is so much more about Christ is that God would like us to be filled with the hope of seeing Him more than His heavenly home. But, as we examine the context of our meditation, we find little to suggest that Paul is speaking about heaven at all. The thought may be that the Lord is, day by day, working out the affairs of our lives, helping us to grow in grace and truth. Our study of the Scriptures provides insights into what God is unveiling in our walk of faith. It is wise to examine and learn how God guided other men and women in the Bible.

> *Don't ask for revelation; appropriate what the Spirit has already revealed.*

Today's Scripture passage is a quotation from Isaiah 64 and is supplied by the Spirit for our instruction. The message of the chapter is that the wisdom of God is made available to all who have the Spirit of God. Many believers continue to seek some further new revelation, something not afforded to less-instructed Christians. These people seem to rejoice in possessing a level of truth not commonly made known to others or recorded in the Scriptures.

But the statement is clearly made: God, by His Spirit, has revealed deep truths to all who will search the annals of revelation. This simple truth challenges us to listen to what the Spirit has said to the churches. We do not need a further revelation than the full and complete message of our Bible. We may imagine and dream and guess without much profit, but as we read, study, memorize, meditate, and digest the truth given to us, our profit is for this world and that which is to come. Don't ask for revelation; appropriate what the Spirit has already revealed.

ଅଠ ———————————— ଓଷ

Father, thank you for giving us the complete and full revelation of the glories of Your Son and the work that He did on our behalf. I commit these verses to memory so that I can meditate on this truth today.

The Miracle of Birth

Of His own will He brought us forth by the word of truth,
that we might be a kind of firstfruits of His creatures.

James 1:18

When a baby is due, mother and father anxiously await its appearance. But spiritual birth takes place according to the will and timing of God, and spiritual birth cannot take place at all without the "Word of Truth."

The Scriptures teach that each individual must "believe," "come," or "receive with meekness the engrafted word which is able to save" their soul. God responds to man's faith by providing him with salvation through the grace of His gospel. Our faith activates God's program by bringing us from darkness to light, just as a baby is delivered from the darkness of the womb to the light of the hospital room.

Yet we must admit that the work of God began long before we surrendered our lives to His control. Similarly, many things have to be in place long before a baby is born. Conception, growth, development, and a host of other specific and spontaneous activities take place in the womb before the day of birth. That is the reason that John writes that to be "born again" is like the wind that comes and goes without our completely understanding how it all works.

The "word of truth" is a designation for the written revelation of God from Genesis to Revelation. But it must not exclude the Word of God in the flesh, which is an official title for the Son of God. The action of the written Word, which is "living and powerful," and the person of God as the Truth, work in harmony to bring life to anyone who believes. We do not save ourselves. We cannot bring eternal life into our being by our own effort. The combined action of the living Word and the written Word is what is needed before we can legitimately say, "He brought us forth."

As important as birth is, that is not the end or goal of any conception. The parents are delighted that birth has taken place. The mother is glad to be relieved of the "burden" of extra pounds. But birth is the beginning of a lifetime of caring, providing, teaching, and disciplining, so that the fruit of the body will be a useful contributing member of society. Our spiritual birth has as its goal Christ-likeness, and every element that is necessary for that development is available in our Lord Jesus.

ಐ ———————————————— ೞ

Father, thank you for bringing me into eternal life by the Word of Truth. I rejoice in the action of Your Word to bring me out of death and into life. I choose to employ the resources of Christ to grow into His likeness.

In the Spirit

*But you are not in the flesh but in the Spirit, if indeed
the Spirit of God dwells in you. Now if anyone does
not have the Spirit of Christ, he is not His.*

Romans 8:9

The litmus test of salvation is the possession of the Holy Spirit of God. This statement, taken at face value, dispenses with the idea that you can belong to God and still not have the Spirit of God dwelling within you. It is a condemning doctrine that teaches that you can gain and lose the Spirit of God. It is a distressing message that you can have your sin forgiven and still not be sure that the Holy Spirit has taken up permanent residence in your being.

When we trust Christ as Savior, we move from a fleshly sphere of control into the sphere of the Spirit. That does not mean that we cannot lapse into a state where the flesh gains a foothold and burdens us under its influence. But it does mean that, since the Spirit has come to permanently indwell us, the flesh cannot enforce full control as it did before we believed.

The statement is clear: the Holy Spirit cannot and does not dwell in a person who is dominated by the flesh. In a person who has not yet believed, the flesh reigns and there is no other force that has the authority to overthrow its influence and power. When a person believes the gospel, God sends His Holy Spirit as a far more powerful force to depose the authority of the flesh and to provide continuing power for victory over the indwelling sinful nature.

We can say with biblical authority that we "are not in the flesh." But conflict with the "old man" still exists every day of our life. Galatians 5:17 reminds us that "the flesh lusts against the Spirit and the Spirit against the flesh." Romans 6 challenges us to reckon the flesh to be dead in our lives day by day. The repetition of this message serves to impress on our mind the reason

Romans 6 challenges us to reckon the flesh to be dead in our lives day by day.

that we can and should have victory over the influence of the flesh. The additional fact needs to be stated affirmatively: we are "in the Spirit." There is reason, moment by moment, for restating this fact so that this truth shapes our thinking, and our thinking shapes our behavior. We need not let the flesh reign in our bodies.

‮ঞ‬ ———————————— ‮ઠ‬

Father, thank you for placing me in the Spirit and the Spirit in me. This fact gives me the basis to hope for daily victory over the flesh. I fill my mind with these truths.

SEPTEMBER

21

God's Purpose for Our Salvation

But we are bound to give thanks to God always for you, brethren beloved by the Lord, because God from the beginning chose you for salvation through sanctification by the Spirit and belief in the truth.
2 Thessalonians 2:13

In Romans 11:34, Paul exclaimed, "Who has known the mind of the Lord" refering to the grandeur of God's plan for bringing us into His family. We must confess that we do not understand all the ramifications extolled in this verse, for the sovereign involvement of God in our salvation predates time and all the activities that brought man's need for salvation. Because of the divine administration of this strategy for mankind, students of the Bible have argued its meaning for generations.

Paul's thanksgiving is that the program for the redemption of mankind works. The people of the Thessalonian church were saved and were being sanctified. That condition is in total correlation with the love of God for them. Yet, how did it all begin? This is a reasonable question emanating from every thankful heart.

A primary ingredient in this scheme was God's choice of these people to belong in His salvation. This is one of the few references of God electing for Himself those who would display His grace and glory, and the only time that the purpose of election is stated as being salvation. One time is enough! However, in the other times, the goal of God's choice is a blameless and holy life. If we did not have this balance, it would be easy to conclude that the only motive of God in choosing them was to go to heaven, and it would not make much difference how they lived.

> *Why did God save us? To conform us to the likeness of Christ.*

On the contrary, it is clear from this verse that the "sanctification of the Spirit and belief of the truth" are the underlying designs in God's salvation. Why did God save us? The answer is to conform us to the likeness of Christ. That is a lifetime exercise. God's choice did not save the Thessalonians. They "turned to God from idols" as part of the activity of believing the gospel and accepting salvation found in Christ alone. Our part is the response of a heart that believes the truth about ourselves (we are sinners!) and believes the truth about God (He sent His Son for our salvation). God's activity predates all of this in His choice made before the beginning of time. I do not argue! I adore!

ॐ ———————————— ☙

Father, thank-you for choosing me. I do not deserve that choice and have not lived up to Your desires in my life. I surrender to Your will.

Blessings Unseen

Whom having not seen you love. Though now you do not see Him,
yet believing, you rejoice with joy inexpressible and full of glory,
receiving the end of your faith—the salvation of your souls.

1 Peter 1:8-9

"The salvation of your souls" must be an all-inclusive description of everything that God promises to all who believe. Our mind can only gather the components one at a time from many biblical texts to give a full expression of our salvation. It is a delight to absorb the meaning of forgiveness from one text, adoption from another, sonship from a few more, citizenship from Philippians, security from Romans—and many other great truths.

This letter from Peter was written to encourage believers who were enduring persecution and suffering because of their faith. Having been driven out of their homeland to present-day Turkey, they had very little around them to bolster their faith. In Jerusalem, they could see the place of the cross and the mountain where He ascended to glory. They could see the empty temple and the empty tomb. They could see the priests carrying out empty rituals, while they enjoyed fellowship with the vibrant church. They could hear the apostolic preaching and pray for brothers and sisters who were being persecuted for their new-found faith.

In place of all that they left in Judea, God gave them an enlightened heart to love the One whom they could not see. God had torn away the fabric of false comforts. Their hearts now rested in loving the One whom they could not see with the human eye. They believed, with active faith, the facts of the gospel and rejoiced in God's inexpressible gifts.

The first chapter of Peter's letter helps these saints turn away from their problems and focus on the Father and His Son, Jesus Christ. They would know true joy if they gazed on the life that they possess in Christ, the resurrection that awaited them, the inheritance stored for them, and their security held by the power of God. These four blessings are salient features of our salvation: new life, new hope, new wealth, and new security. Your joy will be inexpressible, as well, if you focus on these realities of your salvation, believing that the Word of God is the true source of joy. Faith in an unseen Savior is where we begin. That is followed by the present spiritual benefits of belonging to the family of God. The future is guaranteed, as our faith is squarely placed in the promises of God for His children. This lifestyle is full of glory to God.

∞ ——————————— ∞

Father, thank you for helping me to focus on the realities of my salvation. I confess that I am prone to look at my circumstances and problems.

Self Examination

*For it is God who works in you both to will
and to do for His good pleasure.*

Philippians 2:13

It is not unusual for many Christians to ask and plead with God to work. We each have our own concept of the activity that we are sure God ought to do in our lives or in others. We decide what the work should look like, how progress should be measured, and what the end result ought to be. Church leaders and parishioners all come to their own conclusions of the work that God ought to do in and for His church. What a mess!

One of the most common aspects of our intercession is laying out what God ought to change in the lives of those around us. A mother will plead for God to work in the life of her teenager. A wife earnestly prays that the Lord would change her husband. A pastor will pray for a dramatic change in some hardened sinner in his church. But God is not primarily in the business of changing other people—His fundamental work is in changing me.

Today's Scripture follows the words "work out our own salvation with fear and trembling." This is not a guide on how to obtain salvation, but instruction about how to employ the riches of our salvation in our lives. Our work must be in harmony with the will of God and with the Spirit of God, conforming me to the Lord Jesus Christ.

God is not primarily in the business of changing other people. His fundamental work is changing me.

God is not waiting for us to ask Him to start work. He is not a helper with a plan, just sitting around until we ask what His plan is. He is already at work in us.

Again, it is important to realize that He is working in me, not in others. He is not changing others because we decide that it is more reasonable to change others instead of us. This does not mean that God does not work in others. Too often, we are convinced that we are all right and everyone else needs to be changed. We should all carefully examine ourselves and see how we ought to work out our salvation in our own lives. We pride ourselves as building inspectors of other people's work, but God has a plan for *my* life. He is doing in me what pleases Him. Though difficult, we must understand that what pleases Him does not always please us.

ɞ ———————————— ꙮ

Father, thank you for working in me. I offer You my life to work in me the design that You conceive is most like Your Son, Jesus Christ.

Separation, Not Annihilation

And this is the promise that He has promised us—eternal life.

1 John 2:25

God has built into every human being a desire for life. Few people resign themselves to death when there is a fighting chance that they can continue to live. Had it not been for sin, that desire would not be so overwhelming, for God built eternal life into Adam when he was created. The life of God was breathed into that lifeless form, and he became a living soul. He had the life of God!

A characteristic of eternal life is the ability to exist without degeneration or death. Age is evident in scars, sags, and disease, while eternal life is an attribute of God Himself, a life that has no ending. It is eternal.

The quality of eternal life is largely related to the fellowship that Adam enjoyed with his Creator. Life is the absence of death, yet death is often misrepresented by the suggestion that a dead man cannot believe. A spiritually dead person does still exist as a man or woman on earth who, though dead in trespasses and sins, still has the capacity for believing and choosing.

When sin came into the world, Adam died, and this "death spread to all men," as Romans 5:12 describes. Adam was then devoid of the life of God and existed in death, but he continued to function as a person capable of faith and obedience toward God.

To be separated from God is to exist without fellowship with the Creator. Man cannot claim the life of God and be separated from God. The presence of God in our being is in the person of Christ who is "our Life." To receive Christ as Savior is to receive all the riches of divine grace and to receive Him who is eternal life and the source of all grace.

> *The promise of eternal life is a promise immediately fulfilled at conversion.*

The promise of eternal life is a promise immediately fulfilled at conversion. The stark distinction is between those who will perish and those who will not perish. To perish does not mean to cease to exist, but to exist outside the presence of God in what is called eternal death. Each person has a choice to make. To believe in Jesus Christ is to receive eternal life. To remain in unbelief is to remain in spiritual death, separated from God for all eternity.

                        ℘ ———————— ♋

Father, thank you for fulfilling Your promise by giving Christ to live in me. Though I have no physical proof of His residence in me, I claim His life by faith, as I do all the other riches of Your divine grace.

25

Outside the Church's Door

*Behold, I stand at the door and knock. If anyone
hears My voice and opens the door, I will come in
to him and dine with him, and he with Me.*

Revelation 3:20

Although this familiar verse is often misinterpreted, the application of its truths is seldom contrary to the rest of Scripture. Many children have been told that Jesus is at their heart's door and have been urged to invite Him in.

Yet the context is of the Lord speaking to the church, not to wicked and unbelieving sinners. Christ is outside His church and waits for the door to be opened. His promise is that He will come in. We might ask, "Why is the Head of the church outside?" It has happened many times in our declining spiritual society. Often a spiritual man has founded a small gathering of like-minded believers to study and search the Scriptures. The devoted family grows under his leadership of compassion and dedication to the Word. But, after a season, the church drifts from the truth and practices of the Scriptures, and the old pastor is set aside for new ideas, new programs, and new leadership. They reject him and the doctrines that he so clearly taught from the Scriptures. With sadness, he stands outside the direction, administration, and carnal activities of the assembly that he poured his heart into for so long.

The text could be loosely applied to the unbelieving person who lives inside an empty and fruitless house. "Open the door of your life and let the Savior in." No one will dispute that the Lord Jesus will quickly enter any life opened to Him. But that simple and incomplete picture must be supplemented with the understanding that Christ died for sin, and the need for repentance and confession is crucial to the risen Christ entering.

Our promise is that the Lord Jesus, who has been set outside the fellowship of His own church, will enter for the specific purpose of fellowship. A meal in most cultures is the symbol of complete acceptance. To break bread and share the cup is the most holy exercise of the church in fellowship with their Lord and each other. No other activity can be substituted for that sacred feast called the Lord's Supper. This intimate remembrance has been relegated to an occasional ritual, with the Lord outside of its celebration, as saved and lost alike take the holy emblems. This is the Lord's Supper without the fellowship of the Lord. Our prayer must be that He will come in and direct and enjoy the fellowship of the church, and thereby restore His position of headship.

 ₭ —————————————— ℳ

*Father, thank you for your patience and longsuffering with the church. I
commit my energies to restoring your leadership to our fellowship.*

The New Set of Clothes

*And that you put on the new man which was created
according to God, in true righteousness and true holiness.*

Ephesians 4:24

We put on clothes every day, thinking little about it. We select something to wear, push in our arms and legs, and pop our head out the top. The new man is seen in this passage as a suit of new clothes that is waiting for occupation.

Another Scripture reminds us that we also have an old man that must be put off. The common disposal of used or dirty clothes is also a habitual practice. We are glad to put off the old and put on new.

What is different between clothes and "the man" is the personality that makes it distinct from a piece of cloth, sewn in a certain pattern to fit a person. Clothes do not come asking to be filled. A suit is not asked if it wants to be inhabited.

When we trust Christ as our Savior, we become new creatures and are given a new opportunity to be controlled and directed by a new person. Confusion results when people suggest that the new man and the old man produce a split personality. The Bible helps us realize the conscious choice of who will control our actions and attitudes each day.

Obviously, we do not need a new man each day that we live. We were given the new man at conversion, whereas we have had the old man since birth. The conflict is presented by personifying the old and the new, using the concept of clothing. There is no argument in the closet over which suit or dress we will put on today. That is a choice that we make, independent of any thought from the clothes.

But the influence over what we will wear spiritually is bound up in our own personality and the person of Christ in us by the Holy Spirit. There is conflict, as Paul describes in Galatians 5. Every day, the old man wants to be worn, to be displayed, or to be in charge. Every day, the new man seeks the place of control and authority over my behavior.

What is important is that the new man is available and waiting for employment in the war of control. I do not pray for a new man or seek a renewed man. He was given to me when I trusted Christ. The new man is available, just as old or new clothes are. I must decide daily who will clothe my behavior, color my attitudes, constrict my choices, and call people to Christ.

                          ꙮ ——————————————— ☞

Father, thank you for the new man available to me. I choose to put off the old behavior and live today in the power of Christ.

Nearness and Access

*Therefore, brethren, having boldness to enter the Holiest
by the blood of Jesus, by a new and living way which He
consecrated for us, through the veil, that is, His flesh.*

Hebrews 10:19-20

Nearness and access are the doors opened by the blood of Jesus. In the society of Israel under the law, there was neither nearness nor access into the immediate presence of God. Every day, the blood of animals was spilled to remind the Israelites that they could not approach the personal presence of God. The heavy veil, hanging between the holy place and most holy place, blocked man's access into the dwelling place of Jehovah.

Yet God wanted to restore those two vital aspects of His relationship with man, whom He had created. Adam lost both of these special blessings because of His sin. He was driven from the garden and needed to offer a sacrifice of blood to atone for his sin. As God continued to reveal His desire for intimate fellowship, He instituted the sacrifices and ordinances of the law so that His people, the Israelites, could come closer than any other nation of the world. Still, God was not satisfied with the distance and division that separated Him from His people.

The coming of Christ as the perfect sacrifice for the sin of the world laid the groundwork for full and unfettered access into the presence of God. By His life, Jesus proved His qualifications as the only adequate substitute for the sin of mankind. The death and blood of Christ satisfied God's judgment against our sin, and opened the way for all who believe to have full and free access into His presence. The resurrection of Christ broke down the barrier that separated man from God. Christ became the living way into the Holiest. No wonder He could say, "I am the way." Because of our Savior, we can enter "in perfect peace with God."

The price of access into God's presence was very high. The specific act of His body being broken in death was figured in the veil of the temple being torn by God from top to bottom, allowing all to go in and God to come out. The glorious revelation of access was physically demonstrated to the nation of Israel as the veil lay torn and open, and the Lord Jesus' body hung on the cross for all to see. Instead of the fear that priests endured as they entered with the blood of animals, we enter boldly because the blood of Christ has been shed.

Father, thank you for opening the door, allowing me to enter with boldness into Your presence. I claim the nearness and access that You provide as I commune and fellowship in Your presence.

Two Judgments

*And behold, I am coming quickly, and My reward is with
Me, to give to every one according to his work.*

Revelation 22:12

The coming of the Lord in Revelation 22 is one of the concluding comforts for the church. It is also a solemn warning of punishment for the world. Believers in all ages of the church have found mixed consolation in the words of today's Scripture. Some people argue that, because Christ said that He was coming quickly and we have waited 2,000 years, He is not coming back. Yet, as conditions get worse, the church eagerly awaits the coming of Christ to take them out of a hopeless world. Many godly, spiritual Bible teachers have repeated each other by saying, "It can't get worse before the Lord comes again." Others, with equally fervent devotion to the Lord, have declared with confidence, "I will not see death because Christ will come in my lifetime."

"Quickly" does not mean "very soon." As the ages have rolled on for millennia, the sky has not been split by the Judge's appearance. The best understanding of "quickly" is that the judgment will be swift and severe, and there will be no time for any to consider the solemnity of their appearance before the "Judge of all the earth."

What is comforting to the church and threatening to unbelievers is the rule by which all will be judged "according to his work." The absolute justice of this rule has challenged all to "work, for the night is coming, when man's work is done." That night will be lighted by the unapproachable brilliance of the Lord on His throne. None escape the judging eye or His administration of justice.

But we must conclude that there are two very different judgments meant to separate the righteous from the unrighteous when they stand before the Judge. For the believer, there is the judgment seat of Christ where no sin will be reviewed. We will be judged according to our works, which will be tried by fire in that day. That appointment is for every one who has the life of Christ in him. A separate bench of justice will be set at the end of time where all the wicked will be judged according to their work. The Great White Throne will be the gathering of all unbelievers, and is a prelude to being cast into hell to serve their eternal punishment based on their work. There will be no excuse from man and no grace from Christ at this judgment. The rewards for the saved will be as sure as for the lost. The word "reward" may not seem to fit the severe punishment on the wicked, yet it will be swift and severe.

ೞ ───────────── ೞ

Father, I await Christ's righteous review of my life. Thank you for sending Him in Your own time. I am challenged to work faithfully until He returns.

An Undivided Body

So we, being many, are one body in Christ, and
individually members of one another.

Romans 12:5

One of the prominent victories of the enemy of Christ is to divide the church outwardly. After the terrorist attacks in New York on September 11, 2001, rescue workers lined up hundreds of body parts waiting to be united with other members of the same body. The job was horrific, and the task was never completed. Sometimes only one "part" could be found, and it could not be identified as belonging to another "part" with the same DNA.

The body of Christ is outwardly separated by doctrines, practices, rituals, laws, ordinances, and a host of far less important distinctions. Yet, in spite of the "separation," they all share the same life. The birth of a member of the body of Christ is like the addition of a cell in our human bodies. A cell is added spontaneously as our body grows. That act is part of the miracle of birth and growth. The multiplication of cells is reminiscent of the birth and early growth of the church in Acts. All who believed the gospel were added daily by the baptism of the Holy Spirit. The one body manifested unity in diversity as congregations in various cities came together for worship, fellowship, and evangelism.

But it was not long before the disease began that is full blown today. It can be seen in Paul's complaint to the Corinthian church: "I am of Paul," or "I am of Apollos," or "I am of Cephas," or "I am of Christ." Paul asks a question: "Is Christ divided?" Of course He isn't, but sometimes it looks as though He is.

The moment that I trust Christ as Savior, the Holy Spirit unites me to Christ in His body. He also inseparably binds me, individually and indivisibly, to every other believer in His Church. Because of that act, we share the same life, hope, love, Father, forgiveness, peace, future, and all the other blessings made personal to me by the indwelling Christ.

How many are we? The Lord only knows. Jenny and I have had the great joy of visiting believers in more than 75 countries. Each believer is joined to Christ and to us by the Spirit in one body. But the reality is that the body is fighting and devouring each other so viciously that the world turns its back on most of what we say. We say that we are one, but this is betrayed by what we say about each other. Our words and actions often contradict the powerful statement: "We being many are one body in Christ."

— ❧ ———————————————— ☙ —

Father, thank you for joining me to Your Son in such a way that I can never
be separated from Him, or You, or all other believers in Christ.

He Has Triumphed!

*Having disarmed principalities and powers, He made a
public spectacle of them, triumphing over them in it.*

Colossians 2:15

The resurrection of Christ is the greatest spectacle in the history of the world. This presupposes many other events in the record of man, which include the virgin birth of Jesus and His substitutionary death on the cross. No event demonstrates the victory of Christ over the enemies of God as does Jesus "taking His life again" after death!

We are reminded that "through death He destroyed him that had the power of death, that is, the devil." Through resurrection, He showed His superiority over the defeated enemy. In addition to His victory over the devil, Christ also claimed victory over his army with its regimental commanders, called "principalities and powers." The chain of command given here shows the extent of the organization and administration of the enemies of Christ. Yet each one was disarmed and the weapons of war were forcibly torn from their grasp.

To further demonstrate His full and final victory, the Lord ascended into glory. The ascension of Christ is as dramatic as His resurrection, when we consider the realm from which He came and the one to which He went. The devil's sphere of activity is described in one of his names: "the prince of the power of the air." That title helps us to realize the dimensions of Christ's accomplishment when, in His ascension, He traveled right through the realm of the devil's activity. Christ's death and resurrection allowed Him to put His foot on the throne of the devil, as He ruthlessly triumphed over him in His movement from earth to glory.

Christ traveled unhindered and unchallenged from the realm of death to the realm of life, where death can never go. The picture is used by Paul in Ephesians of a victorious returning army, their captives chained to the chariots. Not one could raise a tongue against the victorious general.

The victory of Christ is final. In spite of the activity and seemingly powerful influence of the devil today, the Scriptures declare that he is defeated. Christ's enemies are decimated, fearfully awaiting the day when the divine sentence will be carried out. The devil knows that he is defeated, yet he is still on the prowl. As believers, we should celebrate Christ's victory, instead of crouching cowardly as though the war has not been won. He has triumphed fully and forever.

ഇൗ ———————————— ങ

*Father, thank you for the fullness of Christ's victory. I celebrate His victory
by walking in the power of a living Savior who is seated in glory.*

October

A Closet Of Clothes For The New Believer

". . . let us go on to perfection . . ."
Hebrews 6:1

Let the beauty of Jesus be seen in me,
All His wonderful passion and purity:
Oh, Thou Spirit divine,
All my nature refine
Till the beauty of Jesus is seen in me.
Albert Orsborn

October

Canaan: the Land of Opportunity

Israel's inheritance of the land of Canaan occupies five books of the Old Testament. It must have been of great importance to God to spend so much recorded history on His people's migration to, and occupation of, this land. Some of the details seem laborious and unimportant to us, living almost 4,000 years later.

God's choice to include so many particulars may be because their migration is such a dramatic parallel of our pilgrimage and inheritance in Christ. As Israel was challenged to possess the land, we are reminded that all spiritual blessings are found in Christ. God promised the land to Abraham, and He repeated that promise to Moses and Joshua by saying, "Every place on which the sole of your foot treads shall be yours" (Deuteronomy 11:24; also see Joshua 1:3).

The picture of a foot making systematic progress on the land is a remarkable parallel of our searching and finding truths regarding the person and work of Christ and then placing our spiritual "foot" on that truth and claiming it as ours. Much of the New Testament is a blueprint or map of the blessings found in Christ. We are challenged to go through the length and breadth of this revelation of Christ and claim what has been made available to us by His death and resurrection.

The foundation of this gift to Israel is that God called them His children. God has done the same for us as believers.

Our sonship is based on possessing the life of God through Christ. The guarantee of the inheritance rests on our sonship. An inheritance cannot be bought, earned, or prayed for. It is a free gift. Israel was to possess what had been freely given to them by God. It was theirs as a permanent, personal possession. One day God will finally fulfill that gift, and Israel will possess all the borders of that land given to Abraham, Moses, and Joshua.

For the believer, our inheritance is spiritual and is to be claimed based upon sonship as well. Sonship itself, like the inheritance, is a gift. It must be possessed by faith in the revealed inventory of God.

Israel was poised on the edge of their inheritance when they came to Kadesh Barnea, only a couple of years after leaving Egypt. God offered them the opportunity of entering into their land at that time. But Israel refused to believe God, Joshua, and Caleb. Because of their unbelief, they plunged back into the desert for thirty-eight years of wandering, without progress or possession.

Each believer is offered the opportunity of possessing his blessings in Christ. We can enter into the enjoyment of all that is found in Christ or reject it in unbelief and continue an unfulfilled life of wandering in the wilderness. God offers each of us many opportunities for such enjoyment, unlike that generation of Israel, who had only one invitation to enter and enjoy their inheritance. One difference between an earthly inheritance and our inheritance in Christ is the exercise of our faith. An uncle leaves a sum of money as an inheritance. We receive a check from the estate. Little faith is involved as we go to the bank to cash the check and spend the money. I suppose we might wonder whether the check is really good, but most of us would believe if we really knew the uncle. Do we find it easier to believe an uncle than to believe God?

For the believer, the gifts are detailed in the Scriptures which must be searched, understood, and believed before we can "go to the bank" with our claim of an inheritance in Christ. One of the keys to our inheritance is a thorough knowledge of Christ and a strong faith in the Word of God. If we know Christ well, we will not doubt that He has given us such a lavish inheritance. But if we do not know God and Christ, we may wonder whether we are really possessors of such wonderful blessings. Israel lost their inheritance solely through unbelief.

If our faith is small, we may think that such great blessing can only be obtained by being good, praying earnestly, or a host of other requirements. But the inheritance is ours because of sonship, not effort. Enjoyment of the inheritance is the result of effort, just as Israel had to defeat their enemies in the land in order to possess every place they trod. There are enemies in the land that God has given us; we must defeat the world, the flesh, and the devil before we can enjoy the land of opportunity given us in Christ. So Hebrews says, "Let us therefore be diligent to enter that rest." Be diligent this month in believing the Word of God. Such faith will lead you to enjoy all that He has given to you.

Freed to Follow Christ

*There is therefore now no condemnation to those
who are in Christ Jesus, who do not walk according
to the flesh, but according to the Spirit.*

Romans 8:1

In the early chapters of Romans, God communicates His displeasure with sin and sinners. He defines the only adequate response to His offer of salvation through His Son. The universal sinfulness of man requires faith just as universally. No other offering of man is suitable. No meritorious work is acceptable. No legal requirements can be proffered. Faith alone is what God desires from man's heart.

In Romans 8, Paul describes a life lived in faith in God's Son. That faith results in God Himself removing any condemnation against us, and opens a road on which we are to walk in the power of the Holy Spirit.

It is crucial to know that the first step of faith, the one that brings salvation, is not the only step. Many Bible passages remind us that the first step is to be followed by a lifelong walk in the same reliance on our Savior. God did not save us just to remove the condemning accusations of the law and sin. He saved us to "walk in newness of life." That life is the opposite of the life that we lived under the influence of the flesh that previously ruled our behavior.

The blessing of silencing all condemnation against us is ours because we are now in Christ. The unity that we enjoy in Christ is possible because any judgment due us was borne fully by our substitute. When Christ died, we died with Him. When Christ rose, we rose to walk in a new life. When Christ ascended, we were set free from the manacles of the old life. When Christ sat down, we were seated with Him. Since there is no condemnation against Him, there is none against us!

But what about condemnation for sin committed after we believe? This, too, is set aside because of the adequacy of the work of Christ. There is no condemnation for the past, the present, and the future.

All the judgment due us for our sin and disobedience was borne by Christ. God was satisfied and demonstrated that He was pleased by raising Christ from the dead. Walking according to the Spirit is not the basis for removing the condemning words of God. Rather, it is the result of being set free from such culpability. Freed from punishment, we can live in the power of the indwelling Spirit. He gives me the power to set aside the lifestyle that characterized my life before I trusted Christ.

⁞ ———————————— ⁝

*Father, thank you for removing any condemning charges and setting me free
from bondage to the flesh to live by Christ in the Spirit.*

Bloom, Blossom, and Bear Fruit

That you may walk worthy of the Lord, fully pleasing Him, being fruitful in every good work and increasing in the knowledge of God.
Colossians 1:10

It's a special delight to spend time in a garden that has been artistically designed, full of well-chosen plants, and cared for regularly. It's a striking fact that, in the midst of all of the gardener's work, the plants cooperate with God in the production of flower, fragrance, and fruit. The gardener can perform all his usual responsibilities, but he is dependent on the inbred capacities of each plant to contribute their part to the mosaic that makes them so beautiful and productive. How attractive . . . how inviting . . . how special!

Paul prayed that the Colossians would develop the graces, or fruitfulness, of Christ in the midst of their daily activities. The illustration of the plant helps us recognize that the Lord has made available to us the ingredients necessary to produce the likeness of Christ in our lives. There was no thought that, in answer to this prayer, God would give the Colossian "plants" special food, more intense light, added minerals, or a greater insulation from pests. All that was necessary for them to fulfill His purpose was available to them, and it is to us too. We possess in Christ "all things richly."

The plant does not need to ask for a special diet because the gardener makes sure that it has all the necessary food. Our Gardener has provided all the necessary care for full production of fruit. It is our responsibility to draw on the resources that He supplies so that our fruitfulness will fulfill His purpose and bring special pleasure and glory to the Gardener.

> *The Lord has made available to us the ingredients necessary to produce the likeness of Christ in our lives.*

Being fruitful is the result of every believer drawing on the nutrients of the "soil" and accepting the process that turns that food into life, made evident by fruit. Our health is manifested by fruit which declares that we are "rooted in Christ." We do have a choice where we are rooted and whether we appropriate the food necessary for producing fruit that will last. The Savior has given us all things necessary for a full flower, fragrant aroma, and gracious fruit. A well-designed, colorfully arranged, fruitfully productive garden brings praise to the One who works it so industriously. We are His garden to show forth His excellent skills and the vibrant life of His Son.

⁓ ———————————— ⳩

Father, thank you for giving me all the ingredients for a useful, productive life in Your garden. I find all my needs met in Christ.

Creations of Christ's Sacrifice

*Having abolished in His flesh the enmity, that is, the law of
commandments contained in ordinances, so as to create in
Himself one new man from the two, thus making peace.*

Ephesians 2:15

The indescribable blessings made possible by the cross will occupy our eternal worship of Him who died and rose again. The Holy Spirit gives a glimpse of some of these blessings in Ephesians 2:15. Three special accomplishments are reiterated for our understanding, enjoyment, and appropriation.

First, Christ abolished the enmity. This is not the only time that God reminds us that the law actively opposed the development of righteousness in man. The law was just and good, but it could not meet the righteousness demanded by a holy God. The law was abolished by the work of Jesus Christ on the cross. This does not mean that it ceases to exist, as we still see it reflected in almost every legal system in civilized society today. But it is not acceptable for righteousness in the program of God, who demands perfect righteousness. By His life He fulfilled the law. By His death He abolished the law.

Christ's righteous life silenced the law's demand for a person who could demonstrate absolute obedience. His obedience qualified Him to represent us, in that His righteousness fulfilled the law, setting it aside as a means of attaining acceptability with God. Christ's death and resurrection cancelled the law and introduced His risen life as the only legitimate righteousness acceptable to God.

Second, by His death and resurrection, Christ created one new man. He unified two peoples, Jew and Gentile, into one. When Israel received the law, they demonstrated their tendency toward sin and disobedience. The Gentiles, who were not under the law, still knew sinfulness because of their inability to live up to any standard of righteousness that they established. All men were declared sinners; all continually fall short of the glory of God. The institution of salvation by grace through faith opened the one door through which both Jew and Gentile must pass to be declared righteous. This was established as a creative act by the living Christ, adding to Himself all who will come to God by Him.

Peace, the third blessing, is the condition that ensues from the first two. It is both personal peace for all who become part of the body of Christ, and corporate peace for that body made up of both Jews and Gentiles. We can then rightly say, "In Christ is neither Jew nor Gentile but one new man."

☙ ——————————————— ❧

Father, thank you for setting aside the law which I cannot obey in my own effort. You accept me because of Christ. Help me to never lose sight of this.

Blessed, No Matter What

But even if you should suffer for righteousness' sake, you are blessed. "And do not be afraid of their threats, nor be troubled."
1 Peter 3:14

Most of us think that being "blessed" means escaping all the problems that might come into our life. It would be hard to say to a person that the Lord had blessed him if many trials and tribulations came his way. We pray for the Lord to "bless so-and-so" as they travel, go into surgery, and so on. What we mean is for God to keep anything from happening that would be traumatic or cause loss of health, wealth, or possessions. We want life to be easy and convenient. We may not say it exactly that way to God, but the word "bless" means that to most of us.

Peter was comforting believers who were suffering "for righteousness' sake." They were in fact blessed even as they suffered. Most of us would not argue with God about this, but we might be disappointed that our prayer to "bless so-and-so" was not answered, since so many troubles overtook them. We therefore find it difficult to agree with Peter. It's only when things work out as we had hoped and prayed that we respond by saying, "Isn't the Lord good!" The fact of the matter is: the Lord is good even if things do *not* turn out to be a source of happiness.

This is the lesson that Peter is teaching his readers, and us today. Our tendency is so ingrained in our thinking that we only say "the Lord blessed" if He answers our desires and prayers the way we want. But life for these suffering believers needed to be seen as blessed even though they were in tribulation and trials. It would be easy for these suffering saints to think that God was out of touch with their pain or had forgotten them.

Blessing has nothing to do with our current level of discomfort, pain, or loss.

No, writes Peter. Even in the midst of trials and suffering, God blesses us. Surely it should not be hard for any believer to make a long list of our blessings in Christ, whether we are suffering or all is going well. Blessing has nothing to do with our current level of discomfort, pain, or loss. Blessing rests on us because we are in Christ, and that position of blessing cannot be changed.

May we learn that fear or a troubled heart need not overcome us. The Lord knows, allows, or sends the circumstances of our life. We stand blessed, whatever they are.

ℰℛ ———————————— ℭ℥

Father, thank you for blessing me in Christ. I confess that I often value Your blessings by how easy life is for me and my friends.

Sword Drill

And take the helmet of salvation, and the sword
of the Spirit, which is the word of God.

Ephesians 6:17

An old African maid prayed after hearing her mistress reading the Bible, "Speak to me as you do to her." She knew that the white lady believed that, when she read the Bible, God talked to her, but the maid could not read and, therefore, could not "hear" Him for herself.

God has given us the sword of the Spirit as part of our armor for spiritual victory. It comes from God, is about Christ, and is made available by the Holy Spirit. We do not need to ask it to do the work that it was designed to do. The appeal to "take," in today's verse, suggests that we are the ones to act, taking the sword from the display case where we have put it, removing it from the scabbard where we have sheathed it.

> *The sword is ready, waiting, and willing to be used for spiritual combat and victory.*

Just as there are many weapons in any arsenal of combat, so the Word of God suggests to our imagination many uses: as a scalpel by the surgeon, as a knife to cut bread, a spear to throw at a distance, a pocket knife to carry, a pen knife to conceal, a sword to defend. We need to use it to practice our skills, and to apply it to the enemy as our Lord did with the words, "It is written." The Word of God can be employed in many areas of our life.

"Take" also suggests availability. The sword is ready, waiting, and willing to be used for spiritual combat and victory. As soon as we learn to listen or read, the Word can speak. The maid looked at the black marks on the page and they meant nothing to her, much like our trying to read strange writing. When she learned to read, she heard the Word of God. The Word did not change; she did.

God is waiting to work in our lives and declare victory. We must take the Word into our hands and read it, into our minds and learn it, into our emotions to be thrilled by it, into our wills to walk by it, and into our hearts to confront sin with it.

The sword is living and effective. When we take it, it springs into action, sharp and vital. It is available to act, if we are willing to use it.

ઠ ———————————— જી

Father, thank you for the Sword of the Spirit. Today I take it as part of my armor to live in victory, as it speaks to me and through me.

Forever Forgiven

If we confess our sins, He is faithful and just to forgive us our sins and to cleanse us from all unrighteousness.

1 John 1:9

Forgiveness is the primary work of God toward those who believe the gospel of the Lord Jesus Christ. To forgive means to send away, to cancel, to refuse to count anything against us, all possible because a payment has been made. Because God's justice has been satisfied, He is free to forgive sin and bestow all the blessings of His salvation. The redemptive act of God is to pay the penalty for sin and then to forgive all trespasses when we receive Jesus Christ as our Savior.

To know that we are forgiven removes the anxiety and burden of guilt, which rests on all who come into the world by Adam. This is an instantaneous act of God that puts our sin as far as the east is from the west. It means that God separates us from our sin forever. All our past, present, and future sins are sent to "the sea of God's forgetfulness," never to be recalled again.

> *My confession at the point of conversion cleanses me from all sin.*

But some will say, "If I do not confess, will God still forgive?" Many grow restless and anxious, thinking that if they forget to confess their sin, God will not forgive them. They believe that, if God holds any sin against them, they will be lost. With that idea, confession of sin becomes so important at the end of the day or the end of life. Their fear is: "If I don't confess, I will not be forgiven, and I will be lost." Is that what this verse teaches? *No!*

This chapter discusses the restoration of fellowship between God and His people. My confession at the point of conversion cleanses me from all sin. After that transaction by God, no sin will be charged against me. God requires no further punishment. But sin will break fellowship between my Father and me. That break in *fellowship* does not destroy my *relationship* with my Father. 1 John 1:9 reminds us of the intimate connection between the Father and His children. The prodigal son went his own way in sin and rejection of his father's fellowship, but no matter what he did he was still a son of his father. The father was not pleased with his son's behavior, but he still offered restoration without any punishment. Our Father points to the sacrifice of His Son as adequate for the punishment of all our sin. What forgiveness is mine!

— ❧ ———————————————— ❧ —

Father, thank you for forgiving all my sin. I rest in that pronouncement, and I enjoy rest and confidence because Your Word says that this is my personal possession. I am forgiven. I celebrate that forgiveness.

Built to Last

*For we know that if our earthly house, this tent, is
destroyed, we have a building from God, a house
not made with hands, eternal in the heavens.*

2 Corinthians 5:1

We are prone to live for the present and the visible more than for the eternal and the unseen. Our problem is that we do not think about what the Lord is preparing for us. Let's take a moment to think about what our future, immortal bodies will be like.

Today's Scripture describes our new body as a building. It will be glorious in splendor, personal in identity, and matching our Lord's body because "we shall be like Him." Abraham looked for a city which had foundations, and we, too, will be willing to put off the old tent and put on the new which has foundations. Even the repair and restoration of the old seems fruitless, knowing that a new one is waiting.

Our suffering in this old house is not worthy to be compared to the glorious enjoyment in the one awaiting us. We cannot conceive of the beauty and splendor of the house made possible by His resurrection. What a move from the old one, described in Ecclesiastes 12, to the new one of 1 Corinthians 15. Moving day is the climax of a life of sorrow and suffering. Although worms will eat our flesh, the new one will have no enemy. Time destroys the old, but the new is eternal. The preparation is elaborate, begun before the foundation of the world, carried on by the death of Christ, guaranteed by His resurrection, confirmed by His ascension, and consummated by His coming again. With that accomplished, the natural will put on the spiritual, the weak the powerful, the mortal the immortal, and the dishonorable the honorable.

> *As sure as death is, so sure is the union of our soul and spirit with our new body.*

As sure as death is, so sure is the union of our soul and spirit with our new body. Not all the details have been provided. As John says, "It has not yet been revealed what we shall be." Still, we trust His creative power for the new body more than we marvel at the capacities of the old. What glory that will be!

The destruction of our earthly "house" is certain unless the Lord returns to take us home before we die. But our new building is also sure for all who have received the Lord Jesus Christ as Savior. His resurrection is our guarantee.

₱ ———————————— ℣

Father, thank you for this old body which is decaying so rapidly. Thank you, too, for the new one waiting for me. I confess to wanting to stay in the old longer rather than anticipating the new one.

Christ's On-Going Work

*For Christ has not entered the holy places made with
hands, which are copies of the true, but into heaven
itself, now to appear in the presence of God for us.*

Hebrews 9:24

C hrist sits as the great High Priest of His people who are still on earth. The fact that He is seated reminds us that His work of sacrifice is done. He has finished the work that His Father gave Him to do. He offered one sacrifice for all sin—yet His work is still not done in another aspect of service to His people. What is important for us as His redeemed saints is His present activity on our behalf. Twice in the New Testament we are reminded that He, in His resurrection life, is interceding for us. How encouraging to know that my Savior is praying to the Father for me.

If any one of us sins, Christ acts in our defense, since He bore that sin in His own body on the tree. He is an Advocate with His Father on our behalf. This does not give us the liberty to engage in a loose and lawless life. God's goal for us is holiness, as He is holy. But if we fall, Christ is there for us.

The sacrifice of Christ on the cross was the purchase price required to declare all believers as His possession. Because I am His, He has a special interest in me. Because He has taken up residence in me by the Holy Spirit, I have a special importance to Him. Because He bought me, He has a unique obligation to actively engage in my maintenance. He does all that on my behalf.

He was received by the Father and sat down because His work was adequate and complete, and the Father was satisfied. As I come to a greater understanding of the effectiveness of this work, I am satisfied as well. He is there now for me. He is fully occupied with the care, provision, and maintenance of His people. Paul reminds us in Romans 8, "If God be for us, who can be against us?" Faith in this amazing summary brings enjoyment and satisfaction in the fullness and finality of the work of God in Christ.

> *How encouraging to know that my Savior is praying to the Father for me.*

ᴇᴏ ─────────── ᴄᴢ

Father, thank you for receiving Christ into heaven and seating Him at Your own right hand. I am comforted by the fact that He is there on my behalf in the same way that He came to earth for me.

Suffering for the Name

If you are reproached for the name of Christ, blessed are you,
for the Spirit of glory and of God rests upon you. On their
part He is blasphemed, but on your part He is glorified.

1 Peter 4:14

The believers to whom Peter was writing were suffering for their faith. They were being persecuted because they accepted the derogatory name of "Christian." Many of them lost most of their possessions and had been driven from their homes to a land now called Turkey. Many times over, the New Testament reminds us that if we live out the behavior of Christ we will face suffering, trials, persecution, and reproach. The word *reproach* means to be spoken against, defamed, railed at, chided, taunted, and reviled. It does not imply acts of violence, so much as words that bite and hurt. Most of us experience at least a few of these hurtful words.

What is amazing is Peter's assessment of the situation. He says that we are blessed if we are the recipients of harsh words from those who hate Christ. The word "blessed" here is often translated "happy." Happy and taunted; blessed and blasted; rejoicing and railed against—these were occasions for the ministry of "the Spirit of glory and of God."

Peter no doubt remembered the words of the Lord Jesus in the upper room: "If the world hates you, you know that it hated me." Now, some 30 years later, Peter had a more spiritual perspective on the conditions that faced these believers. They had taken the name of Christ and were being persecuted for their faith. They might easily have been asking themselves whether the Lord was aware of the reproach that they were suffering. Peter comforted them by reminding them that the Lord not only knew but also had predicted that kind of treatment for all who lived like Him in the world.

God chose suffering as a showcase for His glory and the ministry of His Spirit.

God chose suffering as a showcase for His glory and the ministry of His Spirit. This does not mean that those who are not called to suffer like these believers do not have the Spirit of glory and of God. Rather, their suffering was a backdrop for the excellent display of God's glory. Just as a rainbow against a very dark cloud displays its colors to a better advantage, so the reproaches of Christ falling on these believers gave a sharper picture of the Spirit of glory.

Father, thank you for the example of these believers who displayed Your glory. I pray for believers in Turkey who suffer for Christ today.

Forever His Child

*Not with the blood of goats and calves, but with His
own blood He entered the Most Holy Place once
for all, having obtained eternal redemption.*

Hebrews 9:12

Redemption is one of the "big three" words that God uses to help us understand our salvation (propitiation and reconciliation being the other two). To *redeem* simply means "to buy back and set free." The word is used often to give a full perspective of such a grand provision for the human race.

The first picture of redemption that the divine artist draws for us is found in the book of Exodus. The children of Israel were in bondage to Pharaoh and had no ability or power to free themselves. God saw their state and had a plan to redeem them. At the center of His plan was the lamb that each family would select and kill, applying the blood to the doorposts of their houses. The family would then roast the lamb and feast on it in their houses, while the angel of death passed through the land. All who placed the blood on the doorposts were "redeemed by the blood of the lamb." This event began the amazing migration of the Israelites from Egypt to Canaan.

> *We belong to Christ because He bought us by His own blood.*

A second picture is played out in the story of Ruth and Boaz. Ruth became heir to a piece of property that she was unable to claim because of poverty. It needed to be redeemed or purchased, and Boaz qualified as a kinsman redeemer to buy it. Three requirements had to be met for the transaction to be accomplished. The proposed redeemer had to be close of kin; he had to be willing to make the transaction, accepting the responsibilities of the possession; and he had to be capable of paying the redemption price. Boaz, a worthy relative, redeemed the piece of property and also took responsibility for Ruth, who became his wife.

Christ qualified as our Kinsman-Redeemer because He was near of kin, having taken on the form of man when He came to earth. He was willing to give all that He had in order to set us free from our bondage to sin, self, the world, and our flesh. He gave His life to redeem us and rose from the dead to prove that He had "obtained" His purchased possession. Israel belongs to God, and Ruth belonged to Boaz because of redemptive acts. We belong to Christ because He bought us by His own blood. Our purchase was not only very costly, but it will also last for eternity. We are forever redeemed.

ဆ ─────────────── ℭ

Father, thank you for redeeming me from all iniquity and reserving me for eternal blessing as Your purchased possession.

Blessings All Mine

To me, who am less than the least of all the saints,
this grace was given, that I should preach among
the Gentiles the unsearchable riches of Christ.

Ephesians 3:8

Paul's view of himself was more denigrating than exalting. He realized that he himself was not of much use or value, except that the Lord had saved him and called him to important service. He looked back on his life before he knew Christ and realized that his determination to destroy all who followed "the Way" had made him less than likely to receive God's grace. Yet Paul not only received it but also became the one who understood and appreciated it more than all others. Recognizing its value, he was obedient to the heavenly vision and began to preach about the riches that he had discovered in Christ.

Grace is one of the key words that help us understand the vast array of God's provision for man's salvation. Understood as "divine enablement" in this context, Paul was given abundant grace, especially in that he received and employed a spiritual gift in the preaching of the good news. His message was "the unsearchable riches of Christ." Can there be a more picturesque description of the extraordinary blessings that God gives to all who come to Christ by faith? Paul met Jesus in the prime of his life and became an accountant of the vast treasures of Christ. His discovery of the spiritual wealth that God gives in Christ set him on a course to proclaim the availability of the exhaustless spiritual provision for all believers.

How many of us would abandon the personal comforts of such wealth and journey across the globe, proclaiming the unspeakable riches found in Christ? Unlike Paul, many who discover this wealth never sense the urgency of proclaiming to the poverty-stricken world this vault of indescribable wealth. Paul was called, commissioned, and challenged to make known to the nations the fact that the death of Christ has opened the flood gates, unlocked the storehouse, released the riches, and removed the barrier to any who will come and claim the unmatched riches in Christ.

Another Scripture passage reminds us that these treasures are hidden in Christ, but this does not mean that they are locked away or barred from being taken. This book of daily meditations is a tool to help make known some of the riches that are yours in Christ. These *blessings* are all yours, and 10,000 besides. Take, claim, enjoy, employ, and exclaim to the nations that these riches are available to all who will believe.

∞ ———————————— ∞

Father, thank you for opening to me the indescribable wealth in Christ. I commit my life to knowing and appropriating these blessings.

Compassion and Mercy

*Indeed we count them blessed who endure. You have heard
of the perseverance of Job and seen the end intended by the
Lord—that the Lord is very compassionate and merciful.*

James 5:11

Compassion is the ability to understand the burdens of others, to empathize emotionally and to relieve them meaningfully. *Mercy* is withholding judgment from those that deserve it. The context here is about Job's continuing in faith and God's dealings with him. But, since no one deserves God's mercy, the main principle relevant to all mankind is that we are dealt with according to *divine* mercy. If we all got what we deserve, we would all perish.

The Lord's compassion is demonstrated by His leaving the glories of heaven to understand our burdens, to enter into them emotionally, and to relieve them by His suffering and death. The mercy of God was available to Job because God could look beyond Job's situation, see His Son slain from the foundation of the world, and act in the light of that glorious sacrifice. The substitution of Christ set God free to act in mercy to all who call on Him in truth.

The unsaved are sometimes encouraged to pray, "God be merciful to me, a sinner" (sometimes called "the sinner's prayer") as fitting words pleading for God's forgiveness and salvation. Yet, as we look back on this statement of the publican (Luke 18:13), we are reminded that he did not have the sacrifice and death of Christ on which to base His petition for forgiveness and mercy. A sacrifice had been made in the temple court and the blood carried annually into the Holy of Holies and sprinkled on the mercy seat. He was asking God to view the blood-spattered mercy seat and, therefore, to forgive his sin.

We who live long after the cross can, with everyone else since that day, proclaim that the mercy of God has been poured out on all who believe. We do not need, as the seeker is often instructed, to plead for His mercy. God cannot be more merciful than He is! The sacrifice of the cross is the greatest evidence of God's attitude toward my sin. I *claim* the mercy of God, I don't *plead* for it. In the dawn of revelation, Job could only hope for divine mercy. We, with confidence, may invite anyone we meet to run to the refuge of a compassionate God who has poured out His mercy on all flesh. The river of mercy flows, and any who come by faith to that river can draw and drink as much as they desire from His undiminished supply.

Father, thank you for pouring out such an abundance of Your mercy. I have drunk deeply from this fountain and rejoice in Your supply.

Mighty in Meekness

*Now I, Paul, myself am pleading with you by the meekness
and gentleness of Christ—who in presence am lowly
among you, but being absent am bold toward you.*

2 Corinthians 10:1

Jesus Christ perfectly displayed the attributes of God. When the world saw Jesus, they saw God in human flesh. When they heard Jesus, they heard the words of God. When they were in the company of Jesus, they were in the presence of One who perfectly displayed the meekness and gentleness of God.

Yet Jesus strongly condemned the scribes and Pharisees as fools and hypocrites. He called the leaders of the people a "brood of vipers." He made a whip and thrashed those who sold merchandise in His Father's house. He planted His footsteps in the sea and walked on the raging waves. Timid? No! Gentle? Yes! He took a little child in His arms and held him, commending any who would come to Him with child-like spirit and faith. In the garden, He sweat droplets like blood in the vigorous battle for our souls. Weak? No! Meek? Yes!

The strength of the Creator and Sustainer of the universe, and the meekness of a child, were wrapped up in one person. The force of His words stilled the storm and canceled the ravages of pain and disease. His hands steadfastly tore bread for hours to feed 5,000, yet He sat on the well of the father of the Jews in weariness. He never used His might to insulate Himself from the strain of life as man, nor did He elevate His privation as a means of seeking relief from suffering. He could have called 10,000 angels to defend Him in the garden. We tend to misconstrue meekness with weakness, gentleness with timidity. Jesus Christ was neither weak nor timid.

Christ has taken up His residence in us with the specific goal of displaying that same meekness and gentleness in and through us. Paul equates these graces of Christ with lowliness and boldness, both of which He demonstrated perfectly in beautiful combination. Lowliness and meekness display power and strength under control. A powerful man may hold a delicate egg without crushing it. Christ could take the abuse and scathing words of His enemies without a word. When He was reviled, He did not threaten in return. Because we have Christ, we also possess "the meekness and gentleness of Christ."

He is waiting for us to confess our inability to control ourselves and to allow Him to use our being as a display of His meekness and gentleness.

⁎ ———————————— ⁖

Father, I confess that I display my own distortion of Your graces. Thank you for giving Christ and all He is to me. Be my gentleness, my meekness!

Resources at the Ready

Epaphras, who is one of you, a bond servant of Christ, greets you, always laboring fervently for you in prayers, that you may stand perfect and complete in all the will of God.

Colossians 4:12

The prayer of Epaphras for the Colossian believers is a suitable guide for each of us in our intercession for others. Notice how different it is in phraseology compared to our customary prayers.

Epaphras assumed that the Colossians had the resources available to them to "stand perfect and complete," and that the will of God was available and had been revealed to them. As believers, we have difficulty accepting either of these premises. Most times, we pray that God will reveal His will and provide the resources to enable the person we pray for to be perfect or mature as a child of God. The difference is patently clear. We are waiting for God to provide so that the believer can stand mature and complete. Epaphras wanted the Colossians to appropriate what he knew they had and so stand complete.

> *The burden of maturity does not rest on God, but on us.*

Careful analysis is not often welcomed in this regard. Epaphras did not ask God to do anything; rather, he prayed fervently that *they* would do or accept or apply that which God has already provided. This expressive phrase is one of the great keys to maturity and one of the primary reasons for this book of meditations. What has God done? My simple answer is that God has provided all that He needs to in order that I "may stand mature and complete in all the will of God," to enable me to be what He wants us to be. What must I do? Appropriate all I have in Christ and employ all the resources available in Christ.

Earlier in this letter, Paul said that the Colossian believers "are complete in Him," a statement of fact that Epaphras assumed when he prayed. The burden of maturity does not rest on God, but on us. When we tell children to grow up, we are not expecting them to eat another meal or stretch their limbs. We want them to appropriate all the instruction and words that we give and employ their mind, emotions, and will to demonstrate maturity that is consistent with their age. As parents, we do not need to do anything more. Children need to do what they know and stand in the fullness, knowledge, and powers that they possess. Growth is spontaneous and dependent on appropriation.

୫୦ ——————————— ଓଃ

Father, thank you for all that You have given me in Christ. With these resources, I have what I need to be mature and filled with Your will.

Knowledge Worth Having

*Now concerning things offered to idols: We know that we all
have knowledge. Knowledge puffs up, but love edifies.*

1 Corinthians 8:1

One of the primary aspects in the transaction from death to life is the acceptance of the knowledge of the truth. Paul elsewhere reminds his readers that to come to the knowledge of the truth is to believe the gospel of the grace of God. God desires that "all men come to the knowledge of the truth," and there can be no question that this message looks back to the Lord's own words, "I am the Truth."

Paul later writes in more detail about "the gift of knowledge" given to some in the early church before the canon of Scripture was completed. That gift cannot be the subject of this statement since Paul flatly says that we all, including all the Corinthians, have knowledge. It is instructive that the Corinthian believers had knowledge even though they were living a precarious kind of Christian life in a climate of confusion about so many areas of teaching. Obviously, having knowledge is not based on holiness, maturity, prayer, behavior, or the practice of truth.

This gift is the common blessing of all believers. It was announced by Paul, the chief apostle to the ignorant, misunderstanding Corinthians. What, then, is this knowledge? We can be guided by Paul's comprehensive statement about it in Colossians 2:3: "In whom [that is, Christ] are hidden all the treasures of wisdom and knowledge." The gift of Christ is the gift of all knowledge because all knowledge is resident in Him. The *appropriation* of knowledge is waiting for those who, like miners, excavate the treasure from the mine. The work and energy to dig for what is hidden may be extensive, just like extracting gold from deep in the heart of the earth, but it is rewarding!

There is a danger, however, for any who study the Scriptures, making the effort to seek out knowledge hidden in Christ: he or she may become lifted up with pride. Paul is formulating the couplet that has been a help to so many: "To know Him is to love Him. To love Him is to serve Him." There are many, though, who profess to serve one whom they do not really know. Their service may be born out zeal and will often wane if not founded on true knowledge. This knowledge begins by accepting Christ as the Truth and progresses to maturity as each aspect of knowledge is appropriated and employed in a loving behavior that reflects and radiates true knowledge of Him. That process is indeed *humbling!*

           —————————————————————

Father, thank you for the knowledge that is found in Christ. I confess that I have not valued that knowledge as I should. I want to know Him more.

Sufficiency for Unselfish Service

Not that we are sufficient of ourselves to think of anything as being from ourselves, but our sufficiency is from God.

2 Corinthians 3:5

It would be hard for any of us to say that we have enough of anything. For instance, who in our society would say, "I have enough money"? Even the richest of men do not seem content with what they possess. Most of us look longingly at our neighbor who has something a little bigger or a little nicer that ours. We buy things that we do not need because we are infected with a disease of "I just want it." Possessions, money, power, clothes, cars, tools, land—the list is endless of things that we covet. The advertising world knows how acute our lust is to have more than we possess. With the most glamorous messages, models, and merchandise, they tempt us to succumb to the ravages of the disease of greed. Even "Christian" philosophies feed the lust of the eyes by a "name it and claim it" doctrine, so that all my "sanctified" greed can be satisfied.

This message, whether it comes from Christendom or the world, is designed to coax us to seek satisfaction in and for ourselves. Paul, as he so often does, directs our attention away from ourselves to the supply of "life resources" that come through the Lord Jesus from the Father. The Lord teaches us about our inadequacy as He calls us to service that, to us, may seem impossible. A situation that demands greater than human energy or effort forces us to cast ourselves on God for His provision. Unfortunately, we often do not learn this until we have failed repeatedly by doing it in our own strength or from our own resourcefulness. At that point, we then confess, as Paul does, that we are not "sufficient in ourselves."

The adequacy for all that we are called to do is from God.

The adequacy for all that we are called to do is from God. The need for all believers is to understand, appreciate, and appropriate the resources that are in God. An important point is stated again, as it is so often—"from God." God the Father is always the source of supply for the needs of the believer. The Lord Jesus released these blessings by His death. His resurrection and ascension made these resources available. The ministry of the Spirit is to administer and apply these blessings to us in Christ. The Spirit is given "that we might know the things that are freely given to us by God." We are challenged to know the Lord Jesus Christ and the sufficient supply of all things from God.

          ॐ ———————————— ಞ

Father, thank you for the adequacy of Your supply. I confess that I am not sufficient for what You have asked of me. You are entirely sufficient for me.

No Better Prize

I press toward the goal for the prize of the
upward call of God in Christ Jesus.

Philippians 3:14

Our life is a struggle for accomplishment, satisfaction, and acceptance. The philosophy of our world is to seek self-sufficiency in the accolades and awards of our society. But with every new position or prize accumulated, a greater trophy must be sought and put on display for approval.

Into that climate of competition comes God to offer peace and satisfaction that can only be found in Christ. Few people were as energetic in his world as Paul. He would recount his accomplishments many years later, both personal and professional. He had been tempted to glory in his position in the Jewish community, as well as in achievements that he mastered through personal determination. Yet he set all this aside for a calling that was higher and, in the end, richer than any monument to his abilities—the prize held out to him by his new Master, Jesus Christ.

Much of Philippians 3 is a review of what God did to change Paul's ultimate life goal, which had previously been for personal distinction and stature. Now in Christ, the plunder of life was not material, or even social, but spiritual. All tangible awards were to him like rubbish compared to that which, though unseen, was eternal. Into our materialistic world comes the uncompromising message that Christ is the highest prize of intellectual pursuit, emotional drive, and volitional conquest. The only satisfactory accomplishment is to "know Him and the power of His resurrection . . ." That all-consuming challenge was taken up by Paul and, to the best of our knowledge, attained to the highest degree. But such attainment was empty of personal glory.

The Lord Jesus comes to all who place their faith in Him for salvation, and He gives them a perspective on life that completely reverses their path of pursuit and ultimate life goal. We all must set aside personal desires that are self-oriented to devote our energies totally to the call of Christ: to know Him.

Paul records in detail the cost of striving for this goal in 2 Corinthians 11. The challenge to meet that call *from* the Lord and *to* the Lord demanded that he employ all his resources. The call itself was to full glory *in* Christ and complete likeness *to* Christ. The call to us is away from "things on the earth" by setting our affection on "things above," where Christ is waiting for us to finish the race. The prize at the end of the race is Christ Himself. "Looking unto Jesus . . ."

⅋ ———————————— ℭ

Father, thank you for placing Christ in front of me as the goal of my life's race. I confess that I often look away and lose sight of Him.

All-Encompassing Thankfulness

*Giving thanks always for all things to God the
Father in the name of our Lord Jesus Christ,*

Ephesians 5:20

The blessing of giving thanks is a great encouragement to faith. Realizing that my condition is of the Lord's choosing gives me confidence to thank Him that it is right for me at this time. We find a sister verse in 1 Thessalonians 5:18: "In everything give thanks: for this is the will of God in Christ Jesus for you." The two parameters are defined as giving thanks *in* all things and *for* all things.

The designation of offering thanks *in* all things suggests my general sphere of life. "In" reminds me that my environment is designed by God for my good. Think of the weather as a climate that is shaped by a host of things including wind, rain, temperature, pressure, humidity, clouds, and other atmospheric factors. These are arranged by God for me. I can enjoy air conditioning or heat to alleviate any physical discomfort, but the weather is something that I cannot change. The life I live as a child of God is also arranged by Him and designed to help me grow and display the life of Christ in my mortal flesh. Just as God prepares the weather for my body, so He also prepares the climate of circumstances for my soul. If I complain about the weather, I probably won't give thanks for it. If I complain about the circumstances of my soul, I am probably not going to give thanks in these things either.

Ephesians 5:20 says, "Giving thanks always for all things." This is a command to specifically isolate all the things that God gives me to experience or face. For the pleasant things, we find no difficulty in expressing thanks. But the unpleasant are not only hard to face but also tough to acknowledge that they have been allowed or sent by God. A long list of distasteful things can happen. The most common is disease. Add to that losing a job, friends moving away, death of a loved one, financial collapse, a rebellious teen, auto wreck, or a church split. Make your own list, then stop and, one by one, give thanks for each specific thing instead of asking God to change them.

> *I can give thanks knowing that God is in control.*

We can do this because we firmly believe that nothing happens in the life of a child of God without Him screening it and allowing it. Because of this principle, I can give thanks knowing that God is in control and working "all things" together for my good and His glory. Give thanks *for* all things! Give thanks *in* all things!

ဆ ———————————— ‍ဆ

Father, thank you for what You will bring into my life today. I choose to use those events to grow spiritually and display Your grace to others.

All Things New

Then He who sat on the throne said, "Behold, I
make all things new." And He said to me, "Write,
for these words are true and faithful."

Revelation 21:5

In most cases, new is better than used. We may tend to hold on to various items that are old because we become attached to them, but, in the spiritual realm, the new is beyond comparison to the old. The old is ready to pass away. The old cannot grant righteousness. The old is corrupted. The old has been set aside. The old is condemned.

These concluding words from the final book of the Bible are like a fountain from which pure, fresh water continues to bubble. The great work of making all things new began with the resurrection of the Lord Jesus. Without that event, there would be nothing truly new. We have, by His resurrection, a new way, a new life, a new man, a new creation, a new heart, a new spirit, a new covenant, a new commandment, a new song, new wine, a new name, the New Testament, New Jerusalem, new heaven, and a new earth—all because He came out of a new tomb!

> *In the spiritual realm,*
> *the new is beyond*
> *comparison to the old.*

In today's Scripture, it is as though God is summarizing all the new aspects of His work that flow from the sepulcher of His beloved Son. Like the river flowing from the throne, a current of blessings gushes from the only tomb ever opened from the inside. He "abolished death and brought life and immortality to light through the gospel" on that glorious morning.

Many other new things may be added to the long list of new things wrought for us by a living Christ: a new family in place of old fellowships; a new permanent forgiveness replacing a temporary covering of sin; a new freedom in Christ which is "the glorious liberty of the children of God;" a new practice of the Lord's Supper replacing the old Passover; a new house "not made with hands, eternal in the heavens;" a new message that must "be preached in His name among all nations;" a new hope that is secure for all within the veil; a new inheritance reserved in heaven.

Must we wait until we get to glory to partake of this inheritance? No! The down-payment on all that is new has been granted to us among the "exceeding great and precious promises." And, because God is seated on the throne of His glory and has spoken with such authority, none dare challenge His promise. Truly, for the believer, everything is new!

ও ———————— ৪

Father, thank you for the promise of making all things new. I enjoy many of these blessings now and wait in hope for the reality of the rest.

Prison Provisions

*For I know that this will turn out for my deliverance through
your prayer and the supply of the Spirit of Jesus Christ.*

Philippians 1:19

We should view God's resources as more like a river than a bank account. A person with even a huge account may be cautious about spending the principal, fearing that the limited endowment will not be enough in a time of crisis.

The flow of water from the rock was adequate for all the children of Israel to quench their thirst in their migration from the wilderness to Canaan. The river from the throne, recorded by Ezekiel, was full for all no matter how much was appropriated. The gift of the Spirit of Jesus is a fountain that wells up into eternal life and continues to flow for the enrichment of all who possess that life. The adequacy of the Spirit's supply does not depend on our prayer for that supply or our pleading for more of what was given to us fully. The fountain flows. The river rolls because the fountainhead is the Spirit of Jesus Christ sent into the heart of every believer.

Paul was writing to the church at Philippi, expressing his thanks for a financial gift that they had sent him. The circumstances in which Paul found himself were not comfortable on a "human rights" scale. Some might think that he would ask every believer to plead with God for his release. Instead, Paul accepted the condition as coming from God and under His superintendence.

Few of us will be imprisoned for preaching the gospel, but many of us are in "prisons" of other descriptions which have been allowed by God. Your prison may be a body debilitated by disease, a relationship that you cannot change, a level of education that you cannot effect, a position of financial hardship from which you cannot extricate yourself, or employment that you are locked into.

In our experience, these kinds of situations are regular items for prayer, both personally and in the church. Most of us want deliverance as quickly as possible. We want to instantly decrease the level of pain and suffering. Yet nowhere does Paul ask any church to pray for his deliverance from prison. He accepted the prison and knew that, as the Philippians prayed for him, he would appropriate the supply available by the Spirit of Jesus Christ who resided in him as an ever-flowing river of blessing.

If we follow Paul's example, we will accept the "prisons" that God has allowed and learn to appreciate and appropriate the supply of the Spirit of Jesus Christ who is adequate for every circumstance of life.

℠ —————————————— ∓

Father, thank you for the supply of the Spirit of Jesus Christ. I claim His fullness and His resources in the prison that You have placed me in.

Nothing But the Truth

*If indeed you have heard Him and have been
taught by Him, as the truth is in Jesus.*

Ephesians 4:21

One of the most familiar titles belonging to Jesus is "The Truth." To the disciples in the upper room, it may have been a title without profound meaning, since they had not believed what He said at other times. To choose not to believe is to suggest that either the speaker is not telling the truth or the claims are too preposterous to accept.

For us in a world where there is so much deception, this title of Christ's is of the utmost importance. Pilate asked Jesus the pointed question, "What is truth?" This is a question that is asked less frequently in our culture of relativism. In fact, the world has come to the "intelligent conclusion" that there is no absolute truth. We face—even in Christian circles—the claim that Jesus is insufficient as the source of truth. In education, the blending of the world's philosophy with the truth of Scripture seems to be a satisfactory mix. It is acceptable to wed the psychology of atheists to the truth of the Bible and not be offended. It is "common sense" to claim that the Scriptures are insufficient without the introduction of human wisdom. The absolute sufficiency of Jesus as the living Word and the Bible as the written Word seems absurd to many "thinking" people. For this reason, we return to this Scripture passage to hear the Spirit declare through Paul that all truth is found in Jesus.

> *Jesus stands alone as the only one who could claim to be the Truth.*

It is instructive that Paul, who was not in the upper room when Jesus proclaimed Himself to be the Truth, uses the human name of Jesus here as the repository of truth. We have heard Him and have been taught by His Word since He lives in us by the Holy Spirit. The need to reaffirm this message is repeated throughout the Scriptures. The beginning of time was marked by Adam's choice to reject truth for the lie of the enemy. In the midst of the apocalyptic time, the lie will be accepted as truth by many. Jesus stands alone as the only One who could claim to be the Truth and to have resident in Him all of the truth. All that Jesus said came from the fountain of the Truth and, therefore, can only be absolute. He claimed what He is—the Truth!

☙ ——————————————— ❧

Father, thank you for the Truth that I have found in Jesus. I commit myself to refuse any mix of error and truth in my life and doctrine.

Fully Blessed

*But I know that when I come to you, I shall come in the
fullness of the blessing of the gospel of Christ.*

Romans 15:29

Two Old Testament prayers come to mind when I think of the phrase, "the blessing of the gospel of Christ." The first is Aaron's benediction in Numbers 6:23-27. This directive from God through Moses to Aaron is a comprehensive description of the blessing of the gospel in prayer. It was God's way of setting before the children of Israel everything that He wanted to pour out on them in blessing. As all the world would be blessed through Abraham's Seed, so each phrase of this glorious benediction is poured out on every believer through Christ, Israel's Messiah. Read it and enjoy the fulfillment of the blessing of God in you.

The second prayer has been called the Prayer of Jabez and is found in 1 Chronicles 4:9-10. This prayer has become popular, touted as a great advance in the Christian's relationship with God, when in fact it is a reversion to the most simple and childlike cry of a newborn. All that Jabez asked for in strong faith was granted because God is so desirous for all His children to enjoy His blessing. Yet the answer of God to Jabez is completely fulfilled in the blessing of the gospel. All that Jabez asked for is contained in the fullness of Christ. God was pleased with Jabez' prayer because, in a material sense, he asked for all that God would give, in a spiritual sense, to every one of His children. Jabez received it long before Christ was raised to distribute those blessings in and through Himself.

The first clause of Jabez' prayer is fully declared to be mine in Christ: "O that you would bless me indeed." Several times in the descriptions of the blessing of the gospel, God declares that we are blessed. Ephesians 1:3 states that we are "blessed with all spiritual blessing." Repeating this prayer of Jabez may indicate a failure to appreciate and appropriate the fullness of the blessing given to us in Christ. Can God give us more than the fullness of the gospel? This fullness is found in Christ, as Colossians 2:9 states. The fullness is mine by faith, not by praying the prayer of Jabez.

Anyone who preaches the good news offers the blessing of the gospel of Christ, and anyone who receives the good news receives the fullness of the blessing of Christ. Paul rejoiced in what he was offering and knew that everyone who believed would receive the same fullness. What an adequate gift.

వం ———————————— ౧

Father, I confess that I have not entered into the fullness of Your gospel, but I commit myself today to appropriate more of what You have revealed to me of Christ. You blessed me fully in the gospel of Christ.

A Redemption Story

And they sang a new song, saying: "You . . . have redeemed us to God by Your blood out of every tribe and tongue and people and nation."

Revelation 5:9

A pawn shop provides insight into God's activity in redeeming us. If someone wants immediate cash, he can take a valuable item, such as a watch, to a pawn shop where they will give him a percentage of the watch's value. For a limited time, the owner can return with the same amount of money, plus a hefty fee, and get his watch back. He has then redeemed it.

As believers, we were once free like the watch, but we sold our souls to sin by our father Adam. All of us were born into bondage to sin. Christ came to the market of sin and paid the price with His blood to set us free. Christ, our new owner, allows us to be free until the day that He takes us home to be with Himself. We do not belong to ourselves but to Him who redeemed us to Himself.

> *We do not belong to ourselves but to Him who redeemed us to Himself.*

When I was in college, I would buy Bibles at a second-hand store and distribute them in my ministry. One day, a very nice Bible was for sale for a few dollars. I bought it, took it to the jail, and gave it to a new believer there. He later asked for a Bible with footnotes and center references. I found one and took it in exchange for the other one, which I left in my car for future use.

A few months later, I went again to the second-hand shop in search of more Bibles. There, to my amazement, was the first Bible I had given to the prisoner several months before! It had been stolen from my car and sold to the same second-hand shop. I explained to the shopkeeper the story of the stolen Bible, how I had purchased it previously and that it was mine. I showed him the name of the prisoner written on the front page. He said that he was sorry, but if I wanted it I would have to buy it again. I paid the price and took the Bible home. A friend put a new leather binding on it. We still use it at home.

That Bible is so much like our story. Owned, lost, and bought again, rebound with a new cover, and at home with the owner. The Lord Jesus bought us and will one day put a new "cover" on us when we will be at home with Him forever. Believers of every nation will sing their song of redemption that day.

☜ —————————————————— ☞

Father, thank you for redeeming me. Thank you for helping me to proclaim the redemption story to friends that do not know You.

We Will Behold Him

*For if we believe that Jesus died and rose again, even so
God will bring with Him those who sleep in Jesus.*

1 Thessalonians 4:14

We eagerly await the day when we will be reunited with those who have gone on before us. The prospect of seeing "my mansion" in the Father's house is not as satisfying as anticipating being with Christ. We are prone to think more of things in heaven than of the Person who fills it with His glory. We should, however, want to go to glory because of the One who is there, not because of the rewards that we imagine we will receive, the surroundings, or the company of loved ones.

Paul was comforting believers who had the impression that they and their loved ones had missed the coming of Christ. They were filled with sorrow until they received Paul's letter explaining that the Lord had not yet come and that the day of wrath had not yet begun. These saints were wondering what happened to their loved ones who had died and who, according to Paul's prior teaching, were now with Christ. A touching explanation was made to provide hope and comfort to that church and to us today. The Lord's future return to take His church out of this world is detailed in this context. The Lord will descend from above, and the dead will be raised and join Christ. The living will be "raptured" and all will be reunited in that moment.

"Those who sleep in Jesus" is a phrase that helps us understand that death is not annihilation. The disciples did not understand the word "sleep" in John 11 until Jesus said, "Lazarus is dead." The word "sleep" communicates the precious thought that to die in Christ is to be like one who sleeps. They will be raised from sleep and regain the awareness of life when they awake. So those who die before the coming of the Lord are "asleep in Jesus." The body is in repose, though it returns to dust. The same body, no matter what condition it is in, will be raised and reunited to the soul and spirit that indwelt the body before death. That reunion is what Paul was explaining to the church at Thessalonica.

There was no doubt that these saints believed that Jesus died and rose again. That fact is the basis of hope that our body will be raised from the grave, transformed like His glorious body, and prepared to receive our soul and spirit which has been with Christ since death. Humanly speaking, that reunion will be great, but seeing Christ Himself will likely distract us from our hoped-for reunion with Christian family and friends.

ಯ ———————————— ೮೩

Father, thank you for the promise of the coming of Christ. I eagerly await the joy of seeing Him.

Tempted, as We Are

*For we do not have a High Priest who cannot
sympathize with our weaknesses, but was in all
points tempted as we are, yet without sin.*

Hebrews 4:15

The temptation of Christ has been a subject of theological debate for generations. At issue is whether the Lord Jesus Christ could have sinned while on earth in His human body. It can be answered simplistically by asking, "Can God sin?" Although the obvious answer is no, this opens other questions that are continually argued about: Was Jesus God while on earth? Did He shed His divine attributes and prerogatives during His earthly pilgrimage? If we answer the first in the affirmative, then it is clear that Jesus could not sin. This verse is a categorical affirmation of the absolute innocence of our Savior. He did not commit sin.

We choose to also affirm that He could not have sinned even though the temptations that He faced were very real. That is not entirely impossible to fathom, if we are honest in our mind. This we accept by faith. In addition, Christ was tempted in every area that His creatures are tempted. His temptations were not individual aspects of every branch of sin, but general areas that all human beings face. The construction of today's Scripture introduces a Greek practice of using a double negative to highlight a very strong positive. The impact of the two negatives is part of the sentence structure which accurately renders the Greek text. Some paraphrases remove the negatives and offer one positive, thereby losing the force of the original words.

What is also declared in this text is that the Son of God took on human flesh and so was intimately related to the human race that He created. Of the three official offices He accepted from His Father (He is also the Prophet and the King), the position of High Priest is described as adequate for Him to completely enter into our struggles and, therefore, fully able to understand our temptations and human frailties.

These temptations qualify Him to understand and enter into our struggles with a perfectly sympathetic heart. He is, as God, so far above us that we cannot comprehend it. As man, He humbled Himself so low as to bow lower than any of us have, either by choice or by force. He is the perfect God-Man who was prepared by His earthly pilgrimage to enter fully into our temptations. No other high priest endured the circumstances that Christ withstood in preparation for His ministry as the perfect High Priest to His redeemed people.

80 ———————— CR

Father, thank you for the perfection that You have announced regarding Your Son. I claim His sympathy for the struggles that I face today.

26 OCTOBER

Our Spiritual Food

As newborn babes desire the pure milk of the word, that you may grow thereby, if indeed you have tasted that the Lord is gracious.

1 Peter 2:2-3

Peter uses one of our most spontaneous appetites to help us understand the availability of the best solution to hunger. With a baby, it is striking indeed that the one who gives birth, the mother, is the same one who is physically designed to meet the hunger of her newborn. The bonding that has taken place in the womb over nine months finds its first physical expression outside the womb by the baby desiring and being satisfied with the balanced food designed by God for the health of that little body.

The parallel to spiritual birth and development is equally important to note. In the previous chapter in verse 23, Peter reminds us that the spiritual new birth is effected by the living Word of God. The profound meaning seen by putting these two thoughts together is the correlation between spiritual birth from above and the growth that immediately follows. We are born spirituality by the living Word of God as we believe and obey its truths. The Word of God is not only the matrix through which we must pass into new life, but it is also the balanced diet needed for that life. As with physical life, birth and growth come from the same source in the spiritual life.

The spiritual birth is affected by the living Word of God.

Another prominent point is that hunger is automatic. God built into every baby the desire for milk from the mother's breast. God also builds into the life of every new believer a hunger for the Word of God. The balanced nutrition of the mother's milk is meant to point to the balanced provision found in the Word of God.

Some people wrongly suggest that after this new life of God is imparted, it can be nourished by experiences, feelings, or other sources of food. "No!" says Peter, for the source of life is the same one that adequately gives food for growth. This food, we are taught, carries us through life, although not always as milk because, as we develop, we need meat to attain to the full stature of likeness to Christ. "The word is near you, even in your mouth and heart" says Paul affirming Peter's beautiful analogy. The Word of God that gave birth must be read, ingested in our mind, digested in our heart, and processed in our behavior if we are to grow.

₧ ———————————————— ℧

Father, thank you for the desire to know Your Word. I confess I am tempted to seek other sources, but Your Word is entirely sufficient for me.

God's Personal Property

For if we live, we live to the Lord; and if we die, we die to the Lord. Therefore, whether we live or die, we are the Lord's.

Romans 14:8

A goal of God in the work of Christ was to reclaim ownership of His property. The creation of man resulted in ownership, as we see in Psalm 100:3: "It is He who has made us, and not we ourselves." Some claim to be self-made, but no one truly is because both the materials and the abilities to "make" oneself come from the Creator.

We chose, through Adam, to take ourselves out of God's control and reject His ownership. We went our own way. Although God did not interfere with our petty plans, His heart hurt as He awaited our return. In the meantime, He sent His Son into the world to reclaim His possessions and to bring "many sons to glory."

From our standpoint, when we decided to obey the gospel, we returned ownership of our lives to the One who created us for His enjoyment and glory. That transaction, facilitated by the Word and the Spirit, officially signed over the full responsibility of our salvation and care to the One who died for us. The grandeur of that salvation enthralled us from that day until now, but when He claimed His superintendence in our lives we learned that His plan for us was not always what we expected or wanted.

We try to avoid the difficulties. We choose to question the problems. We attempt to pray away the trials. We try to blame failure on others. We second-guess the wisdom of our Owner. We struggle to understand what ownership means. Our fear of Him was much stronger than our faith in Him. We made longer-range plans, insuring ourselves against unforeseen events, hiding away a sizable sum of money for a rainy day, working overtime to guarantee the pleasures of life, and fulfilling many obligations that we assumed our Owner had put on us.

But the time came when we realized that our Owner is, in fact, more concerned for our welfare than we are. The days that we faced life, we were reminded that we belong to Him. The times that we faced death, we were taught that we are His and He is ours. When persecution came knocking at our door, we let Him take the duty of opening it. When disease grew up in the garden of our life, we knew that He was our Gardener and could handle it. We are learning that living or dying is not as important as basking in the knowledge that we are the Lord's!

❧ ───────────── ☙

Father, thank you for taking me into Your family. I rejoice in being owned by You and in the responsibility that You assumed for my life and death.

God's Grace Is with You!

*Brethren, the grace of our Lord Jesus
Christ be with your spirit. Amen.*

Galatians 6:18

Grace is perhaps the most far-reaching and multifaceted term describing the blessings of God's salvation. The grace of God appeared when Christ was born. The grace of God was manifested when Jesus went about doing good. The grace of God was shown when Christ became poor. The grace of God is unveiled when salvation is offered to all. The grace of God is dispersed when anyone believes the gospel. The grace of God is communicated when the Holy Spirit takes up residence in each believer. The grace of God is experienced when we see a sinner saved. The grace of God is explained when we are justified. The grace of God is realized when we confess that we are weak. The grace of God is our food when we grow. The grace of God is administered when we humble ourselves. The grace of God is approached when we come to the throne of God. The grace of God is employed when we serve God. The grace of God is enjoyed when we speak as Christ spoke. The grace of God is ministered when we hear the Word of God. The grace of God is appropriated when we understand more of our Savior.

After all of these uplifting glorious evidences of the employment of grace, Paul's use of the little word "be" is especially interesting. What does the word "be" mean to us, as Paul concludes this great treatise of the grace of God? Is he saying that dispensing the grace of God in the future is dependent on anything that I can do? Does the word "be" mean that this grace may be unavailable for some unknown reason? Is uncertainty added to the equation by the word "be?"

That idea would be preposterous! The grace of God flows like light from the sun; though clouds shield it from our eyes, they do not stop it from emanating out of that fiery globe.

In this Scripture, the word "be" is in italics. It was italicized by translators to help us understand the text. We can rightly and justifiably translate it as "is." "The Grace of our Lord Jesus Christ *is* with your spirit." That truly helps us understand the grace of God which flows from God through Christ and is applied by the Holy Spirit unhindered, unchanged, and unchallenged. Although it may not always be appreciated or enjoyed, His grace *is* still continually with us.

ဆဝ ──────────── ၿ

Father, thank you for the adequate supply of Your grace for my needs. I count it as always available for my life. Thank you for reminding me that Your grace is sufficient for my spirit. I claim Your grace by faith.

The Perfect Plan

*. . . being justified freely by His grace through
the redemption that is in Christ Jesus.*

Romans 3:24

God's plan of salvation was conceived long before man sinned. In fact, the means of salvation and the ones who were to be included were arranged before the foundation of the world. Being locked into a time-conscious frame of mind, it is hard for us to realize that the triune God was aware of what was going to happen and how He would rectify the situation.

Two great words, *justified* and *redemption*, are used to help us enter intellectually and personally into the way that God's plan was carefully carried out in time. Man's sin in the garden influenced everyone born into this world of natural parents. This sin became the root from which all men produced sinful behavior that is unacceptable to a holy God.

The end result for God was to allow sinners to stand justified in His presence. Man has always attempted to justify himself by his own good works or to defend his actions and blame his culture. God rejects any excuse for failing to live a perfect life which would be the basis of man's self-justification.

With God rejecting every attempt of man to present himself acceptable to God, He must have His own solution for bringing man into a position where he can stand justified. God's plan centered in the suffering and death of His only begotten Son. God gave His Son as a substitutional sacrifice that was adequate for the sin of the entire world. The words "God gave" describe the means by which justification would be imputed to sinful man.

Because man's plan of earning justification fails, God extended His grace to all who would receive the free gift of His salvation. Christ died on the cross to demonstrate the extent of the grace of God. That grace, displayed in Christ's suffering and death, could be no greater. Man sees God's grace and either receives it by faith or rejects it.

But what about man's sin? The very act of God in offering His Son in grace as a substitutional sacrifice for the sin of the world meant that the price was fully paid by Christ. Redemption took place as "Christ died for our sins." Anyone who receives Christ stands before God justified, because full redemption is in Christ. To believe in Christ is to be given all the adequacy of the sacrifice of Christ. God sees the death of His Son as sufficient for my sin. God responds to my faith by declaring me righteous in Christ. I stand justified.

      ℆ ———————————— ℅

Father, thank you for giving Your only Son for my sin. I claim His death as the price for my redemption. I enjoy my justification from Him.

Who We Are in Him

But you are a chosen generation, a royal priesthood, a holy nation,
His own special people, that you may proclaim the praises of
Him who called you out of darkness into His marvelous light.

1 Peter 2:9

Thesese four glorious statements stand as foundations to the house of God. The city of God has four corners, and each of the corners is held up by a pillar of truth, so nobly stated that they should never be forgotten. Each of these four, like the four gospels or the four points of the compass, stands complete in its declaration of the unique position that the people of God have been given by their Savior. The profound description of the responsibilities of believers demonstrates that God's plan was not some stroke of luck for a few who were in the right place at the right time.

"A chosen generation" causes us to focus on our glorious Lord who made a choice before the foundation of the world. This generation is not a collection of people of some golden age, but a group of sinners who have come from every era of time and who belong to a spiritual heritage that is set apart by faith.

"A royal priesthood" binds two of the greatest positions in life: the position of royalty is ours because our King intervened in the affairs of life and proclaimed us His. We are priests to God and have the capability to present sacrifices of praise as well as to intercede with God.

> *We are not special because of who we are but because of the One who loves us.*

"A holy nation" is the highest occupation for a people who are sinful by nature and practice. Who wouldn't want to live in a land occupied by a multicultural, ethnically-mixed race of redeemed sinners whose lives are saintly? No country under heaven can claim this lofty calling.

"His own special people" removes all privilege, and groups all believers in a common family who receive from the Lord Himself the individual care and comfort of a perfect, loving Father. We are not special because of who we are but because of the One who loves us.

With these blessings proclaimed by God, can we remain silent about such position, such privilege, such purpose, such provision? Sound these four trumpets loudly. They proclaim not your accomplishments, but the passion of the One who called you out of darkness and death into light and life. "Praise Him, praise Him, Jesus our blessed Redeemer."

⁎ ———————————— ℞

Father, these thoughts are high and lofty. I confess that I have failed to understand, and my mouth has been silent. I choose to declare Your truth today.

Not a Particle of Darkness

*This is the message which we have heard from Him and declare
to you, that God is light and in Him is no darkness at all.*

1 John 1:5

T he contrast between light and darkness is the most graphic possible. Light and darkness cannot coexist in any context, just as truth and error do not belong in the same room. Likewise, God and Satan cannot and will not coexist in the same culture eternally.

It is the Lord Jesus who made the irreversible decision to enter a darkened world and declare, "I am the light of the world." Before the moment of the incarnation, God had revealed Himself in the light of nature and the Schekinah glory. This caused man to be responsible for that declaration of His eternal power and Godhead.

The Palmist profoundly writes, "The heavens declare the glory of God and the firmament shows His handiwork." Can the heathen stand under the burning sun and estimate its size without knowing in their hearts the existence of a Creator? Will the lesser light which rules the night not speak of the One who rules both day and night? Do not the spheres, that follow their assigned orbits, proclaim the One who threw them there? Will not the lightening, that crackles across the darkened sky, write a script that is understood in every language? Look up and know that "God is light!"

Look within your own heart and see the Light of Life who has taken up residence.

From such lofty heights to the simplest fire that burns the waste of society, the voice of nature says, "God is light." Often, the burning action of fire is descriptive of the nature and activity of God. His feet are like brass in a furnace. His face shone as the sun, His clothes are white as the light, His eyes as a flame of fire. From His head to His feet, the light of fire speaks to any whose eyes are open to see the Lord shining in His strength.

Not a particle of darkness is found in Him. Look within your own heart and see the Light of Life who has taken up residence, cast out darkness, and brought immortality to light through the gospel. Will the Lord Jesus Christ, who is the Light, share your throne room with a demon or an evil spirit? A thousand times *NO*, for the Light displaces the darkness.

☙ ─────────────── ෴

Father, You have given us light of every form to remind us that Christ is the Light. We confess that we love darkness more than the light.

November

BLESSINGS OFTEN OVERLOOKED BUT STILL AVAILABLE IN CHRIST

". . . to be conformed to the image of His Son . . ."
Romans 8:29

Born of the Spirit with life from the above
Into God's family divine,
Justified fully through Calvary's love,
O what a standing is mine!

. . . And it's because of that wonderful day
When at the cross I believed,
Riches eternal and blessings supernal
From His precious hand I received.

John W. Peterson

November

Digestion

Eating is one of the delights of living. It's a practice we think little about as we sit down several times a day to consume what has been provided for us.

If we think little about eating, then we think far less about digesting what we have eaten. The body processes what we take in, making it a part of our organs and sending the rest on its way. Some of what we send down is unacceptable, and we experience heartburn and other unpleasant reactions. (We can even take some medicine before we eat as a warning that something is on the way down that the stomach may not like.)

So much food seems to be predestined by the body to hips and other bulges, unattractively perched in unacceptable places on the body. We then try to adjust the content in an effort to make sure that it settles on the body part where we want it. This is a science and study which involves a significant amount of time, special expense, and personal exercise.

Some folks choose more balanced, less fatty, greater fiber-content meals, until the most horrible tasting food is the most nutritious. Eating becomes punishment instead of a delight. We visit a doctor to find out where the food is landing in the process of metabolism. We pay the doctor, the nutritionist, the health club, the personal trainer, and the health food store where we buy the most nutritious food—all in the name of health.

By contrast, we devour—in our mind, emotions, and will—a smorgasbord of ideas that end up in our soul. Few of us are as concerned about the digestive process of ideas in our soul as we are about foods in our body. As a result we are spiritually unhealthy, but physically fit. The sad fact is that the body will last only a few years, but the soul and spirit will carry on forever.

One of the goals of these daily meditations has been to whet your appetite for a balanced diet for your soul and spirit. A popular series of books is entitled Chicken Soup for the Soul. It is popular because it is not very healthy spiritually. The mixture of the soup includes the bones of philosophy, a dash of New Age, a spoonful of religion, a sprinkling of common sense, a bouillon of banter, and some seasoning from sociology—with a residual trace of Scripture.

Few discerning souls will find true food in this soup for a healthy Christian life. A diet of this soup will breed spiritual weakness and will easily take the place of the meat of the Word. Nor will the reading of meditations from this book take the place of personal discovery of pure milk, living Bread, or strong meat available in the Scriptures.

This kind of food must be prepared under the direction of the Holy Spirit and partaken of under the care of the Father. This kind of food is not always tasty and delightful to the spiritual palate. Some will be like medicine, and others like the proverbial "spinach" that is "good for you" but not sweet to the taste buds.

Truth that is taken into the mind, processed by the emotions, and dictated to the will, results in real growth. The Word of God is the Truth. It is ingested by reading, meditating, memorizing, and choosing by faith to be occupied with it, obeying its patterns and precepts. In this way, we digest the Word of God. Jeremiah 15:16 says, "Your words were found and I ate them, and Your words became for me a joy and the delight of my heart." It is a nice feeling to eat just enough of a balanced meal to be satisfied. You sit back and relax while your body sends the food to various places where it is needed. The body grows, is strengthened, and conditioned for life.

Feeding on the Word of God and having a balanced meal results in an appreciation of the food, appropriation of the truth, and a conscious application to our life as we move about in our service to the Lord and His people. Physical food is digested almost unconsciously. Spiritual food is digested through regular conscious choices and decisions about changes in behavior.

These daily devotional thoughts have been designed to stimulate your hunger for strong meat. If you eat nothing but these meditations, it will be like reading an advertisement for some special food without responding and choosing to experience the food itself. May these meditations urge you to give as much thought to spiritual food as you do to your physical food. Your hunger will then be satisfied.

Grace for Today

Let us therefore come boldly to the throne of grace, that we may obtain mercy and find grace to help in time of need.

Hebrews 4:16

The words *grace* and *gift* derive from the same Greek term, *charis*. The work of Christ on the cross has made it possible for us to come to the throne of grace. The resurrection of Christ from the grave has made it possible for Him to sit on the throne as the dispenser of all His grace and gifts.

It is striking to note that the throne is not a place to come asking, but rather of obtaining or receiving grace and mercy. That is often a foreign idea for most of us. Just the vision of a throne suggests that we must put together a special list of all the things that we want. That is too much like the world dreaming of a card that they could put in an ATM machine, withdrawing any amount that they want from a wealthy man's account. God is not offering to satisfy our every dream like an ATM machine.

What rest to come to the throne and believe that the Lord knows what we have need of before we speak.

Rather, God is dispensing the daily needs of grace and mercy, through Christ, to all who will come for help. Even as believers, we think of the throne of grace as the place of prayer for any request. Scripture is clear that we come in time of need, not for any want or desire that might enter our head.

The throne is not a place where we ask for grace and mercy. It is a place where we receive what is needed for the present. Like the Israelite who collected more then a day's supply of manna, we will find that we cannot live tomorrow on today's grace. Instead, we continually approach the throne of gifts and receive a continual supply for the need of the moment, knowing that the throne will not be closed and that the supply will never run out.

What rest to come to the throne and believe that the Lord knows what we have need of before we speak and that He fills our hands with the exact amount required for each day and hour. Why should we plead for what we think we need when, in His wisdom, He can proportion enough grace and gifts and mercy for the present? The next time we come, we will find the same adequate supply from the same throne and from the same person. Receive all the help you need!

Father, thank you for opening the throne room of Your glory and extending the invitation to the throne itself. I am here again today for an adequate supply of grace and mercy. I take it by faith.

Good Fruit Needs Good Soil

But the fruit of the Spirit is love, joy, peace, longsuffering,
kindness, goodness, faithfulness, gentleness, self-
control. Against such there is no law.

Galatians 5:22-23

God does not give us the fruit of the Spirit as though He were handing us a bunch of grapes. God gives us the resources through Christ to produce the fruit of the Spirit. The idea of fruit opens a panorama of pictures to our imagination.

To fully appreciate this word picture, we must also consider Christ's words in John 15, "I am the vine, you are the branches." This verse distributes the responsibility of producing fruit to both the Lord Jesus and to us as branches. The vine, with its roots deeply embedded in the rich soil, delivers the nutrients to the branches that produce the fruit of the vine, or the fruit of the Spirit.

The branch, as we are told, can do nothing in and of itself. Union with the vine is necessary before fruit can be produced. Communion with the vine is essential to transform the resources that the vine furnishes into much fruit.

The fruit of the vine is not automatic. Some people who are united to the vine don't produce. Many are producing fruit that does not remain, while others draw from the vine for a small harvest. A few bring forth much fruit.

Nor is the fruit immediate. The farmer must wait a week for leaves, a fortnight for flowers, weeks for fruit, and months for harvest day. Patience is rewarded when the ripe fruit is drawn from the branch and processed into wine. The farmer is then satisfied and glorified.

The complicated process would best be understood if we lived with a vine-dresser for a whole season. We would then know of the threatening frost and heat, the menacing blights and pests, the damaging droughts and floods, and the varying conditions of the soil.

We understand the threats to the fruit of the Spirit being formed in us if we examine the climate of our own life. The soil is the key to good fruit. Not every soil produces quality fruit. So Paul reminds us that we are to be "rooted and built up in Him," the source of all nutrients necessary to produce the fruit of the Spirit. The natural process is akin to the spiritual process. Draw deeply on the nutrients found in Christ, and from our lives will spring the fruit of the Spirit. The Word of God opens to us the glorious resources found in Christ which we must employ to produce the fruit of the Spirit.

&ca; ———————————— &cb;

Father, thank you for uniting me to Christ and for releasing all His resources into my life for Your glory and the display of His life in me. I commit myself to do nothing on my own today.

A Helper Indeed

So we may boldly say: "The Lord is my helper;
I will not fear. What can man do to me?"

Hebrews 13:6

How often in our prayers do we ask the Lord to "be with us?" We sometimes forget—or fail to believe—that He is with us and that He will never forsake us. We repeatedly ask the Lord to help us in some way. "Please help" is a call that frequently escapes our lips. Yet, in this simple statement of Hebrews 13:6, God affirms for us that He is our Helper.

The writer of Hebrews repeats this promise from the Old Testament to encourage all believers. A more familiar Scripture comes a verse earlier: "I will never leave you nor forsake you." Our text uses the most glorious name attributed to our God: Lord. There can be no greater helper regardless of the task or responsibility. No trial or test, no tribulation or trouble can overwhelm us when the Helper is with us—helping us.

Can we conceive of the Lord giving us a heavy burden and not sharing the load? Will He stand by after He puts a load on our life and watch us struggle to walk or climb? Surely we must affirm that the burden we bear has been allowed by our Helper, or He has Himself brought it and put it on us. It is true that the burden may come from a friend or foe, but it will not be dropped on our back without His permission and without Him sharing the load. The burden is never more than we can bear together.

Our prayers often reflect the idea that some heavy trial or test has been brought by the enemy without the Lord knowing that the burden is being dumped on our back. The weight of the burden is so great that we call out to the Lord, who is standing there waiting for us to ask. And if we do not ask, we fear that He will remain out of sight, distant, and detached. Perish the thought! He is waiting on us, not us waiting on Him.

The burden is never more than we can bear together.

We perceive the Lord standing over us as the enemy seeks to burden us down, and if it weren't for Him we would be crushed. We thank Him for bearing the lion's share of the burden, and gently allowing a portion of the weight to fall on our shoulders so that we know that He is carrying most of the load. The Lord is surely our Helper!

Father, You have protected me from loads that You know I cannot carry. Thank you for sharing in the burdens that You allow in my life.

A New Citizenship

For our citizenship in heaven, from which we also
eagerly wait for the Savior, the Lord Jesus Christ.

Philippians 3:20

T he citizens of Philippi were also citizens of Rome—even though they were born many miles from Rome. The laws for that colony of Philippi came from Rome itself, and the Philippians were under the direction and protection of that great city. Their allegiance was to Rome.

This concept is transferred to every believer born into the family of God. To be born of God is to receive citizenship to the "land" where God dwells. Our citizenship is proclaimed when we accept Christ as our Savior. We are saved from a citizenship of the world, which is ruled by the evil one, to the kingdom of the Son of God.

Citizenship has special privileges and responsibilities. Perhaps the greatest blessing is the right to enter and reside in the land of our citizenship. Many people are driven out of a country of residence because of war or turmoil and return to the land of their birth. God has included this right in our citizenship. One day we will find the conditions in the land of our residence unbearable because of our own mortality, and we will be ushered from the land of our residence to the land of our birth. The Lord Jesus will, one day, evacuate all His own, and we will be forever at home with Him.

But how is heaven the land of our birth? The Lord Jesus answered this question by saying to Nicodemus, "You must be born again." A literal wording is, "You must be born from above." To be born from above is to be born of heavenly life through the truth. Each believer is born of the power of God by the life of the Son of God, and this rebirth gives each of us a new citizenship. When a child was born in Philippi, his citizenship was recorded in Rome. Our citizenship is recorded in the Book of Life. One day, either by death or rapture, we will be brought to the home of our spiritual birth and be welcomed as full-fledged citizens. This citizenship cannot be bought, earned, or traded. Our passport gives the right of residence. It is signed by the blood of Christ. The Father will say with delight, "Welcome home, my child."

Our citizenship is recorded in the Book of Life.

ଅଠ ———————————— ଛଘ

Father, thank you for giving me citizenship in Your country. I eagerly wait to go home! I rejoice in that prospect today in this sinful world.

Never Reconsidered or Revoked

For the gifts and the calling of God are irrevocable.
Romans 11:29

All of us at some time wish that we had not given someone a gift. We may have wished that we had kept it for ourselves, or maybe we thought that the recipient did not appreciate it as much as we had hoped. We feel that we need the item in our own life more than they do. We wonder if we should have spent that much time or money on that person.

But God has never regretted giving so lavishly all the gifts of salvation. In Romans 11, Paul reminds us of the promises that God gave to His people. No other nation under heaven has had such privileges as Israel. Yet Scripture chronicles the repeated disobedience and unthankfulness of God's people.

In spite of the rebellion and idolatry of Israel, God has never once recalled His gifts or His promises of blessings to them as a nation. One generation after another forfeited the enjoyment of the gifts, yet He is still awaiting the day when all His gifts will be poured out on the Jewish people that bear His name. It would be so easy for us to say that God should forget the promises to Israel and pass on the blessings to others who are more worthy.

Many liberal theologians suggest that God has done that very thing. These students of Scriptures teach that all the blessings that are promised to Israel in the Old Testament are passed on to the church. They suggest that God is in fact finished with Israel and is now fulfilling His promises to believers at the present time. This argument jeopardizes His promises to the church. Will He set aside His gifts and calling to the church because we are not appreciative or because we fail to appropriate His grace? It is impossible to harmonize that idea, however, with the clear statement that God will again take up His people Israel and prove that all the gifts and promises will be fulfilled.

> *God has never once recalled His gifts or His promises of blessings.*

What of us who are not "of Israel?" Is this promise categorical for all His gifts to all His people, or just to the house of Israel? Can we not accept that this promise flows from the very nature of God and is true of all His gifts? Surely no gift of God will be reconsidered and revoked. He will not take back that which He has given. God has called us His Church and so it will be. "His divine power has given to us all things that pertain to life and godliness." He will not recall!

ဢ ———————————— 03

Father, thank you for Your faithfulness in the past. We depend on that same faithfulness for all that lies ahead of us today and every day.

Focus of His Master Plan

*Yet for us there is only one God, the Father, of whom are
all things, and we for Him; and one Lord Jesus Christ,
through whom are all things, and through whom we live.*

1 Corinthians 8:6

Every resource for our life is found in the Lord Jesus Christ. This fact is the key to every aspect of life in Christ. God is aware of the conflict in every one of His children in their desire to be what the Father wants for them.

The resources for accomplishing those goals are found in God, yet each of us attempts to use our own abilities and capacities to do His will. The discord is between all that Christ provides and all that we have in ourselves. If we choose to do things in our own strength, then we can claim the praise for ourselves. Since we can do nothing apart from Christ, we are then dependent on Him.

This synopsis reminds us of the chain of supply. God the Father is the source of all things. He is the originator, the cause, the fountain, the architect. His Son is the means by which all the Father's plans are possible. Christ is the builder and the supplier. He Himself flows in the fountain of His fullness to all His people. He is the life of God and the channel of that life. The Holy Spirit is the applier, the agent for appropriating and enjoying. He is the one who points out the riches of Christ and communicates all that is in Him

God is our Savior, the source of our salvation. Christ is the one who accomplished or procured our salvation. The Holy Spirit is the one who brings the fullness of that salvation into our lives.

God is telling us that we are for Him: created for Him, predestined for Him, called for Him, redeemed for Him, justified for Him, sanctified for Him, nourished for Him, and we will be glorified for Him. All that we are and have is for God.

Our Father's fulfillment is not wrapped up in His angelic beings, nor in the animal kingdom, nor in His plant creation, but only in the human race. The whole of His salvation revolves around Christ. In response, the whole of our occupation should be centered in Him and His Son. This leads us away from self worship to the worship of God. This should drive us from seeking praise for ourselves to praising Him. Glory be to God!

ॐ ──────────────── ○β

*Father, thank you for choosing us as the focus of Your master plan. You have
given Christ to us to fulfill Your purpose. We have the Holy Spirit as the
facilitator of all that You want from us.*

Standing Justified

*"Knowing that a man is not justified by the works of the law but
by faith in Jesus Christ, even we have believed in Christ Jesus,
that we might be justified by faith in Christ and not by the works
of the law; for by the works of the law no flesh shall be justified.*
Galatians 2:16

One of the important words found in Paul's writings is *justification*. The justification of man is central to God's plan of salvation. Man's original state in the Garden of Eden was perfection. They were not God, but they stood in God's sight as perfect. To eat the forbidden fruit meant death, while to refrain from eating of that one tree meant that they would continue to live in holiness and righteousness.

But man was disobedient and trusted the word of the serpent more than the Word of God. Adam chose unrighteousness. In that state, they were unfit for God's presence and were denied access to the tree of life. From that time on, everyone born naturally into the world lives in unrighteousness.

Man has conceived of many different ways to earn acceptance before God. All these ways have been rejected by God as unworthy of His righteous standard of perfection. Man's sin keeps him from even coming close to the "glory of God." Even though the law was given by God as a rule of life for the Jewish nation, the works of the law are inadequate for a righteous life acceptable to God. No one could keep the law perfectly. All are unrighteous before God. As the Scriptures declare, "All our righteousnesses are as filthy rags," and "there is none righteous, no not one."

Into this wicked world came the Lord Jesus to offer Himself as a sacrifice for the sin of all mankind. But before He did that, He lived a perfectly righteous life. He was tested by man and the devil, and no one could find fault with Him. His perfection qualified Him to bear the sin of the world. Because God accepted that substitutionary work on the cross, He could then offer the value of Christ's perfect life to any who would receive Him.

Believing in Christ did not make anyone righteous. Rather, God looks at each one who believes and sees him in Christ and justifies him. Justification means to declare a sinner righteous on the basis of his faith in Jesus Christ. I stand justified because I believe that He died for me. One day I will *be* righteous, as God sets aside my sinful nature when I see Christ. Until then, I am justified!

৮০ —————————— ৪

*Father, thank you for seeing me in the Lord Jesus. You placed me in Him, and
I partake of all the blessings of that union and justification.*

Our Glorious Dwellings

Now He who has prepared us for this very thing is God,
who also has given us the Spirit as a guarantee.

2 Corinthians 5:5

Jesus promised His disciples, "I go to prepare a place for you." Our thoughts generally latch onto the idea of "many mansions" or dwelling places that He went to prepare for us. We are even sometimes tempted to compare our own promised mansion with those that we think others might deserve.

But might it be that He is speaking, not about an elaborate building for us to dwell in, but rather a glorified body for us (our soul and spirit) to dwell in? The mansion for us to dwell in is not necessarily a house of gold, silver, and precious stone, as much as a body "like His own body of glory." The cross and the resurrection were necessary for Him to build a body of glory, like His, for us. It might be that His words of comfort were for the disciples who had a difficult time understanding spiritual things such as the resurrection and glorification of their precious Master. "I am going to the cross to die, so that My Father can forgive your sin. But ultimately I want to bring all of you into my Father's house with glorious abodes just like mine." That will be a glorious dwelling place for our redeemed soul and spirit—a body just like His!

The spirit is the guarantee of our ultimate likeness to Christ, both His glorious body and likeness in soul and spirit.

In today's Scripture passage, Paul is not talking about God preparing a place for us; he is telling us that God is preparing us for the dwelling place. In the previous verses, he has written about an eternal house, not made with hands, that is waiting for us. It has been readied because of our Savior's victory over death and the grave. But now He is preparing us for a house not made with hands. He has given us His Spirit as an abiding presence. The Spirit is sanctifying us through His work, as He told the disciples in the upper room. He will guide, teach, remind, comfort, convict, and direct our gaze on our glorious Savior. He will take the things of Christ and show them to us. The Spirit causes us, through the Word, to behold the glory of the Lord and to be transformed into the same image of our blessed Savior. The Spirit is the guarantee of our ultimate likeness to Christ, both His glorious body and likeness in soul and spirit. Love, joy, peace, and other graces make the likeness of Christ a reality in our behavior.

• ———————————— •

Father, thank you for giving Your Holy Spirit to live in me and prepare me for heaven.

In His Might

Strengthened with all might, according to His glorious
power, for all patience and longsuffering with joy.

Colossians 1:11

Most of the apostle Paul's prayers were for the spiritual growth and development of believers. That is in stark contrast to the prayers that often come from our lips. One of the most common phrases in our prayers is for strength to handle some special effort or trial; yet this kind of request is amazingly absent from most Scriptural prayers.

The Lord commands His people to "be strong," rather than to ask God for strength. He also tells that we are to find that strength "in the Lord." Colossians 1:11 is in complete harmony with that exhortation. The point of Paul's prayer is that the "glorious power" of Christ should be the reservoir from which we draw our needed strength.

So often our thinking is conditioned by our own misunderstanding of the spiritual nature of the Christian life, rather than by the words of Scripture. We are more comfortable asking God for strength and power than we are in employing the power which Christ offers in Himself. The primary reason for such mistaken ideas is that we prefer to ask the Lord to do for us what He has commanded us to do ourselves. So, rather than obey His command to "be strong," we pray for strength. We shift the responsibility from ourselves to the Father. He in turn says, "I have given you His glorious power, and as you appropriate it you will be strengthened with all might."

The command to "be strong" is given many times in the Word, from the experience of Joshua to the conflict described in Ephesians 6. And, just as frequently, we are told that the source of our strength is "in the Lord."

Two words are used in today's Scripture to remind us of the amazing resources available to us, and the responsibility to employ them in our lives. "Strengthened" and "might" are translations of a root word from which we get the English words *dynamo* and *dynamics*. A dynamo makes electricity available to all who are connected to it.

Through Christ, spiritual power is available to all believers. Peter did not say that this "might" is to be seen by walking on water or by healing the sick, but by showing three graces that are found in the Lord Jesus: patience, longsuffering, and joy. The power of the dynamo is available for the dim night light as well as for the powerful searchlight. So in Christ we are strengthened for patience and preaching, longsuffering and loving, joy and justice. He is available for all.

＊ ———————————— ＊

Father, thank you for giving Christ to me with all His amazing power.

Directions to His Love

*Now may the Lord direct your hearts into the love
of God and into the patience of Christ.*

2 Thessalonians 3:5

In the above verse, Paul does not pray that the Thessalonians will *have* the love of God, but that the Lord will direct their hearts *into* His love. Clearly, the Lord gave us these blessings when we received Christ as our Savior, but our heart is not always occupied with Him or His love and patience. More often than not, we are controlled by our own selfish desires and impatience.

Numerous verses remind us that the love of God is our present possession. We need to soak our mind in God's love, to "abide in His love." The Lord Jesus continued to abide in His Father's love, and we need to do the same. It is abiding, not obtaining, that is at the heart of the believer's communion with the Father. To abide or consciously contemplate the Father is to be occupied with the many aspects of His being—chiefly love, since God is love. Surely, if we listen, the Lord will direct our hearts to the love of our God. However, if we refuse His still small voice, we will miss the enjoyment of the blessing of His love and be overcome by our sinful nature.

> *The patience of Christ is our present possession.*

Because we have Christ, we have the "patience of Christ." Many weary believers pray for patience, but only receive tribulation in answer to their prayer. Those trials may be a source of learning. To be occupied with Christ is to be taken up with His patience, which is an essential aspect of His person. If we are immersed in the life of Christ, His patience will be manifested in our daily walk. The patience of Christ is our present possession. The Lord is actively directing our hearts, waiting for us to turn from the empty cisterns of the world.

When a person has lost his way, he asks for directions, perhaps even from a stranger. The Thessalonians seemed to have lost their way in the mystery of the coming of Christ and the order of events. Could a God of love leave behind some of His precious children? Must the ones "left behind" persevere in daily life? The Lord answers their prayer for direction by guiding them into the love of God and the patience of Christ.

Is your heart questioning the love of God or the pathway that He has given you to tread? Follow the guidance of the Lord, directing your heavy heart into the unchangeable love of God and the unsurpassed patience of Christ. These twin spheres are your closet in time of trouble and questions. Rest in them.

ಏ ———————————— ೞ

Father, thank you for Your immeasurable love and the wonderful patience of Christ. I choose to fill my heart today with these blessings.

So Complete a Salvation

For Christ also suffered once for sins, the just for the
unjust, that He might bring us to God, being put to
death in the flesh but made alive by the Spirit.

1 Peter 3:18

This is one of the most succinct summaries of the means by which God brought salvation to sinful man. These truths are expanded in many other texts, but each of the five phrases of this verse sheds light on our salvation. We will examine and compare each phrase so that every measure of divine inspiration can be understood. Appreciate!

Christ's sacrifice is directed toward our sins. The word *sins* is the term most often used to give an exhaustive summary of all our disobedience, transgressions, rebellion, offences, trespasses, and all other violations of the character and law of God. Such a list might suggest that a compilation of all the sins of the world required the cumulative price paid by the Savior. In reality, the same sufferings would have been required of Christ if I were the only one who had sinned. Calculate!

The designation of being unjust lays the blame squarely in the heart of everyone born in sin and guilty of sinning against God's justice. All mankind is unjust: God is the only one who can be declared truly just. Substitution is that the Just One died in place of all those of us who are unjust. Our unjust thoughts and actions demanded a just substitute. Contemplate!

The purpose of God's plan of salvation is to bring back those who have gone astray. God has not moved, and He did not need to be reconciled. Man was driven from the presence of God because of sin, and he remained separated from His presence until God sent His Son to "bring many sons into glory" where God dwells. Celebrate!

The supreme price of such reconciliation is the death of the Son of God. He became human flesh in order that He might be a faithful High Priest and offer Himself as the perfect final sacrifice for sin. The price is infinite because Jesus was and remains perfect God in human flesh. He took on our body to submit to God's punishment in the flesh, paying for sin committed in the flesh. Ruminate!

The Spirit's involvement is added to the work of God in accomplishing our salvation. The Father sent the Son to be the Savior of the world. The Son gave Himself for our sin. The Spirit raised the Son from the dead and applies all His blessings to the heart of each believer. Appropriate!

꙰ ──────────── ꙰

Father, thank you for the completeness of my Salvation. I glory in each aspect of such universal and personal provision for sin.

He Is Coming!

Looking for the blessed hope and glorious appearing
of our great God and Savior Jesus Christ.

Titus 2:13

Jesus Christ is coming again! In every generation, there have been believers who have held tenaciously to the promise of His coming. In contrast, the majority of the world scoffs at the spiritual idea that our planet is in any way affected by Christ, and it ridicules the notion that God is at all involved in our affairs on this tiny globe.

But the promise of the Lord's coming, far from uniting the church in hope and patience, has divided her and undermined the unity that Christ prayed for in John 17. Is the coming of Christ pre-tribulation, post-tribulation, amillennial, mid-tribulation, partial-rapture, or not at all? Each camp has its theological champions who seek to influence the thinking of others—and make money in the bargain. All this is sad when the promise of His coming was to promote hope.

Grammarians tell us that a rule in the Greek language indicates that "the blessed hope" and "glorious appearing" must refer to the same event. That brings a debate about the "secret rapture" of the church which has been a contentious issue between proponents and opponents. Suffice it to say that the coming of Christ for His church seems to be an event that will not be hidden for long, even if it is secret. Why do we spend precious emotional capital in arguing these fine details while the Hope of the world is lost in this turmoil and chaos?

No matter how much flack the church receives from an unbelieving world, she must never lose the power of the promise of Christ's coming. God intended a profound impact on everyone because of the announcement of the coming of Christ. For the world, the promise of His coming should instill a powerful reason to consider the fact of their appearance before the Judge of all the earth who will judge everyone's works.

For the believer, the promise of His coming is to have an impact on every thought, word, and deed. He is fully aware of all of those things in our lives. We are to be buoyed along in a world of wickedness and disaster by the promise that all believers will be caught away from a perishing world into an eternal world. We will be transferred from Satan's world to our Father's house, from a decaying body to an eternal body, from time to eternity, all because of "the blessed hope."

&— ☞

Father, thank you for the promise that You will send Jesus Christ for me. I confess that I do not always live as though I believed it. I do indeed believe it and yearn for Christ's return.

Circumcised Without Hands

In Him you were also circumcised with the circumcision
made without hands, by putting off the body of the
sins of the flesh, by the circumcision of Christ.

Colossians 2:11

God commanded the men of Israel to be circumcised for several reasons. There are proven medical benefits validated by the history of man. All that God commanded His people Israel was "for their good." We should not routinely reject that principle, even in the Christian community.

One regularly considered issue is the spiritual correlation for all of mankind in the act and meaning of circumcision. The references in the New Testament cannot be ignored when we see the spiritual justification for this interesting physical surgery.

Clearly the piece of flesh that is cut off after the birth of a male child teaches the need for every believer to set aside anything that resembles or relates to "the flesh" which was born into man through Adam. We are all born in sin and brought forth in iniquity. That sinful trait is a component of our being that enslaves us to sin, demonstrated by disobedience and rebellion. That power cannot be removed without the new birth or overcome without the conscious putting off of the flesh and its lusts. That act is once and for all in Christ, but it is worked out as a daily determination to set aside all evil desires and to employ the Spirit's victory over the indwelling sin nature.

But how can that be done when conflict with the flesh is so fierce, even after we have been born from above by the Holy Spirit? The answer is contained in the physical act of circumcision. Jesus was circumcised according to the Law of Moses. It was a physical act, as much as His death was physical. When Christ died, we died. When He rose, we rose. When He ascended and sat down, we did so also in Him. So, when Christ was circumcised as a baby, we, being "in Christ," were circumcised in Christ. This act is referred to in today's Scripture.

But the physical act on Christ's body represents a spiritual act in our being. The putting off of the sin of the flesh is a spiritual operation done without hands. We have been circumcised in Christ. The personal spiritual effect of that act must be reckoned as having been accomplished, because we are in Christ. It must also be reckoned as having the profound effect of giving us reason and power to set aside the desires of the flesh, because the flesh has been separated from us.

ଏ ———————————— ଔ

Father, thank you for placing us in Christ to be included in all aspects of His
work. I count my circumcision effective for spiritual victory.

He is Always with Us

That good thing which was committed to you,
keep by the Holy Spirit who dwells in us.

2 Timothy 1:14

Why do we need to be indwelt by the Holy Spirit? The New Testament epistles are sprinkled with announcements that believers have the Holy Spirit in their hearts.

Perhaps the reason that this truth is repeated is that we so easily forget and develop habits which contradict what we know and what the Word says. We hear people pray, "Lord be with so-and-so." This is often in reference to ourselves as we start the day. It is frequently a prayer for others who may be going through difficulties, trials, or sufferings. The request is repeated over and over by the most knowledgeable and seemingly "spiritual" of believers.

The Word of God reiterates with amazing regularity the fact that the Holy Spirit and Christ permanently reside in every saved person. As believers, we know that God is with us. There cannot be a simpler truth or a more basic way of communicating it to us. Some have argued this point saying, "God understands," or, "Don't bug me," or, "He wants us to come as little children." One church took a whole Sunday service to dispute the idea that we don't need to ask the Lord to be with us.

Maybe a review of the ministry of the Holy Spirit would develop in us the habit of communion with the person of the Holy Spirit. Why is He in us? He is our teacher, guide, comforter, helper, counselor, reminder, leader, intercessor, advocate, and applier of the Word to our lives.

Possibly, because we do not commune with Him, we are not conscious of His presence and work in us. Perhaps we go weeks and maybe months without any interaction of listening, communing, obeying, longing, or learning of Him, and forget that He is waiting for us while we go on our way, oblivious to His presence. Have we forgotten that He is there?

Perhaps we do not really think when we pray. After I spoke about this trend in our prayer life, someone remarked, "You want us to think when we pray?" We have become so thoughtless in our prayer life that our personal fellowship with the Spirit is bland and repetitive. Another person said to me, "I will never pray in front of you again." I am not the judge of prayer. Our prayers more than anything else reflect our knowledge of the Word and our level of spiritual maturity. Stop and ask, "Am I praying according to the will of God, the Word of God, and by the Spirit in me? Am I thinking when I ask Him to be with me?" My dear brothers and sisters, thank Him for His presence!

☙ ——————————————— ❧

Father, thank you for the residence of Your Holy Spirit in my life. I confess that I neglect Him and forget that He dwells within me.

Weapons for Warfare

*For the weapons of our warfare are not carnal but
mighty in God for pulling down strongholds.*

2 Corinthians 10:4

Our spiritual conflict is real combat. The confrontations of enemies in the life of the believer are not always subtle or mysterious. There are times when we receive a frontal attack, while other times the assault is from within. Our enemies include the world around us that we encounter every day, as well as the flesh which is in every believer and has access to our mind, emotion, and will.

In most cases, Satan is singled out as the primary enemy that we face in spiritual battle. This excuse can be a source of discouragement. It is easier to blame the devil for all the defeats in our lives than to accept the truth that the flesh in me, which I can control, is responsible for much of the failure in my life.

In many encounters we feel powerless to gain the victory over any of these foes. We attempt various means of defeating the world, yet fall back defeated. We think that we have put the flesh to death, but the next morning it is alive and on the offensive again. Many times, we are defeated in spiritual clashes because we are using weapons that are carnal or worldly. Keeping the law is a popular weapon. Asceticism is a tool of the flesh. Staying out of the world is a common approach. Blaming the devil for everything is a favorite accusation. Activity often proves ineffective. Even service for the Lord may seem a spiritual proposal. Each of these is carnal as weapons in spiritual warfare.

What weapons has the Lord given us? The Spirit leads us to Ephesians 6 where He reiterates the list of armor provided for each believer. Understand that all are in some way related to the Truth. Each piece is designated for a vulnerable area of our life. Because they are all related to the Truth, we must consider the activity of truth in our conflict. None of the armor suggests activity, isolation, service, blaming someone else, or even keeping the law as a means of victory. We assume responsibility for taking the whole armor of God.

Our weapons are powerful and effective! The key to victory is knowing and employing those weapons. Obviously, our weapons include our blessings in Christ, the ministry of the Holy Spirit, the power of the Word of God, prayer, faith, the unity of believers, and fellowship in the family of God. Do we know and employ them? They are mighty!

⠀⠀⠀⠀⠀⠀⠀⠀ℰ❍ ———————————— ᏻ

*Father, thank you for the powerful weapons that You have provided for my
daily victory over the world, the flesh, and the devil.*

Believing His Promises

So then those who are of faith are blessed with believing Abraham.
Galatians 3:9

This is one of the grandest statements of our blessing, packaged in an illustration taken from the life of faith that Abraham pioneered for us all. We can say authoritatively, "We are blessed!" We should repeat this again and again for our instruction and encouragement: I am blessed! You are blessed!

Why? The simple answer is recorded almost incidentally, as Abraham's step of faith is examined and explained in terms of New Testament Christianity. Those who have placed faith in the person, work, and Word of Christ receive blessings.

The story of Abraham is used in several contexts to emphasize this truth. Romans 4 adds a powerful passage reinforcing the grand similarity between all believers and this patriarch. Abraham believed God's promise of a son. He lived day by day dwelling on that statement, taking strength from its truth, soaking his soul in the prospect of fatherhood, absorbing the possibilities, rejecting the doubts, refusing to feed his questions, praising the one who made the promises, repeating the words spoken to him, basking in the glory of the Lord. Of course, we know that he failed, but at least He believed.

We are blessed because of our faith in the same God, blessed through Abraham's greater Son, so that we, too, can practice the attitude of faith. Repeat the statements of truth. Memorize the messages of fact. Meditate on the adequacy of God's provision. We do not know how it will all take place, but, like Abraham, we are counseled to "stagger not at the promise of God in unbelief."

Too often we feed our fears, multiply our questions, double our doubts, work out our worries, advance our anxieties, and wonder why we do not accept the fact that we are blessed. In turn, we plead with God to bless us and bless everyone else we pray for. How sad our great God must be when He speaks to us of the astonishing array of blessings that He has freely given us in Christ, only to see us turn from all of these and say to Him, "Lord, bless me." Do we believe?

We must learn to drive out our doubts by repeating, "I am blessed." A full inventory of all the blessings of Christ will drown any lagging shred of unbelief. The long catalogue of resources for life will parade before the eyes of our understanding and, as each passes, we salute it and offer a thank you to the giver of every good and perfect gift.

დ ———————————— ჩ

Father, thank you for blessing me. I will never fully understand all that You have given to me in Christ. I seek to know more of Christ my Lord.

Christ, the Power of God

. . . but to those who are called, both Jews and Greeks,
Christ the power of God and the wisdom of God . . .

1 Corinthians 1:24

It is not unusual to hear a believer pray for strength or power for a special set of circumstances: strength to overcome temptation, power for victory over habits, strength through a surgery. What spawns the prayer for more strength or power is separating what Jesus Christ is from what Jesus Christ *gives*. We might say it very simply, "Christ is what He gives."

We are the called of God, and He has given us the fullness of Christ as a permanent possession. Christ lives in me, and all that is found in Christ is also found in me as a child of God. Can I have Christ and not have the power of Christ or the wisdom of God? The answer is emphatically no!

The center of God's provision is Christ Himself. God does not weary of repeatedly telling us that all the resources of our salvation are found in His Son, our Savior. He urges us to find our sufficiency in the knowledge and grace of Jesus Christ.

Many are called to accept Christ as Savior. Several times we are reminded that those who believe are the called of God. Elsewhere we are reminded that, in Christ, there is no difference between the Jew and the Greek, because all are one in Christ Jesus. The blessings of salvation are not different for any member of the family of God. All receive the same blessings.

Christ is the power of God. This demonstration of the Father's power was revealed in and through the Lord Jesus Christ. In His earthly ministry, Christ reminded the disciples and the Jews that all He did was in the power of His Father. His miraculous works were a revelation of the power of God. The words that He spoke were the wisdom of God. The result was amazement at what He did and what He said.

> *God does not weary of telling us that all the resources of our salvation are found in His Son, our Savior.*

Does this mean that because we have Christ we should be regularly performing miracles and uttering profound words? It is not God's intention to duplicate Jesus walking on water or raising the dead. What was unique about Christ's life was that it was explained only in terms of His Father. What God wants for us is for our lives to be explained in terms of Christ. Power is there, but it is God's power available to us in Christ. Wisdom is there, available to us in Christ. Christ is my power. Christ is my wisdom.

⊰ ———————————————— ⊱

Father, thank you for giving me Christ and all the power that I need to live in His strength. I confess my weakness and use His power and wisdom.

Breaking the Law

Who also made us sufficient as ministers of the
new covenant, not of the letter but of the Spirit;
for the letter kills, but the Spirit gives life.

2 Corinthians 3:6

The primary work of the Holy Spirit is to give life to every one who comes to Christ. All of us were abiding in death because of sin before we received the Lord Jesus Christ as our Savior. The Father sent the Spirit, who proceeds from His presence as the emissary of Christ, to give us life in exchange for death.

In 2 Corinthians, Paul faces the challenge of preaching the new covenant of grace and peace. This was a monumental responsibility, proclaiming a message of the grace of God to a nation that was living under the law. That law was ordained by God and was perfect and just and good. To replace that divinely sanctioned rule of life with grace seemed incomprehensible to the Jewish mind. But that was the Lord's calling and challenge for Paul.

Paul's challenge was twofold: One, to convince the nation of Israel that the Law of Moses kills. The second truth was that the Holy Spirit gives life. Paul was to reveal to Israel that the transition from death to the Person who brings life is possible only through Christ.

The law was given by God through Moses. The Holy Spirit was sent by Jesus, who lived amongst them, died, and rose again. Would Israel accept the idea that what was ordained by God had been replaced by the work of Christ?

> *The Spirit gives life to all who accept God's grace and forsake the law.*

For 1,500 years, the law was a minister of death. God had said, "This do and you will live." But no one could do all that God commanded. So, then as now, the letter or legalistic rule of behavior only brings death and kills the spirit of man, and the end is spiritual death. No one can claim to have life in Jesus Christ by keeping the law or ordering his or her conduct by the Ten Commandments. The letter of the law brings death. The keeping of the law is the work of the flesh, which God now condemns. It is the opposite of receiving "the gift of God which is eternal life through Jesus Christ." The law kills the spirit of man, because he is unable to perfectly perform every precept required. The Spirit gives life to all who accept God's grace and forsake the law.

ଅ ———————————————— ଊ

Father, thank you for giving me Your life by sending Your Spirit into my heart. I choose to live a life of faith and reject the law as my rule of life.

Able to Help

For in that He Himself has suffered, being tempted,
He is able to aid those who are tempted.

Hebrews 2:18

The life and ministry of Jesus Christ had a manifold purpose in the plan of God. Major W. Ian Thomas summarizes it: "The life that He lived qualified Him for the death that He died. The death that He died qualifies us to receive the life that He lives."

The perfection of Jesus was declared by seven different people. No one could find fault in Him. He faced a host of temptations that exceeded any that we face. No one can say that He does not understand. None can claim that He has never been through what He is putting us through. Every tendency of human nature has been met by Christ, with the exception of sinning.

Christ's temptations and sufferings were very real. This concept, proclaimed by the Scriptures, is beyond our comprehension, but it can be accepted by faith and appreciated by every believer. The temptation of the Lord Jesus was not to see if He *would* sin but to prove that He *could not* sin. Those who suggest that Jesus could have sinned must answer the question, "Can God sin?" Any biblically minded person must answer, "God forbid!"

The preparation of Christ for the work of the cross was not the only reason for a life of sorrow and deep suffering. Though we cannot comprehend the depth of His suffering, we are the beneficiaries of His grief and affliction. The Lord Jesus rose from the grave to live in the power of an endless life. That life has been communicated to us because God gave His Son to live in every one of His children. Why is He there? One of the reasons is "to aid those who are tempted." That includes all believers. Though none of us escapes temptation, none of us is without aid.

Christ is able to help. His characteristics are an encouragement to all believers. He is able to save, able to make, able to keep, able to do, able to comfort, and able to raise. But we ask, "Is He willing?"

Can those words be framed by our lips before we realize how inappropriate they are? What makes Him willing? Our pleading? Our holy life? Our level of need? If we try to survive the temptation on our own, He may allow us to stumble. But confessing our weakness and thanking Him for His help opens to us all the wealth of His power. He is able and willing, because He shared every temptation of life.

Father, thank you for the gift of the One who has been through it all, even before we faced our temptations.

Living as Sanctified Heirs

By that will we have been sanctified through the
offering of the body of Jesus Christ once for all.

Hebrews 10:10

The will of God is that we be sanctified, according to 1 Thessalonians 4:3, "For this is the will of God, your sanctification: that you should abstain from sexual immorality." Sanctification is one of the glorious works of the Lord Jesus through His death on the cross. Considerable misunderstanding exists because of the way that the words are used. How can it be that we are sanctified by the will of God while still living an unsanctified life?

The word "sanctified" means "to set apart." The root Greek word is used in at least three different ways in the New Testament, and it is also translated "saints" and "holy." Each of these words presents the same difficulty. How can we be saints, and then be told to live a saintly life? How is it that God says that we are holy, and then commands us to "be holy"?

An important principle for us to understand is the profound position that God gives us because we are in Christ. Because we are children of God, we are set apart as His special people.

When the king of a country has a son born to him who will be the next king, he is set apart for that position and is called the heir to the throne. That does not mean that his behavior is always "kingly." He must go through a period of development and a curriculum of training like any other child. Though he has been sanctified or set apart by birth to be the next king, he must still learn and develop his physical and mental skills to rule wisely.

We were born into the family of God as His children and have been designated by the will of God as "sanctified" or set apart by God for Himself. As soon as that position has been granted to us, we begin a long and often arduous program of discipline and study to develop the character that God wants to see in us as His children.

Jesus fulfilled the will of God, as the previous verse tells us. We, like Him, must do the will of our Father, not to earn the designation of "sanctified," but because we *are* sanctified. We have been sanctified and stand in that position. Our standing before God cannot be undone, just as the finished work of Christ cannot be canceled or reversed.

⃣ ———————————— ⃤

Father, thank you for setting me apart as Your own possession. I confess that I do not always act as though I have been sanctified. Thank you for helping me live a life worthy of You.

Don't Ask for Forgiveness

*And you, being dead in your trespasses and the
uncircumcision of your flesh, He has made alive together
with Him, having forgiven you all trespasses.*

Colossians 2:13

The forgiveness of sin is a message repeated throughout the epistles. Yet, if we are not forgiven and cleansed, the Holy Spirit cannot come and make us alive. The preparation of our body as a residence for God begins with full and total cleansing. That is the act of a moment, coupled with all the other blessings of our salvation.

What is important is that God has forgiven all our trespasses. But many will ask, "Why, then, do we ask for forgiveness for sin if they are all forgiven?" That question has a misconception in it. Nowhere are we urged to "ask for forgiveness." We are directed to "confess our sins." The difference may seem small, but attention to the words of Scripture will enlighten us. We are charged to agree with God about our sin, and He is faithful to forgive our sin. The context of that command in 1 John 1 deals with restoration of fellowship, not the "sending away" of sin.

The salvation that God provides sends away all our trespasses. That removal is a permanent personal possession which cannot be reversed. No sin can be charged against us once we have been made alive by Christ. Does that mean that we can continue to live in sin after we have believed? Paul answers that question with a resounding "God forbid" in Romans 6:1. The characteristic of the Christian life which stands out prominently is that we put away sin and begin a life of holiness which is pleasing to God. If we do sin, we have an Advocate who faces every charge with His substitutional sacrifice on the cross. Jesus paid it all!

If we did not know the forgiveness of our sin, we would live in fear as many do. Some are hounded by the possibility that they will die without having remembered and confessed all their sins. Many will ask for forgiveness every time they pray, just in case they may have missed one in their forgetfulness. We must not be so ignorant of the Word of God to think that daily forgiveness is dependent on our poor memory. When we believe the gospel for salvation, all our trespasses are forgiven—past, present, and future!

When we confess our sin, the Lord affirms that His blood, shed on the cross, has already been applied, and He refuses to let any charge stand against us. We are fully forgiven!

ფ ———————————————— ൠ

Father, thank you for the forgiveness of sin and the life that You have planted in my being. What a wonderful change in my life has been wrought since Jesus came into my heart.

Helping Us to Pray

Likewise the Spirit also helps in our weaknesses. For we do not know what we should pray for as we ought, but the Spirit Himself makes intercession for us with groanings which cannot be uttered.

Romans 8:26

O ne of the most common words in our prayers is "help." In times of special trouble, we may cry out *"help!"* Under more normal circumstances, we may ask for help in a decision or an especially difficult trial. More often, perhaps, we ask God to help others whose needs we know. Yet it may be that the cry for help is inconsistent with the ministry of the Spirit, who is our Helper.

> *He is helping us in prayer, not because we ask or plead for help, but because that is His ministry to us.*

Four times in the upper room discourse, the Lord Jesus told the disciples that "the Helper" was going to reside in them and perform a multitude of ministries in their life and service. Those ministries are explained and expanded for us as we read the letters that those apostles and Paul wrote in our New Testament. Many of those aspects of service are considered in these meditations.

The specific employment of the Spirit in today's Scripture is to help us in prayer. One of the most amazing blessings of our salvation is ready access to the Father by the work of Christ in prayer. The Holy Spirit is the one who guides us in praying. We are commanded by God through Jude's letter to be "praying in the Holy Spirit."

The problem that Paul addresses is common to us all in our exercise of prayer. "What should we pray?" We are asked that question countless times as we visit believers around the world. Most do not know our day-to-day activities or the special conditions under which we might be living or ministering.

The Spirit helps in many ways. He brings to our attention a specific situation and guides our thoughts and words in prayer. As we listen to the Spirit of God, we can be sure that we are praying in harmony with the Word of God and the will of God. The Holy Spirit will bring to our minds various Scriptures that will be the basis of our communion, worship, and intercession. This same Spirit engages in intercession for us with sounds that we cannot hear or understand. But His thoughts are always in harmony with the will of God for us and the Word of God that we have before us. He is helping us in prayer, not because we ask or plead for help, but because that is His ministry to us.

೮ ———————————— ೮

Father, thank you for the presence and ministry of the Holy Spirit as my Helper. I confess my need of His help and believe that He is helping!

The Guarantee of Our Inheritance

. . . who is the guarantee of our inheritance until the redemption
of the purchased possession, to the praise of His glory . . .

Ephesians 1:14

The Holy Spirit is the "who" of our verse, the one who seals us in Christ. His sealing demonstrates two things: ownership and security. Both ownership and security are marked by the sealing of each believer, just as hot wax sealed important papers in the first century.

The person of the Holy Spirit, more than His work, is referred to as the guarantee. We can understand how someone would give a piece of paper, which is properly signed and sealed, as a document of guarantee. Many of us have such warrantees which have little or no value. More than a document, God has given to us His Holy Sprint as the guarantee.

How much more is the person of the Sprint to us as the guarantee of our inheritance? Many wealthy people spend a long time making sure that their will is properly documented and safely secured until they die. That piece of paper is not in force until the death of the author. Then, in their absence, the document is brought out and read. "He, being dead, yet speaks" through his last will and testament.

God has written the last will and testament of our blessed Savior. Christ died to make the will effective and to put it in force. Then, blessing above all blessings, He rose from the dead and sent the promise of the Father into our lives so that we can cry "Father!" That Spirit, by His daily ministry, reminds us of the opulence of the riches of our inheritance. It is true that we will not enter into all the riches until we are absent from the body or alive with Christ at His coming.

We have a document that declares all the riches of our inheritance.

However, we do have a document that declares all the riches of our inheritance. We are commanded to study the Word where the inventory of blessings is recorded. The Spirit has been given to us "that we might know the things that have been freely given to us by God" (1 Corinthians 2:12). He is not a document, but a person with mind, emotion, and will. He is talking to us, unraveling the mysteries of His glorious provision. He is living in us, unfolding the fabric of blood-washed linen whereby we may be clothed. He is uncovering the riches hidden in Christ. He is walking with us, unveiling the path that leads to our full inheritance and our final redemption. He is our guarantor.

℘ ———————————— ℃

Father, thank you for giving the Spirit to me. I confess that I have neglected His ministry of revealing the riches of Christ to me. I choose to listen!

Carrying Me through Temptation

And the Lord will deliver me from every evil work and preserve me for His heavenly kingdom. To Him be glory forever and ever. Amen!

2 Timothy 4:18

It might seem at first glance that this verse promises clear sailing through the Christian life and arrival in the eternal kingdom, unscathed by the problems and afflictions common to all people. However, many other reminders are recorded for believers, teaching us that we are not exempt from the circumstances ordinary to all mankind. Even if we pray fervently for such afflictions to be kept away from us, the calamities of our world may still come to the children of God. We are not exempt because we are believers or have great faith.

What we are promised is that the spiritual enemies cannot harm us as children of God. There are many "evil workers" who may be released by my Father to afflict and persecute me. My temporal enemies are allowed by God to bring trials and agony. Paul himself never claimed that he was being insulated from the onslaughts of those who were "enemies of the cross of Christ." He did ask the Thessalonians to pray "that they [Paul and his company] may be delivered from unreasonable and wicked men." Yet, in 2 Timothy 3, he recounts many calamities and tribulations that he faced, and he proclaims that "out of them all, the Lord delivered me."

> *The Lord knows our capacity to endure temptation and so superintends all our affairs, encouraging us in the trial to use the resources for victory.*

The balance is delicate. The Lord knows our capacity to endure temptation and so superintends all our affairs, encouraging us in the trial to use the resources for victory. In areas where we are weak, He may keep us from the trial. In other circumstances, He may deliver us in the middle of the test. In still different conditions, we may need to go through the difficulty to the end. He is in charge, and I can trust and give Him thanks for overseeing my situation.

The Lord does not keep us from sin. Although we are able to submit to sin, our Father gives us the resources to confront sin. In the power of the Spirit, He enables us to reject temptation by quenching all the fiery darts of the wicked one. We are not promised to be kept from death, which is common to all people. For us, physical death is not a judgment that we must endure but a means of travel into the fullness of life with Christ in glory.

ഇൗ ────────────────── ൽ

Father, thank you for the personal care of the details of my life. I know that You allow things to come that I would never choose. I trust Your wisdom.

Head of Church and Home

For the husband is head of the wife, as also Christ is
head of the church; and He is the Savior of the body.

Ephesians 5:23

No matter what arguments are made or how many times it is contradicted, the Bible unequivocally says, "the husband is head of the wife." This has been repeated in marriage ceremonies for generations without being challenged. But, in our progressive and rebellious society, it has been denied, rejected, discarded, and, perhaps most abhorrent of all, it is no longer considered to be true. Yet that does not change the fact of the Word of God.

The parallel truth is also considered archaic and out of touch with human wisdom that has been accumulated in the past generation. Christ is the head of the church. The church of which Christ is head is an organism, not an organization. The difference is clear. The church is alive because He has given His life to every member—just as in a human body every member shares the same life. The head of the church is not a man who holds an office, such as pastor, bishop, or pope, but rather the Man who rose from the dead to redeem His church from death.

The failure of the church to accept the truth of the headship of Christ has influenced husbands to reject it as well. The breakdown of the church has led to the breakup of marriage commitments. If each local church proclaimed and accepted the absolute headship of Christ as revealed in the Scriptures, it would be difficult for husbands to refuse the position and responsibility to be the head of his wife.

At the same time, the rejection by the wife of the headship of her husband adds to the confusion in the church and the family. Our liberated society thinks that it knows better than the God who created marriage. It seeks to set all women "free" from "bondage" to such enslaving concepts as the headship and authority of the husband over his wife. The added biblical injunction to obey him has been almost entirely lost in our culture. But God remains firm in His injunction both to obey and to accept the headship of the husband.

It seems that our world will never recover the divine formula for peace in the home and a radiation of the glorious relationship of Christ to His church. The truth will not change. He is head of His church and will remain so, no matter what man says! The husband is the head of the wife, regardless of how it is challenged.

꧁ ──────────────── ꧂

Father, thank you for giving me and my church a divine Head from whom we
choose to get direction and authority for life and faith.

26

Works of Man or Fruit of Christ?

He who sins is of the devil, for the devil has sinned from the beginning. For this purpose the Son of God was manifested, that He might destroy the works of the devil.

1 John 3:8

The "works of the devil" stand in stark contrast to "the fruits of righteousness which are by Jesus Christ." The word "works" reminds us of a factory where raw materials come in one end of a building and the finished product appears at the other end. In between is the cacophony of machines and human inventions, playing out their amazing clamor. The shop floor is littered with used materials, excess parts, and a layer of dust, while a pandemonium of noise echoes from the works of man's hands.

The word "fruit" takes us to a garden where, silently and spontaneously, the nutrients of the soil are being transformed both day and night by the process of photosynthesis into flower, fragrance, and fruit.

What a beautiful transformation of a few acres of land when an old manufacturing plant—with its chimneys belching out smoke and pollution, the rumbling of trucks and machines, employees hurrying in and out—is all replaced by a lovely park with grass, shrubs, flowers, and trees. Here families and friends enjoy each other and appreciate the sights and sounds of the Creator. The works of man are replaced by the fruits of the Creator.

The works of the devil have been manufactured since his plant was established. It started with his hunger for independence from his Creator. His desire for independence led to pride and arrogance and the aspiration of equality with the One who made him as the covering cherub.

Into the perfect Garden of Eden came this destroyer who began his works by deceiving Eve, resulting in the downfall of mankind. Adam's act of greater trust in the devil than in God led to the introduction of all "the works of the devil." The list of his works is long, and the showrooms of his products are the lives of men and women, deceived from the beginning to this very day.

The Lord Jesus appeared in conflict with the devil, and the showdown was finally appointed on a hill outside Jerusalem. There, the Son of God was displayed in humility, suffering, and death. But, on the third day, He rose victorious over the devil and all his works. The reclaiming of his stage began with tearing down the domain of this defeated foe. The Son's ascension through the realm of the devil was His ultimate evidence of victory. What a beautiful garden God has created in Christ Jesus.

ॐ ———————————————— ☙

Father, thank you for the victory of Your Son. I claim His victory in my mind and choose to display the fruits of His victory in my life today.

Our Blessed Inheritance

And whatever you do, do it heartily, as to the Lord and not
to men, knowing that from the Lord you will receive the
reward of the inheritance; for you serve the Lord Christ.

Colossians 3:23-24

Rewards are an element of life that drive us to excel. Many Christians are looking forward to rewards and crowns that they contemplate enjoying in eternity. Others are committed to casting them at the feet of Jesus. The revelation about rewards is not entirely clear in the New Testament, but what is sure is the review at the judgment seat of Christ. Paul draws a picture describing a huge gathering of all believers, each with a pile of goods that he has accumulated during his lifetime as a believer. All will be tested by fire.

This picture is sometimes a haunting nightmare. Very few people feel that they have done enough to warrant rejoicing at the prospect of our works being tried in the furnace. The solemnity of this appearance at the judgment seat of Christ should affect our stewardship. The reminder in 1 Corinthians 4:5 can be comforting: "Then each one's praise will come from God."

Another aspect of today's Scripture is that the reward is related to the inheritance. It may be that the more honorable the service, the more sizable the portion. That is fitting in our practice of distributing wealth. A favored son gets a greater amount. It could be that the reward is in keeping with the faithfulness of service that we have rendered in life. Each of these uncertain considerations may give us uneasy feelings about what we might receive, either in rewards or inheritance.

But we "serve the Lord Christ" is a statement that immediately relieves any anxiety, as we consider the judgment seat of Christ. We serve one who Himself served faithfully and perfectly. Not one act or attitude was out of line, as He always did those things that pleased His Father. He also is a faithful judge and will review righteously.

It is challenging to serve under the eye of man without considering what effect our dedication merits. "You serve the Lord" is a reminder that we are to employ all our resources under His eye and not man's. Our relationship in His service cannot be challenged. We serve the Lord! We do not choose to do so. We cannot resign, refuse, or retire. It is a blessing that we have, and we are responsible to Him.

        —————————————————

Father, thank you for employing me in Your service. I may be ashamed before
Christ at His coming, but I seek to serve heartily. I choose to take my eyes off
other servants and look only to Your Son, my Lord.

Resources of Christ-likeness

To know the love of Christ which passes knowledge;
that you may be filled with all the fullness of God.

Ephesians 3:19

The ultimate goal of God for His children is to be like His Son, Jesus Christ. Some suggest that the primary reason that God saves us is that we might go to heaven. There is no question that this was one of the foremost objectives in the mind of God when His plan was conceived before the world began.

But many of us who believed in Christ for salvation are still here on earth. He must have a special purpose in leaving us on earth after we are born again. He would have saved Himself a lot of sorrow by taking some of us home before we messed up so many times and stumbled so often. But here we are!

The primary purpose in God's saving us is to make us more like Christ. God is not satisfied in doing the job instantly. Instead, He has us playing a large role in this work of reconstruction. One of the reasons for this being an important part of the plan is the fact that His Son is absent from this world. He left us here to develop and portray the life of Christ to our world. Each generation is responsible to proclaim the gospel of a living Christ, not only by their mouths but also by their behavior.

> *The resources that God has given us are described in the Word of God.*

The resources that God has given us in His glorious storehouse are described in the Word of God. This great book is the source of knowledge about Christ. The Bible is akin to an inventory of all that is hidden in Christ. As we gain knowledge of Christ, the fullness of God opens to us, and we are then free to appropriate any and all of the things provided for life and godliness. If we do not know what God has provided, we will be unable to employ that blessing in our life. We cannot develop likeness to Christ without a knowledge of Christ. We are told that the wealth of Christ's love passes knowledge. Does that mean that we should not seek a fuller understanding of that love? No! It means that we will never fully comprehend the fullness or richness of that love provided for us in Christ. A lifetime is spent researching the unsearchable riches of divine grace. The more we know, the more we can employ! The more we employ, the more we grow into likeness to Christ, which glorifies God.

— ☙ ——————————— ☜ —

Father, thank you for providing a storehouse of spiritual blessings. You have given me all the wealth necessary to make me more like Christ.

Entering the Land of Rest

For we who have believed do enter that rest, as He has said: "So I swore in My wrath, 'They shall not enter My rest,'" although the works were finished from the foundation of the world.

Hebrews 4:3

The context of our meditation is the history of Israel as they were transplanted from Egypt to the land of Canaan. This migration is one of the greatest illustrations of the deliverance and progress of each Christian from bondage to the possession of their inheritance in Christ.

Israel was promised the land of Canaan as far back as the Lord's covenant with Abraham, and that promise began to be fulfilled when He redeemed Israel from under the domination of Pharaoh. The pilgrimage of that horde could easily have taken a few short weeks, but, because God had many lessons for them to learn on the journey, it was extended for two years. After that, Israel was given the opportunity to enter the land of rest. This was to be a rest from servitude and bondage into a glorious liberty provided for His children. He had saved them from the house of slavery in Egypt, and they were rightfully His own special people.

After two years, they finally stood on the edge of the Promised Land—yet, even then, the people refused their inheritance. They chose not to believe the Lord and enter the land. They were turned back by the Lord into the wilderness to wander for 38 years, until a new generation grew up to enjoy the land. The opportunity to possess their inheritance was lost because they did not believe.

The author of Hebrews presents this picture so that we can know that the same opportunity is available to us in Christ. The land of Canaan is not a picture of heaven for us. It is, rather, a metaphor of all the riches that are available for us in Christ. We, like Israel, have been redeemed out of bondage to sin and self, and set free into the glorious liberty of the children of God. We left behind the land of our birth and slavery to sin, self, the world, and the flesh on a pilgrimage to the land of rest. This rest is available to all who have come out of Egypt by Christ. Yet not everyone will enter this land of rest because they do not believe that it is available or because they are happy living like the world.

Living in rest can only happen by believing that the Lord has given us all these blessings in Christ. All the resources of Canaan are a glorious picture for us of our wealth in Christ.

಄ ⸺⸺⸺⸺⸺⸺⸺⸺ ಬ

Father, thank you for giving me the inheritance of rest in Christ. I confess that I live in turmoil and anxiety instead of enjoying Your rest.

The Two Seeds

*Whoever has been born of God does not sin, for His seed remains
in him; and he cannot sin, because he has been born of God.*

1 John 3:9

Sinless perfection is not attainable in this world of sin. The apostle John wrote in the preceding verse, "If we say that we have no sin, we deceive ourselves, and the truth is not in us." It is clear that no one but our Lord Jesus could claim to be without sin. We can stand in God's presence fully justified with no sin charged against us only because we are in Christ, who is fully righteous.

Is John contradicting himself by writing that the person who is born of God cannot sin? We must note with care that the word "His" is capitalized in our text. This can only mean that it refers to the Lord Jesus Christ Himself. "His seed" refers to the implanted life that we received when we were born from above by the Holy Spirit. The seed is a metaphor that helps us understand this powerful statement by John.

The word seed is introduced a few other times regarding the person and work of Christ. In John 12:24, Christ speaks about Himself, describing the simple choice of holding a seed or planting it. If you hold it, it remains alone and never multiplies as God intended. If you plant it, multiplication takes place and spontaneously produces many more seeds. When we receive Christ as our Savior, God places Christ's seed in us. That seed remains in us—this being the life of God in His Son. Now we know why that seed cannot sin—because it is the life of Christ in us, and there is no possibility of sin coming from that seed. That seed unites with our life and we choose its impact in our behavior.

> *Adam's seed has a tendency only toward sin, in the same way that Christ's seed has a tendency only toward perfection.*

Yet still we exclaim, "We do sin even though we have His seed in us." When Adam sinned, he received a nature prone to sin which he passed on to every one of his descendants. Adam's seed has a tendency only toward sin, in the same way that Christ's seed has a tendency only toward perfection. With these two seeds in us, a conflict results. Which seed wins the conflict—Adam's or Christ's? We are not schizophrenic, but we have a choice as to who will control our mind, emotion, and will. Because we have the prerogative of control, we bear the responsibility for sin.

80 ———————————— 03

Father, thank you for placing Your seed in me. I claim His power to produce the life of Jesus in my mortal flesh.

December

A Cornucopia Of
Resources For Living

"... a perfect man, to the measure of the
stature of the fullness of Christ."

Ephesians 4:13

Learning every day from His Word of grace.
Growing every step in this glorious race.
Taking from His treasure 'til I see His face,
These are the blessings of my special place.

F. L. K.

December

Oil Under Poor Dirt

Jeremiah Cole was poor—dirt poor. Or as he liked to put it, "I'm dirt poor because of the poor dirt." He lived on a piece of poor dirt that stretched as far east, west, and south as you could see from the main road. His grandfather bought the land cheaply because nothing would grow and nothing could live on it. His father and mother lived on it the rest of their lives. He and his wife lived on it all their lives.

Their house was like a sieve in the winter, as the cold and snow seemed to blow right in the door. In the summer, the wind whipped the "poor dirt" through the cracks all around the house. They had no need for electricity, and he pumped water from the well when needed. The phone was down the road; it cost too much to run the lines bringing it to the old house. Things hadn't changed much for the Cole family in nearly a hundred years.

People came to the door, talking about oil down in the dirt that they wanted to extract. "I can't be bothered and don't really need any change," he

would say. "My Pa lived this way. My Grandpa lived this way. I might as well live this way, too." Finally, a pushy young man asked if he could drill a well and see what was down there. Cole told him, "We went down a long way to find water and there ain't much of that." But he finally agreed, as long as the well was just outside his back door.

A few days later, all the trucks and men arrived to drill. Down they went for two days. Nothing but "poor dirt." On the third day, a loud noise and a huge gusher ripped loose and sprayed the old house, soaking the bleached timbers. "Thar she blows!" the big man shouted. Oil. A lot of oil!

Now Mr. Jeremiah Cole lives down the road in a big new house with electricity, a phone, and running water. A new car is in his big garage, and all the conveniences of life in his home. This was available to him all his life if only he had believed that it was there. He could have enjoyed the riches of life instead of eking out a lowly existence.

Dear Mr. Cole is much like so many believers today. The land has been given to them by their Father and His Son. In that land are "hidden all the treasures of wisdom and knowledge." The wealth is available to all who will believe that they have received "every spiritual blessing in the heavenly places in Christ."

Most of us would be far more ready to drill a well to see what is down there than to look up and see the riches of divine grace that are centered in our Lord Jesus Christ. All the treasures that are hidden in Christ can only be claimed by faith in the Word of God. These meditations are a collection of some of the "barrels of oil" that belong to us because we belong to Christ. Each is labeled so we that know where it came from and its inventory can be counted and compared. The resources are unlimited, since the Father gave us His eternal Son and, with Him, He will "freely give us all things."

Mr. Cole began to "really live" because he finally believed that the wealth was his. So we, too, can employ the Christ-life for our life because we believe that "His divine power has given to us all things that pertain to life and godliness." The task before us is that "we might know the things that have been freely given to us by God."

These treasures are hidden in Christ. The process of discovering and developing the riches involves a significant investment of time and effort. In oil recovery, the exploration company that drills the well gets a percentage of the riches, and the owner of the property gets a portion. In the Christian life, the explorer and owner are one and the same. No one else can explore or recover your riches. It is for you to dig and discover and deploy the blessings of Christ. Another believer may point the riches out to you, but you must dig for yourself.

Israel inherited Canaan, and every place where the sole of their foot landed was theirs as a gift from God. Christ is our Inheritance. Let us explore and claim "the depth of the riches both of the wisdom and knowledge of God."

Dead to the Flesh

And those who are Christ's have crucified the
flesh with its passions and desires.

Galatians 5:24

This verse comes immediately after the well-known list of the fruit of the Spirit. Paul declares that no one can produce the fruit of the Spirit without belonging to Christ.

Furthermore, Paul lets us know that believers have shared in His crucifixion, putting to death the passions and desires of the flesh. This event is part of our salvation, being imparted to us on the basis of our faith. Some people suggest that this is an experience that follows salvation, as a sort of "second blessing." But as we discover the impact of our crucifixion with Christ, we find peace and joy, proving that this is not a second work of grace.

As believers, we fight a running battle with the flesh. It is hard to understand the basis of our crucifixion. We misunderstand the meaning of death, when physical death seems to declare "the end." Because what follows death is only known by faith, we are prone to think that death is final, approaching non-existence or annihilation.

But Scripture is clear that death is best defined as "separation." Death is not the end of existence, but separation from worldly influences. When an alcoholic dies, a friend may offer a drink to the body in the casket. There is no response because the desire has been removed or separated from the intoxicant. As we comprehend the crucifixion that we experienced with Christ, we gain a handle on the reason that we can have victory over the flesh (Galatians 5:20).

When Christ died, our old nature died with Him. When Christ was raised from the dead, we were raised to walk in the newness of His life. It is His life that enables us to produce the fruit of the Spirit. The end result of our death with Christ, which was made active in us by our faith in Christ, is that the passions and desires of the flesh have been separated from our new life in Christ.

Does this mean that we are no longer tempted by the flesh? No! The flesh is alive, but it has been put at a distance by our death with Christ. We can choose to enjoy fellowship and enjoyment of Christ, or yield to the flesh and worldly desires. We can choose to enjoy our intimate relation with Christ, or exchange it for the strong passions of temporary pleasures. There is a danger of those desires coming to life, even though I died to them once with Christ.

Father, thank you for placing me in Christ so that I may fully share life in Him and separation from the call of my flesh. I choose Christ!

Grace Revealed

For the grace of God that brings salvation has appeared to all men.
Titus 2:11

God's grace has appeared! This program of God has been fully implemented by the coming of the Lord Jesus Christ to die on the cross for our sin. Nothing in the hands of men could thwart that purpose, accomplished in and through the wrath of His creatures. The spectacle of the Lord Jesus hanging on the cross, while God "made Him who knew no sin to be sin for us," is the fullest revelation of the grace of God.

This grace of God has appeared to all men. We think of a population of over six billion and wonder if that grace has appeared to all of them. Have the many millions of people who lived in the past also had that grace unveiled to them? We must conclude that they have, since it "has appeared to all men" of all time.

But many will ask about those who have never heard the gospel of God's grace. Titus 2:11 does not say that all have heard, but that it has appeared to all. Grace has appeared! We must declare that appearance.

What is clear is that there is no need for God to again reveal His grace in another way or at a different time. The cross was adequate for all men, for all time. Yet, sometimes we think that if only God would further reveal His grace in some dramatic way, more people would come to accept the salvation that is in Christ Jesus. The revelation was full and final. God will not send an army of angels to reveal His grace. Grace is fully seen in the sacrifice of Christ.

Why don't all men know that He is a gracious God and offers salvation to all who will believe? The problem lies with us. It is our responsibility to preach that salvation which is by grace and through faith. God is waiting for us to do what Christ commanded us: Go! God has placed the burden of telling the gracious message to those who have already had the grace of God revealed. Paul asks, "Have we received that grace in vain?" Have we accepted it without carrying it to the ends of the earth? Has the truth of His grace "died" in our hands? The cross of Christ stands as the greatest demonstration of God's willingness to give all that He had so that we can receive His wonderful grace.

> *God will not send an army of angels to reveal His grace.*

Father, thank you for a complete revelation of Your grace through Christ and His cross. I rejoice in the fullness of Your grace and commit myself to show it to others today. Shine Your grace through me!

The Builder of All

For every house is built by someone, but
He who built all things is God.

Hebrews 3:4

God is the builder. From "eternity past" into the eternity that spreads out before us, God has created all things. Most of us reading this truth focus on the creation of the world, with God as the architect of all that was made. In the same way, we can read further in Hebrews that our faith is properly placed when we accept that "the worlds were framed by the Word of God."

> *We must not forget that each stone of the church is a building in and of itself.*

The context also causes us to realize, however, that God is the one who intervened in the history of man and built a nation of one man: Abraham. That nation flourished and grew in the land of Canaan and then in Egypt. Later, God remembered His promise to Abraham from 430 years earlier and came down to deliver His people from the land of Egypt and the hand of Pharaoh. On this occasion, He began to rebuild that nation of slaves into His own special possession. With a mighty hand and an outstretched arm, He built a community of people redeemed by the blood of the lamb. Delays in the final steps of building were because of the unbelief of the multitude. But eventually He planted them and provided for their every need in His land flowing with milk and honey. He built and defended the building, as long as they were faithful and obedient.

We would be remiss if we only saw our God as the builder of big things, such as our universe and His nation. God is also in the small things. The telescope is a window into the vastness of His building program, accomplished by the Word of His mouth. Similarly, the microscope allows us to observe the smallest aspect of His creation and see His signature on every atom. He built all things, big and small.

He also built the church as a habitation for Himself by the Spirit. God does not dwell in houses made by hands. He has chosen stones from the quarry of humanity, ignited them with His life through faith, and prepared them for the glorious temple that He is building. That building cost Him His Son!

We must not forget that each stone of the church is a building in and of itself. The microscope of God points out the wonderful construction process that He used to make us a living stone, in a living building for a living Creator.

—————————————— ❧

Father, thank you for building me as You saw appropriate. What value You put on my life to purchase my soul!

Once and Forever

*But this Man, after He had offered one sacrifice for sins
forever, sat down at the right hand of God, from that
time waiting till His enemies are made His footstool.*

Hebrews 10:12-13

Forever is a concept that is difficult for the human mind to comprehend, yet the Bible teaches us, as in this passage, that our salvation, our forgiveness, and the reign of Christ are all "forever." Does the author of Hebrews say here that Christ's sacrifice for sin was once and forever? Or is he teaching that Christ sat down forever after the sacrifice? Both of the messages are true!

For us, it is a glorious blessing to know that no additional sacrifice is necessary for the removal of sin. Many religions demand that humanity make some further sacrifice for the full forgiveness of sin. Others suggest that only if we personally give a sacrifice of time, money, or devotion can we expect to feel that our sins have been forgiven. Yet none of these schemes offers the finality of Christ's sacrifice and the resulting peace which His work has brought.

Though declared so clearly in Scripture, many Christians still base their peace on feelings. Such feelings are based on the Christians' evaluation of their own sacrifice, and as such they are no better than the religions of the world. Faith in the sufficiency of Christ's work on the cross will produce lasting peace.

> *Many Christians still base their peace on feelings.*

The believer accepts this declaration, resting in Christ's work by refusing to add anything of his own to what Christ has finished and God has accepted. What wonderful peace and rest results in our hearts when we simply believe that the work is done. Christ has offered a full, final, fervent, faithful sacrifice—not only for our sin, but also for the sin of the entire world. God always wants to direct our attention to the cross and Christ's sacrifice, rather than to ourselves and what we are tempted to add to His finished work.

Most alternatives to the finished work of Christ do one of two things. They either try to *add* to the work of Christ, or they *take away* from the person of Christ by rejecting His deity. Either undermines the adequacy of the sacrifice of Christ. If we add baptism, we say that Christ did not do it all. If we say that Christ is not God, then His work was insufficient. Once forever is the only statement that satisfies God. Only the sacrifice of our Lord Jesus Christ on the cross lasts eternally.

❧ ━━━━━━━━━━━━━━━ ☙

Father, thank you for demanding and accepting the full and final sacrifice of Christ. I choose daily to apply the value of that sacrifice to my life, as you have done to my sin. I am satisfied.

Appropriating the Spirit

*That the God of our Lord Jesus Christ, the Father
of glory, may give to you the spirit of wisdom
and revelation in the knowledge of Him.*

Ephesians 1:17

The word "may" is a key to understanding this line of the prayer of Paul. It is considered a conditional clause and is repeated in many of the New Testament benedictions. Since it is conditional, we must determine the specific condition alluded to by the Holy Spirit.

Several conditions could be considered. If this request is not offered or answered, is the "spirit" not given? If the condition is personal holiness, is the "spirit" not universally available? If the willingness of God is under question, is the "spirit" given only in response to pleading? Is the condition one of hunger or acceptance on the part of each believer? Is the "spirit" always available and the only condition one of belief? Is the "spirit" a part of the overall gift of God in Christ and only awaiting our acceptance? Can we answer all those questions?

The other key word, "wisdom," is found elsewhere as a personal characteristic of Christ Himself, given to us by God. We can conclude that the only condition is our own personal appreciation and appropriation of this spirit "who became for us wisdom from God." To receive Christ is to receive the "spirit of wisdom." But to receive Christ does not mean that all that is in Christ is also practically applied in our life. Just because a plate of food is in front of us does not mean that we have partaken of it or eaten it. We must appropriate it. This does not negate the instruction that we find in James 1. That is an opportunity to receive a special endowment of wisdom for special circumstances.

Paul is praying that each believer would grow in the knowledge of Christ and thereby be made aware of the wisdom and revelation that Christ possesses. Knowing the riches in Christ is necessary before we make the gift of that wisdom practical in our lives. We are not waiting for the Father to give us the spirit of wisdom. The Father is waiting on us to increase in the knowledge of Christ so that we can enjoy and deploy the wisdom of Christ. God has made available to us all the gifts in Christ, and it is our faith that releases that spirit of wisdom so that our lives will radiate the person of Christ and all His characteristics.

❧ ⎯⎯⎯⎯⎯⎯⎯⎯⎯⎯ ☙

Father, thank you for giving me the "spirit of wisdom." I hunger to know more of Christ so that His wisdom is released in my life by decisions that I make.

The Law and Its Curse

Christ has redeemed us from the curse of the law,
having become a curse for us (for it is written,
"Cursed is everyone who hangs on a tree").

Galatians 3:13

Paul is addressing the Jews who had held to the law in spite of the wonderful provision of God through the cross. The death of Christ was the central event in the history of the world, followed by His glorious resurrection.

The Jews who had come to Christ for salvation wanted to hang on to the provisions of the law, given to Israel through Moses. They hoped to be saved by the grace of God and sanctified by keeping the law. God had proclaimed the work of Christ fully adequate, not only for salvation but also for conforming each believer to Christ's image.

These Jews thought they could keep the law as a rule of life and yet not come under its curse. It is convenient to accept law for guiding our behavior if there are no repercussions for failing to obey all its ordinances. The simple answer from God is that we cannot have law without the curse of punishment. Then how do we escape the law and the punishment that it pours out on all who are disobedient to its demands?

The only place to go is to the cross and see again that Christ did away with the law and also its curse on all law-breakers. The curse of the law was death, and hanging on a tree was the most despicable display of death. So God, overseeing the whole process from His vantage point, states that Christ would be crucified and so bear the full curse of the law, even though He had never sinned.

Anyone who believed the gospel was set free from the judgment of God against lawlessness by Christ's death on the tree. The Jews, who were stuck between two positions, were challenged by Paul to turn from the law as a means of salvation and sanctification. Legalism has been a curse on the church since Christ died to put it away. Many "Christians" are forced under the law as a means of sanctification and pleasing God. They are prone to exalt themselves as superior to others, comparing themselves and belittling those whose lives are set free into the liberty of the children of God. No curse rests on us who believe. The law and its curse have been born by Christ for us. The standard for believers today is far higher than the Law of Moses—it is Christ!

ଅ ———————————— ଓ

Father, thank you for setting aside the law and its requirements. I confess that I cannot fulfill the law. I accept Christ's sacrifice against the law and celebrate His victory over the law and its curse.

Death and Resurrection

Blessed be the God and Father of our Lord Jesus Christ, who according to His abundant mercy has begotten us again to a living hope through the resurrection of Jesus Christ from the dead.
1 Peter 1:3

The resurrection should be the most celebrated event in the history of the world. The Lord's Supper is a service of remembering Christ and His death, and is regularly observed by most Christian churches. Yet the resurrection of our Savior is often relegated to a special, once-a-year celebration on Easter Sunday. If Christ had not been raised from the dead, we would still be lost in sin, our faith would be vain, we would be miserable, and our preaching useless.

Perhaps the enemy is pleased that the church remembers the death of Christ more regularly than it celebrates His resurrection.

The church should make some recognition of the importance of the resurrection every time it meets. A Sunday service should not pass without a celebration of the effect that the living Christ has on our faith. It is easy to carry on our daily lives without reference to the victory of Christ over death and the grave. It is all too frequent that we hear the gospel presented without any mention of the resurrection. How sad that we have become so familiar with the gospel that we do not miss the exclusion of the most important event making the gospel powerful.

I have often listened to someone give the salient features of the gospel about God's love for man, man's utter sinfulness, the death of Christ for all, the requirement of faith in Christ, and the blessing of salvation for all who believe. Then an invitation is issued to "receive Him" who died for them. This is an invitation to a dead Christ! If there is no resurrection, there is no "living hope" because we cannot be "begotten to a living hope" if Christ is dead. Every blessing made available to the believer is dependent on the resurrection of Christ. As our living Lord, He distributes the fruits of Calvary.

Perhaps the enemy is pleased that the church remembers the death of Christ more regularly than it celebrates His resurrection. The death of Christ "destroyed him that had the power of death," while the resurrection of Christ demonstrated the finality of that victory and released the life of God to be passed on to everyone who believes. "Because I live, you will live also!"

Father, thank you for sending Your only Son to die for my sin. I praise You for that sacrifice. I celebrate His life, given to me as a living hope. I commit to living today in the power of His resurrection.

Grow Up!

*Therefore, if anyone is in Christ, he is a new creation; old things
have passed away; behold, all things have become new.*

2 Corinthians 5:17

The spontaneous development of a child is a miracle of growth. The early years are almost perceptible as they "grow in wisdom and stature and in favor with God and man." How does a dose of milk disperse its nutrients throughout the little body, growing a nose and nails as well nerves and knees? Yet it has happened to all of us and continues to do so. What joy to see baby things pass away and new capacities discovered.

Similarly, the development of the Christian life is demonstrated in our being as "we receive with meekness that engrafted word" and drink with "desire the pure milk of the word." Those spiritual nutrients manifest themselves in patience and power, peace and perseverance. As we continue in the faith, grounded and settled, our progress will become evident to all.

But how does this wonderful process get started? The initial prerequisite is to be "in Christ." The fact of being placed "in Christ" guarantees results. Paul reminds the Corinthians in his previous letter that, when a believer grows to maturity, he puts "away childish things." We see this exchange in our lives as we mature in age. It is also a hallmark of spiritual development.

It is a sad condition when a youth is still practicing the habits of babyhood. The author of Hebrews condemned the believers for failing to eat spiritual meat and being content to be taught elementary truths, when they should have been teachers of the great doctrines of Christ. Many Christians can look back to an event when they were placed "in Christ" at spiritual birth, but today they are satisfied with milk and have no desire for strong meat. They remain satisfied to practice comfortable, childlike habits. Although they should be strong in faith, they are weak in knowledge, and so are still "babes in Christ." The old things remain, and nothing new is manifested.

The new creation, that we received when we trusted Christ as our Savior, sets us free from the bondage to old things of babyhood and enables all things to become new. We seek to change our child by good food, personal training, regular discipline, adequate sleep, challenging exercise, and lavish love. God, as our perfect Father, does the same but does so faultlessly. It is our responsibility to respond to the abundant provision for spiritual growth. How delighted the Father must be when baby things pass and new things become standard practice.

❧ ─────────────── ❧

Father, thank you for my position in Christ. I am blessed beyond my understanding. I choose meat so that I will grow into the likeness of Christ.

Anointed as Priests

But the anointing which you have received from Him abides in you, and you do not need that anyone teach you; but as the same anointing teaches you concerning all things, and is true, and is not a lie, and just as it has taught you, you will abide in Him.

1 John 2:27

Anointing has a rich history in the rituals of the nation of Israel. The kings of Israel were anointed with oil at the start of their reigns. David, for example, was anointed by Samuel. It is striking that the New Testament gives all believers the titles of both "priest" and "king." We receive these titles, not because of our prayers or our behavior, but because of the relationship that we have with God through His Son. We have been redeemed by the blood of Christ, and that is what qualifies us for ministry and service to God.

Anointing is once and for all, a rite that is not generally repeated. The anointing of a priest took place at the outset of his ministry. The anointing of each believer takes place at the point of salvation. That act is not to empower, but to designate our offices. Yet the figure of anointing is closely connected with the ministry of the Holy Spirit, of whom oil is a spiritual type. The indwelling of the Holy Spirit in the life of every believer is a cardinal truth reiterated many times, explaining the grandeur of our salvation.

The activities of the Holy Spirit include indwelling, sealing, filling, empowering, abiding, convicting, teaching, guiding, and anointing. The multiplied ministries of the Spirit of God are summed up by the Lord Jesus in John 16:14: "He will take what is mine and declare it to you." All the combined services of the Spirit to the believer are guaranteed by the glorified Christ and given "that we might know the things that have been freely given to us by God." We do not need a fresh anointing any more than we need to ask for a fresh indwelling. The anointing was received without asking and is manifested by a changed life.

The anointing was received without asking and is manifested by a changed life.

These ministries are not a result of prayer or pleading for an extra endowment for service, but are the normal duties of the Spirit, as promised by the Lord Jesus. We do not pride ourselves in the fact that we have been anointed, as though we earned or deserve this recognition. But we can repeat this truth with thankfulness. We are anointed!

❧ ───────────────── ☙

Father, thank you for designating me personally as a king-priest in Your service. I want to minister humbly in the power and energy given in Christ. Thank you for the Spirit who guides me in my anointed service.

Praying in the Spirit

*Now He who searches the hearts knows what the
mind of the Spirit is, because He makes intercession
for the saints according to the will of God.*

Romans 8:27

The New Testament commands all believers to pray for one another. Most of us ask those that we fellowship with to pray for us, and at times we even tell them exactly what to pray. Only occasionally do we ask them to pray "according to the will of God."

The Lord Jesus concluded His poignant prayer in the garden of Gethsemane with the words "not My will but Yours be done." In Romans 8:27, we find that He follows the same pattern by interceding for us in harmony with the will of God. The previous verse reminds us that we do not know what to pray as we should, but the Holy Spirit helps that infirmity. His help is not to whisper some words in our ear that feel right or seem best to us. He will guide our thoughts to the Word of God, and through the Scriptures He will instruct us in our words to the Father. As we follow the Spirit's guidance, we will pray in harmony with the will of God and according to the Word of God.

The saints are Christ's special concern, as He sits beside God the Father and focuses on those whom He redeemed by His precious blood. Those who are the special concern of the Lord's prayers are not a select group of people, singled out from among all believers. The word *saints* is a simple and oft-repeated name in the New Testament for sons and daughters in the family of God. This verse is not teaching that only those who are the most holy receive the prayerful attention of their Savior. The words "saints" and "holy" come from the same Greek term. The word saint is used to designate the position that we enjoy because we are redeemed by Christ and, by God placed in Christ.

Perhaps the focus of His prayer is that we might honor the name that God has given to us. None of us behaves in a perfectly holy or saintly way. The goal of the ministry of the Spirit is to build into the Father's children the character and graces of His Son. Christ knows our hearts and searches them, seeking a pliant spirit that will respond to the teaching of the Word and the ministry of the Spirit. Christ and the Holy Spirit, in harmony with the Word of God, are promoting a spiritual response to the truth that will influence our lives and behavior, leading us toward Christ-likeness.

ༀ ───────────── ༀ

Father, thank you for the intercession of my Savior. I choose to pray for the saints according to Your will and in harmony with Your Word, while listening to the Spirit speak to me.

Loving as Christ Loved

Husbands, love your wives, just as Christ also
loved the church and gave Himself for it.

Ephesians 5:25

Christ demonstrates the proper love of a husband by His love for His own bride, the church. Yet as husbands, we fail to live up to this example. It is instructive that the words in this verse are not a suggestion or advice, but a divine command. It is easy to hope that God means for this love to be reciprocal or dependant on how "lovely" or obedient our wife is. We somehow want to change the meaning, or find a paraphrase that will let us off this sharp hook.

The standard is perfection. Wives should be comforted by the fact that husbands are given a higher standard by which to live and love. The church, as the bride of Christ, is to be obedient to her head, the Lord Jesus. Wives are instructed to imitate that example in their obedience to their husbands. Yet a wife's failure does not give husbands any excuse for not rendering the love that is commanded in this verse. This is a matter of obedience, not feelings.

It is challenging to fully understand the love that the Lord had for His church. Meditating on the highest expression of love known to man will increase our determination to love more perfectly. The more we look at our love, the less satisfying is our effort. The more we gaze on Christ giving His life for the church, the more we are empowered to love as He loved.

Even a wife may be more tolerant of her husband's failure to live up to the standard when she bathes her soul regularly in how much Christ loved her. His love and devotion gives her a perspective that is much different than when she frets about the lack of fulfillment that she experiences from her husband. We can spend a lot of time being subjective in our view of our own satisfaction with the spouse that the Lord gave us. The alternative is to dwell deeply on the example of Christ and to be satisfied in Him.

Linger longer on the love of Christ.

Most couples who face dissolution and divorce must realize that their focus was primarily on the failure of the other member and the lack of self-fulfillment. Decline begins when we turn from fulfilling the needs of our spouse to examining the emptiness in our own life. Linger longer on the love of Christ than on the lack of love in your marriage partner. Christ's love is still the standard, no matter how much any of us fail. Obedience is possible, not by lowering the standard, but by letting Christ love through us.

Father, thank you for the command to love my wife as You have loved me. I receive this coming from One who loves me more than anyone.

12
DECEMBER

The Rod of Iron

Now out of His mouth goes a sharp sword, that with it
He should strike the nations. And He Himself will rule
them with a rod of iron. He Himself treads the winepress
of the fierceness and wrath of Almighty God.

Revelation 19:15

God's ultimate judgment is a message that the world does not accept or want to hear. Through "political correctness," the mouths of many preachers have been closed for fear of being accused of extremism. The voice of government has spoken harshly to those who preach a singular means of salvation, an exclusive code of behavior, or the severe judgment of all the wicked. But the revelation of Christ is so clear in His judgment of all who violate His law that there can be little room for rejecting this truth.

Three metaphors are used to demonstrate the severity of Christ's rulership over the whole earth. The sword points to a powerful military attack. The rod of iron introduces His governmental authority. The winepress provides a picture of thorough devastation.

Revelation 19:16 announces His auspicious titles, "KING OF KINGS AND LORD OF LORDS." These titles distinguish His authority over the nation of Israel and the church. He is King of Israel and Lord of the church. Both titles describe His sovereign control over all.

> *The rod and staff are our constant companions.*

His appearance to the *church* is that of the Shepherd who died for the sheep and who lives for them. His appearance to the *ungodly* and wicked world is described metaphorically by a sword, a rod, and a wine press. Figures of speech are used because words are inadequate to convey His wrath and anger against disobedience.

His rod of iron is in contrast to the rod and staff which are our constant comforting companions. He ministers to His sheep as the Good Shepherd who gave His life for the sheep. The sword of His mouth shows the power of His words against the rebellious words that have flowed from the mouth of impious man against the Son of God. What a dramatic demonstration for the wicked, as the rod of His anger flashes forth, smiting them on the back and hobbling their legs, bringing them to their knees until they proclaim with their mouths, "Jesus Christ is Lord!" The blood will flow from His enemies as wine from the winepress. His absolute domination is manifest as the Almighty puts everything under His feet.

„ ———————————————— –

Father, thank you for the promise that I am not appointed to endure Your wrath against the nations that have rejected You and Your Word.

Awaiting Our New Bodies

Who will transform our lowly body that it may be conformed
to His glorious body, according to the working by which
He is able even to subdue all things to Himself.

Philippians 3:21

Today's Scripture states clearly that the Lord is sovereign over all things. Yet we are often tempted to wonder whether the Lord really does know what is taking place in our lives. We add to that the question, "Is He in control of all things?" This is one of many reminders in the Word that there is nothing that escapes the eye of the Lord. Hebrews 4:13 says, "And there is no creature hidden from His sight, but all things are naked and open to the eyes of Him." This is a very encouraging and challenging message for us.

The differences between our lowly body and His glorious body help us realize that our body, though fearfully and wonderfully made, is not worthy to be compared with His glorious body. Many times we consider that the Lord has put us in a prison called our body, and the bars and doors and locks frustrate our desire to do what we want. The suffering of the body should have a profound impact on our outlook on life in this body and the promise of a glorious body like His.

If we did not experience a fair amount of decay, we might want to linger longer in this old house in this old world. But our decline and the ravages of time are the messengers of God, urging us to repeat more fervently, "Even so come, Lord Jesus." A daily dose of reflection in the mirror should encourage us to consider the new eternal house, not made with hands, waiting for us in the heavens. Our glorious body does not mean that we will all be clones of Christ in appearance, but like Him in character, capacity, capability, in purity, in fullness, in separation from evil, and in service to the Father.

We must note that the resurrection is the foundation of this work on our behalf. Enough emphasis cannot be placed on the importance of the resurrection of Christ. The message of God, through Paul, places this event above all others in relation to our salvation. Even the death of Christ would not have its desired effect without His resurrection. His resurrection guarantees our transformation. His work will reverse decay, destroy death, and define likeness to Christ over whom death has no power.

The absolute authority of the Lord in all affairs tends to make us wonder whether He is interested in our mundane problems. The answer is in this promise which is universal to all believers and also personal to each of us.

꙳ ———————————— ꙳

Father, thank you for the aging process that makes me look up and say,
"Perhaps today." I long to see my Savior and be like Him forever.

14
DECEMBER

All-Sufficient Grace

And He said to me, "My grace is sufficient for you, for My strength is made perfect in weakness." Therefore most gladly I will rather boast in my infirmities, that the power of Christ may rest upon me.

2 Corinthians 12:9

God's grace is adequate. The New Testament tells us again and again that God has given us, through Christ, all the grace that we need for life and godliness. The Greek word is translated as *thanks*, *gifts*, and *grace*, giving us a complete picture of the Lord's provision for all our needs.

The God of all grace and the throne of grace suggest that the Father is the source of all grace. Both the Old Testament and the New refer to the Spirit of Grace. But it is Christ who is the reason that grace can be supplied so fully to all believers equally.

> *God's grace is enough.*

The important point is that, in the most difficult situations and in the midst of the most trying circumstances, God's grace is enough. So many of us receive Christ and then turn to God in prayer, asking for an additional infusion of His grace. We do not need to plead for more. His provided grace is sufficient. All grace abounds from God, through Christ, who is "full of grace and truth."

When we become aware of our own weakness, we are then willing to set His grace free in our lives. When we are absorbed in our adequacy, we are not in a condition to confess our insufficiency. Many times the Lord must bring us to our knees before we admit our emptiness. It is then that we confess our infirmities and accept His fullness of grace.

We must be content to accept the axiom that "Jesus Christ is what He gives." He is love and gives love. He is peace and gives peace. He is joy and gives joy. He is grace and gives grace. God does not give grace apart from His Son Jesus Christ. This is why Christ can boldly say to Paul and to us, "My grace is sufficient for you." The word "my" suggests that it belongs to Him, was made possible by His death, is applicable because of His resurrection, is available because of His ascension, and is as sufficient as He is in His person. What power and provision in Christ!

The hard part is to be willing to confess our weakness and inadequacy in and of ourselves, and to accept by faith His gracious gift of divine strength. The confidence of Paul is recorded in Philippians 4:13: "I can do all things through Christ who strengthens me."

Father, Your intervention in my life has pointed out my tendency to be sufficient in myself. Thank you for exposing my weakness and opening my eyes to Your all-sufficient grace. I rest in You.

Being Truly Thankful

And whatever you do in word or deed, do all in the name of the
Lord Jesus, giving thanks to God the Father through Him.

Colossians 3:17

This is one of the many times that we are commanded to give thanks. The word *thanks* indicates dependence and acknowledgement of a gift. As believers, we need to realize that, in the midst of all our activity, our constant response should be, "Thank you!"

This command is in the context of whatever comes out of our mouth or whatever is done by our hands. The mention of these two activities is intended to be inclusive of all that we, as God's children, engage in while serving Him. It is not limited to just words or the function of our hands, but includes every activity that we perform. God has saved us for His glory and His service.

There is to be no glory or praise for us.

Yet some people might think that it is time for God to give us thanks for all that we do for Him. We teach a Sunday school class and the class says, "thanks." Why doesn't God do the same? Someone offers himself for missionary service and crosses the sea to a very difficult living environment. Does God lean over the banister of heaven and say, "Thanks for the sacrifice for My sake"? Instead, after we have taught a class, after we have shared the gospel, after we have gone around the globe, we reply, "thank you!" But for what?

God is impressing on us that all we do or say is in the power and through the provision of God. He gave the words. It is His Word that we give to others. It is His gospel that we preach. Every aspect of the will of God is to be done in the name of the Lord Jesus. His name echoes with every godly word that we utter. His name is the signature on our every godly deed.

There is to be no glory or praise for us! And, in a real sense, there is to be no thanks from Him for all that we say and do. Yes, we are reminded that in that day when we stand before Christ everyone will receive praise from Him. But the parable in Luke 17 asks whether the master will thank his servant. "I think not," Christ says. It is our joy to realize that every act and word is done in His power and with the provision of God Himself. "He does the work," said Christ of His Father. We can say with thanks, "He does the work" of Christ who is our life.

& ———————————— og

Father, with special joy I say thank you. By so doing, I acknowledge that all I say and do is a result of my dependence and Your provision. You gave Christ to me, and I inscribe His name on all I say and do.

16

DECEMBER

Growing from Temptation

No temptation has overtaken you except such as is common to man; but God is faithful, who will not allow you to be tempted beyond what you are able, but with the temptation will also make the way of escape, that you may be able to bear it.

1 Corinthians 10:13

We are called upon to endure temptation. Neither this verse nor any other suggests that we should plead or pray earnestly for God to remove a temptation. The repeated message of God's dealing with His children is to develop strength *in* the temptation, rather than to escape *from* the temptation.

The Lord prayed in John 17 that we should not be taken out of the world. However, a movement is affecting many believers by counseling them to "get out of the world and let it go to hell." Removing believers from the temptations of the world is an affront to the Lord's own words. Today's Scripture puts the temptation and the escape in such close relationship that they both exist for our strengthening and victory. "With the temptation" tells us that the will of God is not to take away the temptation. Yet it is proposed that our prayer should be for a wall to be built or a hedge to grow around all the people of God, so that no one has to endure temptation.

God's will is to endure temptation. James writes, "Blessed is the man who endures temptation." Is it possible that one of our blessings is to endure temptation? It is clear that God expects us to face temptation and also to experience victory over it. Does this mean that God has taken a position of disinterest in our temptations? He says that He will "not allow us to be tempted beyond what we are able," which shows that He is personally involved in allowing and determining which temptation we can handle.

Each of us grows spiritually stronger at different rates and in different areas. God may not trust me with the kind of disease that another brother is facing. You may be stronger in a certain area where another brother or sister would fall. God, who is not the author of temptation, is tailoring each temptation to our strengths, knowing our weakness.

Yet someone might object, "No one has been though what I have." God says that your temptation is common to all mankind. Where is God? He is determining the specific areas of our life that need to be strengthened, allowing the enemies to attack where He knows we are strong in Christ. He never designs a temptation to bring us down. That is the enemy's tactic. We rejoice in our "Personal Trainer" who is molding us to be like Christ.

⁂ ——————————————— ⁂

Father, thank you for overseeing my personal conflicts. I confess that I am fearful in temptations. You have provided the resources for victory.

Freedom of the Spirit

Now the Lord is the Spirit; and where the
Spirit of the Lord is, there is liberty.

2 Corinthians 3:17

The ministry of the Holy Spirit is to set people free—both positively and negatively. The negative aspect of the Spirit's work is to set people free from slavery, sin, the world, and self. That great work is a fulfillment of the promise of the Lord Jesus in John 8:36: "If the Son makes you free, you shall be free indeed."

Many have a skewed view of liberty or freedom.

When we admit the Son into our lives, the Holy Spirit is sent to dwell in us. The bondage that every person experiences before believing is one of the reasons for salvation, including freedom from slavery. This freedom needs to be claimed, not prayed for. The blessings of salvation include liberty by the ministry of the Spirit.

The liberty described in 2 Corinthians 3:17 seems to be of a positive nature. The freedom is not only away from the bondage described above; it is also to "be delivered from the bondage of corruption into the glorious liberty of the children of God." That freedom can be enjoyed by every child of God because of the presence of the Spirit of the Lord. There is no need for additional prayer asking for liberty or pleading or earning this gift. Let us, in holiness, claim this liberty in Christ without offending other believers by our freedom.

But where does this freedom lead? Many have a skewed view of liberty or freedom. Even in the political realm, some suggest that liberty means the freedom to do anything one wants without regard to law and order. That is not the thrust of human liberty, and it is not spiritual liberty, either. As liberty in human relations must abide by law and order, so liberty provided by the Spirit must be exercised within the confines of biblical principles.

Although our text says that the presence of the Spirit brings liberty with Him, some people argue that this means that anything that feels good for the believer must be of the Spirit. Spiritual liberty is not the freedom to do anything or to claim that any activity is the work of the Spirit. Other people want the Spirit to perform miracles and healings to prove that He is present. The enemy has the capacity to imitate almost everything that the Holy Spirit does. Only the spiritually wise are willing to compare the teaching of the Scriptures with what is claimed to be of the Spirit. The liberty of the Spirit is regulated by the Scriptures and its parameters are dictated by the Father, who sent the Spirit. We must know the Word and will of God by the Spirit of God.

꙰ ———————————— ꙮ

Father, thank you for the residence of Your Spirit. I claim liberty, and choose
to let the Spirit operate in my life in harmony with Your Word.

Our Father's Likeness

Beloved, now we are children of God; and it has not yet been revealed what we shall be, but we know that when He is revealed, we shall be like Him, for we shall see Him as He is.

1 John 3:2

No one has come into this world without being a child. All of us were at one point a child. Our pilgrimage began the moment that we were placed in our mother's arms. The development of our appearance was gradual. As we learned the language of our parents, we spoke like them. They guided us to develop skills and abilities that they thought were necessary.

The spiritual birth of every believer begins when each one puts his trust in Jesus Christ as Savior. That birth takes place spiritually with about as much understanding as when we were born physically. We knew some small truths that brought us to Christ or drove us to escape eternal judgment. We appreciated those elementary blessings, and thought that we knew it all. Then, as we grew in grace and in knowledge of the Lord Jesus, through the study of the Bible and fellowship with other growing believers, we learned our ultimate goal as children. Likeness to the Lord Jesus who saved us is the final goal of every child of God.

As we study and are nurtured by truth and our Christian family, we grow into likeness of our Father, just as we do physically to our earthly father. It is a spontaneous development physically as we eat properly, exercise, learn discipline, keep clean, and use our abilities. Spiritually, we grow spontaneously into likeness to the Lord Jesus. We should eat right by studying the Word. We must discipline ourselves by obedience to the Lord. We must keep clean by receiving forgiveness for sin. We must exercise by employing our gifts and abilities in service to the Lord and His people. We must appropriate the resources available to us in Christ.

> *When we see Him, we will instantly be like Him, and God will be fully glorified in us.*

But ultimately, when we see Him, we will instantly be like Him, and God will be fully glorified in us. This is not something that we pray for or earn by obedience and holiness. This is a blessing waiting for us when we see His face. No believer will miss this blessing promised to all who are the children of God! We still must employ all the resources available, which leads to becoming more like Christ while waiting to see Him.

⁘ ──────────────── ⁘

Father, thank you for my birth by Your Spirit. I choose to employ all that You have given me at birth which will lead to likeness to Your Son.

God's Cupboard

*The cup of blessing which we bless, is it not the communion
of the blood of Christ? The bread which we break,
is it not the communion of the body of Christ?*

1 Corinthians 10:16

A cup is a common household item. Yet, in spite of its commonness, the Scriptures use it graphically. There is a long list of cups that God uses to help us understand His way with us. Some are sad in their connotation, such as a cup of trembling. A cup of fury fires the imagination. The cup of His indignation is terrifying. The cup of salvation runs over, as David said. A cup of consolation is inviting. Others are mentioned in Scripture, displaying the collection of cups in God's cupboard. The cup of blessing is one of the most suggestive in all of Scripture.

Our Lord used the cup to describe the cross when He said in John 18:11, "The cup that my Father gives me, shall I not drink it?" We will never be called to drink His cup. But the cup that is in front of us is ours and ours alone. We do not always know what is in the cup which He has mixed for us. We all can look back to the experiences that He poured in for us. Had we known the contents, we might have drawn back. But the same Father who mixed our Savior's cup has overseen the mixture of our cup. What is going to be offered to us in the days ahead? Regardless of what comes, it's important to remember that the cup is handed to us by our loving Father. No cup comes to us that He has not handled, ordained, or permitted.

> *Our cup, handed to us by God, has been blended for our good and growth in grace.*

Our cup, handed to us by God, has been blended for our good and growth in grace. If we could mix our own cup, it would not be a compound of joy and sorrow, happiness and suffering, prosperity and poverty, opulence and obstacles. But the Father knows our needs best. Though He mingles ingredients that we find distasteful, there is one cup which is common to us all: "the cup of blessing." That cup, made possible by the blood of Christ and handed to us at spiritual birth, has all the resources for the life-long journey that He has mapped out for us. Along with other cups that we take from His hand, He always offers the cup of blessing. All the requirements for life and godliness are in this cup. Our response is to bless that wonderful cup by saying thank you to the Father who mixed and presented it to us. Drink deeply.

Father, thank you for mixing my cup today. I take it from Your hand as I do the cup of blessing, and thank You for them both. I drink with joy!

Saying Thanks

*. . . giving thanks to the Father who has qualified us to be
partakers of the inheritance of the saints in the light.*

Colossians 1:12

Each of our meditations concludes with a suggestive prayer that almost always begins with "thank you." This is a habit that is hard for a young child to learn. It is neither natural nor spontaneous for any child to say thank you. It must be taught, and the habit is often learned through sorrow or deprivation. In the Christian life, the habit must be developed and drilled into our minds daily.

In Colossians 1:12, Paul assumes that we are conscious enough of blessings that we are giving thanks regularly for the resources available to us as the children of God. Paul's actual words are the conclusion to his prayer for the church in Colosse. His prayer is a pattern for our intercession and personal communion with our Father. Thanks should be one of the most oft-repeated words in our prayer life.

*What belongs
to Christ
belongs to me
as a joint heir
with Christ.*

As children, it took many years before we spontaneously changed our habit from our first cry of "gimme" to "thanks." How long it was before we set aside the monotonous phrase, "I want," for some more polite way of asking. Being sheep in the flock of the Lord, we are taught "I shall not want" because we are "fully blessed" in our perfect Shepherd.

When we trusted Christ as Savior, God qualified us as recipients of an inheritance that will not pass away. The requirement to share in this inheritance is to be a member of the family of God. By spiritual birth into Christ, we have been fully established to receive our share of the riches of divine grace. It is a source of great joy that the proportion for each of His children is equal. No one child gets more than another. We are "joint heirs with Christ!" Who can complain with that arrangement? What belongs to Christ belongs to me as a joint heir with Christ. Have you said "thanks" for that recently?

We may not fully appreciate the inheritance until we are with the Lord in the unapproachable light which we cannot now endure. But until that day, we need to know these riches, master their use, employ them daily, appreciate them fully, and give thanks regularly. That habit is not easily learned when we pray thoughtlessly.

⁎ ———————————————— ∛

Father, thank you for qualifying me for the inheritance that You give me. I claim it because I am Your child. Thank you for all the riches of Christ.

The Light of the World

And the city had no need of the sun or of the moon to shine in it,
for the glory of God illuminated it, and the Lamb is its light.

Revelation 21:23

Everywhere the Lord Jesus goes, He brings light. The Gospel of John begins by revealing that the Word brought truth and light. He gives light to every man who comes into the world. One of His primary ministries is to bring light to a darkened world. Our text is the culmination of that glorious responsibility which the Father delivered to the Son when He came into the world.

His appearance was as common as any other man. He was cut from the same bolt of cloth, receiving the same human frame with the same physical capacities as we—yet without sin. When we saw Him, there was no unusual beauty that we should want to be with Him. In that temple of clay resided the full light of the glory of God, which found a window for display in His countenance. Only on the Mount of Transfiguration did the Father open the skylight of His face to shine as the sun. On another occasion, those same features were marred more than any man's.

At the cross, where the Lamb died, the light seemed to be extinguished by the brutality of man. Rather, it was the building up of the darkened cloud that limited the full radiance of His divine glory. With ever-expanding refraction, the Light now moves into the heart of everyone who believes.

The darkness was dispelled, and that powerful regenerating Light sought out every evil deed and every iniquitous thought and swept them from my soul. For the first time in my life, I was fully lighted, as John tells me that the life in Him "was the light of men." The darkness was gone; the true Light now shone.

That wonderful regeneration, which resulted in glorious restoration, was a microcosm of the day when this same light will be the light of the city of God. In that day, His life and face will be the focal point when every eye will see Him. All the glories of the Son will find full expression in the One who created light. The Lamb, who died and poured out His soul unto death, is a fuller radiance than the sun, which ruled the day for thousands of years. The moon, which has the limitation of reflection, will not be needed, for the full radiation of the Son will shine without restriction from within the One who alone could say, "I am the light of the world." What He did in my soul, He will do for the New Jerusalem and the world.

ɞ ———————————— ☙

Father, thank you for sending the Light into the world and into my heart. I rejoice in the Light, and await the day of His full radiance.

That Which We've Committed

For this reason I also suffer these things; nevertheless I am not ashamed, for I know whom I have believed and am persuaded that He is able to keep what I have committed to Him until that Day.

2 Timothy 1:12

Safekeeping is an enormous challenge. A bank used to be called a "trust company." But, with failed banks and corruption in their administration, the word "trust" has lost its value in the banking business. Many other aspects of life are challenged by the legal system. A will must be properly written with the right language and sealed to await the day of death. But with the arrival of that day, it seems that lawyers come out of the woodwork to make it say something very different than was intended. Someone wisely offered this advice: "Do your giving while you're living, then you'll be knowing where it's going."

> *We gave to Him that which we could lose in this life in order that He might keep it in a world where it cannot be lost.*

The confidence that a believer has in God and His Word means that anything committed to His trust will never bring shame. Isaiah writes in 2:22, "Cease ye from man, whose breath is in his nostrils: for wherein is he to be accounted of?" Even in the Christian community, the lack of confidence that we have in those who proclaim the name of Christ makes us hesitant to entrust much to our fellow believers. Is there anyone that we can trust?

The idea of stewardship is one of the missions that the Lord Jesus gave to His disciples. Several of His parables reminded them of the responsibility of faithfulness in the gifts entrusted to them. God obviously more than lives up to the standard that He sets before us. God has entrusted to each of us gifts and talents, time and money, physical and mental abilities for which we will have to give an account.

But what have we entrusted to God? The primary thing that we have committed to Him is our soul. We placed the future of our being in this life and the next in the hands that were pierced for us so long ago. God has taken on the sole responsibility, as a faithful Father, to care for us now and to secure our souls for eternity. What a day that will be when He offers back to us that which we have entrusted to Him. We gave to Him that which we could lose in this life in order that He might keep it in a world where it cannot be lost.

Father, thank you for Your faithfulness. I choose to trust You with my life, possessions, money, family, career, and the security of my soul. I commit to You today things that I have been holding onto myself.

Fully Justified

*Who shall bring a charge against God's
elect? It is God who justifies.*

Romans 8:33

The fullness of God's justification means that no charge can be placed against any of His children. When we look into the Word of God, we face the mirror that shows our inconsistencies and inadequacies, as well as our failure and frustrations. But we also clearly see our sin of disobedience, unfaithfulness, lying, stealing, lust, and a host of other sin that we chose to do. The purpose of the Word is to show our sins and cause us to see the necessity of confession and enjoyment of our restoration of fellowship with God.

There are two spheres of activity in our relationship to God, our Father. Our view of ourselves in the world is the practical day-to-day living where I often fail. This is the "reality show" which I know so well, even though those around me may not be aware of my wickedness. I know, and of course God knows. In that sphere, I see that I fail and need to confess and receive the restoration of my fellowship with the Father.

The other sphere in which my life is exposed is the presence of God. There, in glory, is my loving Father, offering all the resources necessary for my victory over every temptation, and providing the assistance through the Spirit to keep me from falling. Beside Him, on His throne, is my precious Savior, Jesus Christ. In this perfect throne room of glory is a place for me where I am "seated with Christ." In this climate, a charge may be hurled against me by the enemy relating to what I am doing and how I am living on earth.

> *God has fully justified me in His own sight.*

The charge hurled against me is true from the viewpoint of my behavior on earth. But as soon as the "accuser of the brethren" has spoken, my Advocate, seated with me, speaks to His Father and reminds Him that that sin has been fully paid for. The charge is thus dismissed.

God has fully justified me in His own sight. Justification means to be "declared righteous." I am seated in the presence of God because of this monumental act of God. I am absolved of all sin because of the work of Christ and my faith in Him. I am "declared righteous" by God Himself. One day I will be fully righteous when I see Him face to face. Until then, I stand fully justified, and no charge can ever be laid against me.

    ✆ ———————————— ☙

Father, thank you for fully justifying me and forgiving me of all my sin. I claim my seat in Your presence by virtue of the righteousness of Christ.

Resting in Christ

Therefore, since a promise remains of entering His rest, let us fear lest any of you seem to have come short of it.

Hebrews 4:1

We live in a world filled with turmoil, trouble, and tumult. The sad reality is that believers seem to be as anxious and worried as the rest of the world who do not know Christ. Believers and unbelievers go to the same counselors, psychologists, and psychiatrists, who offer the same worldly advice to cope with the chaos in life. Yet the rest and peace of God is available to all who have been redeemed.

When the Israelites were slaves in Egypt, God promised them deliverance through the blood of a lamb which was to be displayed on each house. On that Passover night, Israel was delivered out of the house of bondage. This started their pilgrimage from Egypt to Canaan, which was their home of rest. They came to the edge of the land and, in disobedience and unbelief, they refused to enter it, and so came "short of it." God says that the promise of that land of rest remains available to us today.

Obviously, the nation of Israel has never fully enjoyed the prosperity, blessing, and rest that God offered them. One day, God will plant them in the land forever. In faith, they will accept the promise and enjoy the prosperity of God's provision in Christ, their Messiah.

> *It is not a retirement kind of rest, but a reliance on Jesus for all our needs, problems, and conflicts.*

All this is a picture of our condition before God. We, too, were slaves of the enemy, but we have been set free by the blood of the Lamb who took away our sin. We are set free into the liberty of the children of God. We are offered His rest, made possible and available by His work on the cross. It is not a retirement kind of rest, but a reliance on Jesus for all our needs, problems, and conflicts. Just as the Lord gave the land to Israel as a gift by inheritance, so God has given us as our inheritance all the blessings found in Christ. Just as Israel refused to enter and enjoy the land of Canaan, so there is the danger of believers today refusing to trust and obey the command to enter and enjoy all the riches of His grace. Fear took hold of Israel, and they were driven by anxiety, worry, alarm, dismay, dread, panic, and terror. These same emotions drive us from enjoying the Lord and His rest to accepting a pilgrimage of wandering in the wilderness and away from the rest of God. Choose this day to enter into and rest in the riches of Christ.

꙰ ———————————— ꙮ

Father, thank you for the rest that You offer from the fear and worry that so often besets me. I choose in faith to enjoy and employ this rest and peace in Christ.

Learning from Suffering

Though He was a Son, yet He learned obedience
by the things which He suffered.

Hebrews 5:8

Jesus is fully God and fully man. Many aspects of the perfect union of God and Man create, for our simple minds, a puzzle that we cannot master. We tend to emphasize the humanity of Jesus over His deity, or we give priority to His deity and minimize His humanity. Either extreme leads to heresy. The balance is perfect, even if we cannot reconcile the apparent contradictions. Let us in faith accept rather than argue! If we do this, we will learn the lessons before us.

Christ's learning process was affected by suffering. Most of our prayers are directed to God, pleading for Him to alleviate or remove suffering. We tend to think that all suffering is allowed without reason, and we consider escape the only sensible solution to our problem. That assessment leaves out God's plan and program for our lives. God, as the perfect Father, had a perfect Son whom He allowed to suffer more than any of us. That fact jettisons any suggestion that all suffering is the result of our own personal sin, or that the Father is not in control of what comes to us as His children. Since the perfect Son was sent suffering from a perfect Father, how can we suggest that our curriculum of suffering is not ordained or permitted by our Father? Is all that happens in our life directed by fate or by the enemy?

Add to that popular opinion the idea that we can learn obedience without suffering. Many best-selling books promote the idea that God intends us to be free from problems and filled with prosperity. We enjoy hearing messages about all sorrows being dissolved by our faith, and all His material riches being accepted by that same faith. But this assertion is hollow and untrue when measured against the Word and by the life of Jesus Christ.

If any one could have escaped suffering, Christ could. Yet, despite the physical and spiritual pain, He accepted the will of God and the resulting sorrow and suffering. How can we believe that we will become like Christ without walking the same path? How will we develop into the likeness of Christ without the same program? We do not learn as much in a climate of opulence as we learn in a context of tests and personal exams.

We are blessed by His perfect example in suffering, but more so because He lives in us and is capable of living through us in the same suffering. His presence in us provides a curriculum of learning in the midst of suffering.

ುಲ ——————————— ೞ

Father, thank you for allowing Christ to endure suffering. I claim His victory
in suffering as a resource for learning in the suffering that I face today.

Sharing in His Resurrection

Buried with Him in baptism, in which you also
were raised with Him through faith in the working
of God, who raised Him from the dead.

Colossians 2:12

Baptism is a graphic picture of death. As we watch a believer go under the water, we see how foreign that element is to normal life. The message of baptism is a declaration that this person is rejecting the old life and proclaiming his intention to walk in a new lifestyle, empowered by the risen Christ. The death and resurrection of Christ is also a part of the reason for immersing a person in water. The resurrection of Christ is the reason that we can leave the condition of spiritual death behind and know that we share His resurrection life.

But the act of water baptism does not in any way add to our salvation. It is an act of obedience which is the answer of our heart and conscience to God's gift of salvation.

Colossians 2:12 gives us an added item of importance. We were baptized with Christ and raised with Him. This is a most difficult concept to understand and apply. How were we baptized with Christ—or, as Romans 6:8 says, "we died with Him"? Even though we were not even born, we still shared in His death and resurrection.

Let me illustrate. If your grandfather died at the age of four, who else died? The answer is you! Because you descended from your grandfather, if he had died that young, you would not be here. If that man were miraculously raised from the dead a year later, you also were raised. You would be given the new life of your grandfather through your father. If you eat a seed, you eat all the seeds that could have been produced by that seed if you had planted it. In the one seed you eat is a multitude of seeds that could be produced by its death and "resurrection." Your life is dependent on the life of the parents from whom you came.

When Christ died, we died because we were in Him. That is the operation of the working of God. Only God could do that in a seed, and He does it in the Seed who is Christ. If you have faith in Christ as your Savior, you shared in His death and resurrection because God put you in Christ just as He put seeds in every seed. Christ gave His life to you by His death and resurrection in just this way. Because you have Christ, you are provided the resources to walk in resurrection life.

თ ──────────────────────── ა

Father, thank you for the death and resurrection of Christ. I am coming to understand how important His resurrection is to my life.

Paul's Benediction

*Now may our Lord Jesus Christ Himself, and our God
and Father, who has loved us and given us everlasting
consolation and good hope by grace, comfort your hearts
and establish you in every good word and work.*

2 Thessalonians 2:16-17

A benediction is the communication of some blessing from one person to another. At the end of a church service, a pastor will often raise his right hand and give the benediction. In this particular example, I am not sure that there is an actual endowment of blessing. Do we leave with some aura of help or assistance that we did not previously have? A pastor is not called to bequeath a blessing that he has no authority to transfer. He is called to make known "the unsearchable riches of Christ," to train and encourage his flock to know and understand the blessings that they can enjoy. Thankfully, there are many pastors who, in their benediction, invite their congregation to appreciate and appropriate the blessings of their salvation in Christ.

But the benediction in 2 Thessalonians 2:16-17 is the voice of God Himself, through Paul, announcing to all believers the endowment of the two special blessings of consolation and hope. The Thessalonians had been taught an incredible amount in the few weeks that Paul ministered to them as their teacher. Few churches in the New Testament availed themselves of such a large percentage of Paul's words. The confusion that existed about the coming of Christ had affected many of them, and the previous letter was written to correct some misconceptions.

This verse is like a bountiful feast of spiritual food for the soul. Unlike "chicken soup" for the sick, this is meat for maturity. The two special blessings are consolation and hope. Each is an aspect of the character of God. He is called both "the God of all comfort" (2 Corinthians 1:3) and "the God of hope" (Romans 15:13). The words *consolation* and *comfort* come from the same root Greek word, used by the Holy Spirit in many verses. As titles for Him, they are both a radiation of His nature and aspects of His being. Because they are so intimately tied to who He is, He cannot be present without offering consolation and hope.

The Thessalonians, in the midst of their spiritual struggles about the coming of Christ, needed to know that the comfort of God was theirs, even if they lost loved ones through death. They also needed to know that the future was full of hope, and that they must commit themselves to every good work in the service of their coming Savior.

Father, thank you for the comfort that You provide. I claim its power in my life. I rest in Your hope for every aspect of my future.

Access to God

For through Him we both have access by one Spirit to the Father.

Ephesians 2:18

Prayer is one of the glorious privileges given to every child of God. Man was driven from the presence of the Creator when he sinned. Adam lost the wonderful fellowship and place of communion with his Father as a son of God. He was also driven from the presence of God and had no access unless he brought an animal sacrifice to God, as his son Abel did.

The Lord was not pleased with the estrangement between Himself and mankind. Yet God could not let them come back without a plan that fully paid the price for his sin. When an offering was presented which removed sin and fully cleansed the sinner, the way of access to God's presence was fully opened.

The death of Christ was the only sacrifice adequate to forgive and cleanse the sinner. God sent His Son "to take away our sin" and to open the way for all who are forgiven to come to God in prayer. This access is for both believing Jews and Gentiles, as today's Scripture reminds us.

Prayer is addressed to the Father, through the Son, under the direction of the "one Spirit." Many people offer their prayers to Jesus and forget that our prayers are to be addressed to the Father. Adoration and worship may well be presented to Jesus Christ, but confession, intercession, petition, adoration, and worship are brought to the Father. There are others who, with little regard for the Word of God, address prayers to the Virgin Mary, thinking that she is more sensitive to our needs, has closer access to Christ, and will bring our requests to Him. This is a false idea of prayer, and elevates Mary above Christ.

All the aspects of prayer are made possible and available because of the work of Christ. The Father is waiting and willing to hear the prayers of all believers. He is committed to listen to His children. It may be that He will hear the cry of those who reject His Son, but He is not bound by covenant to answer the prayers of rebellious, ungodly unbelievers. Of course, when the heart of anyone comes to God in faith and confession, He is waiting to hear that cry, forgive their sin, and give them full privileges of access to His presence by His Son. The Holy Spirit is active in His ministry of guiding us in our prayers, so that our words and petitions are in harmony with the Word of God and according to the will of God. What a blessing access to the Father is for every child of God.

ɞ ———————————— ☘

Father, thank you for opening the way for me to come into Your presence, bringing my worship, confession, thanksgiving, and intercession.

The Greatness of Christ

You are of God, little children, and have overcome them, because
He who is in you is greater than he who is in the world.

1 John 4:4

God could have removed all conflict in our lives when we were born again, but He didn't. Even if we pray for deliverance from the onslaught of the enemy, God may choose to allow him freedom to challenge us. If we pray for a hedge or a wall to be built around us, God may still permit the devil and his army to have access to us. From our standpoint, it is more reasonable to confine Satan in a cell block from which he cannot operate than to allow him freedom of movement in the affairs of the church and believers in general. But that is not God's perspective.

Many believers live a defeated spiritual life because they are unaware of the nature of the battle—and both the enemy and God are misrepresented. Too may times, Satan is presented as outside the control of our Lord. This idea brings shipwreck to one's faith and disaster to one's life.

> *Christ, who is in us, is greater than the devil, who is in the world.*

The apostle John declares that, since "we are of God," we have overcome "the spirit of the Antichrist." To believe in Christ is to reject the spirit of the enemy, which is anti-Christ. The work of salvation is proof that we have refused the deception of the enemy and accepted Christ as our Savior, placing Him in charge of our life. This conversion is the foundation on which all other aspects of the Christian life are built.

That work of God in saving us also endows us with all the resources necessary to defeat the enemy in our life and behavior. The daily manifestation of victory over the enemy is through the life of Christ in us.

Instead of God taking away the conflict in our life, He has given us the resources for victory. The result is glory to God, who gave us the means for spiritual victory. When Jesus prayed for Peter in Luke 23:32, He did not pray for a wall around him or deliverance from temptation. Rather, He prayed that Peter would be strong in faith in the temptation. Today's Scripture reminds us that Christ, who is in us, is greater than the devil, who is in the world. The devil is not limited by a wall that we pray will be put in place. He is limited by the strength of our faith! The goal is greater faith in Christ than in the enemy around us. We have the shield of faith by which we can douse all the darts of fire from the evil one.

∞ ———————————— ∞

Father, thank you for placing Christ in me as a permanent residence. I claim
His superiority and victory over all enemies in the world.

Known by the Shepherd

*For the Lamb who is in the midst of the throne will
shepherd them and lead them to living fountains of waters.
And God will wipe away every tear from their eyes.*

Revelation 7:17

Tears are good for us in many ways. They release emotional pressure, clear the ducts that channel water to our eyes, demonstrate emotions to others who might not know our heart, and communicate sympathy with those who weep. But what a day that will be when all tears will be wiped away. And, greater still, it will not be just a day, but all eternity!

Part of the shepherding ministry of God is to deal with the tears of His lambs. Christ is described as a Lamb in many places in Revelation. His close identity with us as His lambs is consoling. His knowledge of sheep is both from His perspective as the Shepherd and also as the Lamb.

The context of Revelation 7:17 is for believers who are martyred for their testimony during the great tribulation. In His presence, they will never be faced with hunger, thirst, sun stoke, exhaustion, or tears. In that glorious climate, where the Lamb is resident and president, His people will serve Him day and night.

What a prospect for these who endure so much physical, mental, and emotional persecution because of their faith in Christ. The promise of the Shepherd is that He will do for His people all that the word *shepherd* suggests. Shepherding is foreign to many of us, but for the readers of Revelation in the first century this vocation was a way of life, full of meaning and pregnant with benefits to every lamb. All the vicissitudes of the sheep come into view, as they do in Psalm 23, where the sheep speaks in terms of the ministry of his Shepherd.

Is this ministry limited to the heavenly realm and the select company of believers who have "washed their robes and made them white in the blood of the Lamb"? Surely it cannot be that we, who have not experienced such sorrow and grief, should miss out on this ministry. Does He lead only the martyrs to the "living fountains of waters"?

No! My dear fellow lambs, we too share in that ministry which the Chief Shepherd administers to all who are called by Him. We can claim a foretaste of that maintenance because "we are His people and the sheep of His pasture." Surely He will not begin a ministry only then, but will continue the upkeep that He began when we became His lambs.

ಬಿ —————————— ಜ

Father, thank you for my Shepherd. I delight in His maintenance of my life. I confess that I am still prone to go astray. I long to be before Him.

All Things

As His divine power has given to us all things that
pertain to life and godliness, through the knowledge
of Him who called us by glory and virtue.

2 Peter 1:3

The wealth of God's treasures has never been fully measured, and their extent has never been fully comprehended. Peter here tells us of some of our marvelous blessings in Christ, and in the next verse he reminds us that "exceedingly great and precious promises" have been given to us. These twin truths alone should satisfy our hearts and minds in Christ Jesus.

Elsewhere we are told that the power which raised Christ from the dead is employed to make available all the riches of God's grace, purchased by the death of His Son.

The abundant blessings are a gift to every child of God. These resources cannot be bought or earned, nor do we need to pray that God will release them to us. They are ours because we have Christ. We can appropriate them by increasing in the knowledge of Him who bought them, possesses them, and distributes them—the Lord Jesus Christ.

> *We will never be like Christ if we do not have His life and if we do not respond obediently to the training of our Father.*

Our experience as followers of Christ is summed up by the descriptive words "life and godliness." Life must refer to all the vicissitudes that God allows, to teach and train us as growing members of His family. Parents provide not only life, but also a culture of living, as our Father does. Godliness is the end result of the operation of the life of God in us. These two things shape us physically, personally, and spiritually. One element is the life that we were given from our parents at conception and is played out no matter how we are raised. The other shapes us by the training, discipline, teaching, and correction that we receive from those who are responsible for our care. These ingredients produce likeness to our parents. God has given us spiritual life which, when worked out by the Spirit, produces God-likeness or godliness.

All things are given to us in Christ to shape us into the likeness of Christ. We will never be like Christ if we do not have His life and if we do not respond obediently to the training of our Father. "All things" have been given to us, and it is our responsibility to know Him and to employ all the treasures found in Christ.

80 ———————— ८३

Father, what abundance You have given to me as Your child. Thank you for giving me Your life. I choose to respond to Your training today.

Endnotes

Book title taken from the hymn, "Great is Thy Faithfulness" by Thomas O. Chisholm, Copyright © Hope Publishing Co. Used by permission.

"Heaven Came Down and Glory filled My Soul" © Copyright 1961, renewed 1989 by John W. Peterson Music Company. A portion of this hymn is printed on the November chapter page using the first four lines of stanza two and the last four lines of stanzas three. All rights reserved. Used by permission.

Additional Resources

Below are additional books that will be of help in understanding and employing the riches of divine grace.

All books by F. B. Meyer

The Life and Land of Rest, W. Graham Scroggie

Paul's Prison Prayers, W. Graham Scroggie

Joshua, Alan Redpath

Victorious Christian Faith, Alan Redpath

Vital Union with Christ, A. T. Pierson

The Divine Unfolding, James Graham

Let Us Go on to Maturity, John E. Hunter

Knowing God's Secrets, John E. Hunter

The Saving Life of Christ, Major W. Ian Thomas

The Mystery of Godliness, Major W. Ian Thomas

If I Perish I Perish—Esther, Major W. Ian Thomas

The Principle of Position, Miles Stanford

Principles of Spiritual Growth, Miles Stanford

Abide Above, Miles Stanford

The Green Letters, Miles Stanford

The Reckoning that Counts, Miles Stanford

Notable Quotations

"Only the power of God through the Holy Spirit can free us so that our actions are not conditioned by the behavior of other people but by Christ. To react to others is to let them control us and determine our moods and courses of action. To be committed to Christ and filled with His love is to let the Lord chart our desires and behavior as we respond to Him. Difficult? Yes, but possible when we give ourselves to Him and let Him do in us and through us what we cannot do ourselves."

Author Unknown

ဆ ──────────────────── са

"As you leave the whole burden of your sin and rest upon the finished work of Christ, so leave the whole burden of your life and service, and rest upon the present in-working of the Holy Spirit.

"Give yourself up, morning by morning, to be led by the Holy Spirit and go forward praising and at rest, leaving Him to manage your day. Cultivate the habit, all through the day, of joyfully depending upon and obeying Him, expecting Him to guide, to enlighten, to reprove, to teach, to use, and to do in and with you what He wills. Count on His working as a fact, altogether apart from sight and feeling. Only let us believe in and obey the Holy Spirit as the Ruler of our lives, and cease from the burden of trying to manage ourselves, then the fruit of the Spirit appears in us, as He wills to the glory of God."

From the fly leaf of the Bible of Harold Wildish (1903-1982)
Missionary in South America, the West Indies and Jamaica

Scripture Index

ECS Ministries

As the largest correspondence school in the world, ECS Ministries remains committed to equipping people with quality, Bible-based resources.

The correspondence courses, books, booklets, study guides, and other materials that ECS publishes are of tremendous value in areas such as Christian growth, doctrine, and evangelism.

Over 25,000,000 students have used ECS courses to study the Bible and grow in the Christian faith. As you spend time reading God's Word and answering questions, you too can become involved in bringing "The Word to the World".

Publisher Of:
Correspondence Courses
Christian Books
Booklets
Study Guides,
Prison Resources

ECS
MINISTRIES
The Word to the World

www.ecsministries.org (563) 585-2070